STUDENT LEARNING ABROAD

STUDENT LEARNING
ABROAD

What Our Students Are Learning, What They're Not, and What We Can Do About It

Edited by Michael Vande Berg,
R. Michael Paige, and Kris Hemming Lou

Sty/us

STERLING, VIRGINIA

COPYRIGHT © 2012 BY
STYLUS PUBLISHING, LLC.

Published by Stylus Publishing, LLC
22883 Quicksilver Drive
Sterling, Virginia 20166-2102

Library of Congress Cataloging-in-Publication Data
Student learning abroad : what our students are learning,
what they're not, and what we can do about it / Edited By
Michael Vande Berg, R. Michael Paige and Kris Hemming
Lou.—First Edition.
    pages   cm
  Includes bibliographical references and index.
  ISBN 978-1-57922-713-5 (cloth : alk. paper)
  ISBN 978-1-57922-714-2 (pbk. : alk. paper)
  ISBN (invalid) 978-1-57922-715-9
  (library networkable e-edition)
  ISBN (invalid) 978-1-57922-716-6 (consumer e-edition)
  1. Foreign study.   2. American students—Foreign
countries.
I. Vande Berg, Michael, 1948–   II. Paige, R. Michael,
1943–   III. Lou, Kris Hemming, 1959–
LB2376.S775   2012
370.116—dc23   2012005525

13-digit ISBN: 978-1-57922-713-5 (cloth)
13-digit ISBN: 978-1-57922-714-2 (paper)
13-digit ISBN: 978-1-57922-715-9 (library networkable
e-edition)
13-digit ISBN: 978-1-57922-716-6 (consumer e-edition)

Printed in the United States of America

All first editions printed on acid-free paper
that meets the American National Standards Institute
Z39-48 Standard.

Bulk Purchases

Quantity discounts are available for use in workshops
and for staff development.
Call 1-800-232-0223

First Edition, 2012

10   9   8   7   6   5   4   3   2   1

We dedicate
Student Learning Abroad
to all those students and educators
whose curiosity about the world
has inspired us to produce this volume.

CONTENTS

PART THREE: PROGRAM APPLICATIONS: INTERVENING IN STUDENT LEARNING

PREFACE

For decades U.S. higher education has largely relied on two types of "evidence" to document success in study abroad. The first is the simplest of metrics: the increasing number of students that individual colleges and universities, and more generally the United States as a whole, annually send abroad. The more students an institution sends abroad, the more it is said to be "succeeding." The second metric is the number of returning students who not infrequently report that studying abroad has "transformed" them. The second has traditionally been taken as evidence that corroborates the first; that is, sending more and more students abroad makes sense because some of them are telling us, when they return, that they have learned abroad in special ways—in ways they presumably would not have had they stayed at home.

Both of these metrics have seemed to make sense because much of the U.S. study abroad community has traditionally embraced the view that students normally and naturally learn valuable things through participating in an educational experience in another country. This has especially made sense when programs have been structured to "immerse" students while they are abroad: housing them with host families, enrolling them directly in host university courses, organizing buddy systems and *intercambios*, and so on. If the number of students studying abroad has increased from one year to the next, if the students are enrolling in programs that take steps to "immerse" them, and if a fair number return to campus telling us that they have been "transformed," then, ipso facto, students are learning as their faculty and study abroad advisors expect they will.

However, this traditional reliance on increases in enrollment, student self–report, and structural immersion practices is now meeting with growing doubts about what students abroad are or are not in fact learning abroad. Increasingly, faculty and staff are becoming frustrated by conflicting reports and evidence about student learning; dubious about claims that students are learning in ways traditionally associated with studying abroad; unclear whether their skepticism about student learning is justified; and uncertain what can be done about it, if their doubts are justified.

Our first and overarching aim in editing and writing parts of this volume has been to collect and share credible evidence about learning abroad so that our colleagues in the study abroad community will be able to make informed decisions in designing and delivering programs, and in advising students about their options. Like many members of the large and growing study abroad community, we are cautiously optimistic about student learning abroad: We believe that many students *may* learn abroad in ways they will not if they stay at home. But also like many of our colleagues, we are more than a little uneasy about the extent to which most students currently are learning and developing in these ways. In fact, we believe that a dispassionate review of the evidence will leave little room for doubt: Far too many U.S. undergraduates are not learning and developing in ways that most members of our community typically believed they did as recently as a decade or two ago.

In saying this, we do not mean to suggest that students are typically not learning anything. This is clearly not the case: Those statements from returning students to the effect that "studying abroad changed my life" surely must mean *something*. And many students clearly do return home sharing disciplinary knowledge they acquired abroad—sometimes through enrolling in courses and in disciplines they might not have had they stayed at home—and giving a strong impression that they changed in some ways while abroad. The important questions, though, are not about whether students are learning anything or not; they are about what students are learning, about how they are learning, and about whether the process—the *experience*—of learning abroad is allowing them to develop competencies they might not have if they had stayed at home. This volume, then, embraces the concept of "deep" and "surface" learning that originated in Europe in the 1970s, and that by two decades ago was emerging in U.S. study abroad circles through discussions about learning that was "student centered," "experiential," "developmental," "constructivist," and "holistic."

There is, of course, a considerable amount of evidence that bears on student learning abroad, and no single volume or a whole series of volumes devoted to the topic could begin to exhaust it. Credible evidence does point to answers, and our aim here is to tell a story about student learning abroad that is very different from the stories that many members of our community have traditionally told each other.

The second aim of this book is to be as clear as possible about the standards we are applying when we give more weight to some sorts of "evidence" than others—when we say that not all evidence is created equally.

We find some of the evidence that has traditionally been offered to be very persuasive, some less so, and some not persuasive at all. We offer, in support of our story, three types of evidence we believe to be very persuasive: research findings on student learning abroad, insights from a broad range of disciplines that together offer new understandings about human learning and development, and six concrete examples of study abroad courses or programs that intervene in the learning of students abroad by applying the interdisciplinary insights and research findings.

We find the research record to be compelling: In highlighting recent studies that focus intentionally on student learning abroad, we have taken care to select those whose instruments are valid and reliable, and whose methodologies are well designed and rigorously carried out. We find the interdisciplinary evidence that the authors of this volume contribute to be no less compelling. They offer key insights and findings from a wide range of academic disciplines and traditions that converge to offer us new understandings about how human beings—including, of course, students abroad!—learn and develop. We suggest that the six examples of courses and programs that appear in Part Three offer another type of compelling evidence, showing concretely how educators are now applying theoretical insights and research findings to help students abroad learn and develop effectively and appropriately.

We offer these diverse kinds of evidence in the hope that some of our colleagues in the study abroad community—in weighing the evidence against increases in student enrollment, student self-report, and a belief that students learn through being "immersed"—will reconsider long-held assumptions, beliefs, and practices about teaching and learning in study abroad.

We have chosen to focus almost exclusively on the intercultural learning and development of undergraduates for several reasons. We are, first, not discussing learning domains that, like second-language acquisition, have been treated at considerable length elsewhere. And although ours is not the first volume to focus on intercultural learning and development in study abroad, it is the first to examine such study through the lens of a large number of disciplines that are together reframing our beliefs and attitudes about human learning, and against recent research findings that provide empirical support for this interdisciplinary perspective.

More than anything else, though, we have chosen to focus on intercultural learning and development because we have come to recognize that nearly everything students learn abroad is informed by the way they frame their interactions in the new cultural contexts within which they find themselves. Even formal "academic" teaching and learning take place in particular cultural contexts that are often very different from the academic contexts in which the students learn at home. In these new academic contexts, students need to deal with unfamiliar cultural values and beliefs to the same extent that they need to contend with them in home stays or in any other interactions during their time abroad. What they experience in their classes, for example, is hardly culturally neutral: Assumptions and beliefs about teaching and learning are culturally grounded and inform how teachers teach and students learn. Study abroad students taking a history class in Buenos Aires or Shanghai approach the learning of history differently from the Argentinian or Chinese teachers and students with whom they are interacting. Put simply, we are focusing on intercultural learning and development because how a student responds to the differences and commonalities in a new cultural context will determine how, and to what extent, he or she learns anything in that environment—including even historical facts, to say nothing of historical interpretations. As we will see in examining the interdisciplinary and research evidence, most students abroad are at this point not learning to negotiate cultural differences, whether inside or outside the classroom, unless educators intervene in their learning in ways that help them develop the types of knowledge and skills that will allow them to shift perspective and adapt behavior to new and often challenging cultural contexts.

We have divided our volume into four parts. Part One, "Setting the Scene," consists of two chapters. In the first, we, the editors, lean on Thomas Kuhn, and on four of this volume's authors—Milton Bennett, David Kolb, Bruce La Brack, and Douglas Stuart—in arguing that U.S.-sponsored study abroad has been framed through the unfolding of three successive paradigms, each of which has provided the study abroad community with a set of basic assumptions that has dominated theory and practice during a particular period. In the second chapter, R. Michael Paige and Michael Vande Berg review the research record, focusing on recent studies that offer convincing evidence about what and why undergraduates are or are not at this point learning and developing interculturally through studying abroad. These studies also point to ways that faculty and staff can intervene to improve student learning.

Part Two, "Foundations of Teaching and Learning," consists of eight chapters, each of which helps us trace the evolution of beliefs and attitudes about study abroad to the convergence of theoretical and experimental evidence from a range of key academic disciplines and developments: developmental theory (chapter 3), intercultural relations (chapters 4 and 5), experiential learning theory (chapter 6), neuroscience (chapter 7), anthropology (chapter 8), psychology (chapter 9), and the scholarship of teaching and learning (chapter 10). Insights and findings from these disciplines converge to offer an account of human learning and development that is very different from the accounts that underpin earlier study abroad paradigms—an account that emphasizes that humans do not learn as the environment imprints itself on them, but through individually constructing, and, through their membership in various cultural communities, coconstructing the world through the very act of perceiving it.

Part Three, "Program Applications: Intervening in Student Learning," consists of six chapters authored by faculty and staff who have developed innovative and successful approaches to intervening in student learning and development abroad. Each of the authors discusses, in specific terms, what an educator will need to know, and what he or she will need to be able to do, in order to increase the likelihood that his or her students will learn and develop effectively and appropriately through studying abroad. In chapter 11, Laura Bathurst and Bruce La Brack discuss the University of the Pacific's well-known pre– and post–study abroad training program. In chapter 12, Lilli and John Engle introduce the American University Center of Provence's multilayered approach to training. In chapter 13, R. Michael Paige, Tara A. Harvey, and Kate S. McCleary chronicle the development of the multistage Maximizing Study Abroad Project. Kris Hemming Lou and Gabriele Weber Bosley, in chapter 14, discuss the asynchronous online training courses that they offer, respectively, to Willamette University and Bellarmine University students at home and abroad. In chapter 15, Adriana Medina-López-Portillo and Riikka Salonen describe the development of the training program that they and other members of the training team embedded into the curriculum and cocurriculum of The Scholar Ship. Finally, in chapter 16, Michael Vande Berg, Meghan Quinn, and Catherine Menyhart discuss the evolution of the Seminar on Living and Learning Abroad, an on-site intercultural training course that is offered to students enrolled in most of the Council on International Educational Exchange's semester programs abroad.

Part Four, "Conclusion," consists of a brief chapter in which Kris Hemming Lou, Michael Vande Berg, and R. Michael Paige offer a series of specific recommendations for faculty and study abroad advisors who are interested in maximizing their students' learning abroad.

A final word: Increasing numbers of faculty and staff are now persistently asking questions such as the following and raising concerns about student learning abroad:

- What should we make of student reports that studying abroad is "transformational"?
- What does recent research tell us about what and how students typically learn through studying abroad?
- How can we judge whether some research findings are more useful than others in guiding decision making?
- Do some programs promote student learning and development more successfully than others?
- What do I need to know, and what do I need to be able to do, to help my students abroad learn and develop more effectively?

In responding to these questions, we are addressing what has become a central and growing concern for the study abroad community: the extent to which students are learning what they could—and should—through studying abroad. Many of our colleagues wonder whether their students typically learn and develop well on their own, or whether they need well-trained educators to intervene in support of their learning. And when the evidence shows that students do in fact benefit significantly when they enroll in programs abroad that intentionally intervene in their learning, faculty and staff wonder, too, who will be doing the intervening for their students, and what concrete forms the interventions might take. The authors of this volume offer what we believe are well-considered responses to these questions and concerns.

Michael Vande Berg, CIEE: Council on International Educational Exchange
R. Michael Paige, The University of Minnesota–Twin Cities
Kris Hemming Lou, Willamette University

PART ONE

SETTING THE SCENE

STUDENT LEARNING ABROAD

Paradigms and Assumptions

Michael Vande Berg, R. Michael Paige, and Kris Hemming Lou

T he literature on study abroad has recently been growing exponentially. One estimate places the number of scholarly publications about study abroad during the past decade—books, dissertations, articles, chapters, monographs—at more than a thousand (Comp, Gladding, Rhodes, Stephenson, & Vande Berg, 2007), and commentaries about students abroad appear regularly in the popular press. Much of the literature focuses on student learning and development, with authors offering a wide range of views about the ways that students do or do not learn and develop through studying outside the United States. These authors often speak from their own experience as students, from their experiences teaching in or visiting programs abroad, or from conversations they have had with students who have returned to the home campus. Sometimes their views are grounded in popular wisdom. And sometimes they are informed by theories and supported by research evidence. A central purpose of this book is to sort through the literature and make sense of these various claims about student learning abroad.

One common view about studying abroad is that when students travel to and are "immersed" in a place different from home, they learn many interesting and useful things on their own, and do so rather effortlessly. Much of what we hear and read about study abroad encourages us to embrace this perspective. We have all talked with returning students who tell us that studying abroad has "transformed" them, or that seeing new and different things has "changed their lives," or that being abroad has been "the best experience" they have ever had. Many students talk enthusiastically in blogs and in online education abroad magazines about the things they have done and learned. On college and university websites and in institutional viewbooks, groups of U.S. students smile and pose in front of iconic study abroad images—the Eiffel Tower, the Sydney Opera House, the Roman aqueduct in Segovia, China's Great Wall—conveying the message that they and their U.S. friends are learning happily and easily as they are exposed to the new and different. The common assumption that education abroad provides knowledge and helps students develop skills that they need in order "to compete in the globalized workplace" reassures parents; anxious about the spiraling costs of higher education, they are relieved to hear that studying abroad will make their sons or daughters more mature, as well as give them the knowledge and skills that will land them a good job after graduation or get them into a highly ranked graduate or professional school.

We are frequently assured, implicitly and explicitly, that our institutions are meeting a worthy goal in sending more and more students abroad. After all, with students learning valuable things abroad that they are not likely to learn if they stay at home, who would not wish to send as many of them abroad as possible? The Institute of International Education's annual *Open Doors* report lists the U.S. colleges and universities that send both the largest number and the highest percentage of students abroad (Chow & Bhandari, 2010); the very simplest metric, the number of participants, is the primary marker of success here. Presumably mindful of the marketing advantages that annual institutional rankings confer, college and university presidents urge their faculty and administrators to send still more of their students abroad. Admissions and public relations staff boast that 20%, 40%, 50%— and, in at least one case, 100%—of their institution's students are, or soon will be, studying abroad. What is all too often not addressed is whether core assumptions about student learning are warranted. In the press to expand, learning is simply a given.

Federal government funding programs provide tacit support for the assumption that students normally learn effectively and easily abroad, whatever the type of program in which they participate. Each year significant numbers of students receive generous federal funding to study abroad in the form of Fulbright Program travel grants, Gilman scholarships, and National Security Education Program scholarships. Most of the students who receive these grants or scholarships participate in programs that offer little intentional support for their learning, beyond formal classroom instruction. As this book goes to press, Congress is still considering passage of the Paul Simon Act, an ambitious scholarship bill whose principal goal, within 10 years of passage, is to quadruple the number of U.S. undergraduates who study abroad. Here again, the metric of success is a continuing increase in education abroad enrollments, not the extent to which students are learning through studying abroad.

Not all faculty and staff are convinced, however, that most students are more or less automatically gaining the sorts of knowledge, perspectives, and skills that are important for living and working in a global society, merely through being exposed to the new and different in another country. As annual enrollments continue to soar—data show that more than five times as many U.S. undergraduates now study abroad as did 25 years ago (Chow & Bhandari, 2010)—voices inside and outside higher education are persistently asking questions about what all of those students are in fact learning over there. Faculty and staff at home and abroad have long questioned whether coursework at study abroad sites is as academically rigorous as it ought to be (Bok, 2006; Engle, 1986; Hoffa, 2007; Vande Berg, 2003, 2009). Recent studies on language acquisition cast doubt on the traditional view that students typically make remarkable gains in second-language proficiency through studying abroad (Collentine & Freed, 2004; Freed, 1995; Segalowitz et al., 2004). Similarly, studies on culture learning have shown that students enrolling in most education abroad programs are, at best, making quite modest gains (Paige, Cohen, & Shively, 2004; Vande Berg, 2009; Vande Berg, Connor-Linton, & Paige, 2009). Some commentators have observed that U.S. consumer culture is being transported abroad and that programs are being structured in ways that allow students to avoid meaningful engagement with the host culture. However, this approach undermines their ability or desire to learn about the host country or form relationships with their hosts (Citron, 2002; Engle, 1986, 1995, 1998; Engle & Engle, 2002; Ogden, 2007; Vande Berg, 2007b).

Other commentators ask if much of current study abroad practice offers experiences that differ from taking vacations to other countries and if so, in what ways (Gardner, Gross, & Steglitz, 2008; Woolf, Battenberg, & Pagano, 2009). When students return home excitedly sharing stories about the traveling they did and the friendships they formed with other U.S. students, skeptical faculty wonder why presidents and other campus leaders are urging them to send still more of their majors abroad (Engle & Engle, 2002; Vande Berg, 2003, 2004; Vande Berg et al., 2009). Doubts about student learning are compounded by reports that highlight student drinking and related forms of misbehavior abroad (Blankinship, 2010; Kowarski, 2010). Studies that question whether studying abroad typically helps students develop the types of skills and perspectives that employers look for in prospective employees contribute further to a sense that students are not learning as the education abroad community has traditionally believed (Gardner et al., 2008; Trooboff, Vande Berg, & Rayman, 2008; Van Hoof, 1999). Considered together, the findings of these studies and reports offer the beginnings of a counter-narrative to the view that students normally learn effectively simply through studying elsewhere.

Various metaphors about learning abroad have entered the discourse during the past two decades, as faculty and staff seek ways to express the growing perception that students are all too often failing to engage with, and learn effectively in, the host culture. Perhaps the most common of these portrays education abroad as a swimming pool. Here, educators work to get students to learn in the host culture—whether they are learning academically, linguistically, or interculturally—by "throwing them into the deep end," "immersing" them in the new culture through such practices as direct enrollment courses, language pledges, and home stays. The metaphor goes on to suggest that too many students fail to thrive in this "sink-or-swim" environment; it depicts them fleeing the deep cultural waters, leaving the pool as quickly as possible to avoid further unpleasant and threatening exposure to the new and unfamiliar (Lou & Bosley, 2009; Vande Berg, 2007a, 2009; Vande Berg et al., 2009). Another metaphor depicts students abroad as "colonials"; like elite British administrators in India during the Raj, today's students all too often lead lives of ease and privilege, sitting comfortably on the veranda and observing the locals from a safe distance (Ogden, 2007). Still other metaphors depict education abroad as a "safety net" (Citron, 1996), with students living in highly protected U.S. American "ghettos," taking their courses in English, and traveling in groups with other U.S. students, in "packs" or cultural "bubbles" (Engle, 1986; Ogden, 2007).

Returning students themselves sometimes report that they did not learn or accomplish what they had thought or had been told that they would (Zemach-Birsin, 2008), offering a counterpoint to reports by other students about being "transformed" through studying abroad. Liza Donnelly's lampooning of education abroad in a recent *New Yorker* cartoon highlights what for many is an open secret: that students are too frequently treating their time abroad as something very different from a learning experience. The cartoon depicts a college student telling her roommate, "For my junior year abroad, I'm going to learn how to party in a foreign country" (2010, p. 64). In a recent *Chronicle of Higher Education* back-page essay, John Burness, a visiting professor at Duke University, expresses the kind of doubts about the aims and outcomes of education abroad that growing numbers of faculty and staff are feeling:

> I've talked with enough students from various institutions to develop a concern that the study abroad experience, in many cases, is not all it should or could be. As a very smart student now on a Marshall fellowship—someone who clearly appreciates the value of internationalism—told me last year, "For many students, study abroad is a semester off, not a semester on." (2009, p. A88)

Increasingly cautious about traditional reports that study abroad transforms student lives and develops critical knowledge and skills, many faculty, staff, employers, and members of the general public are now questioning what it is that the rapidly growing number of U.S. students abroad are in fact typically learning through the experience.

Three Paradigms

These two very different takes on study abroad—an optimistic and often enthusiastic view that students normally and naturally learn a lot of useful things, and a more skeptical and sober appraisal that too many of them are at this point not learning very well—have uneasily coexisted for decades. Conflicting aims for and claims about student learning have in fact been a feature of U.S. study abroad since at least the early 1960s (Hoffa, 2007), and it is clear that members of the study abroad community are now increasingly questioning whether study abroad "is all it should or could be." We are in the midst of a long, drawn-out, and now accelerating reappraisal about how we conceive of learning abroad, and about the extent to which we should more systematically involve ourselves in our students' learning.

This accelerating evolution from earlier to newer ways of framing study abroad recalls Thomas Kuhn's (1962) description of a shift between "paradigms"—a transition from one "accepted model or pattern" to another, with the movement to the new paradigm occurring because it is "more successful . . . in solving a few problems that the group of practitioners has come to recognize as acute" (p. 23). Kuhn describes a successful paradigm shift, the eventual elimination of the old paradigm by the new, as a "scientific revolution." The ensuing decades have shown that the dynamics Kuhn describes, the specific ways that a "community of practitioners" (p. x) comes to embrace a new paradigm, powerfully account for major changes of perspective, belief, and practice that occur within academic disciplines as well as other domains, such as study abroad.

The concerns that the study abroad community is increasingly voicing about the aims, methods, and outcomes of study abroad are an expression of a classic paradigm shift; increasing awareness and complaints that students are not learning what they have long been assumed to learn represent what Kuhn (1962) calls "anomalies, or violations of expectation [that] attract the increasing attention of a scientific community" (p. xi). When such anomalies persist and begin to seem "more than just a puzzle," and more and more members of a community turn their attention to solving them, "the transition to crisis . . . has begun" (p. 82). And once the search for answers to such persistent anomalies proceeds beyond the crisis point, a new paradigm emerges, one that "reconstructs" the field:

> The transition from a paradigm in crisis to a new one . . . is far from a cumulative process, one achieved by an articulation or extension of the old paradigm. Rather it is a reconstruction of the field from new fundamentals, a reconstruction that changes some of the field's most elementary theoretical generalizations as well as many of its paradigm methods and applications. . . . When the transition is complete, the profession will have changed its view of the field, its methods, and its goals. One perceptive historian, viewing a classic case of a science's reorientation by paradigm change, recently described it as "picking up the other end of the stick," a process that involves "handling the same bundle of data as before, but placing them in a new system of relations with one another by giving them a different framework." (pp. 84–85)

Kuhn's description of the "reconstruction of the field," the dynamic by which one paradigm shifts to another, is epistemological—that is, he is describing the process by which a community of practitioners passes from an older to a newer worldview about the structure of knowledge, about its likely limits, and about how knowledge is learned and taught. This dynamic process includes profound shifts of perspective regarding the theoretical orientations we use to explain and understand phenomena, the core assumptions we accept about our field, and the research methods or tools that we use to create and assess knowledge.

The questions we are asking in this book frame the history of study abroad epistemologically. What does the education abroad community mean by "learning," at home or abroad? When our students return home, what do they know and understand, and what are they able to do, that they did and could not when they departed? How do they learn abroad? Does the process of learning abroad differ essentially from the process of learning at home? What is the proper role of educators in helping students abroad learn? In calling on Kuhn to help us respond to these and related questions, we are exploring the ways that the "bundle of data"—in the case of study abroad, theories about learning and teaching, assumptions about the aims and roles of educators and students, the goals and objectives of different program models, even the very nature of study abroad itself—has been and is being significantly reconfigured. Put differently, members of the study abroad community have responded and continue to respond very differently to the questions we are asking, according to which set of paradigmatic assumptions they have used or are using to frame learning and teaching abroad.

In an earlier discussion about changes in the study abroad field, Vande Berg and Paige (2009) described a shift from a traditional "teacher-centered" to a "learner-centered" education abroad paradigm and identified a number of historical developments that have contributed to this transition. These include the increasing importance of assessment in higher education, the impressive body of theoretical insights and research findings known as the Scholarship of Teaching and Learning (SOTL) and the increasingly important role that centers of teaching and learning are playing in disseminating these SOTL findings at universities in the United States and abroad (Robinson, chapter 10, this volume), and the coming-of-age of intercultural relations as a legitimate area of academic inquiry (for other earlier treatments of paradigm shifts in study abroad, see Vande Berg 2003, 2004, 2009; Vande Berg et al., 2009).

In assembling this volume, in reading and reflecting on the contributions of its authors, we have come to two new understandings about the ways that different assumptions about teaching and learning have shaped and changed study abroad over time. First, these shifting assumptions are not limited to the field of study abroad: Changing views of teaching and learning abroad represent only one manifestation of a much broader paradigm shift in the ways that theorists, researchers, teachers, and practitioners in many parts of the world are coming to new understandings about how learners learn, and about how educators can best intervene to help them learn. To be broad enough to take in all of the disciplines, traditions, and practices represented in this book, our paradigm shift needs, then, to be described in terms other than "teacher-centered" and "learner-centered," terms that might suggest that its reach is more or less restricted to theory and practice within the fields of education and study abroad. This chapter offers a different and more comprehensive language of paradigms for describing the profound changes occurring in the study abroad field.

Second, placed in historical perspective, we can now see that during the nearly 100 years of its existence, study abroad has evolved through three significantly different accounts of the nature of knowing and learning—from "positivism" to "relativism" and then to "experiential/constructivism." There is nothing new about describing the history of the past century as a progression across three periods; it has long been commonplace in the humanities and social sciences to describe recent history as an evolution from traditional to modernism and then postmodernism (see, for example, Kegan, 1994). However, we most clearly owe our own framing of study abroad as a three-paradigm progression to four of this volume's authors: Milton J. Bennett (see chapter 4) for his characterization of the evolution of intercultural relations as a progression from "positivism" to "relativism" and then to "constructivism"; David A. Kolb (see chapter 6), whose seminal work on Experiential Learning Theory (ELT) has strongly informed contemporary study abroad theory and practice and has led us to refer to the third paradigm as "experiential/constructivist"; Bruce La Brack (coauthor of chapters 8 and 11; personal communication, June 10, 2010), who describes the evolution of intercultural relations in the work of the cultural anthropologist Edward T. Hall, a founder of intercultural communications, as a three-stage progression from a "Traditional" to an "Ethnography of Communication" and then to a "Coordinated Management of Meaning" paradigm; and Douglas K. Stuart (see chapter 3), who in discussing Robert Kegan's developmental model of human consciousness has helped us to understand why so many members of the study abroad community continue to embrace positivist and relativist assumptions in their work in spite of the convincing interdisciplinary evidence that supports the experiential/constructivist paradigm.

Important changes in study abroad theory and practice that we are now experiencing—innovations in the design and delivery of programs abroad; growing enrollments in nontraditional destinations; a growing willingness to award credit for experiential learning; increasing calls for assessing student learning; structured facilitation of student learning prior to, during, and after study abroad; the use of online technologies to teach and train students before and during study abroad—need to be understood, then, as more than events strung along a chronological chain, with earlier events preparing for or "causing" others farther down the line. Kuhn reminds us that change does not always occur incrementally, with each successive discovery refining or improving those discoveries that preceded it. While a straightforward history of study abroad would represent the evolution of study abroad as chronologically ordered "facts" or "events," our own approach to understanding these as more epistemological than historical, with ongoing shifts occurring within an unfolding progression of three paradigms, throws into sharp relief the nature and meaning of what Kuhn (p. xi) would call the "anomalies or violations of expectation" that have challenged and continue to challenge the study abroad community.

Introducing the Chapters in Parts Two and Three

The authors in Part Two, "Foundations of Teaching and Learning," speak to the ways that their disciplines have contributed to the convergence of our assumptions about teaching and learning around the experiential/constructivist paradigm:

- Douglas K. Stuart discusses the increasingly important role of developmental models for our understanding about how individuals learn—models that play an important role in the experiential/constructivist paradigm. Exploring the significance of Robert Kegan's developmental model, he identifies parallels between it, on the one hand, and Bennett's Developmental Model of Intercultural Sensitivity (DMIS) and Hammer's Intercultural Development Continuum (IDC), on the other.
- Milton J. Bennett begins with a three-paradigm account of the evolution of intercultural relations; then, grounding his DMIS in constructivism—as he points out, a core concept of the emerging third paradigm—he discusses the implications of each of the three paradigms for intercultural learning and development and characterizes the continuing presence of the three in current study abroad theory and practice as "paradigmatic confusion."
- Mitchell R. Hammer discusses each of the five stages of his IDC, a revised version of the DMIS that he has published following his research on the original model. He summarizes applications of the Intercultural Development Inventory (IDI) (the instrument that he and Bennett codeveloped in the mid-1990s, and that continues to play a prominent role in current research) in study abroad practice and argues that a growing body of IDI-based research seriously undermines what he calls the "global contact hypothesis."

- Angela M. Passarelli and David A. Kolb introduce ELT, outlining its primary assumptions and describing both Kolb's Learning Style Inventory and his "learning spiral," a multilinear developmental model that, like the DMIS, continues to play a key role in disseminating experiential/constructivist assumptions into study abroad. They describe "deep learning," whether at home or abroad, as experiential, developmental, holistic, and dialectic.
- James E. Zull discusses recent neurological evidence that provides striking empirical support for Kolb's theories on preferred learning styles and the learning spiral. Emphasizing the importance of emotion in learning abroad, and linking the processes of learning in the brain to the learning spiral, he notes that "the challenges of study abroad cannot be met simply by studying more" (see page 163) and explores ways that educators can use this knowledge to adapt their teaching to the needs of different types of learners.
- Bruce La Brack and Laura Bathurst discuss the roles that two very different theoretical and research traditions, cultural anthropology and intercultural communication, have played in the emergence of "interventionism" in study abroad. Tracing what they describe as the largely diverging paths of these two traditions, they conclude by discussing how the two are coming to converge in current training programs.
- Victor Savicki opens with an overview of the history of psychology, showing how theory and research have over time become increasingly oriented around constructivist principles. He relies on a framework that distinguishes between the affective, behavioral, and cognitive dimensions of psychological experience; contrasting "learning by chance" and "learning by design," he suggests ways that educators can apply research findings in helping their students adapt effectively to living and learning abroad.
- Jennifer Meta Robinson discusses the development of SOTL as a growing movement in higher education in many parts of the world; she argues that the study abroad "learning community," whether working with students at home or abroad, will benefit by applying SOTL insights and evidence in program design and teaching.

The authors in Part Three, "Program Applications: Intervening in Student Learning," provide us with six important examples of study abroad programming that demonstrate the nature of teaching and learning within the experiential/constructivist paradigm. These six "training interventions" appear in chronological order:

- Laura Bathurst and Bruce La Brack discuss the University of the Pacific's study abroad approach to training, the oldest continuously operating study abroad training program in the United States. Launched by La Brack in 1976, the program quickly evolved to assume its current form: pre- and post-study abroad courses, both offered for academic credit, and both required of Pacific's School of International Studies students. Pre- and post-IDI testing allow faculty to understand to what extent student learning outcomes are being met. This study abroad program is unique: The locus of learning is not abroad—as is the case with virtually all other programs—but on campus. Following their return to campus, students in the reentry course apply what they have learned, before and during the experiences abroad, to their lives at home.

- Lilli Engle and John Engle chronicle their development of the American University Center of Provence (AUCP). Active planning began in 1993; launched in Aix-en-Provence in 1994 and several years later in Marseille, the AUCP is arguably the first study abroad program designed in its entirety to help participating students meet clear learning outcomes. Before taking any other steps, the directors identified two outcomes, intercultural development and French language acquisition, to guide their choice and development of all elements of the program. Courses, housing, community engagement, a required intercultural relations course, and more—the entire program is designed to challenge and support students as they work to meet these predetermined learning outcomes. The directors have relied on pre- and post-IDI testing for more than 10 years to inform ongoing adjustments in program design and delivery.

- R. Michael Paige, Tara A. Harvey, and Kate S. McCleary describe the development of the Maximizing Study Abroad Program at the University of Minnesota. The project began in 1993, when Paige and other members of a project team conducted research on student learning, the results of which then guided their writing of three guides—for, respectively, students, instructors, and study abroad professionals— designed to support student learning of second-language and intercultural development strategies. From 2002 to 2005, the team conducted a research study that used the IDI and other instruments to assess student learning. The results informed their development of an online course, first called Maximizing Study Abroad, and now called Global Identity; trained instructors at the University of Minnesota use the *Student Guide* to facilitate the language learning and intercultural development of many of the university's students abroad.

- Kris Hemming Lou and Gabriele Weber Bosley discuss their development of the Intentional, Targeted Intervention model, two online, elective, and asynchronous courses designed to support the intercultural development of Bellarmine University and Willamette University students who while abroad are organized into small learning communities. Intentionally focused, since 2003, on experiential/constructivist theory, Lou and Bosley teach students from their own campuses; students abroad as well as a number of international students studying on the two home campuses are eligible to enroll. Each of the courses begins with a required pre-departure and concludes with a required reentry program. For the past eight years Lou and Bosley have conducted pre- and posttesting and continue to use the results to guide improvements in course design and delivery.
- Adriana Medina-López-Portillo and Riikka Salonen discuss their participation, as members of the design and training team, in the development of The Scholar Ship, a shipboard education program whose goals and outcomes included the development of students' intercultural competence through the creation of a shipboard learning community. The team worked to align the learning outcomes with all elements of the program: courses, housing, excursions, counseling, and cocurricular activities. Even the operation of the on-board judicial system was informed by experiential/constructivist theories, including the DMIS and Personal Leadership. The team used the IDI in training faculty and staff, as well as students, and relied on the instrument in the pre- and posttesting of students during the two semesters that The Scholar Ship operated.
- Michael Vande Berg, Meghan Quinn, and Catherine Menyhart discuss the ongoing development of the Student Learning Program, which began in 2006 with two preparatory projects: a learning outcomes project, followed by the On-Line Pre-Departure Orientation project. The development of an intercultural course, the Seminar on Living and Learning Abroad, followed. The course focuses on three learning outcomes: increasing students' awareness of themselves as

cultural beings, enhancing their awareness of others in their own cultural contexts, and developing their capacities to bridge cultural differences between self and other. The seminar was launched in 2008, and the Council on International Educational Exchange now offers this elective course to students enrolled in most of its semester programs abroad. The authors, who have learned through IDI pre- and posttesting of students enrolled in the seminar that instructors need a lot of support to learn how to facilitate this experiential, developmental, and holistic course, devote considerable time and energy to training and coaching them.

Three Master Narratives

Borrowing a concept from critical theory, we frame positivism, relativism, and experiential/constructivism as competing "master narratives." These narratives provide the members of the extended study abroad community—those who design and deliver programs and conduct research at those sites, other faculty and staff at institutions and organizations who simply "know things" about study abroad, the students who enroll in programs abroad, their parents, and employers who hire students who have studied abroad when they graduate—with a coherent account of the study abroad "world." Cultural communities do not normally reflect on their master narratives. We offer the narratives here because we believe that bringing them into awareness can help us understand the current state of study abroad practices and policies, and in the process shed light on how we have arrived at them.

It is important to note that although master narratives help us organize our lives into meaningful patterns, they can also limit our capacity to adapt to new conditions and take advantage of new opportunities. The social force of a particular narrative leads us to selectively perceive those things that tend to confirm its assumptions and to ignore, deny, minimize, and otherwise explain away things that fall outside it.

The Positivist Narrative: Learning Through "Experience" and Basic Exposure to the New and Different

Our students learn through being exposed to a world that is stable, unchanging, and profoundly material. This external and objective world is the primary agent of learning, and students come to know things through their physical senses, a universal process that is known as "experience." As a student experiences the new and different abroad, he or she acquires significant fragments of these experiences as they imprint themselves on and are stored in his or her mind.

Because our students learn through the force of an outside agency—the physical environment—we need to make sure they have a reasonably good knowledge of the local language before they depart: The better their language abilities, the more they will be able to benefit from the broadening influences that the environment will give them.

It is in the nature of things that some human societies are superior to others in this paradigm. Through a process of natural selection, these "civilized" societies, most of them located in Western Europe, have come to dominate less advantaged groups. We wish to send our students to these privileged places so that they will acquire valuable knowledge through reading edifying works, visiting famous landmarks, and attending university lectures at the summits of human civilization. Our students acquire desirable social skills in such places as well, becoming more seasoned, refined, and cultivated as they come into contact with the types of sophisticated people who live there.

Before the students depart, we offer them tips about the ways that local people behave—"lists of dos and don'ts"—so that they can avoid making embarrassing social gaffes that could prevent them from taking full advantage of the experience.

Study abroad offers valuable ways to enrich and diversify the home campus curriculum: The disciplinary or interdisciplinary knowledge our students acquire abroad will supplement what they learn at home.

Students who have demonstrated on the home campus that they are academically serious and socially mature—the ones who have earned good grades and respected campus conduct policies—deserve to go abroad and will benefit from the experience. If they return home without showing evidence that they have acquired desirable knowledge and skills, we need to increase the minimum GPA, the number of semesters of language, or take other steps to improve our selection process so we can weed out those who are undeserving.

The positivist narrative reached its high watermark during study abroad's formative decades; but while the European Grand Tour provides the signature program model for the narrative (Vande Berg, 2004), we can see, in beliefs and practices embraced by some educators today, that positivist assumptions are still to a significant extent informing the contemporary study abroad community.

The Relativist Paradigm: Learning Through Being "Immersed" in a New and Different Environment

All cultures are equal: No single culture or perspective is inherently superior to any other. Each culture is also unique: Its members have over time responded differently to a common set of human needs and desires. However, the essential things that all humans share—our common humanity—is more important than any differences that we encounter in another culture, differences that might at first glance seem to keep us apart.

Our students often find it difficult, though, to deal with differences when they go abroad. They have trouble understanding that if they would simply "engage" with the new and different they would quickly come to discover the commonalities that bind them and the members of the host culture together.

Because we have learned that many of our students are unable to engage on their own while abroad, we take steps, whenever we can, to help them engage by "immersing" them in the new culture. We design programs, structure the student experience, so that they will spend as much time as possible engaged in the host culture and with host nationals. For example, we encourage them to study abroad for longer, rather than shorter, periods of time; to live with host families; to enroll directly in host university courses; to spend all of their free time with host nationals; and so on.

Students are normally "transformed" through studying abroad. We know this is true because our students themselves confirm it: When they return home, many of them tell us that study abroad has indeed "transformed" them or has "changed their lives."

Because students are learning abroad in ways they will not if they stay at home, colleges and universities should send as many of them abroad as possible.

Students who are academically serious and socially mature—the ones who have earned good grades on campus and who have respected student conduct policies—are the types of students who will be transformed through the experience. It sometimes happens that students return home without having been transformed; in these cases, they have no one to blame but themselves.

As we bring the relativist narrative into awareness, we can appreciate the extent to which many of our current practices and policies are informed by relativist assumptions—and the extent to which the enduring force of those assumptions allows many members of our community to ignore, deny, minimize, or explain away the problems about student learning—the "anomalies, or violations of expectation"—that we reviewed in the opening section of this chapter.

The Experiential/Constructivist Paradigm: Learning Through Immersion and Cultural Mentoring

The world is no longer stable and unchanging: Now a learner individually creates and together with other members of his or her several cultural groups cocreates the world even as he or she perceives and experiences it. Learning does not occur as the environment imprints itself on the mind; it occurs through ongoing transactions between the individual and the environment, with humans the principal agents of their own learning.

The meaning of things is not "in" the environment; the environment "modulates," but does not determine, what humans learn. The things that a learner "brings to" an event—habitual ways of perceiving and behaving that have been informed by genetic makeup, prior experience, and present needs and requirements—determine his or her cognitive, affective, perceptual, and psychomotor capacities and play a fundamental role in shaping his or her experience of what is "out there."

When our students study abroad, they may learn things and learn in ways that they will not if they stay at home. Although disciplinary and interdisciplinary learning abroad is important, intercultural learning is foundational—among other things, it allows students to understand that new and different teaching and learning norms and practices are grounded in the values and beliefs of the local culture.

The primary goal of learning abroad is not, then, simply to acquire knowledge but to develop in ways that allow students to learn to shift cultural perspective and to adapt their behavior to other cultural contexts—knowledge that will allow them to interact more effectively and appropriately with others throughout their lives.

Intercultural learning is experiential, developmental, and holistic. The appropriate emblem for learning abroad is not a yard light equipped with a motion sensor that is tripped when a student enters the yard, so that he or she is suddenly bathed in the light of new knowledge. Learning is more like a dimmer switch. As the student enters a dark room, he or she needs to find the switch and begin to experiment with the effects of moving it up or down. Each student's genetic makeup, previous learning experiences, and current needs and interests have equipped—"structured"—the student differently; the differing capacities of students as learners mean that each of them will experience, in unique ways, both the act of manipulating the dimmer switch and the very qualities of the room that are illumined through that act.

Students who learn well at home do not, therefore, necessarily learn or develop effectively abroad. Some of them come to the study abroad experience with the capacities to learn and develop effectively on their own in new and different cultural contexts—but most do not. Most students learn to learn effectively abroad only when an educator intervenes, strategically and intentionally.

Educators who intervene in student learning and development in these ways need to be trained to do so effectively.

When students return home without having learned and developed effectively, educators do not immediately assume that the students are at fault. Although this may be the case, they are also aware that adjustments in the program may need to be made so that future students participating in it will be more likely to succeed.

Unlike positivism and relativism, the experiential/constructivist paradigm is characterized by the efforts of theorists and practitioners to bring its assumptions into awareness. In this regard, then—the commitment to helping learners and teachers alike become conscious of and explicit about their teaching and learning assumptions—the third paradigm is profoundly different from the other two. Each of the authors in this volume is informed by and speaks from an experiential/constructivist worldview.

The Emerging Experiential/Constructivist Paradigm: Some Important Implications for Teaching and Learning Abroad

Today an increasing number of programs are grounded in experiential/constructivist assumptions about teaching and learning. As we will see in Part Three, those educators who are developing such programs, and who are teaching and assessing students enrolling in them, understand the limitations of three key beliefs and practices from the positivist or relativist paradigms. The first concerns the nature of student learning abroad, the second the role educators play in supporting such learning, and the third their orientation to assessing it.

Moving Learners Beyond Habitual Ways of Experiencing and Behaving

As we will see in chapter 2 (Paige & Vande Berg), recent research assessing and comparing the learning of students enrolled in experiential/constructivist, versus more traditional, programs helps us appreciate how difficult it is for most individuals to get outside the worldviews that they have created and cocreated. Like all of us, students abroad experience the world in habitual ways, strongly informed by the cultural contexts in which they have lived. They do not begin to experience themselves and others differently, they do not begin to develop interculturally—gaining the capacities to shift cultural perspective and to interact more effectively and appropriately with culturally different others—simply by virtue of going abroad and crossing national (and sometimes linguistic) boundaries. Experiencing "the new and different" does not in and of itself change deeply engrained perspectives and behavior. As John Dewey (1897) began to discuss more than a century ago, and as recent research findings and theoretical insights from the disciplines and traditions represented in this book show, experience is simply not the same thing as learning. Rather, each of us learns through transactions between ourselves and the environment; what we bring to the environment—that is, our genetic makeup, our cultural makeup, and the ways that these have equipped and conditioned us to learn and to know—is ultimately more important than the environment in determining how we will experience it, and what we will learn from it.

The Limitations of "Immersion" as a Learning Strategy

As we have seen, the relativist narrative holds that students learn effectively when educators take steps to "immerse" them in the host culture because this presumably increases the likelihood that they will engage with the new and different. Within the context of this paradigm, students are more likely to learn when educators manipulate the learning environment—through placing them in home stays, for example, or by directly enrolling them in host university courses. However, when viewed through an experiential/constructivist lens, we see that immersion in experience abroad will not, in and of itself, lead students to learn effectively. As the review of recent research in the next chapter will show, students do not simply and automatically learn when they are, for example, placed in home stays abroad. The extent to which they learn and develop through this familiar "immersion" strategy is a function of how relatively developed they are interculturally—which is, to say, of the ways that they perceive and experience cultural similarities and differences in their interactions in the home stay. The research record shows that other common immersion strategies that much of the study abroad community has for decades applied in developing programs are also in only limited ways predictive of student development.

Most students do not, then, meaningfully develop either through simple exposure to the environment or through having educators take steps to increase the amount of that exposure through "immersing" them. Instead, students learn and develop effectively and appropriately when educators intervene more intentionally through well-designed training programs that continue throughout the study abroad experience. Although the empirical evidence suggests that students who are "immersed" in a new culture do develop interculturally somewhat more than students who are simply left to learn on their own, the research also shows that the gains students make in programs that seek to "immerse" them are quite modest when compared with the gains students make when trained educators intervene, throughout the study abroad experience, to help them develop the capacities to deal effectively with crossing cultures.

The data, in other words, suggest three progressively greater "levels" of intercultural development. Within a positivist framework, in which students are presumed to learn through coming into contact with, or being exposed to, cultural difference, the research findings show that students develop interculturally, on average, little if at all. Within a relativist framework, in which students are said to learn through being "immersed" in cultural difference, students learn somewhat more than they do when they are left to their own devices—but the gains are not impressive. Only when students are learning within a context informed by experiential/constructivist perspectives—only when they are immersed in another culture and receive meaningful intercultural mentoring and opportunities for reflection on meaning-making—do most students develop to an impressive degree. Put differently, the data show that students learn and develop considerably more when educators prepare them to become more self-reflective, culturally self-aware, and aware of "how they know what they know." In developing a meta-awareness of their own processes of perceiving and knowing, students come to understand both how they habitually experience and make meaning of events, and how they can use that newfound understanding to help them engage more effectively and appropriately with culturally different others.

Reports That "Study Abroad Transformed Me"

What should we make, then, of student reports that they have been "transformed" through studying abroad? We as a community have traditionally placed a lot of value on such anecdotal reports about learning abroad, using them as evidence in order to assure ourselves and others that our students are in fact learning effectively. It is tempting to accept such self-reports at face value—and not only because we hear this sort of thing from a fair number of students. It is also simply tempting to accept that a student has been "transformed" when she sincerely and enthusiastically tells us this is the case. However, there are at least three good reasons why we should respond cautiously when students tell us that study abroad has "changed their lives," three reasons why we should not take such self-reports as "evidence" that they have learned as profoundly as their words suggest.

First, we do not rely on self-reports to assess student learning in other domains; why, then, do we do so where learning and development abroad is concerned? If a student at a home campus in the United States came to us complaining that she had received a B in, say, Advanced French, rather than the A she thought that she deserved, it is unlikely, to say the least, that we would simply conclude that the student deserved the A. No matter how sincere and enthusiastic she was in telling us that the grade did not accurately reflect her abilities, we would not pick up the telephone and call the faculty member in the French Department who had taught the course, and ask him or her to change the grade. If we did decide to call the instructor to inquire about the final grade, we might ask him or her to confirm whether it had been computed correctly, but we would not presume to ask that the grade be changed. We would instead assume that he or she had relied on some external standard or standards in assigning it. If the grade, for example, represented the average of all of the student's work throughout the semester, then the standard might be the French grammatical structures, vocabulary, and functions that the instructor had covered in the course. If the final grade also reflected his or her assessment of the student's oral proficiency in French at the end of the course—or, more specifically, the extent to which the student's oral performance had improved by the end of the term, as measured through pre- and posttesting—then the external standard he or she relied on might be the American Council on the Testing of Foreign Languages (ACTFL) oral proficiency scale, and the instrument used in the pre- and posttesting, perhaps the Simulated Oral Proficiency Interview, would also be based on the ACTFL scale.

A second reason we should be cautious when our students tell us that study abroad has "transformed" them is that self-reports are notoriously unreliable in the sense that an individual may not have enough knowledge about the topic being discussed to draw valid conclusions about it. Developmental theorists—including Jean Piaget (1952), Kurt Lewin (1951), David Kolb (1984; chapter 6 of this volume), William Perry (1970), Mary Belenky

(Belenky, Clinchy, Goldberger, & Tarule, 1986), Milton Bennett (1993; chapter 4 of this volume), Mitchell Hammer (2009; chapter 5 of this volume), and Jack Mezirow (2000)—have been exploring the nature of "transformation" for decades and have provided us with theories that provide convincing explanations and descriptions about what the phenomenon is and how it develops (see Stuart, chapter 3 of this volume). Mezirow's (2000) Transformation Theory, for example, offers useful insights about the ways that emotional responses to crises can serve as catalysts that lead to "frame shifts," a developmental capacity that intercultural relations typically places at the core of intercultural competence. For Bennett (see page 102 of this volume), "The crux of communication . . . [is] the ability to transcend our own limited experience and embody the world as another is experiencing it"; for Hammer (2009), cultural adaptation is "the capability of shifting perspective to another culture and adapting behavior according to cultural context" (p. 209; see also chapter 5 of this volume).

When a student tells us that she has been "transformed," she may be describing or sharing experiences that are deeply meaningful to her, perhaps sharing her sense that she has, for instance, gained greater self-reliance or independence while abroad. However, unless we have good reason to believe that she is reporting on a capacity to shift her frame of cultural reference—the developmental capacity to begin to experience events from the point of view of another person—then we should suspect that what she is describing is something other than "transformation," as this concept is now framed within the context of developmental and intercultural theory. If we do discover, in talking with her, that she is in fact describing "transformation" as such theories define it, and if through testing her (with the IDI, for example) we conclude that she does seem able to shift her frame of reference in different cultural contexts to that of culturally different others, we will still not necessarily be in a position to conclude that "study abroad has transformed her." That is, unless we had tested her at the beginning and at the end of her study abroad experience, using a valid and reliable instrument like the IDI, we cannot assume that she developed this core intercultural capacity through studying abroad.

Self-reports can be and sometimes are unreliable on a third count as well: The person making the report may not be telling the truth. In raising this possibility, we are not suggesting that students are simply lying—in the sense that they are "making it up"—when they tell us they have been transformed. We are, however, suggesting that a student who tells us that studying abroad has been "the best thing that has ever happened" to her may, consciously or unconsciously, be exhibiting what testing experts call "social desirability bias"; that is, she may be telling us what she believes we want or expect to hear. Consider this: If just about everybody the student had ever talked with about study abroad had told her that the experience would change her life—if her institution, the instructors and staff organizing her experience abroad, and her parents embrace a relativist master narrative that frames learning abroad as "transformational"—then perhaps we should not be surprised when she returns to campus and tells us that she has, in fact, been transformed.

In saying that there are good reasons why we should respond with healthy skepticism to student reports about being transformed, we are not suggesting that students are not learning anything through studying abroad. This is clearly not the case. Faculty and staff who work with students while they are abroad or after their return home often find that they "know when and why study abroad fails or succeeds" (Brewer & Cunningham, 2009, p. 1), and the sincerity and enthusiasm of those students who tell us that study abroad has succeeded is unmistakable, strongly suggesting that some, perhaps even many, of them are learning, and understand that they are learning, through studying abroad. Anyone who attends an annual Forum on Education Abroad conference and listens to the formal presentations by recipients of the Forum's Undergraduate Research Award will very likely come away understanding that some students learn very well indeed while abroad. We as a community have a bad habit, though, of leaping from that fact—that certain students learn a lot—to the untenable conclusion that most if not all students therefore learn a lot. What we are suggesting is that we, as a teaching and learning community (see Robinson, chapter 10), need to pay much more attention both to the ways we are framing the concept of "student learning" and to the sorts of evidence we are relying on before we conclude that students, in general, are "learning well abroad," or that they are learning more "successfully" in one program rather than another.

The unfolding of the three paradigms that we have briefly described in this chapter has not occurred in anything resembling a neat and tidy historical chronology. Some members of the study abroad community are still working from positivist or relativist assumptions, even though increasing numbers of their colleagues are coming to embrace experiential/constructivist perspectives. And consistent with Kuhn's theory of paradigm shifts, some faculty and staff were responding to anomalies within positivism well before most of their colleagues had even begun to consider examining or changing their own practices, while others had come early to the understanding that relativism's core study abroad assumption—that students abroad learn effectively through enrolling in programs that aim to "immerse" them in new and different experiences—was simply not working as well as predicted.

What these "early adaptors" understood, and what other members of the community are increasingly coming to realize, is that educators need to intervene in focused and intentional ways, throughout the study abroad experience, if most students are to learn and develop effectively and appropriately. The authors of this volume, representing a wide range of disciplines and traditions and study abroad programs, converge around the core perspectives of the experiential/constructivist paradigm, embracing and enacting the view that effective and deep learning (Fink, 2003; see also chapters 6 and 14 of this volume), whether students are at home or abroad, is necessarily experiential, developmental, and holistic.

References

Belenky, M., Clinchy, B., Goldberger, N., & Tarule, J. (1986). *Women's ways of knowing: The development of self, voice, and mind.* New York: Basic Books.

Bennett, M. J. (1993). *Towards ethnorelativism: A developmental model of intercultural sensitivity.* Yarmouth, ME: Intercultural Press.

Blankinship, D. G. (2010). Students learning abroad increase drinking: Study. *Huff Post College: The Internet Newspaper.* Retrieved from http://www.huffingtonpost .com/2010/10/12/students-learning-abroad-_n_759158.html

Bok, D. (2006). *Our underachieving colleges: A candid look at how much students learn and why they should be learning more.* Princeton, NJ: Princeton University Press.

Brewer, E., & Cunningham, K. (2009). *Integrating study abroad into the curriculum: Theory and practice across the disciplines.* Sterling, VA: Stylus.

Burness, J. (2009, September 21). Study abroad is often not all it should be. *The Chronicle of Higher Education.* Retrieved from http://chronicle.com/article/Colleges-Should-Focus-on-th/48486/

Chow, P., & Bhandari, R. (2010). *Open doors report on international educational exchange.* New York: Institute of International Education.

Citron, J. L. (1996). *Short-term study abroad: Integration, third culture formation, and re-entry.* Annual NAFSA conference, Phoenix, AZ: NAFSA Conference Paper.

Citron, J. L. (2002). U.S. students abroad: Host culture integration or third culture formation? In W. Grünzweig & N. Rinehart (Eds.), *Rockin' in Red Square: Critical approaches to international education in the age of cyberculture* (pp. 41–56). Piscataway, NJ: Transaction.

Collentine, J., & Freed, B. (Eds.). (2004). Learning context and its effects on second language acquisition [Thematic issue]. *Studies in Second Language Acquisition, 26*(2), 153–363.

Comp, D., Gladding, S., Rhodes, G., Stephenson, S., & Vande Berg, M. (2007). Literature and resources for education abroad outcomes assessment. In M. Bolen (Ed.), *A guide to outcomes assessment in education abroad* (pp. 97–135). Carlisle, PA: The Forum on Education Abroad.

Dewey, J. (1897). My pedagogic creed. *School Journal, 54*, 77–80.

Donnelly, L. (2010, September 6). Cartoon. *The New Yorker*, p. 64.

Engle, J. (1986, October 22). Study abroad: It's good for students if it's well-planned. *The Chronicle of Higher Education, 33*, 88.

Engle, J. (1995, March 17). Critical attention for study abroad. *The Chronicle of Higher Education*. Retrieved from http://chronicle.com/article/Critical-Attention-for-Study/85649/?key=Sjl7eVdvZCBIN3I3fnJBLnBXYXV6cUMpantCMSka YVlQ

Engle, J. (1998). At century's end, it's time to re-think international education. Breakfast Plenary, Council for International Educational Exchange International Conference. El Paso, TX.

Engle, J., & Engle, L. (2002). Neither international nor educative: Study abroad in the age of globalization. In W. Grünzweig & N. Rinehart (Eds.), *Rockin' in Red Square: Critical approaches to international education in the age of cyberculture* (pp. 25–39). Piscataway, NJ: Transaction.

Fink, L. D. (2003). *Creating significant learning experiences: An integrated approach to designing college courses*. San Francisco, CA: Jossey-Bass.

Freed, B. F. (1995). *Second language acquisition in a study abroad context*. Philadelphia, PA: John Benjamins.

Gardner, P., Gross, L., & Steglitz, I. (2008). Unpacking your study abroad experience: Critical reflection for workplace competencies. *CERI Research Brief, 1*(1), 1–10.

Hammer, M. R. (2009). The intercultural development inventory: An approach for assessing and building intercultural competence. In M. A. Moodian (Ed.), *Contemporary leadership and intercultural competence* (pp. 203–217). Thousand Oaks, CA: Sage.

Hoffa, W. (2007). *A history of U.S. study abroad: Beginnings to 1965*. Carlisle, PA: Frontiers Journal.

Kegan, R. (1994). *In over our heads: The mental demands of modern life*. Cambridge, MA: Harvard University Press.

Kolb, D. (1984). *Experiential learning: Experience as the source of learning and development*. Englewood Cliffs, NJ: Prentice Hall.

Kowarski, I. (2010). Colleges help students to translate the benefits of study abroad. *The Chronicle of Higher Education*. Retrieved from http://chronicle.com/article/Colleges-Help-Students-to/123653/

Kuhn, T. (1962). *The structure of scientific revolutions.* Chicago, IL: The University of Chicago Press.

Lewin, K. (1951). *Field theory in social sciences.* New York: Harper & Row.

Lou, K., & Bosley, G. (2009). Dynamics of cultural contexts. In V. Savicki, (Ed.), *Developing intercultural competence and transformation* (pp. 276–296). Sterling, VA: Stylus.

Mezirow, J. (2000). *Learning as transformation: Critical perspectives on a theory in progress.* San Francisco, CA: Jossey-Bass.

Ogden, A. (2007). The view from the veranda: Understanding today's colonial student. *Frontiers: The Interdisciplinary Journal of Study Abroad, 15,* 35–55.

Paige, R. M., Cohen, A. D., & Shively, R. (2004). Assessing the impact of a strategies-based curriculum on language and culture learning abroad. *Frontiers: The Interdisciplinary Journal of Study Abroad, 10,* 253–276.

Perry, W. G., Jr. (1970). *Forms of intellectual and ethical development in the college years: A scheme.* New York: Holt, Rinehart and Winston.

Piaget, J. (1952). *The origins of intelligence in children* (M. Cook, Trans.). New York: International Universities Press.

Segalowitz, N., Freed, B., Collentine, J., Lafford, B., Lazar, N., & Díaz-Campos, M. (2004). A comparison of Spanish second language acquisition in two different learning contexts: Study abroad and the domestic classroom. [Thematic issue]. *Frontiers: The Interdisciplinary Journal of Study Abroad, 10,* 1–18.

Trooboff, S., Vande Berg, M., & Rayman, J. (2008). Employer attitudes toward study abroad. *Frontiers: The Interdisciplinary Journal of Study Abroad, 15,* 17–33.

Vande Berg, M. (2003). The case for assessing educational outcomes in study abroad. In G. T. Hult & E. C. Lashbrooke (Eds.), *Study abroad: Perspectives and experiences from business schools* (pp. 23–36). Oxford: Elsevier.

Vande Berg, M. (2004). Introduction. [Thematic issue]. *Frontiers: The Interdisciplinary Journal of Study Abroad, 10,* xii–xxii.

Vande Berg, M. (2006). Direct enrollment and the resident director. In *Notes from the field* (pp. 1–3). Portland, ME: CIEE.

Vande Berg, M. (2007a). Interventions. In *Notes from the field* (pp. 1–3). Portland, ME: CIEE.

Vande Berg, M. (2007b). Intervening in the learning of U.S. students abroad. *Journal of Studies in International Education, 11*(3), 392–398.

Vande Berg, M. (2009). Intervening in student learning abroad: A research-based inquiry. *Intercultural Education, 20*(4), 15–27.

Vande Berg, M., Connor-Linton, J., & Paige, R. M. (2009). The Georgetown Consortium Study: Intervening in student learning abroad. *Frontiers: The Interdisciplinary Journal of Study Abroad, 18,* 1–75.

Van Hoof, H. (1999). The international student experience: A U.S. industry perspective. *Journal of Studies in International Education, 3*(2), 57–71.

Woolf, M., Battenburg, J., & Pagano, M. (2009). Study abroad changed my life and other problems. A presentation at the annual conference of the Forum on

Education Abroad, Portland, OR. Retrieved from http://www.insidehighered
.com/news/2009/02/20/studyabroad#ixzz1gKaGHO58 Inside Higher Ed

Zemach-Bersin, T. (2008, March 7). American students can't be global citizens. *The Chronicle of Higher Education*. Retrieved from http://chronicle.com/article/
American-Students-Abroad-Cant/25527/

2

WHY STUDENTS ARE AND ARE NOT LEARNING ABROAD

A Review of Recent Research

R. Michael Paige and Michael Vande Berg

In this chapter, we examine the research literature on student learning in study abroad programs. Our focus is on intercultural learning and development, but the key findings have generalizability to other outcomes such as language learning, engagement with global issues, and learning in the disciplines. Periodically, we refer to other learning outcomes as they pertain to intervening in student learning. The purpose of this review is to provide readers with an empirical foundation for the arguments being advanced in favor of intervening in the study abroad learning process. Two central questions are addressed in this chapter:

1. What is the impact of interventions on intercultural learning and development in study abroad above and beyond the impact of the study abroad intercultural experience itself?
2. What is the nature of the interventions that have the greatest impact?

These questions guide our inquiry, and the answers from the literature have enabled us to better understand the intervention-related factors that have an impact on student learning in study abroad programs. The studies also permit us to examine the competing assumptions of the immersion and intervention models of learning.

This review of the literature is targeted on intercultural interventions, which we define as *intentional and deliberate pedagogical approaches, activated throughout the study abroad cycle (before, during, and after), that are designed to enhance students' intercultural competence.* Hence, this review does not discuss in depth all of the possible explanatory variables that can also have an impact on intercultural development, though we are cognizant of the fact that other variables play a role in student learning. These include *personal factors,* such as age, gender, prior intercultural experiences, and second-language proficiency. Also included are *contextual variables,* such as destination, attitudes of host nationals toward internationals, degree of cultural similarity and dissimilarity of the host to the home country, degree of cultural isolation from home country peers while abroad, and the overall psychological intensity of the intercultural experience (Paige, 1993). Instead, this review focuses on *programmatic factors* that we can design into our study abroad programs: program duration, intercultural coursework, cultural immersion opportunities, on-site and online cultural mentoring; planned intercultural contact; and regularly occurring reflection through journaling, written assignments, peer-to-peer feedback, and other mechanisms.

It should also be pointed out that we do not propose that this chapter serve as an exhaustive review of the study abroad literature over the past 50 years. For the broader historical perspective on study abroad, the reader is referred to the two-volume publication, *A History of U.S. Study Abroad* (Hoffa, 2007; Hoffa & DePaul, 2010), supported and published by The Forum on Education Abroad. For our purposes, most if not all of the relevant research literature regarding our two central questions on the nature and impact of interventions has been published since 2000. This is not to discount the importance of earlier, noteworthy studies such as Koester's (1985) large-scale survey of Council on International Educational Exchange (CIEE) students, the Study Abroad Evaluation Project (Carlson, Burn, Useem, & Yachimowicz, 1990), and the Institute for the International Education of Students' 50-year retrospective survey of past participants (Akande & Slawson, 2000; Dwyer, 2004). The emphasis of those and other earlier studies, however, was not exclusively on intercultural learning, nor was the focus on intervention as an explanatory variable. As Bennett (2010) points out in his review of intercultural learning in study abroad over the past 40 years, there certainly was considerable interest in developing such programs. But before 2000, well-designed research studies on how study abroad programs could affect intercultural learning were lacking. At that point in time, a body of knowledge that could guide study abroad design was badly needed.

Today, that situation has changed dramatically for the better. The research literature on this topic is growing rapidly. Study abroad itself has become a global phenomenon, and there is great interest throughout the world in providing programs that have a demonstrable impact on learning outcomes among secondary, tertiary, and professional school students. There is indeed an emerging accountability imperative within higher education institutions, private study abroad program providers, and youth exchange organizations that is translating into investments in research and program assessment.

Our understanding of intercultural learning and development derives in considerable part from the work of scholars and practitioners from the fields of intercultural communication, intercultural relations, anthropology, psychology, and intercultural education and training, many of whom have contributed to study abroad programming. The conceptual and empirical literature related to intercultural training is particularly salient to our interest in intercultural interventions (Landis, Bennett, & Bennett, 2004; Landis & Bhagat, 1996).

In conducting this literature review, we sought to identify research studies that meet several criteria. First, the study must adhere to rigorous research design and methodological principles. Second, the study must utilize instruments with demonstrated validity and reliability that measure key intercultural constructs. Third, the findings must be generalizable, providing a basis for comparisons across studies. Fortunately, the trend in study abroad research during the past decade has been oriented toward these criteria.

The Intercultural Development Inventory (IDI) (Hammer, 2007; Hammer & Bennett, 1998) is an intercultural instrument that exemplifies this trend. It has been shown to be a valid and reliable measure of intercultural competence (Hammer, 2011; Hammer, Bennett, & Wiseman, 2003; Paige, Jacobs-Cassuto, Yershova, & DeJaeghere, 2003) with a strong conceptual and theoretical foundation: Bennett's (1993) Developmental Model of Intercultural Sensitivity (DMIS). Its use in research makes it possible to evaluate the many approaches to developing intercultural competence in study abroad and to determine what approaches are more or less effective, something that could not be done if every study used its own instrumentation exclusively. The IDI is also being used to help design programs and guide intercultural learning (see chapters 5, 12, 13, and 16 of this volume; DeJaeghere & Cao, 2009).

By way of contrast, the student self-report or evaluation at the conclusion of a program, a mainstay of study abroad, provides us with an important narrative, a story, an account of what the students *feel* the program has meant to them. These narratives give voice to the study abroad experience. But they are ultimately unique to the student and lack generalizability because there is no external criterion with which to evaluate them (see chapter 1). Empirical research, of the type reviewed in this chapter, allows us to say, with increasing confidence, "This is what works if you wish to support intercultural learning among your students."

Maximizing Study Abroad Research Project: Curricular and Online Interventions

We begin the review with an examination of the University of Minnesota's Maximizing Study Abroad (MAXSA) project. Sponsored by the university's Center for Advanced Research on Language Acquisition and begun in 1993, MAXSA has played a key role in advancing, as well as researching, intercultural learning and development in study abroad. The MAXSA project has included (a) textbook development (1999–2002), (b) research program (2002–5), (c) text revision (2005–9), and (d) study abroad course development (2002–present). In chapter 13, Paige, Harvey, and McCleary describe the MAXSA curriculum project in greater detail. For our purposes, we lead this chapter with the MAXSA project because it is one of the first with intervention in intercultural learning as an explicit and central element of its design.

The MAXSA research program (Cohen, Paige, Shively, Emert, & Hoff, 2005; Paige, Cohen, & Shively, 2004), conducted between 2002 and 2005, set out to test rigorously the effectiveness of a new text designed to support language and culture learning: *Maximizing Study Abroad: A Students' Guide to Strategies for Language and Culture Learning and Use* (Paige, Cohen, Kappler, Chi, & Lassegard, 2002). The text was used as the basis for an online course that was taken by one group of study abroad students, who were then compared with a second group of students who did not take the course. Change scores for intercultural development, second-language learning, culture learning strategies, and language-learning strategies were compared for these two groups.

Intervention

The intervention for the experimental (E-group) students was conducted primarily online. Following a one-day pre-departure orientation (which included learning about speech acts and being introduced to the *Students'*

Guide), the students had to complete weekly assigned readings on language and culture from the *Students' Guide* throughout the semester abroad plus biweekly reflection papers (*n* = 7) pertaining to the students' responses to the assigned readings, their use of the *Guide* while abroad, and their open-ended reflections on their language- and culture-learning experiences. Students had an instructor to whom they sent their papers and with whom they could interact if they wished. On-site study abroad staff members, however, were not involved in the intervention.

Research Design

The research program utilized a true experimental design in which students (*N* = 86), all of whom would be studying abroad for three months, were randomly assigned to either the experimental (E or intervention) group (*n* = 42) or the control (C or nonintervention) group (*n* = 44). By design, the C- and E-group participants shared the experience of studying abroad for a semester in a French- or Spanish-speaking country. What differentiated the two groups was the intervention.

Pre- and posttest administrations of four instruments were conducted for all of the research subjects. The study utilized the IDI (Hammer & Bennett, 1998); the new Speech Act Measure of Language Gain (Cohen & Shively, 2002, 2002/2003); and research adaptations of the original MAXSA culture-learning and language-learning inventories, the Strategies Inventory for Learning Culture (Paige et al., 2002) and the Language Strategy Survey (Cohen, Oxford, & Chi, 2002). These are described in greater detail in chapter 13 of this volume and in Cohen et al. (2005).

Findings

Regarding intercultural development, the first finding was that the gain for all students of 4.47 points on the IDI was statistically significant. Thus, studying abroad, in and of itself, was associated with intercultural learning. The second finding showed that there was no statistically significant difference between the E-group and C-group on their intercultural development. The results of the qualitative post–study abroad interviews, however, showed that the E-group students felt that the MAXSA materials and assignments had given them a better understanding of culture in general and of their specific host culture in particular. Student after student provided examples of how the knowledge that they had gained about different cultural variables, such as communication styles, was helpful in navigating their daily interactions in country.

The language results showed, first, that the gain for all students between the pre- and posttest was statistically significant ($p < .001$) on the combined "overall success" score of all 10 speech act vignettes. On 9 of the 10 vignettes, the gain in "overall success" from the pretest to the posttest was also statistically significant, at $p < .05$ or higher. When the E- and C-groups were compared on the Speech Act Measure using categorical data (negative gain score, positive gain score, no change), the results were statistically significant ($p < .05$) in favor of the E-group. The raw data results showed E-group students outperforming C-group participants ($p < .05$) on three indicators ("appropriate level of directness": all requests; "overall success": meeting professor vignette; and "fit between vocabulary and level of formality": meeting professor vignette). The language results indicate, then, that the MAXSA intervention did have a positive impact. From an intercultural learning perspective, it is encouraging that the E-group students gained more in handling these situations in which language and culture intersect than did the C-group students.

To summarize, the MAXSA research project provides us with findings that support the intervention hypothesis, though, as we will see, the gains in intercultural competence that the E-students made were modest compared with the gains of students enrolled in a number of the other research studies that we are describing in this chapter. MAXSA stands now as a pioneering effort that has served as an important foundation for intercultural interventions in study abroad.

The Georgetown Consortium Project: Studying Immersion in Depth

The Georgetown Consortium Research Project (see chapter 16 of this volume; Vande Berg, 2009; Vande Berg, Connor-Linton, & Paige, 2009; Vande Berg & Paige, 2009) is the most comprehensive examination of immersion and its impact on intercultural development and language learning yet undertaken in study abroad research. Over a four-year period, 2003–7, the researchers examined the experiences and learning outcomes of students on 61 different study abroad programs, using a comprehensive conceptual model consisting of 14 potential explanatory factors. As seen in the research findings, among the 61 programs, the American University Center of Provence (AUCP) was the only one with a comprehensive intervention strategy, one that included intensive cultural mentoring.

The Georgetown Consortium Research Project was carried out during the same years as the MAXSA study and explored similar questions: Does immersing students in the new culture abroad help them develop interculturally? Do particular aspects of the study abroad immersion experience affect intercultural development more than others? What types of intervention can enhance learning beyond that provided by the immersion itself? The MAXSA research project provided important evidence that study abroad participants were making only limited gains in their language and intercultural development even when they had specialized materials to guide their learning. The Georgetown Consortium Research Project broadened the analysis to include a wider set of immersion-related factors that might be influencing student learning.

It is more than mere coincidence that both studies focused on the factors influencing student learning outcomes in a study abroad environment and were conducted at about the same time. As we saw in the previous chapter, by the end of the last century the study abroad community was divided about the extent to which students were learning effectively abroad on their own, and the tension between those two camps was growing acute. By examining the degree to which immersion practices and intervention approaches were advancing student learning, these two studies were representative of a paradigm shift in which researchers, first singly and then in groups, began to focus on an anomaly (Kuhn, 1962, pp. 19, 82): that students immersed in the study abroad environment were not learning as well as expected. In both testing and challenging the immersion paradigm, these studies represent, then, an accelerating shift from the relativist to the experiential/constructivist paradigm.

Research Design

The Georgetown Consortium Project utilized a pre-posttest comparison group design with the instruments administered at three points in time: before, immediately after, and some five months after the study abroad program. Two research instruments were utilized for the learning outcomes: the IDI (Hammer & Bennett, 1998) and the Simulated Oral Proficiency Interview (Stansfield, 1991, 1996).

Intervention

The Georgetown study explicitly focused on the role of immersion and intervention in student learning abroad using the seven program design elements proposed by Lilli Engle and John Engle (2003; chapter 12 of this volume). These were the program design elements or "defining components" they felt that educators needed to take into account to ensure that students would learn and develop interculturally. In the Georgetown Consortium study, these design elements were incorporated into the larger conceptual model of 14 predictor variables, operationally defined, and tested. The seven "defining components" were as follows:

1. Length of student sojourn,
2. Entry target language competence,
3. Language used in course work,
4. Context of academic work [In the study this meant whether students took classes with other U.S. students; host country students; non-U.S. international students; or a mixture of international, host, and U.S. students.],
5. Types of student housing [This meant being housed with other U.S. students, host country students, international students, or a host family.],
6. Provision for guided/structured cultural interaction and experiential learning, and
7. Guided reflection on cultural experience (2003, p. 8).

The research sample of 1,297 students included study abroad participants ($n = 1,159$) and a control group of non–study abroad students ($n = 138$).

Findings

The findings provide very little support for the immersion hypothesis. Overall, the IDI gains were not statistically significant for those students in the 60 programs that lacked an intervention strategy—in particular, cultural mentoring. Their average IDI gain was only 1.32 points, and the non–study abroad students gained a mere .07 points. To put this in perspective, the IDI scale has a 90-point range and a standard deviation of 15 points. Clearly, neither students abroad nor those at home developed interculturally in this study. By contrast, the students enrolled in the AUCP program, the only program in the study with a comprehensive intervention strategy, made a most impressive average IDI gain of 12.47 points. When the AUCP data are included, the gain for the study abroad group as a whole increased to 2.37 points.

The study showed no support at all for two of the study abroad community's preferred immersion practices: housing students with host families (thereby presumably providing the deeper social experience of a host country student) and enrolling them in host university courses (thereby presumably providing the academic experience of a host country student). The findings showed that of the four types of housing—homestays, living in an apartment or dorm with host students, living in an apartment or dorm with other U.S. students, and living with international students—only students who lived with U.S. students made statistically significant, though modest, IDI gains (3.37 points). The gain of students who lived with host families (1.07 points) was not significant. It is worth noting, however, that when students chose to *engage with* someone in the host family ("time spent with host family"), the gains were significant; those who spent 26–50% of their free time with their host family gained 3.37 points and those who spent 51–75% of their free time gained 4.95 IDI points.

Of the four classroom environments—direct enrollment in host university courses; courses designed specifically for U.S. students; courses designed specifically for international, including U.S., students; and a mixture of these three environments—direct enrollment courses fared the worst; the 349 students enrolled in these courses gained just .71 points on the IDI scale. By comparison, those studying with other international students gained 4.99 points.

One of the Engle and Engle (2003) defining components, program duration, was significantly correlated overall with IDI gains ($F = 2.65$; $p = .037$), but the gains were quite modest. Program length mattered the most for students who studied abroad for a semester (13–18 weeks): they gained a relatively small 3.4 points on average. Yet this group gained more than those who studied for shorter or longer periods of time. This study indicates that another preferred immersion practice—program duration—does not predict intercultural development as clearly or dramatically as many members of the study abroad community have traditionally supposed.

Of the seven Engle and Engle (2003) variables, the one the Georgetown Consortium study shows to be most predictive of intercultural development is cultural mentoring, that is, "guided reflection on the students' cultural experience." Students were asked how often they had received cultural mentoring on-site, either individually or in groups. For both individuals and groups, as cultural mentoring increased in frequency from "never" to "very often," the intercultural gains increased (from .83 to 5.02 for group mentoring and from .78 to 5.47 for individual mentoring). Except for those who did not receive any mentoring, these intercultural gains were statistically significant at or near the .05 level. In fact, analysis of the findings has revealed that the group of students who received the most individual and/or group mentoring made greater IDI gains than any other group.

The practice of providing cultural mentoring on a regular basis, throughout the study abroad experience, is not supported by the assumptions of either the positivist or relativist paradigms. It is, however, a central feature of the experiential/constructivist paradigm, which, as we will see in discussing other research studies in this chapter, predicts that students abroad learn most effectively—and appropriately—when educators take steps not only to immerse them, but to actively facilitate their learning, helping them reflect on how they are making meaning from the experiences that their "immersion" is providing.

In contrast to cultural mentoring, participation in guided/structured experiential activities was not significantly related to either the intercultural- or language-learning outcomes. This finding seriously challenges the immersion hypothesis; it suggests that providing students with experiential learning opportunities alone is insufficient for intercultural learning to occur. Finally, pre-departure and on-site-arrival orientation programs, long a staple of study abroad programs, did not show a statistically significant relationship with intercultural or language learning.

The Georgetown Consortium study gives us a tantalizing hint at the power of reflection and the importance of guiding the learning process. Regardless of the other characteristics of the study abroad program, the student, or the setting, it is clear that cultural mentoring makes a difference. The consistency of the cultural mentoring finding for both intercultural development and language proficiency is striking. What the Georgetown Consortium study does not tell us is how to structure interventions designed to support intercultural learning. Those insights come from several studies that we now discuss.

The American University Center of Provence: Comprehensive, On-site Intercultural Intervention

The pioneering efforts being undertaken at AUCP, begun in 1994 by Lilli and John Engle, are particularly important to this inquiry for three major reasons. First, the program directors from the very beginning were quite systematic and deliberate in facilitating linguistic and intercultural competence. These outcomes are at the core of what are now two AUCP programs, one in Aix-en-Provence, and the other in Marseille (see chapter 12). Second, these AUCP programs provide us with an important example of the numerous ways that intercultural competence can be facilitated on-site. The MAXSA project showed that online language and intercultural interventions can contribute to student development in those areas. The AUCP program allows us to see how intercultural interventions can be structured on-site. Moreover, the Georgetown findings showed that cultural mentoring supports intercultural development, but not how. AUCP provides answers to the question of how such learning can be organized and delivered by professional staff on-site. Third, AUCP staff have conducted rigorous research about student learning on their programs for a number of years, the results of which (see chapter 12; Engle, 2009; Engle & Engle, 2004) are directly relevant to this chapter.

Intervention

AUCP promotes French-language competence and intercultural competence, among other things, through intense cultural immersion, a French-only language pledge, and ongoing cultural mentoring. For cultural immersion, students participate each week in a series of community-based, experiential learning activities called French Practicum (see chapter 12). Student learning is supported by a 15-week intercultural communication course, French Cultural Patterns (Engle & Engle, 2004; see chapter 12). In the words of the directors, "The leading program components here—consistent use of French, coursework, required intercultural contact, guided cultural reflection, individual housing—are intended to combine to form a synchronized, harmonious whole" (Engle & Engle, 2004, p. 221). In chapter 12, Engle and Engle discuss the three defining orientations that guide the AUCP intervention model: (a) challenging and supporting the students, (b) utilizing a holistic program design (drawing on and integrating into the program a wide variety of learning approaches), and (c) mentoring for intercultural competence. With respect to the first, students are regularly challenged by being deeply immersed in the culture and using the French language at all times, both of which, as Paige (1993) points out, can be very stressful. On the other hand, the program staff provides continual cultural mentoring on-site, space in the intercultural course for discussions of intercultural issues, and culture content to help the students better understand their experiences.

Research Design

Since 2002, AUCP has been systematically researching its own semester- and year-long programs with pre- and post-program administrations of the Test d'Evaluation de Français for French language proficiency, and the IDI (Hammer & Bennett, 1998) for intercultural competence. The early IDI results (Engle & Engle, 2004) were impressive, and the more recent findings (Engle, 2009) even more so.

Findings

In the first AUCP research report, Engle and Engle (2004) found that for the 187 AUCP students in the sample, intercultural competence increased during the one-semester program. In their article, the authors use "percentage of achievable progress" (AP) to report the IDI results. For all students, the average gain was 36% of their AP. Of these students, 25.6% ($n = 48$) gained between 50% and 100%, 26.7% ($n = 50$) gained between 30% and 49%, and 25.1% (47 students) gained between 10% and 29%. Only 27 students (14%) declined during a semester. In the first study of full-year students ($n = 25$), Engle and Engle reported that the students achieved 28% of the AP in the first semester and 40% of their remaining AP in the second. Based on their research, Engle and Engle conclude, "Two factors lead to the clear development of cross-cultural competence in the American student group: as much direct, authentic contact with the host culture as possible, and skillful mentoring which guides, informs, inspires, and stimulates the experiential learning process" (2003, p. 232).

At the 2009 Forum on Education Abroad conference, Lilli Engle (2009) presented AUCP research findings for the period 2002–8. For students in semester-long programs, the average gain on the IDI was a striking 11.97 in Aix-en-Provence ($n = 414$) and 10.81 in Marseille ($n = 73$). Moreover, as the program has developed, the IDI gains have increased. In chapter 12, Engle and Engle report that the average gains between fall 2006 through spring 2011 were 13.43 points.

In terms of intercultural development, these gains translate into movement away from ethnocentrism and into ethnorelativism. Of the students in Aix-en-Provence and those in Marseille, 39.3% and 35.9%, respectively, had reached the Acceptance level of intercultural development at the end of one semester, a notable accomplishment. The results are even more impressive for students in yearlong programs, with 57.6% attaining Acceptance. These are among the largest IDI increases that have been reported. These intercultural gains far exceed those of the Georgetown Consortium students (average IDI gain excluding the AUCP students = 1.32) or those of the MAXSA intervention group students (average IDI gain = 3.82). The AUCP research has provided important evidence to support Engle's (2009) conclusion that "program intervention brings results."

Willamette University-Bellarmine University: Intentional and Targeted Online Intervention

Gabriele Weber Bosley (Bellarmine University) and Kris Hemming Lou (Willamette University) have developed the Bosley/Lou Intentional, Targeted Intervention (ITI) model, an intercultural intervention approach that combines in-person pre-departure and reentry seminars with in-country intercultural programming conducted online (Lou & Bosley, 2008; chapter 14 of this volume). Two of the unique features of the ITI approach are that it is being used with both international students in the United States and U.S. students abroad, and that it utilizes student learning communities in which students contribute to the learning of their peers. Here we look first at the features of the intervention and then at the research findings.

Intervention

The ITI model (chapter 14) begins with a pre-departure orientation that brings U.S. students together with each other, and an arrival orientation at Bellarmine and Willamette for international students that serves the same purpose. Students learn key intercultural concepts, work in groups to develop their ethnographic skills, and develop greater cultural self-awareness by examining their own core values. The orientation sets the stage in terms of group learning processes and substantive intercultural content for the in-country phase. While abroad (the U.S. students) or in the United States (the international students), online learning communities of three to five students are created on the basis of having similar pretest IDI results, with some groups consisting of a mix of U.S. and international students. On a weekly basis, the students participate in activities designed to increase their engagement with the culture, doing relevant readings assigned for that week and writing reflection journals about their experience. Every week, each student in the group gives the others feedback on his or her online journal entries. This process of continual reflection on one's own and others' intercultural experiences is based on Kolb's (Kolb & Kolb, 2005; chapter 6 of this volume) learning theory and is central to the ITI Model. Not only are the students reflecting on their own experiences, but they are also giving and receiving feedback. There are two versions of the model: one that features a course instructor, based at Bellarmine or Willamette, who reviews the journals and provides online feedback to the students; and one that does not rely on an instructor.

The program concludes with a postprogram workshop following the U.S. students' return to the Bellarmine and Willamette campuses that brings all the students back together and explores aspects of reentry, including the transferring of skills and knowledge acquired by the U.S. students abroad, to their home environment.

Research Design

Lou and Bosley (see chapter 14) provide detailed information regarding their research program. They utilized a pre-posttest research design with the IDI (Hammer & Bennett, 1998) serving as the measure of intercultural competence.

Findings

The average IDI gains of 144 U.S. and international students who to date have participated in the instructor-guided ITI program is 8.08 points. When the data for students participating in the non-instructor version of the ITI are included, the gain drops to an average of 6.65 points. This difference between the instructor-guided and noninstructor versions becomes even more striking when we examine the international student results. Those who had an instructor ($n = 29$) gained 10.17 points on the IDI, whereas those who did not ($n = 29$) gained only 1.94 points. At least in the case of international students, the presence of an instructor has proved to be a critical variable in the success of the model.

University of Minnesota Duluth: On-site, In-country Intervention

The intercultural intervention examined by Pedersen (2010) is an in-country, semester-long Psychology of Group Dynamics course that utilizes a multifaceted intercultural pedagogy. The students are participants in the academic year Study in England (SIE) program offered by the University of Minnesota Duluth; they take this (elective) course during their first semester.

Intervention

The course features the following intercultural elements. At the beginning, students take the IDI (Hammer, 2007). The instructor gives them individual feedback about their IDI results; that is, they learn about their "primary orientation" on the intercultural continuum, and the instructor then encourages them to use that knowledge to continue their intercultural development. The course also provides intercultural content, a variety of interculturally relevant classroom activities including group projects, outside-of-class cultural immersions, and guided reflection through written assignments and journaling. Students thus are exposed to and reflect on culture in numerous ways, both inside and outside of class. This intercultural pedagogy model is based on a grounded, constructivist theory of learning that Pedersen (2010) describes as "a process of creating our own knowing and meaning . . . primarily from experience" (p. 73).

Research Design

The researcher employed a pre-posttest control group repeated measures design that included three groups of students: (a) those in the 2006–7 SIE program abroad who took the intercultural course (*n* = 16), (b) those in the 2006–7 SIE program who did not take the course (*n* = 16), and (c) those who stayed on campus in 2006–7 but who had expressed interest in the SIE program. All three groups took the IDI at the start of the academic year, and 9 to 11 months later.

Findings

There are two major findings of this study. First, SIE students in group one, who took the intercultural course, on average gained 11.56 points, whereas students in group two, who had studied abroad but who were not enrolled in the course, gained only 1.22 points. Students in group three, who remained on campus that year, gained 1.43 points. The gain for group one was statistically significant, as were the differences in gain scores between group one and groups two and three. Clearly, the intercultural course had a major impact. Second, the impact was greatest for those students who had not traveled abroad before (IDI gain = 24.9 points). As Pedersen (2010) points out, this group moved "from a denial/defense worldview to just above the mid line of minimization" (p. 76). This finding is consistent with Hammer's (2005) research finding that the major intercultural shift of AFS students in that yearlong program was from Denial or Defense to Minimization.

AFS Intercultural Impact Study: The Effects of a Youth Exchange Intercultural Experience

AFS Intercultural Programs is an international organization best known for its one-year programs for high school–age students from the United States and elsewhere who have the opportunity to study in any of more than 50 countries. The organization has a long research tradition, and during the past decade it has commissioned two impact studies pertaining to intercultural competence, one an assessment of AFS participants in the 2002–3 program (Hammer, undated) and the other a long-term, follow-up assessment of participants who had been in AFS programs from 1980 to 1986 (Hansel, 2008; Hansel & Chen, 2008).

Intervention

The aforementioned studies are of special interest because the essence of AFS intercultural intervention is long-term immersion in another culture (10–12 months) that includes living with a host country family (the homestay experience). As Hansel (2008) puts it, "The AFS Program is first and foremost a program of experiential learning. AFS provides the participant with a direct experience in another culture" (p. 5). In effect, AFS programming relies heavily on long-term immersion and close contact with host culture members by means of the homestay. It is a classic example of the immersion model.

Research Design

In the study of AFS students abroad during the 2002–3 academic year, Hammer (undated) utilized a pretest, posttest, and post-posttest control group design. The sample included students who had been abroad for 10 months and lived with host families ($n = 1,500$), and a control group of "student friends" ($n = 600$) who had not studied abroad. Intercultural learning was assessed using the IDI (Hammer & Bennett, 1998), the Intercultural Anxiety Scale (Gao & Gudykunst, 1990), student journals, and the perspectives of the student's own and host families.

In the long-term impact study (Hansel, 2008; Hansel & Chen, 2008), a posttest control group design was implemented. The sample consisted of AFS participants who had been in one-year or summer programs in 1981–82 ($n = 1,920$) and a control group of high school peers, nominated by the AFS group, who had not been abroad ($n = 511$). The IDI and the Intercultural Anxiety Scale were the primary assessment instruments, which allowed the researcher to compare the 2002–3 and 1981–82 groups. They were also able to address the question, "Would the gains hold up over the years?"

Findings

Hammer (undated) found that the students in the 2002–3 group on average gained 2 points on the IDI during their 10 months abroad. On further analysis, he discovered that the greatest changes occurred among those who had begun the program at the earliest, most ethnocentric levels of intercultural competence: Denial, Defense, and Reversal (DD/R). They gained an average of 8 points, which moved many to the beginning of Minimization. Those who had begun in Minimization (M) or in the ethnorelative orientations of Acceptance and Adaptation (A/A) stayed where they were. The author reports, "Essentially, the DD/R group 'caught up' with the M group on all measures at the completion of the program. These results were maintained six months later (post-post test)" (p. 4). In total, 61% of the AFS participants scored in Minimization on the post-posttest. The author also found that intercultural anxiety was reduced from pre- to posttest and that this reduction had not changed at the time of the post-posttest. It is encouraging that both the gains made on the IDI and the reduction of anxiety, as shown by the post-posttest results, were still maintained after six months.

It appears that the long-term/homestay type of intervention provided by AFS is quite effective for those who are the most ethnocentric initially, but far less so for those who are in Minimization and beyond. This finding suggests that something more is needed, such as a more structured and intense form of cultural mentoring, if further intercultural development is to occur.

The findings from the 1980–86 group are similar (Hansel, 2008; Hansel & Chen, 2008). Hansel and Chen report, "The AFS returnees are somewhat more likely than the controls to be in the M group, while controls are somewhat more likely than returnees to be in the DD/R group" (Hansel & Chen, p. 6). Approximately 65% of the returnees were in the M group, compared with 59% of the control subjects, while 29% of the returnees were in the DD/R group, compared with 36% of the control subjects. Minimization, then, represents the largest intercultural orientation for both groups, though it is slightly smaller (61% versus 65%) for the long-term returnees. Interestingly, more than 33% of those in the long-term group studied abroad again in college; for those who did study abroad, compared with peers who did not, their IDI score in this study was higher, their intercultural anxiety score was lower, and they outperformed their peers on a number of other measures, such as language fluency.

CIEE: Seminar on Living and Learning Abroad

CIEE has been offering its semester-long Seminar on Living and Learning Abroad ("the Seminar") as an option for students in CIEE semester-long programs since 2008 (see chapter 16 of this volume). The CIEE Seminar represents a comprehensive intervention strategy for intercultural learning that includes the On-Line Pre-Departure Orientation Program; deep immersion experiences in the host culture; and regular, structured opportunities for reflection on those experiences.

Intervention

The CIEE Seminar on Living and Learning Abroad is the first study abroad program to systematically utilize what Hammer (see chapter 5) refers to as IDI Guided Development. The concept here is to tailor student mentoring and guidance to the level of intercultural development, at the beginning of the Seminar, and to use that information to support learning that is developmentally appropriate and relevant to each student. This is a challenging pedagogy for the CIEE Resident Directors (RDs) who teach the Seminar. Accordingly, they receive intensive preparation before they begin to teach the course, including completion of the IDI and individual feedback sessions about their own intercultural development, and ongoing coaching during at least the first two semesters that they teach it. By the time the RDs are serving as Seminar instructors, they are very familiar with the intercultural development continuum and with learning activities that are useful for students at different levels. However, unlike the approach used in the University of Minnesota Duluth Psychology of Group Dynamics course abroad, students are not given their individual IDI results at the beginning of the course.

The core content of the Seminar includes culture-general and culture-specific materials. As the course has evolved, in response to student suggestions and RD observations, there has been an increasing emphasis on applying culture-general concepts specifically to the local culture. This has been accomplished, in part, through the use of *Cultural Detective* materials (Saphiere, 2004; see chapter 16), a reliance that contributes to the students' understanding of subjective culture, cultural literacy, and their ability to bridge cultural differences.

Research Design

The research design is a straightforward pre-posttest design that uses the IDI (Hammer, 2007) for assessing intercultural learning. To put the Seminar intervention in a broader perspective, CIEE data are then compared with data from many of the other studies using the IDI that are reported in this chapter.

Findings

During the pilot semester of the Seminar in fall 2008, students on average gained 4.03 points on the IDI. Analysis of data from 13 Seminars conducted in spring 2011, however, showed students gaining, on average, 9.0 points on the IDI. Vande Berg, Quinn, and Menyhart (see chapter 16 of this volume) attribute the increase in student intercultural competence primarily to the preparation, training, and ongoing coaching of the RDs who are teaching the course.

The CIEE case offers important lessons. First, a course specifically designed to foster intercultural development can have a positive and meaningful impact on student learning. Second, the Seminar demonstrates that for this type of course to be successful, the cultural mentors, be they faculty or professional staff, need a great deal of preparation and support to learn how to facilitate it. This is a specialized course that requires faculty to support the development of intercultural competence by taking into account the learning needs and capacities of students, both individually and in a group. As we have seen here, when instructors are well prepared, the results are striking.

Westmont in Mexico Program: A Holistic Approach to Intercultural Learning

The Westmont in Mexico (WIM) program (Doctor & Montgomery, 2010) provides an important example of intervening in learning abroad through the entire study abroad cycle, from pre-departure to reentry. Begun in 2004 by Westmont College, WIM is a three-semester program that includes a three-month pre-departure course, one semester in country, and a three-month reentry course. The program is grounded in Bennett's (1993) theory of intercultural development and Sanford's (1966) pedagogy of challenging and supporting learners.

Intervention

The WIM intervention is multifaceted. First, during the time that students are in Mexico they take courses in Spanish (language, composition, or literature) that are determined by their existing level of Spanish at the time of arrival, as well as a Mexican history course. Second, they live with Mexican families in homestay placements throughout their stay and thus have the opportunity to experience language and culture in a naturalistic setting. Third, they may select from a variety of elective courses, including some that focus on various aspects of Mexican culture. Fourth, they are required to participate in the WIM seminar, the centerpiece of the intervention. In the manner of the CIEE program, there is an RD, in this case a Westmont faculty member, who teaches the seminar and serves as a cultural mentor. The course is tailored to the individual student's needs and level of intercultural development. Students can use English in the seminar and are encouraged to treat it as a place to discuss their engagement with the host culture, for example, in their homestays. In addition, instructors give students other assignments to gather cultural information and discuss what they are learning in the class. In principle and practice, the WIM seminar links experience with reflection to support intercultural development.

Research Design

The WIM research program utilized a pre-posttest comparison group design. WIM students ($n = 52$) and non-WIM students ($n = 18$) comprised the sample and were drawn from programs that ran between 2004 and 2009. The non-WIM students were participants in other study abroad programs. All of the research subjects completed the IDI (Hammer & Bennett, 1998) before and after their study abroad programs.

Findings

The 52 WIM students gained a statistically significant and very impressive 14.4 points on the IDI. Interestingly and contrary to the Georgetown Consortium Project results, the gain for men (18.41) was higher than for women (13.32), and both groups had nearly identical Time 1 scores. The students' 18 non-WIM counterparts gained only .7 points, with women gaining 2.83

points and men declining 4.86 points. The authors also reported that while all students had started, on average, at low Minimization, 43% of the WIM students progressed to the ethnorelative stages, whereas none of the non-WIM students progressed beyond Minimization. Among all WIM students, 33.8% showed no change, 53.8% moved forward developmentally, and 7.7% moved backward. Only 16.7% of the non-WIM students made progress; for the remainder there was either no change or decreased progress.

The WIM approach shares a number of similarities with the AUCP model, in particular, deep cultural and language immersion, intensive cultural mentoring on-site, and a course in which students can reflect on their intercultural experiences. Both programs are showing quite striking results in intercultural development and are providing important evidence regarding the value of a comprehensive intercultural intervention.

University of the Pacific: Comprehensive Intervention for Intercultural Learning

The University of the Pacific (see chapter 11 of this volume) has provided academic coursework to support intercultural learning in study abroad programs for more than 35 years. The work done there by Bruce La Brack and his colleagues has had a profound influence on the study abroad field. This was the very first intervention to systematically link pre-departure with reentry coursework for the purpose of both framing and reinforcing the study abroad experience (La Brack, 1993). These courses have set the standard for pre-departure and reentry programs.

Intervention

Two features of the University of the Pacific's intervention are particularly important. The first key feature is the innovative pre-departure and reentry courses, both of which incorporate core intercultural concepts and are sequenced developmentally. When these were originally developed, a focus on intercultural learning in study abroad was uncommon. La Brack's identification and development of intercultural content and methods, including his successful efforts to get these courses offered for academic credit, represented important innovations that have over time come to have a wide reaching impact on the field of study abroad. Coming at a time when study abroad work was typically positioned at the margins of the academy, his work, grounded in anthropology and the growing field of intercultural communication (see chapter 11 in this volume), gave the courses credibility and helped bring intercultural coursework and study abroad into the mainstream.

The second key feature is the integration of the university's intercultural courses into the institution's broader curriculum. This integration has assured that learning is framed not only during study abroad but also at home, where students can apply understandings gained abroad to the diversity that surrounds them in the context of the disciplines they are pursuing. This is particularly the case in the School of International Studies (SIS), which requires all SIS undergraduates, as a part of their academic program, to study abroad for a semester and to complete the two intercultural courses.

Faculty members are well prepared to teach these Pacific courses through participating in courses at the Summer Institute for Intercultural Communication, auditing for a semester the course they are going to teach, and participating in peer mentoring with a faculty member who is already teaching the course.

Research Design

The Pacific research program uses a pre-posttest comparison group design. The intercultural intervention sample consists of SIS students, all of whom are administered the IDI (Hammer, 2007), first within several weeks of the beginning of their studies, and then again shortly before the end of their senior year. The two comparison groups are (a) University of the Pacific seniors who had studied abroad but were not in the SIS program and (b) seniors who had neither studied abroad nor been SIS students.

Findings

According to earlier research (see chapter 8 of this volume; Sample, 2010), the students' intercultural gains are very impressive. SIS students gained 17.46 points, a statistically significant gain ($p = .000$). Their pretest mean IDI score of 92.13 placed them in early Minimization, while their posttest mean score of 109.60 located them toward the end of Minimization and on the cusp of Acceptance. Their non-SIS counterparts who studied abroad did not fare so well. Starting with a pretest score similar to that of the SIS students, they had a far lower posttest IDI mean score of 95.90, a difference that is also statistically significant ($p = .004$).

Sample (2010) reports data collected for a sample of SIS students ($n = 53$) between 2007 and 2010. The IDI average change score of 19.78 points for this group is statistically significant (p = .000), one of the largest seen in the literature. Comparison of this average IDI gain with that of a random sample of University of the Pacific seniors (n = 35) who averaged 91.31 points of gain provides important evidence that intercultural competence is not simply a function of human maturation or of being a college or university student.

It is important to keep in mind that these results, unlike results in the other studies we have discussed, represent gains made not merely across a semester or a year of study abroad, but over a three- to four-year period. What they show, though, is that intercultural gains are much stronger when study abroad is integrated into the curriculum, as is the case with students enrolling in the SIS. Intercultural learning is deeply embedded and facilitated throughout the curriculum, and this is clearly making a meaningful difference in the learning and development of students.

Related Studies of Intercultural Professional Development

A number of studies related to professional development provide additional support for the power of an intercultural intervention. DeJaeghere and Cao (2009) report the results of an in-service teacher development program designed to enhance intercultural competence. The school district used the IDI for both a baseline assessment that would serve as the basis for designing subsequent professional development activities, and pre- and posttest assessments. As the authors explain, "The district initiative sought to relate specific school professional development to the school's intercultural developmental needs" (p. 440). Beginning in 2003, teachers participated during the first year in a wide variety of intercultural training sessions and in the subsequent years in four half-day workshops annually. These activities constitute the intervention; the average IDI gain over a 2.5- to 3.5-year period was 6.90 points, statistically significant at p = .001 (n = 86). The authors conclude that

> intercultural competence can be developed through district and school-based professional development programs, in which the DMIS and the IDI serve as a process model to guide intercultural development. Given the variance in the change in teachers' intercultural competence, school leaders and trainers should be careful to provide developmentally appropriate training that supports teachers' learning. (p. 437)

Altshuler, Sussman, and Kachur (2003) report on an intercultural train-ing program designed for pediatric residents ($n = 26$) working in an urban U.S. hospital serving a very diverse clientele. Participants were assigned to one of three groups. Intervention group one received didactic cultural con-tent and had a behavioral rehearsal working with culturally different patients, group two participated only in the behavioral rehearsal, and group three received no intercultural intervention. At the conclusion of the training pro-gram, those who were in group one (didactic plus rehearsal) had lower eth-nocentrism scores (Denial, Defense, Minimization) and higher Acceptance and Adaptation scores than those in the other two groups. Contrary to expectations, those in group two (only the behavioral rehearsal) showed a small decrease in Acceptance and small increases in Denial and Defense. In effect, the rehearsal-only model represents an immersion approach without any accompanying cultural mentoring and cultural content to support the learning. We concur with the authors' conclusion that "providing a cognitive framework for cultural differences would promote a greater understanding of such differences and enhance trainees' ability to learn specific communica-tion skills around cultural issues" (p. 400).

Koskinen and Tossavainen (2004) utilized study abroad in England combined with cultural mentoring to increase the intercultural competence of Finnish nursing students. Based on DMIS-oriented content analysis of oral and written materials produced by the students during the program, the authors found that the students' experience of difference ranged from Defense to Acceptance. One very important finding was that "the students adjusted better and learned more in the placements where they had a named nurse mentor and regular meetings with a nurse teacher than in the place-ments where they practised without such support" (p. 117). The authors conclude that

> the host tutors and mentors are probably the key persons in encouraging the students to cross the inevitable language barrier. . . . The tutors and mentors should adopt strategies that encourage direct client encounters and reflect openly on the problems aroused by the inter-cultural differ-ences. (p. 118)

Marx and Moss (2011) discuss the critical importance of cultural mentor-ing and how it works to support intercultural development in the detailed ethnographic case study of one student, Ana. "Ana's program had several important components: opportunities for mentoring and guided cultural reflection, credit-bearing coursework related to cross-cultural issues, and opportunities for intensive immersion into the local culture" (p. 38), including her internship within a school. The data included pre- and posttest completion of the IDI; 400 hours of participant observation; and five "in-depth, open-ended" interviews with a mentor. The data revealed that participation in the program positively influenced Ana's intercultural development, and that having a cultural mentor and guide who was able to provide "a safe space for Ana to engage in the critical cultural reflection necessary for the development of cultural consciousness" (p. 45) proved crucial. The authors conclude that "[the] role of cultural translator and intercultural guide needs to be built into a study abroad experience and should be played by someone who is trained in providing support for intercultural development" (p. 44).

Intervening in Intercultural Learning Abroad: Lessons Learned From the Literature

We summarize this review by identifying some of the most important lessons learned from the literature:

- *Cultural mentoring and the cultural mentor.* The significance of cultural mentoring and the value of having a cultural mentor cannot be overstated. This conclusion is supported by many of the studies in this review, including the Willamette-Bellarmine ITI study, which shows a very wide difference in IDI gains between a first group of students enrolled in an intercultural course taught online by a faculty member and a second group enrolled in the same course without active faculty intervention. As the CIEE findings show, effective cultural mentoring means engaging learners in ongoing discourse about their experiences, helping them better understand the intercultural nature of those encounters, and providing them with feedback relevant to their level of intercultural development. Cultural mentors need to be trained in order to become skillful in providing support and knowledgeable about culture, the process of intercultural adjustment, and the ways in which learners characteristically react to cultural differences. As Paige and Goode (2009) point out, those who work with sojourners do not always possess those intercultural skills and knowledge. The preparation of cultural mentors, whether they are faculty, in-country professional staff, or others, is an essential part of student success in study abroad.

- *The provision of cultural content.* Study after study demonstrates the importance of providing learners with cultural content such as value orientations, communication styles, nonverbal communication, conflict styles, and ways of learning. This knowledge enables them to become more culturally self-aware and more observant of cultural patterns different from their own. Understanding the process of intercultural development is another key component of cultural content because, as Engle and Engle (see chapter 12) suggest, it enables students to chart their progress and direct their learning in order to gain greater intercultural competence. Cultural content anchors the intercultural experience by serving as a foundation for reflection and learning.

- *Reflection on intercultural experiences.* Providing opportunities for students to reflect on their experiences is an essential element of an intercultural intervention. As Passarelli and Kolb (see chapter 6) argue, it is through ongoing reflection that students make meaning of their intercultural encounters. They begin to challenge their own cultural assumptions, consider other cultural perspectives, and shift their frame of reference to the particular cultural context. Many of the interventions described in these studies incorporate journaling and other forms of writing to stimulate the reflection process. Thinking through situations with peers and instructors enables students to bounce their ideas off others. Cultural mentoring and the provision of cultural content drive and support reflection.

- *Engagement with the culture.* Although these studies demonstrate that immersion in another culture, in and of itself, is not as powerful as immersion plus reflection, engagement with the culture is still at the heart of the study abroad experience. Becoming involved with another culture brings abstract cultural concepts to life. Seasoned intercultural trainers are well aware of how difficult it is to discuss culture in pre-departure orientations; many students simply lack sufficient experience with diversity to make sense of these concepts until they are actually in country. Many of the interventions in the studies we examined build opportunities for engagement with the culture into the program such as internships, service-learning projects with host culture counterparts, and studying with host country students in regular courses in the target language. These can be effective as long as a cultural mentor is working with the students to help them process their experiences in such culturally challenging activities and contexts.

- *Intercultural learning throughout the study abroad cycle.* The research on study abroad suggests that the most effective programs are those that work through the entire study abroad cycle. A number of the interventions examined in these studies, including those in MAXSA and in Willamette-Bellarmine, provide for learning before, during, and after study abroad. Pre-departure orientations and readings begin the process and provide cultural frames for continued learning. In-country intercultural programming brings culture concepts and theories to life through cultural engagement and reflection. Reentry programs support study abroad, reinforce earlier learning, and help students make sense of their experiences, particularly with respect to their educational and occupational futures.
- *Online versus on-site intercultural interventions.* The MAXSA and the Willamette-Bellarmine ITI studies have demonstrated that online interventions can have an important impact on intercultural learning. The AUCP, University of Minnesota Duluth, and CIEE studies, among others, provide evidence that on-site interventions can be even more powerful. It appears that intervening online has less of an impact than intervening through a mentor at the site. That being said, the evidence shows that both forms of intervention can in fact support meaningful intercultural development.
- *Comprehensive intercultural interventions.* Several of these programs— WIM, AUCP, and University of the Pacific   make the case for comprehensive interventions for intercultural learning to be fully realized. When intercultural development is woven into the fabric of the larger educational experience, the study abroad experiences take on greater significance than they otherwise would.

It is our hope that the programs and findings discussed in this chapter can serve to inform those working in study abroad, and that through their ongoing efforts they can more effectively support their students' intercultural learning and development.

References

Akande, Y., & Slawson, C. (2000). A case study of 50 years of study abroad alumni. *International Educator, 9*, 12–16.

Altshuler, L., Sussman, N. M., & Kachur, E. (2003). Assessing changes in intercultural sensitivity among physician trainees using the Intercultural Development Inventory. *International Journal of Intercultural Relations, 27*, 387–401.

Bennett, M. J. (1993). Beyond ethnorelativism: The developmental model of intercultural sensitivity. In R.M. Paige (Ed.), *Education for the intercultural experience* (pp. 21–71). Yarmouth, ME: Intercultural Press.

Bennett, M. J. (2010). A short conceptual history of intercultural learning in study abroad. In W. W. Hoffa & S. C. DePaul (Eds.), *A history of U.S. study abroad: 1965–present* (pp. 419–449). Lancaster, PA: Frontiers: The Interdisciplinary Journal of Study Abroad.

Carlson, J. S., Burn, B. B., Useem, J., & Yachimowicz, D. (1990). *Study abroad: The experience of American undergraduates.* New York: Greenwood Press.

Cohen, A. D., Oxford, R. L., & Chi, J. C. (2002). *Language Strategy Survey.* Minneapolis, MN: Center for Advanced Research in Language Acquisition, University of Minnesota.

Cohen, A. D., Paige, R. M., Shively, R. L., Emert, H. A., & Hoff, J. G. (2005). *Maximizing study abroad through language and culture strategies: Research on students, study abroad program professionals, and language instructors.* Minneapolis, MN: Center for Advanced Research on Language Acquisition, Office of International Programs, University of Minnesota. http://www.carla.umn.edu/maxsa/index.html

Cohen, A. D., & Shively, R. L. (2002). *Speech Act Measure of Language Gain.* Minneapolis, MN: Center for Advanced Research in Language Acquisition, University of Minnesota.

Cohen, A. D., & Shively, R. L. (2002/2003). Measuring speech acts with multiple rejoinder DCTs. *Language Testing Update, 32,* 39–42.

DeJaeghere, J. G., & Cao, Y. (2009). Developing U.S. teachers' intercultural competence: Does professional development matter? *IJIR, 33,* 437–447.

Doctor, M., & Montgomery, L. (2010). *Using IDI Guided Development to maximize the study abroad experience: A case study.* Paper presented at the Second Intercultural Development Inventory Conference, Minneapolis, MN.

Dwyer, M. (2004). More is better: The impact of study abroad duration. *Frontiers: The Interdisciplinary Journal of Study Abroad, 10,* 151–163.

Engle, L. (2009). *Intervening in student learning abroad.* Paper presented at the Forum on Education Abroad, Portland, OR. http://www.aucp.org/sous_pages/main/Advisor_docs/Facilitating_Experiential_Learning.pdf

Engle, L., & Engle, J. (2003). Study abroad levels: Toward a classification of program types. *Frontiers: The Interdisciplinary Journal of Study Abroad, 9,* 1–20.

Engle, L., & Engle, J. (2004). Assessing language acquisition and intercultural sensitivity development in relation to study abroad program design. *Frontiers: The Interdisciplinary Journal of Study Abroad, 10,* 219–236.

Gao, G., & Gudykunst, W. B. (1990). Uncertainty, anxiety and adaptation. *International Journal of Intercultural Relations, 5,* 301–317.

Hammer, M. R. (2005). *Assessment of the impact of the AFS study abroad experience: Executive summary: Overall findings.* Ocean City, MD: Hammer Consulting. http://idiinventory.com/pdf/afs_study.pdf

Hammer, M. R. (2007). *The intercultural development inventory (IDI) manual* (Vol. 3). Ocean Pines, MD: IDI.

Hammer, M. R. (2011). Additional cross-cultural validity testing of the Intercultural Development Inventory. *International Journal of Intercultural Relations, 35*(4), 474–487.

Hammer, M. R., & Bennett, M. J. (1998). *The Intercultural Development Inventory.* Portland, OR: Intercultural Communication Institute.

Hammer, M. R., Bennett, M. J., & Wiseman, R. (2003). Measuring intercultural sensitivity: The Intercultural Development Inventory. *International Journal of Intercultural Relations, 27,* 421–443.

Hammer, M. R. (undated). *Assessment of the impact of the AFS study abroad experience. Executive summary: Overall findings.* Ocean City, MD: Hammer Consulting, LLC. http://www.idiinventory.com/pdf/afs_study.pdf

Hansel, B. (2008). *AFS long term impact study. Report 2: Looking at intercultural sensitivity, anxiety, and experience with other cultures.* New York: AFS International.

Hansel, B., & Chen, Z. (2008). *AFS long term impact study. Report 1: 20 to 25 years after the exchange experience, AFS alumni are compared with their peers.* New York: AFS International.

Hoffa, W. W. (2007). *A history of U.S. study abroad: Beginnings to 1965.* A Special Publication of *Frontiers: The Interdisciplinary Journal of Study Abroad* and The Forum on Education Abroad.

Hoffa, W. W., & DePaul, S. C. (Eds.). (2010). *A history of U.S. study abroad: 1965–present.* A Special Publication of *Frontiers: The Interdisciplinary Journal of Study Abroad* and The Forum on Education Abroad.

Koester, J. (1985). *A profile of the U.S. student abroad.* New York: CIEE.

Kolb, A. Y., & Kolb, D. A. (2005). Learning styles and learning spaces: Enhancing experiential learning in higher education. *Academy of Management Learning & Education, 4,* 193–212.

Koskinen, L., & Tossavainen, K. (2004). Study abroad as a process of learning intercultural competence in nursing. *International Journal of Nursing, 10,* 111–120.

Kuhn, T. (1962). *The structure of scientific revolutions.* Chicago, IL: University of Chicago Press.

La Brack, B. (1993). The missing linkage: The process of integrating orientation and reentry. In R. M. Paige (Ed.), *Education for the intercultural experience* (pp. 241–278). Yarmouth, ME: Intercultural Press.

Landis, D., Bennett, J. M., & Bennett, M. J. (Eds.). (2004). *Handbook of intercultural training* (3rd ed.). Newbury Park, CA: Sage.

Landis, D., & Bhagat, R. (Eds.). (1996). *Handbook of intercultural training* (2nd ed.). Newbury Park, CA: Sage.

Marx, H., & Moss, D. M. (2011). Please mind the culture gap: Intercultural development during a teacher education study abroad program. *Journal of Teacher Education, 62,* 35–47.

Paige, R. M. (1993). On the nature of intercultural experiences and intercultural education. In R. M. Paige (Ed.), *Education for the intercultural experience* (pp. 1–19). Yarmouth, ME: Intercultural Press.

Paige, R. M., Cohen, A. D., Kappler, B., Chi, J.C., & Lassegard, J. P. (2002). *Maximizing study abroad: A student's guide to strategies for language and culture learning and use.* Minneapolis, MN: Center for Advanced Research on Language Acquisition, University of Minnesota.

Paige, R. M., Cohen, A. D., & Shively, R. (2004). Assessing the impact of a strategies-based curriculum on language and culture learning abroad. *Frontiers: The Interdisciplinary Journal of Study Abroad, 10,* 253–276.

Paige, R. M., & Goode. M. L. (2009). Cultural mentoring: International education professionals and the development of intercultural competence. In D. K. Deardorff (Ed.), *The SAGE handbook of intercultural competence* (pp. 333–349). Thousand Oaks, CA: Sage Publishing.

Paige, R. M., Jacobs-Cassuto, M., Yershova, Y. A., & DeJaeghere, J. (2003). Assessing intercultural sensitivity: A psychometric analysis of the Hammer and Bennett Intercultural Development Inventory. *International Journal of Intercultural Relations, 27,* 467–486.

Paige, R. M., Rong, J., Zhang, W., Kappler, B., Hoff, J., & Emert, H. (2002). *Strategies Inventory for Learning Culture.* Minneapolis, MN: Center for Advanced Research in Language Acquisition, University of Minnesota.

Pedersen, P. J. (2010). Assessing intercultural effectiveness outcomes in a year long study abroad program. *International Journal of Intercultural Relations, 34,* 70–80.

Sample, S.G. (2010). Intercultural development and the international curriculum. Paper presented at the IDI Conference. Minneapolis, MN: October 29–30.

Sanford, N. (1966). *Self and society: Social change and individual development.* New York: Atherton Press.

Saphiere, D. H. (2004). *Cultural detective.* Retrieved from http://www.cultural detective.com

Stansfield, C. (1991). A comparative analysis of simulated and direct oral proficiency interviews. In S. Anivan (Ed.), *Current developments in language testing* (pp. 199–209). Singapore: Regional English Language Center.

Stansfield, C. (1996). *Test development handbook: Simulated oral proficiency interview (SOPI).* Washington, DC: Center for Applied Linguistics.

Vande Berg, M. (2009). Intervening in student learning abroad: A research-based inquiry. (M. Bennett, Guest Ed.) *Intercultural Education, 20,* 15–27.

Vande Berg, M., Connor-Linton, J., & Paige, R. M. (2009). The Georgetown Consortium Project: Interventions for student learning abroad. *Frontiers: The Interdisciplinary Journal of Study Abroad, 18,* 1–75.

Vande Berg, M., & Paige, R. M. (2009). Applying theory and research: The evolution of intercultural competence in U.S. study abroad. In D. K. Deardorff (Ed.), *The SAGE handbook of intercultural competence* (pp. 404–418). Thousand Oaks, CA: Sage.

PART TWO

FOUNDATIONS OF TEACHING
AND LEARNING

3

TAKING STAGE DEVELOPMENT THEORY SERIOUSLY

Implications for Study Abroad

Douglas K. Stuart

I n the natural world, we are quite comfortable with understanding the life of any creature through a series of radically different developmental stages, such as the path from acorn to seedling to sapling to mature adult of the oak tree, or the path from egg to larva to chrysalis to butterfly. Likewise, the idea of the creation and development of a human being from the union of egg and sperm to embryo to baby, and the path from infant through toddler, child, and teenager to young adult and on through middle and old age is simply life as we know it. The process of numerous sorts of growth and change, as we pass through the traditional stages of life, is discussed in our families, taught in our schools, and passed on as practical wisdom. Somehow, by going through life we change in very significant and broadly predictable ways; these do not seem remarkable, perhaps because the visible signs of such growth are not so different from stage to stage when compared to the insect or botanical world. We can generally recognize the same person in photographs from different life stages; that is not so likely when examining the stages of butterflies or trees. We hold in an interesting cognitive tension the opposite and equal truths that we both are and are not, at each age and stage, who we used to be. Part of that tension stems from the fact that many important changes are not captured in our traditional distinctions. In these increasingly complex times, we need a framework to distinguish patterned developmental differentiations.

This chapter has two goals: first, to examine how our perception of the world, particularly as adolescents and young adults, evolves through the developmental perspectives of stage theories, and how these transformational perspectives affect our engagement with our environment, particularly during study abroad; and, second, to consider why this natural developmental process often falters and stops short of its possibilities, as well as how we can better provoke, encourage, and support it.

A Look at the Concept of Stage Development

The work of the theorists Milton Bennett, whose Developmental Model of Intercultural Sensitivity (DMIS) is the basis for the developmental measurement of the progress of many students abroad (see chapter 4 of this volume), and William Perry will be familiar to some readers. Readers may know about some other developmental theorists as well: There are literally dozens of models with a variety of foci. Here are a few theorists, from Wilber's (2000, pp. 201–208) exhaustive list, whose work I know:

- Needs: Abraham Maslow
- Cognitive development: Michael Basseches, Michael Commons and Francis Richards, Kurt Fischer, Otto Laske, and Jean Piaget
- Self-related stages: Susanne Cook-Greuter, Erik Erikson, Clare Graves, Robert Kegan, and Jane Loevinger
- Self-related stages of morals and perspectives: Carol Gilligan, Karen Kitchener and Patricia King, Lawrence Kohlberg, William Perry, and William Torbert

Most of this work has been done in the last 80 years (since Piaget's early articles), and a great deal in the last 40 years within the Harvard Graduate School of Education. Perhaps because of its recency, stage developmental work is not widely known beyond academia. However, with the increasing need to be able to assess people's capability for placement into various positions or programs, there has been a proliferation and application of assessment instruments, particularly in education and in the workplace, putting some of the developmental knowledge to practical use and encouraging interest in further study. We are likely more aware of the measurement tools than the theory and research behind them.

All such study is based on similar assumptions: that progress, in whatever line of development, occurs in relatively discrete and measurable stages, and that the stages unfold in a particular order, each apprehending greater complexity than the last. This tends to preclude reversal or skipping of stages. An important implication of these developmental theories is that they suggest a fundamental distinction between what we might call horizontal and vertical growth, between learning and developing, between gaining new knowledge or skills—the goals of traditional teaching and training, as achieved in somewhat predictable time frames—and the seemingly mysterious phenomenon of development, which occurs unpredictably while other things are going on, including traditional learning. Otto Laske (2008) described such a developmental shift as a dialectical movement from thesis A (one point in time) to another point, its antithesis or non-A, contributing to the development of a synthesis,

> which is not only *later* than the thesis, but also richer, more differentiated, and more complex. This qualitative *developmental* movement from one time point to another is not one that is "in time" but rather "across time." It connects time points across long distances, such as a lifetime. It seamlessly relates past and future by inconspicuously transitioning through the present. *Humans live across time, not in time.* (pp. 44–45)

Such shifts, whether the result of new experience and/or deliberate intervention, produce perceptual discontinuities, and vast changes in how we perceive our environment, ourselves, and how we interact with the increasingly differentiated objective world. We are looking at the same world but suddenly seeing it differently.

Qualitatively, one might say that one has become a different person as a result of participating in wartime combat, living through a natural disaster, going through a divorce, recovering from a life-threatening illness, or other possibilities. In this sense, the crossing of developmental thresholds as a human being is transformational in ways no less startling than experiencing life through the perspectives of an egg, a voracious caterpillar, a swaddled pupa, and a free-fluttering butterfly. And this insight has revealed itself only this last century, the period within which we began to discover the discrete stages of perception—worldviews—that can unfold during the years of adulthood long assumed to be relatively unchanging.

Stage theories that take account of developmental transformations from various perspectives have a number of things in common. They divide the developmental progression into discontinuous stages and provide detailed descriptions of each, of how people in each stage perceive the world, of how each stage allows the processing of greater complexity and supports enhanced operations in the world as newly perceived. They provide great insight into what it means to be a human being, supporting the dialectical tension that allows us to be complete, whole, and yet radically different at each stage, containing in every moment all that we need to continue our development throughout our lives, as an acorn is no less complete and whole than the oak tree it becomes.

Stage theories are *constructivist* developmental models. Constructivism takes the theoretical position that the world we know is constructed in our mind through our ongoing perception of and interaction with external reality. As our interactions with that reality become more complex, we are gradually pressed to construct more comprehensive worldviews. We can call this the social forcing function (Laske, 2006, pp. 61–62) of the environment, generally met by internal compliance.

Implications of Stage Development for Study Abroad

What we perceive, that is, what we pay attention to and how we interpret it, is strongly determined, initially, by our cultural surround. Obviously, different cultures in different environments pay attention to different things and construct different internal representations of their realities. These representations or worldviews make sense of our world so that we can act effectively in it. These inner landscapes are not necessarily developmentally different from one culture to another, but they provide another fabric, we might say, within which development takes place. Therefore, common sense in one culture may not be common sense in another. This is the essential challenge of intercultural competence: How do we learn to deal with people whose internal woven fabric of reality, whose common sense, is different from our own? Developmental stage theory reveals how such ability evolves.

Developmental models assume that humans proceed through relatively disjunctive stages of development throughout life, with (in some models) no determined upper boundary. We must realize that each successive stage is a viable worldview representing a different and larger perspective on reality. Each stage can be thought of as a screen through which we perceive and operate in and on the world, and each successive screen is more fine-grained than the last, comprehending greater complexity—greater differentiation and interconnection. We first notice the things, then the patterns of the things, and later, perhaps, the patterns of the patterns. Achieving the upper reaches of these stages has clearly not been a historical requirement for most humans to lead satisfactory lives. Nevertheless, our successful participation in our increasingly complex contemporary civilization seems to require further development.

Theorists use the phrase "transcend and include" to indicate that nothing is lost in the transformation from a lower to a higher stage—each perceptive stage is not a view of a different world, but a more inclusive, complex worldview of the same world (constructivism does not make any final claim about whether or not there is an objective reality out there). From the perspective of subject-object theory (explained in more detail later), one could say that we are subject to whatever we cannot differentiate from ourselves, as an infant cannot differentiate itself from its mother. Each developmental stage includes more of what exists as object, as something that we can differentiate from ourselves.

The world of particular concern in this chapter is the human beings of any environment. Thus, not only are the worlds that humans construct in different environments different because the environments are different, the way in which we perceive and interact with other cultures' worlds, as when we go abroad for study or work, also differs according to our developmental levels. The essential realization from a developmental stage model is that our capability to interact effectively with our environment—with other human beings—increases with each stage of development.

The Challenges of Developmental Models

Although stage theories are powerful, they also contain features that are problematic to many. They are absolutely hierarchical, in that each stage both transcends (is more complex, comprehensive, and capable) and includes the one before it. They imply a linear progression in a world that often appears to move backward or sideways as much as forward. They are teleological, implying direction and perhaps destination in a world full of vague and countervailing forces in which many of us abhor hierarchy, oppose assumptions of linearity, and deny teleology—all for good reason. That is, all of these theories are anathema from the postmodern perspective that has recently escaped the rigidities and certainties of the Newtonian universe and is enjoying and occasionally overwhelmed by a newly created anarchic freedom. And, perhaps most challenging, these theories tend to lack a mechanism of change. That is, they describe the nature of the changes quite remarkably, but they do not tell us how we actually proceed from one stage to the next. In that way, human development seems to follow the biological evolutionary model of punctuated equilibria (Eldridge & Gould, 1972), with long periods of apparent stasis interrupted by relatively rapid and significant change—often for poorly understood reasons. We will see, however, how these objections might yield to a larger and perhaps more attractive perspective that provides answers to some of the puzzles of the current paradigm, including the question that birthed this book: Why do not all students develop as a result of their studies abroad? In addition to a brief comparison of two stage theories that will shed light on this question, I conclude by looking briefly at the nature of complex systems for a better understanding of how and why development actually takes place; when it does; and, by the same token, why it often does not.

Within whatever limitations, most of us do accept ideas of change, growth, and progress, both at the individual and at the systems levels. Certainly, no one quarrels with the fact of economic, technological, or social development, of development within the fields of medicine, communication technology, construction, or transportation, just to name a few. We are comfortable with developmental lines being drawn so as to create discrete stages in these developmental paths, conscious of the fact that where the line is drawn between stages is often somewhat arbitrary. We are comfortable with the historical stages of civilization—from hunter/gatherer families, tribes, and clans to agrarian communities to city- and nation-states (less comfortable perhaps with the rise of global corporate dominions)—and we perfectly understand that a later stage does not so much replace as supersede its predecessor, as the industrial age superseded the agricultural age without replacing agriculture, but moved beyond it as a primary focus for human endeavor.

Likewise, we have no problem with the concept of socioeconomic evolution because we are all equally a part of whatever age we live in, and most of us aspire to the upper reaches of the socioeconomic spectrum. In addition, we proceed inevitably through temporal life stages and, although we may value one stage beyond another (youth over age, e.g., in our Western individualistic cultures), we try not to prejudicially discriminate one from another, and accept, perhaps grudgingly, our own aging. The discomfort comes, however, when we are asked to assess individuals with respect to discrete developmental stages that may or may not be in synchrony with life stages. Stage theory does this explicitly.

It can be uncomfortable to realize that developmental stages exist that are only loosely tied to age, and that not all of us proceed equally far, nor at the same pace, along this developmental path. This implies a way of uncomfortably sorting and perhaps judging members of our society. In a national culture that still clings fondly to its founding claim of relative equality, we are loathe to sort people along lines that might cause further dissention in a society already riven by increasing socioeconomic disparity. One of the most prominent of stage theorists today, Robert Kegan (1994) of Harvard, addressed this in his book *In Over Our Heads: The Mental Demands of Modern Life*. He compared constructive developmental theories with others that are solely constructivist. That is, both are about a way of organizing experience and both describe ways of knowing, but the latter distinguishes behavioral or attitudinal differences (the Myers-Briggs distinctions are an example, as are various approaches to differentiating leadership styles). By contrast, developmental theories distinguish successive structures of consciousness:

> Stylistic distinctions by themselves are non-judgmental. There are merely different orientations or preferences; one is in no sense "better" than the other. Subject-object distinctions presume to tell a story of increase, of greater complexity. They are thus more provocative, discomforting, even dangerous, and appropriately evoke greater suspicion. Any time a theory is normative, and suggests that something is more grown, more mature, more developed than something else, we had all better check to see if the distinction rests on arbitrary grounds that consciously or unconsciously unfairly advantage some people . . . whose own preferences are being depicted as superior. (Kegan, 1994, p. 229)

Hence, theorists themselves recognize the challenges of developmental models. Nevertheless, despite our squeamishness about applying a stage theory to the development of human beings (especially individuals), let us consider some possible advantages. Understanding where a group, on average, or an individual is with respect to developmental stage (and assuming that the observer is in the same or a higher stage), one can

- better structure educational curricula and place students within them (Kegan, 1994, pp. 217–304);
- select the most appropriate psychotherapeutic intervention, because different approaches align with different stages of development (Wilber, Engler, & Brown, 1981, pp. 107–159);
- match employees and executives to job requirements (Laske, 2008, pp. 53–79);

- determine the capability of individuals for leadership (Kegan, 1994, pp. 307–334); and
- select organizational officers according to the scope and complexity of projects (Laske, 2008, pp. 411–435).

Tools that can help us match people to the demands of their environment, predict how successfully people are likely to perform in particular environments, and determine how people are likely to develop as a result of their experience in various situations will become increasingly valuable in our ever-complexifying world.

A Prominent Developmental Model

Developmental models, though accessible, with increasing practical applications, are unfamiliar beyond the psychology and business administration communities where the research is conducted. Therefore, this chapter provides a somewhat detailed description of one of the better-known models.

Robert Kegan's Evolving Self

Before turning to Robert Kegan's theory, let us begin with an overview of the developmental arc by the most eloquent of the developmental psychologists, Clare Graves (1981), from whose work the popular Spiral Dynamics educational program was developed, and who introduced the idea of the developmental *center of gravity*:

> Briefly, what I am proposing is that the psychology of the mature human being is an unfolding, emergent, oscillating, spiraling process marked by progressive subordination of older, lower-order behavior systems to newer, higher-order systems as man's existential problems change. Each successive stage, wave, or level of existence is a state through which people pass on their way to other states of being. When the human is centralized in one state of existence (center of gravity), he or she has a psychology which is particular to that state. His or her feelings, motivations, ethics and values, biochemistry, degree of neurological activation, learning system, belief systems, conception of mental health, ideas as to what mental illness is and how it should be treated, conceptions of and preferences for management, education, economics, and political theory and practice are all appropriate to that state. (cited in Wilber, 2000, p. 40)

Several stage theories of human development have been validated through extensive cross-cultural research in both the developed and the developing world. Robert Kegan's model, first outlined in *The Evolving Self: Problem and Process in Human Development* (1982), describes what might be called social-emotional development (to distinguish it from the purely cognitive models). I present this summary of his model through the lens of Otto Laske's (2006) *Measuring Hidden Dimensions: The Art and Science of Fully Engaging Adults*, as well as from Kegan's (1994) *In Over Our Heads* and two intriguing interviews with Kegan. Laske used Kegan's model as one part of a triad of tools for assessing adult development—social-emotional, cognitive, and psychological—particularly as applied in the workplace. Although Laske's (2008) great contribution to stage development theory was to separate the cognitive from the social-emotional strands, to show the relationship between the two, particularly the influence of the cognitive on the social-emotional, and to indicate how cognitive development can be influenced, the constraints of this chapter allow only a focus on the more general and more approachable social-emotional.

Kegan's (1982, 1994) model (recalling the social-emotional portion of Laske's work) is based on subject-object relations theory. From this perspective, a human being grows in consciousness through becoming able to consider more and more of the world, including oneself, as an object of contemplation. We begin in infancy as pure subject; we are the world. Gradually, we become aware of ourselves as distinct from others and the world, and slowly we make more and more subtle distinctions, becoming aware of more of ourselves and of our transforming relationship to the world. The greater our object awareness, the smaller we become, relatively, as subject, and the more skillfully we learn to navigate an increasingly complex reality. This greater object awareness occurs in discrete epistemologies—stages of meaning making—of interpreting the world. We are all subject to that which we cannot yet perceive as object; we are subject to our stage of development, which provides our worldview.

Kegan (1982, 1994) posited five major stages or orders of consciousness, the first of which occurs in childhood and need not concern us. The next four stages, generally beginning in adolescence and unfolding (or not) over the adult lifetime, are not tied strongly to education or very strictly to age. Notice in Figure 3.1 that development oscillates between a focus on independence (self) and a focus on inclusion (others), with similarities, therefore, between stage 2 (S-2) and S-4, and between S-3 and S-5.

Each of these stages comprises a worldview with unique assumptions, values, and beliefs—a perspective on a vertical scale through which the set of horizontal subcultures in which one lives and with which one interacts

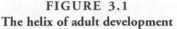

FIGURE 3.1
The helix of adult development

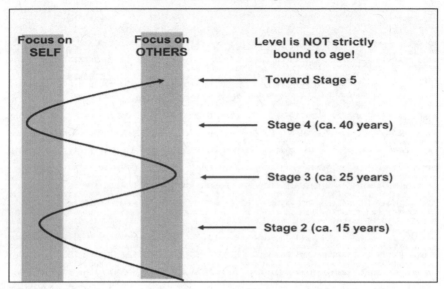

Note: Adapted with permission from Laske (2006, p. 31).

(family, ethnicity, and others) is perceived. The perspective on each of these subcultures shifts with respect to one's position on the developmental vertical axis (as shown in Figure 3.2), and with the shifting worldview come different attitudes toward and interactions within the cultural communities.

Here is Kegan in a 2002 interview speaking on the changing stages of the subject-object relationship:

> It is a fundamental distinction in the way that we make sense of our experience—a distinction that shapes our thinking, our feeling, our social relating, and our ways of relating to internal aspects of ourselves. The subject-object relationship is not just an abstraction but a living thing in nature. What I mean by "object" are those aspects of our experience that are apparent to us and can be looked at, related to, reflected upon, engaged, controlled, and connected to something else. We can be objective about these things, in that we don't see them as "me." But other aspects of our experience we are so identified with, embedded in, fused with, that we just experience them as ourselves. This is what we experience subjectively—the "subject" half of the subject-object relationship. (Debold, 2002, para. 13)

Kegan emphasizes that such changes in the way we create meaning are not just linear accretions of more information about the same thing, like a child

FIGURE 3.2
Intersection of developmental stage and environmental plane

Some of Our Cultural Memberships

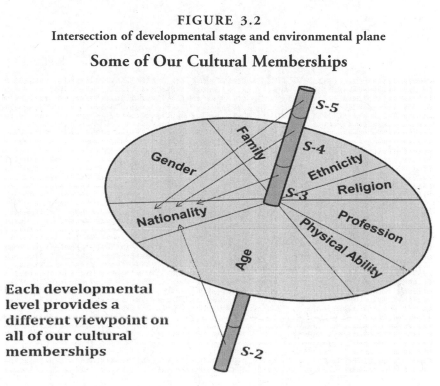

Each developmental level provides a different viewpoint on all of our cultural memberships

collecting more and more rocks or toys or electronic games. They are rather qualitative changes in our lens on the world that allow us to transform the collected knowledge of a past lens upward into observable categories, that is, organized sets of abstractions that can be analyzed, compared, contrasted, and eventually, perhaps, reorganized again at a higher level of abstraction— the next epistemology. Each of these qualitative movements repositions an entire subjective mental structure into an objective position.

Let us look at some of the major distinctions between these stages or epistemologies as shown in Table 3.1. Note that Tables 3.1 and 3.2 are adapted from Laske (2006), who emphasizes that these descriptions must be understood as very simplistic abbreviations of richly differentiated stages of being. These stages are not represented equally in a population. Cook-Greuter's (1999) research indicates, in general, the approximate distribution, as displayed in Table 3.2. Thus, we see that the modal level of adult development is S-3, group contributor. Research conducted by Cook-Greuter (1999) and others suggests that the modal preference for S-3 extends across national

TABLE 3.1

Changing orientations across adult stages

Orientation	S-2	S-3	S-4	S-5
View of others	Agents of their own need, gratification	Needed to contribute to own self-image	Collaborators, delegates, peers	Contributors to own integrity and balance
Level of self-insight	Low	Moderate	High	Very high
Values	Law of jungle	Community	Self-determined	Humanity
Needs	Overriding all others' needs	Subordinate to community, work group	Flowing from a striving for integrity	Viewed in connection with own obligations and limitations
Need to control	Very high	Moderate	Low	Very low
Communication	Unilateral	Exchange 1:1	Dialogue	True communication
Organizational perspective	Carerist	Group contributor	Manager	Leader

Note. Adapted with permission from Laske (2006, p. 32).

TABLE 3.2
The sober reality of adult development attainment

Organizational Perspective	Highest Level of Attainment by Approximate % of Population
S-2: Careerist	10%
S-3: Group contributor	55%
S-4: Manager	25%
S-5: Leader	<10%

Note. Adapted with permission from Laske (2006, p. 35).

cultures, placing primary emphasis on how people relate to each other. Kegan (cited in Debold, 2002, para. 32) talks about S-3, the socialized mind, as the result of a transformation that occurs in adolescence and early adulthood through which we develop the complexity to internalize and identify with the values of our environment. This new epistemology is the key to becoming truly socialized in our community. The socialization process generates a self that feels whole, connected to, and in harmony with a set of beliefs and values that both constitute the self and connect it to its cultural surround. This is Kegan's third-order consciousness.

Note that it is precisely during the time of the protracted transformation from S-2 to S-3 that students go abroad to study. The students are transferring themselves from the nurturing environment of their cultural community, from continuous exposure to the developmental expectations of S-3 level adults in many environments at home (e.g., family, church, school, competitive activities) into what is often a relatively insulated study abroad environment where they are in the comforting company of peers, thereby reducing both external and internal developmental pressures.

Laske (2006) suggests that society pushes individuals to S-3, the socialized mind, but that

> there does not seem to be a social forcing function for getting people beyond S-3 (other-dependent) to S-4 (self-authoring). Nothing but you yourself prompts you to go there, and you do so at a price. Society is already satisfied if you get to S-3, where you constitute a member of the civil community. To go beyond the conventional realm of S-3 is left to everybody him- or herself. (p. 35)

Indeed, as we see in Table 3.2, only 25% of the population reaches S-4 with its capability for management of self, allowing these individuals to step away from the group and to manage others. Although the achievement of third-order consciousness, the socialized mind, by a little more than half the population has clearly been adequate for the rise and expansion of civilizations, the rapid development of technology in the last century has created an environment of ever-increasing complexity, requiring a further generalized development.

Kegan's (1994) *In Over Our Heads*, a "look at the curriculum of modern life in relation to the capacities of the adult mind" (p. 5), amply illustrates how virtually every situation in contemporary life—parenting, partnering, work in many environments, higher education—has become so complex as to require S-4 development for successful participation. Kegan (cited in Debold, 2002, para. 33) discusses the later adult transformation, typically in the period between ages 25 and 50, from the orientation of being shaped by one's surround, to S-4, the self-authoring stage, fourth-order consciousness. Kegan convincingly argues that the rapidly expanding pluralism of postmodern populations produces conflicting demands for loyalty, time, attention, and so on. This cannot be adequately managed from the S-3 stance that assumes a homogeneous definition of who we should be and how we should live. S-3 is insufficient for modern life, the complexity of which requires S-4, what Western culture often calls personal empowerment.

Despite the clear advantages of and necessity for achieving S-4 in today's increasingly complex environment, Kegan (as cited in Debold, 2002) notes:

> The data across a number of studies suggest that a majority of even well-advantaged, well-positioned adults haven't yet reached . . . the self-authoring mind, fourth order consciousness. This means that they do not have the capacities that would enable them to thrive within today's increasingly pluralistic world that requires individuals to exercise a kind of authority that, throughout human history, human beings have never had to do. . . . And only a tiny percentage of people in the studies are beyond the fourth order. (paras. 36–38)

When we consider the dearth of adequate leadership today in government at all levels, in business, in education, and in the military, as such institutions grow larger and more complex, we see the importance of what Kegan is saying about the need for self-authoring. From Table 3.1 it is clear that the authority Kegan describes emerging in fourth-order consciousness provides the emerging capacity for leadership. That is, one has to be able to step outside the group in order to lead it somewhere else. More specifically, Kegan (1994) links the convergence of various conceptions of leadership and criteria for leadership success to two talents:

> an ability to craft and communicate a coherent vision, mission, or purpose; and an ability to recruit people into taking membership in, ownership of, or identification with that vision, mission, or purpose. The first requires powers of conception and communication; the second tests interpersonal skills and capacities. . . . Although these expectations might be directed to different aspects of personal competence, together they form a single demand on consciousness . . . yet another identification of the pervasive modernist demand for fourth order consciousness in yet another domain, this time that of public leadership. (pp. 321–322)

To the old question of whether leaders are born or made we add the complication that although one may be born with an innate capacity, it arises through a developmental process, partially, at least, in response to the forcing function of external circumstances. As usual, we cannot separate nature from nurture. What we can say, however, is that one must proceed through the developmental stages to the level of fourth-order consciousness before the capacity for true leadership emerges.

Implications for Study Abroad

Forms of leadership exist at each stage. We are familiar with the inferior leadership arising from the individuality of second-order consciousness that operates by threat, intimidation, and brute force in criminal gangs, organized crime, and paramilitary forces. Most leadership in civil society is really S-3 management—the leadership of existing groups under normal conditions in which well-respected people are chosen to lead a group with no need for radical change. With reference to the situation of study abroad, it is unreasonable to expect the experience of exposure to another culture to generate the capacity for leadership, whether S-3 or S-4, in young people who are experiencing what may be an interruption in their development from S-2 to S-3.

A Linguistic Challenge in Communicating the Constructivist Stance

In any theory of change it is important to have a mechanism by which change occurs. In a constructivist, as opposed to a positivist or relativist, perspective, reality is constructed within the experiencer, and the arbitrary division between experiencer and what is experienced is dissolved. While it may be a convenient distinction to say causes of change are located outside or inside the person, that inside/outside boundary is realized by, created by, the experiencer. If we understand the person as a permeable system operating within ever-larger systems of permeable systems, any boundaries thought to separate these systems are porous and defined somewhat arbitrarily. As a person changes, the causes of that change cannot be fully isolated as external or internal because the influences between entity and environment are mutual and inseparable. Thus, if my text seems to imply an inside/outside distinction, understand that this is merely a convenience in the particular example. The mechanism enabling the change process is discussed later in this chapter in "How Does Change Happen? Human Individuals as Systems."

A More Detailed Look

In the following sections, I examine Kegan's theory in more detail as well as the implications for study abroad.

Kegan's Theory

Five stages may seem rather inadequate to describe the myriad variations we observe in human capabilities. In fact, Kegan posited four intermediate stages between the main stages, for a total of 20 distinguishable levels across four major stages of adult development, as shown in Table 3.3.

As a specific example, let us examine the developmental movement from S-3 of the "good citizen" to S-4 of the career professional and potential leader and look at brief characteristics of each substage, as shown in Table 3.4. The severe linearity of this model is moderated by the fact that individuals at any point on the scale do not make meaning from a single stage, but oscillate around Graves's (1981) center of gravity. One might be centered at 4(3), for instance, between the higher 4 of "my world" and the conflicts of the lower 4/3, maintaining a sort of "dynamic equilibrium" within three substages that under the right circumstances (environmental pressure and internal capacity) eventually reorganizes and advances to the next three-substage spread. These centers of gravity can be very stable for long periods of time, during which the center of the three substages is our primary epistemology.

TABLE 3.3
Progression from Stage X to Stage Y

Stage	Progression Between Stages (proceeding upward from the bottom)
Y	Being "at" Stage Y
Y(X)	Residual "hanging on" to the lower stage; espousal of the higher stage
Y/X	In conflict, with the higher stage "winning out" (turning point toward higher stage)
X/Y	In conflict, with the lower stage "winning out"
X(Y)	Residual "hanging on" to the lower stage; espousal of the higher stage without really being there
X	Being "at" Stage X

Note. Adapted with permission from Laske (2006, p. 106).

TABLE 3.4
Progression from S-3 to S-4

Level	Characteristics (proceeding upward from the bottom)
4	Fully self-authoring decision maker respecting others; "my world" hypothesis
4(3)	Nearing self-authoring, but remaining at risk for regression to others' expectations
4/3	Conflicted, but with more detachment from internalized viewpoints, resolving to S-4
3/4	Conflicted over and unsure about own values, direction, worth, capability
3(4)	In need of "hand-holding" by physical others to act on own behalf
3	Made up of others' expectations; "our world" hypothesis

Note. Adapted with permission from Laske (2006, p. 130).

Implications for Study Abroad

In more tumultuous times, we exist in a more fragile developmental balance, as one end or the other of the three-substage oscillation strengthens in response to changing conditions. Study abroad circumstances can certainly induce such instability (the student is "falling apart"), with the possibility for either upward or downward movement. Such situations provide an excellent opportunity for deliberate developmental learning interventions, whether to prevent a downward slide by reestablishing stability, or to support upward development.

To return to the general arc of more mature adult development as illustrated in Table 3.4, if one is primarily seeing the world from the 4(3) perspective, one is approaching a new primary worldview (S-4) but not yet quite there, so much effort is expended reassuring oneself and others that one indeed has become independent, has one's own worldview and set of personal values, and is capable of making important decisions even when they conflict with the view of others in one's group. One is essentially espousing a new worldview that has not yet consolidated structurally and is, therefore, experiencing in some situations a strong sense of being independent (4), whereas in other situations a conflicted concern for how one is being perceived (4/3). Eventually, assuming that the environmental pressures continue, the S-4 perspective becomes dominant, and one has the self-assurance to act independently in the world, taking on a professional stance with the capability to manage projects and groups.

In an interview with Claus Otto Scharmer (2000), Kegan suggests that a "third big force" is at the heart of the dynamic evolution from one stage of consciousness to another:

> There's a third big force [beyond Whitehead's entropy and negentropy] in the universe, which I would call dynamic equilibrium. It is neither about everything falling apart nor becoming more complex. It's not about fixity and stasis, either. It's about the dynamic, ongoing, countervailing processes that hold things pretty much as they are. It preserves a certain kind of meaning-making system, the balance of what is subject and what is object. We come up against all kinds of experience and seek to make sense of that experience in a way that preserves the balance, which you could call "knowing," you could call "defending." We run up against perturbing, disturbing experiences which throw the balance off temporarily, but the balance is very hardy and it tends to wave its big arms and right itself. We keep assimilating experience to this balance. Eventually, though, we come

up against experiences that actually disturb the balance sufficiently that, although it feels to us like going off a cliff, actually lead to some higher-order balance. I think the self is participating in these powerful processes, kind of endlessly, restlessly, creatively, ceaselessly. (paras. 87–89)

Kegan's (1982) model provides a context for understanding the "transformation" that students and other individuals returning from an extended period abroad sometimes claim. While one would probably not be able to develop over a full stage, for example, from S-2 to S-3, even during a sojourn of several years in another cultural environment, a movement from one substage upward into another is quite possible and would, in the context of an individual's lifelong development, represent a significant transition. Such a developmental difference can be reliably measured, both by the Subject-Object Interview (Lahey, Souvaine, Kegan, Goodman, & Felix, 1988) developed for Kegan's model, and by the Intercultural Development Inventory (IDI) (Hammer, Bennett, & Wiseman, 2003), which Milton Bennett and Mitch Hammer discuss in the two following chapters. A backward movement is also quite possible, and measurable, depending on the degree of system shock from diving into "the deep end of cultural immersion" (see chapter 1 of this volume) with inadequate developmental support.

A Look Further Down the Scale

Until now we have primarily examined the adult levels of development. Most important in this paper is the socialization process, the movement from adolescence into the adult community.

The Adolescent Challenge in the Study Abroad Environment

Although we understand that the complexifying environment of the postmodern world is trying to push and pull its adult inhabitants inexorably toward S-4, it is still society's primary goal and duty (the forcing function) to raise its children to S-3 so that they are able to join the community as willing and contributing members, having internalized the values and learned the appropriate behavioral responses to adult environments. Table 3.5 provides a description of the transformation from S-2 (early adolescence) to S-3 (early adulthood).

S-2 (like S-4, an "I" rather than "we" stage) is characteristic of early adolescence, where individuals are strongly steeped in their own wants or

TABLE 3.5
Progression from S-2 to S-3

Level	Characteristics (proceeding upward from the bottom)
3	Made up of others' expectations; "our world" hypothesis
3(2)	Able to be influenced by imagined others and their expectations
3/2	Conflicted, but with more detachment from own needs and desires; resolution to Level 3
2/3	Conflicted over risking exposure to others' feelings and thoughts; resolution to Level 2
2(3)	Beginning to be influenced by physical and imagined others
2	Ruled by needs, desires, wishes; "two-world hypothesis"

Note. Adapted with permission from Laske (2005, p. 3).

needs, highly impulsive, and often manipulative. They will follow community rules and conventions when they are convenient or beneficial to them, or when they are likely to be caught and punished if they do not. The development from S-2 to S-3 is frequently, as we are all aware, a stormy and protracted period. Individuals at S-2 require civilizing, and the fact that some 10% of the population never reaches S-3 explains society's need for the policing function. Parenting and education are the primary tools for encouraging and shaping this developmental movement.

From a sympathetic perspective, humans at this stage are undergoing, and at times resisting, their gradual induction into adult society, their transformation into interdependent beings. The struggle to become independent, as we have seen, is the next stage. We now know, from decades of research on the development and function of the human brain, that this entry into the adult world accompanies the internal development of the prefrontal lobes. According to David Eaglemann (2011), a neuroscientist at Baylor College of Medicine, the prefrontal lobes

> balance the debate between the long- and short-term parties of the brain, giving the option of reflection before action to those who lack it. And really, that's all maturation is. The main difference between teenage and adult brains is the development of the frontal lobes. The human prefrontal

cortex does not fully develop until the early 20s, and this fact underlies the impulsive behavior of teenagers. The frontal lobes are sometimes called the organ of socialization because becoming socialized largely involves developing the circuitry to squelch our first impulses. (p. 123)

There is, in addition to this coincidence of the development of the socialized mind and the maturation of the human brain, a further pertinent aspect: brain biology. In a recent issue of *National Geographic*, Dobbs (2011), speaking about the new science of the teenage brain, concluded:

A final key to both [the teen brain's] clumsiness and its remarkable adaptability . . . is the prolonged plasticity of those late-developing frontal areas as they slowly mature. . . . These areas are the last to lay down the fatty myelin insulation—the brain's white matter—that speeds transmission. And at first glance this seems like bad news: if we need these areas for the complex task of entering the world, why aren't they running at full speed when the challenges are most daunting? The answer is that speed comes at the price of flexibility. While a myelin coating greatly accelerates an axon's bandwidth, it also inhibits the growth of new branches from the axon. According to Douglas Fields, an NIH neuroscientist who has spent years studying myelin, "This makes the period when a brain area lays down myelin a sort of crucial period of learning—the wiring is getting upgraded, but once that's done, it's harder to change." . . . So it is with the forebrain's myelination during the late teens and early 20s. This delayed completion—a withholding of readiness—heightens flexibility just as we confront and enter the world that we will face as adults. (p. 59)

Implications for Study Abroad

With the complexity and impact of this biological process of maturation in mind, consider the sending of teenagers into foreign cultures for the express purpose of being transformed by the experience. What an interesting opportunity! In the midst of the turmoil of entry into the interdependent adult society of their own culture, they suddenly leave that milieu and enter a foreign culture where they (a) have the challenge of studying in an unfamiliar environment, (b) may be surrounded by people speaking a different language from their own, and (c) are engulfed in an unfamiliar culture with limited help in figuring out its rules. Considering the flexibility of their young brains, they should be able to develop through mastering these challenges. But we must consider their motivation as well as their capability.

These young people, typically in the developmental substages between S-2 and S-3 (S-2[3], S-2/3), are strongly challenged biologically and socially at home, under increasing adult pressure to persevere in their development. Away from their primary culture, they are freed to a large degree from the socializing pressures of home, with little replacement pressure in their new environment. What a relief: out of the pressure cooker and into a fascinating new environment with little adult supervision! Is it any wonder, then, that many students abroad might choose to minimize unfamiliar challenges to whatever degree possible by (a) clustering with their compatriots, (b) avoiding the language challenge, and (c) exploring the host culture in like-minded groups of other expatriate adolescents? Is there any doubt, considering the developmental state of their brains, about why too many of them "behave badly," while learning little of the new culture and language?

Understanding both the developmental challenges from the social-emotional perspective and the developmental opportunities from the biological perspective provides a strong argument for well-supervised learning with frequent and structured interventions. Considering the forebrain's plasticity at this point, supporting great behavioral adaptability, any effort to encourage structured interaction with the target culture and language, led by well-trained cultural and linguistic mentors, will be powerfully effective in helping induce developmental transformation across substages within Kegan's (1982) framework.

The IDI

Many members of the academic community, especially those associated with study abroad programs, are likely aware of an assessment instrument frequently employed to measure students' pre- and post-scores around their study abroad experiences: the IDI, codeveloped by Mitchell Hammer and Milton Bennett (2009) in the mid-1990s and grounded in the theoretical work of Bennett's DMIS (1986, 1993). Following further empirical testing, Hammer (see chapter 5 of this volume) recently revised the original DMIS, renaming it the Intercultural Development Continuum (IDC), and he has developed a third version of the IDI. This third version measures one's relative development along the five-stage IDC, which represents "a progression from a less complex perception of and consequently a less complex experience of culturally-based patterns of difference to a more complex experience around cultural diversity" (Hammer, 2009, p. 205). As Hammer explains:

> Individuals who have a more detailed set of frameworks for perceiving and understanding patterns of cultural differences between themselves and

others have the capability of then experiencing observed cultural differences in ways that approximate how a person from that other culture might experience the world (Bennett, 2004). The capability of shifting cultural perspective and adapting behavior to cultural context represent an intercultural mindset. In contrast, perceiving cultural differences from one's own cultural perspective is indicative of a more monocultural mindset. (p. 5)

Each culture organizes the world in unique ways, holistically creating its own cultural worldview. People who have grown up in a single culture with little exposure to other cultures have access only to their own worldview; they are able to perceive another culture only through that lens and thus cannot distinguish between their own perceptions and those of culturally different people. Therefore, "the crux of the development of intercultural sensitivity is attaining the ability to construe (and thus experience) cultural difference in more complex ways" (Hammer et al., 2003, p. 423). Each stage on the continuum represents a different cognitive orientation, each represents different affective and behavioral stances toward cultural difference and commonality, and each is more sophisticated and comprehensive than the last. These more complex orientations support increasingly competent intercultural interaction. Denial and Polarization represent what Hammer (see chapter 5 of this volume) calls the more "monocultural" orientations, in which one's own culture forms the basis for reality, while Acceptance and Adaptation, the "multicultural" orientations, represent increasing capacities "to shift cultural perspective and adapt behavior to cultural context" (see page 124 of this volume). Between the monocultural and multicultural orientations lies Minimization, a transitional stage. Bennett and Hammer, in the next two chapters, each describe at greater length their intercultural development models and discuss the applicability of the IDI to student intercultural development.

A Suggestive Comparison of the Models

Kegan's (1982) model is focused broadly on the total human experience, whereas the DMIS and the IDC focus more narrowly on how people construe cultural difference and commonality. Nevertheless, as constructivist developmental models, each describing ascending series of increasingly complex worldviews, the DMIS and IDC parallel Kegan's model in interesting ways. Let us compare Kegan's S-3 (the other-dependent stage) with Minimization, the third stage of the IDC. In Kegan's model, S-3 is a "we," or "sense of community" stage. Self-image is determined entirely by what external or internalized others think. Individuals at S-3 are highly identified with and defined by socially established norms; their values are the values underlying these norms, and they strive to conform to others' expectations. If we consider, for example, the values of political correctness that are often manifested in the diversity movement in U.S. corporate and public environments, values that ask one to overlook or "minimize" differences of culture, race, ethnicity, and so on, in the attempt to reinforce beliefs in "a unified community," the dynamic strongly reflects both Kegan's S-3 and the Minimization orientation of the DMIS and IDC.

At the DMIS and the IDC's Minimization stage of cultural difference, elements of one's own cultural worldview are experienced as universal. Cultural differences are subordinated either within physical universalism, in which the overwhelming similarity of people's biological nature is generalized to other phenomena such as needs and motivations, or through a transcendent universalism that subsumes diverse philosophical and religious beliefs to the belief system of the minimizing individual or group. These Minimization dynamics obscure deep differences, allowing unique cultures to be trivialized or romanticized (Hammer et al., 2003).

This worldview fits comfortably within Kegan's larger perspective, where the concern for fitting into one's community, with everyone sharing the same values, allows one to extend the concept of community quite broadly through an emphasis on cultural similarities. Both S-3 and Minimization are concerned with a communal perspective and the subsuming of different types of human difference into more familiar, and more comfortable, categories.

We also find strong similarities between the Acceptance orientation and Kegan's (1982) S-4 stage. In Acceptance an individual experiences his or her own culture as just one of many complex worldviews; these are experienced as different from one's own, but equally human and valid. One can identify cultural differences over a range of human interactions. Acceptance does not imply agreement with cultural differences; but although individuals may not embrace particular differences—they may choose not to incorporate certain behaviors into their own behavioral repertoire, for example—they will not reject the humanity of the community that does embrace such behaviors. At Acceptance, one stands apart, struggling with the challenge of respecting differences when they reflect values at odds with one's own (Hammer et al., 2003, p. 425). The same challenge can be found in the U.S. diversity movement, in which individuals are often challenged to develop from minimizing to valuing cultural difference, thereby ascending a level on the DMIS and the IDC, as well as Kegan's, scales.

Kegan's S-4 is the independent, fully self-authoring decision maker. At this stage, one can articulate a conscious personal value system and strive for personal integrity. Having succeeded in pursuing S-3 goals, one has earned the right to stand out from the crowd and be noticed and, in turn, show respect for others both for their competence and for their different values and beliefs. The limitation encountered at this stage is that, although far more objective about the milieu from which one has just emerged, individuals will typically exhibit only a limited objectivity in their patterns of interaction with others, will not be able to enter perceptively into the universe of discourse of those others, and may find it difficult to harmonize the shaping of one's own group or organization with one's own principles. In this sense, individuals at this stage struggle with the relativity of values.

The point of this comparison is to reveal, for those more familiar with the DMIS and the IDC, and with the IDI, that the development of intercultural sensitivity and its concomitant intercultural competence fit comfortably within Kegan's (1982) larger framework—a framework in which we are all participating, whether we are focusing on cultural difference and similarity or not. Our relative "position" within this framework will largely determine how we interact with every aspect of our environment, in every aspect of our lives. Movement along these developmental scales is not trivial, nor does it happen without the requisite circumstances.

How Does Change Happen?

To understand how anything becomes something else, we have to identify a mechanism. To help us comprehend the transformation of human socioemotional and cognitive stages, we can look to the study of complex physical systems for very suggestive similarities.

Human Individuals as Open Systems

I have presented a framework in which human development can be understood, implied that measurable development can occur throughout the lives of individuals, and summarized Kegan's perspective that modern life has put us in a pressure cooker, demanding for the first time in human history that we move toward fourth-order development. Insights from another realm of human experience, science, point to answers about why fourth-order development is becoming critically important, and how it occurs. The farther we look into the largest of natural systems (astronomy) and the deeper we look into the tiniest (subatomic physics), including all biological and ecological systems that fall in between, the more we encounter what appear to be universal laws of entropy (order breaking down into disorder), negentropy (the increase of energy and organization), and the dynamic equilibrium of relatively stable systems. Intelligent living systems seem to operate quite similarly to inanimate material systems, and such relative distinctions are under intense scrutiny (Maturana & Varela, 1992). Dynamic systems of differing orders of complexity exist at every level of investigation, and each level reveals its place within an immense transcend-and-include developmental hierarchy, from the smallest systems of subatomic particles to the largest galaxies and the universe itself.

There is no reason to think that the developmental processes described by Kegan, Bennett, and Hammer operate differently, in their essentials, from the evolutionary processes studied by the sciences. The nature of these strikingly similar processes is the focus of systems theory and the sciences of complexity. The fundamental question is: How do open systems transform to higher or lower levels of functionality?

To oversimplify, such systems can exist in three states. The first two states of dynamic equilibrium and near equilibrium are not particularly pertinent, except to note that much of the time we adults (as open systems exchanging matter and energy with our environment) are in near equilibrium—fluctuating between waking and sleeping, eating and breathing—in order to maintain our matter/energy balance, a dynamic that slowly winds down over the course of our lifetimes. What is very pertinent, however, are systems in the third state. The matter-energy systems that emerge in the course of evolutionary processes in the real world, including human beings, are third-state, dynamic systems far from equilibrium (Laszlo, 1987). Such systems are nonlinear and sometimes indeterminate (i.e., end points cannot be predicted). They amplify certain fluctuations and evolve toward a new dynamic regime that is radically different from stationary states at or near equilibrium. Simply put, under the right conditions, they transform.

Change occurs and evolution unfolds because dynamic systems in the third state are not entirely stable. They have upper thresholds of stability. Transgressions of these thresholds produce critical instabilities, and the systems can be moved out of their steady states by changes in some environmental parameters:

> When changes of this kind occur, the systems enter a transitory phase characterized by indeterminacy, randomness, and some degree of chaos.

> Dynamic systems do not evolve smoothly and continuously over time, but do so in comparatively sudden leaps and bursts. (Laszlo, 1987, pp. 35–36)

Furthermore, the end state of transformation is not entirely predictable, for there are multiple possibilities:

> We cannot predict the precise evolutionary trajectory chosen by any system in the third state: all we can say is that the new steady state, if it is dynamically stable, assimilates the disturbance introduced by the destabilizing parameters within *an open structure that is likely to be more dynamic and complex than the structure in the previous steady state* [emphasis added]. (Laszlo, 1987, p. 36)

Implications for Study Abroad

These new, dynamically stable, open structures are what this chapter is about. If we consider "human beings" as systems in the third state, we have an excellent description of the process of human transformation through the developmental stages of Kegan, Bennett, and Hammer. Imagine, for instance, an adolescent student abroad as a system in the third state, far from equilibrium, and now in an unfamiliar environment perturbing the student/system. Depending on the degree of perturbation and the amount of free energy in the student/system (perhaps measurable in the student's emotional state), there is considerable potential for transformation, both upward, say from Kegan's S-2/3 to S-3/2, and downward, from S-2/3 to S-2(3).

Without (a) some design and management of the student's environment (degree and nature of exposure to the local culture), (b) regular structured learning intervention (to manage the internal chaos building in the student/system), and (c) measurement of developmental state, we cannot predict the outcome of the experience. A valid and reliable instrument such as the Subject-Object Interview (Lahey et al., 1988) or the IDI (Hammer, 2009) will allow us to measure the degree and direction of student/system change. However, our ability to predict the outcome will depend heavily on the emotional state of the student/system upon entering the new environment (a partial measure of free energy in "the system"), the student's/system's current developmental stability (the center of gravity in Kegan's [1982] model or the developmental orientation on the IDI), and the degree of environmental control and intervention that educators are able to apply during the experience. Without the elements of measurement, program design with developmental intention, and structured supervision, the developmental outcome of a student's study abroad experience is a proverbial crapshoot.

References

Bennett, M. J. (1986). Towards ethnorelativism: A developmental model of inter-cultural sensitivity. In R. M. Paige (Ed.), *Cross-cultural orientation: New conceptualizations and applications* (pp. 27–70). New York: University Press of America.

Bennett, M. J. (1993). Towards ethnorelativism: A developmental model of intercultural sensitivity. In R. M. Paige (Ed.), *Education for the intercultural experience* (pp. 21–71). Yarmouth, ME: Intercultural Press.

Bennett, M. J. (2004). Becoming interculturally competent. In J. Wurzel (Ed.), *Toward multiculturalism: A reader in multicultural education* (2nd ed., pp. 6–77). Newton, MA: Intercultural Resource.

Cook-Greuter, S. (1999). *Postautonomous ego development: A study of its nature and measurement* (Doctoral Thesis). Harvard Graduate School of Education, Ann Arbor, MI: Bell & Howell.

Debold, E. (2002, Fall/Winter). Epistemology, fourth order consciousness, and the subject-object relationship, or . . . how the self evolves: Interview with Robert Kegan. *What Is Enlightenment.* Retrieved from http://www.enlightennext.org/magazine/j22/kegan.asp?pf=1

Dobbs, D. (2011, October). Beautiful brains. *National Geographic, 220*(4), 59.

Eaglemann, D. (2011, July/August). The brain on trial. *The Atlantic, 308*(1), 123.

Eldridge, N., & Gould, S. J. (1972). Punctuated equilibria: An alternative to phyletic gradualism. In T. M. Schopf (Ed.), *Models in paleobiology* (pp. 82–115). San Francisco, CA: Freeman.

Graves, C. (1981, May). *Summary statement: The emergent, cyclical, double-helix model of the adult human biopsychosocial systems.* Paper presented at the meeting of World Future Society, Boston, MA.

Hammer, M. R. (2009). The intercultural development inventory: An approach for assessing and building intercultural competence. In M. Moodian (Ed.), *Contemporary leadership and intercultural competence* (pp. 203–217). Thousand Oaks, CA: Sage.

Hammer, M. R., Bennett, M. J., & Wiseman, R. (2003). Measuring intercultural sensitivity: The intercultural development inventory. *International Journal of Intercultural Relations, 27,* 421–443.

Kegan, R. (1982). *The evolving self: Problem and process in human development.* Cambridge, MA: Harvard University Press.

Kegan, R. (1994). *In over our heads: The mental demands of modern life.* Cambridge, MA: Harvard University Press.

Lahey, L., Souvaine, E., Kegan, R., Goodman, R., & Felix, S. (1988). A guide to the subject-object interview: Its administration and interpretation. Cambridge, MA: The Subject-Object Research Group, Harvard Graduate School of Education.

Laske, O. (2005). *Developmental coaching, module A: Handouts.* Medford, MA: Inter-developmental Institute Press.

Laske, O. (2006). *Measuring hidden dimensions: The art and science of fully engaging adults*. Medford, MA: Interdevelopmental Institute Press.

Laske, O. (2008). *Measuring hidden dimensions of human systems: Foundations of requisite organization*. Medford, MA: Interdevelopmental Institute Press.

Laszlo, I. (1987). *Evolution: The grand synthesis*. Boston, MA: Shambhala.

Maturana, H., & Varela, F. (1992). *The tree of knowledge: The biological roots of human understanding*. Boston, MA: Shambhala.

Scharmer, O. (2000, March 23). *Grabbing the tiger by the tail: Conversation with Robert Kegan,* Harvard Graduate School of Education. Retrieved from http://www.presencing.com/dol/kegan.shtml

Wilber, K. (2000). *Integral psychology: Consciousness, spirit, psychology, therapy*. Boston, MA: Shambhala.

Wilber, K., Engler, J., & Brown, D. P. (1981). *Transformations of consciousness: Conventional and contemplative perspectives on development*. Boston, MA: Shambhala.

4

PARADIGMATIC ASSUMPTIONS AND A DEVELOPMENTAL APPROACH TO INTERCULTURAL LEARNING

Milton J. Bennett

E very year for at least two decades I gave the same speech at NAFSA: Association of International Educators. It had different titles and contexts, but the basic message was the same: Intercultural learning does not happen automatically during study abroad. The rapid growth and turnover of study abroad programs ensured a continually changing, enthusiastic audience for the topic, although those same factors probably reduced its overall influence. Currently, I call the speech "Turning Cross-Cultural Contact Into Intercultural Learning." As a subjective indicator of change in the study abroad field, it seems to me that audiences are more ready than ever before to accept the premise of the presentation and to move quickly to the question, How can we do it differently and better? The existence of this volume reflects the change and I am pleased to be able to contribute to it.

In this chapter, I define *cross-cultural contact* and *intercultural learning* in relationship to the three major scientific paradigms. In their original physics forms, the paradigms are generally referred to as *Newtonian, Einsteinian,* and *Quantum* (Briggs & Peat, 1984; Kuhn, 1967). In their social science form, I refer to the paradigms as *positivist, relativist,* and *constructivist* (M. Bennett, 1985, 1998b, 2005). I define the terms commonly used in study abroad in the following way, most recently stated in a publication for the Forum on Education Abroad (M. Bennett, 2010):

- The term *international* refers to multiple nations and their institutions, as it is used in *international relations*. When *international* is used to modify *education*, it refers to curricula that incorporate attention to the institutions of other societies, and it refers to the movement of students, faculty, researchers, and other academics across national borders. For instance, "Our international education program incorporates foreign students and returned study abroad students into an effort to internationalize the curriculum of the university."
- The term *multicultural* refers to a particular kind of situation, one in which there are two or more cultures represented. For example, "The international university had a multicultural campus, with more than 15 different national and ethnic cultures represented."
- The term *cross-cultural* refers to a particular kind of contact among people, one in which the people are from two or more different cultures. For example, "On a multicultural campus, cross-cultural contact is inevitable."
- The term *intercultural* refers to a particular kind of interaction or communication among people, one in which differences in cultures play a role in the creation of meaning. For example, "The cross-cultural contact that occurs on multicultural campuses may generate intercultural misunderstanding." The term *intercultural* may also refer to the kind of skills or competence necessary to deal with cross-cultural contact. For example, "Administrators of cross-cultural programs need intercultural skills to be effective."
- The term *intercultural learning* refers to the acquisition of generalizable (transferable) intercultural competence; that is, competence that can be applied to dealing with cross-cultural contact in general, not just skills useful for dealing with a particular other culture. For example, "In her study abroad in Germany, not only did Susan acquire the skill of arguing in a more German than American style, she also learned how to recognize and potentially adapt to a wide range of cultural variation in dealing with differences of opinion." (pp. 214–215)

In the context of usage in this volume, it would be consistent to say that study abroad programs have been part of traditional (positivist and relativist) international education. Often, the expected outcome was positivist—simply increased knowledge. But as a result of the "great debate" in international education during the latter half of the last century (Hoffa, 2000), experientialists who challenged the traditionalists began exercising influence on the expected outcome of study abroad. Administrators and participants of many traditional programs bought part of the experiential package; they conceded that the experience of studying abroad was valuable itself, in addition to the new knowledge gained. In effect, they acknowledged the relativist assumption that knowledge was necessarily limited by perspective, and that it was important to be aware of one's own and others' frame of reference. However, they continued to assume that the cross-cultural contact in itself was sufficient to generate an experiential learning experience. As noted in chapter 1 by this book's editors in their reference to the *New Yorker* cartoon ("For my junior year abroad, I'm going to learn how to party in a foreign country"), in too many cases students indeed had a learning experience, but not necessarily an intercultural one.

In the terminology used in this chapter, the claim that intercultural learning is emerging from a simple cross-cultural program is a case of *paradigmatic confusion*, which occurs when incompatible epistemological assumptions are inadvertently mixed in explanations and practice. In this case, many study abroad programs are lodged in a different paradigm from the outcome that they expect and/or claim. Programs with a positivist base that are focused on knowledge acquisition and simple cross-cultural contact cannot legitimately claim an outcome of intercultural learning, which is based on constructivist assumptions of intentionality and self-reflexiveness. Because of paradigmatic confusion, intercultural learning in such programs is, at best, accidental.

This chapter accepts the premise of the editors that traditional study abroad programs are largely positivist or relativist, and it establishes that intercultural communication has emerged largely from constructivist roots. It is therefore not surprising that our efforts to introduce intercultural outcomes to study abroad have generated a large amount of paradigmatic confusion. This is particularly troublesome for both intercultural relations and study abroad, because both areas rely on "theory into practice" for conceptual relevance. If the paradigm underlying a theory is different from that underlying a related practice, both the credibility of the theory and the effectiveness of the practice suffer (Intercultural Development Research Institute, 2011).

The Positivist (Newtonian) Paradigm

In physics, Sir Isaac Newton (1642–1727) is credited with formalizing the scientific worldview (Briggs & Peat, 1984). By stating clearly that phenomena are governed by "laws of nature" (e.g., the behavior of apples and the law of gravity), he broke with a prescientific worldview pervaded by capricious spirits. The two major tenets of the Newtonian paradigm are (a) linear causality and (b) objective observation. *Linear causality* means that causes and their results run in one direction through time—a necessary assumption for prediction and control of events. *Objective observation* means that an observer is outside the event being observed, and that all observers of similar competence will observe the same events.

The Newtonian paradigm also became the template for social science. Considerations of the human condition had theretofore been mainly religious, spiritual, and philosophic in nature. But with the tools of Newtonian physics it was possible to objectify the human condition and study it as one would any other object in the world—in terms of causes and effects, prediction and control, at both the micro (individual) and macro (institutional) levels. Auguste Comte (1798–1857) formalized this epistemological position as "positivism." Building on and limiting ideas from Aristotle and incorporating some of the then-heretical thinking of Francis Bacon (1561–1626) and the formalization of empiricism accomplished by Newton, Comte (1966) held that all metaphysical speculation is invalid and that the only appropriate objects and criteria of human knowledge are data from sense experience. While Newton focused his attention on the physical world, Comte extended the idea of axiomatic scientific thinking to the study of all phenomena, including social relations. As such, he is often considered to be the father of sociology.

Of particular note for intercultural relations is the teleological implication of positivism. Despite its insistence on only describing empirical phenomena, positivism implies that there is an underlying ideal reality that is being imperfectly described. In the physical world, this ideal state is traditionally that of equilibrium. Thus, when the Nobel prize winner Ilya Prigogine described complex, self-organizing living systems as *far from equilibrium systems* (Prigogine & Glansdorff, 1971), he was departing sharply from this traditional scientific view.

Implications for Intercultural Theory

There are three rather dismal implications of positivism for the idea of "culture" itself. One is that culture is the kind of metaphysical speculation that is precluded from study. We can only describe behavior; we cannot speculate on the patterns of such behavior that might be shared by groups of interacting individuals. Patterns do not exist outside of our observation, and therefore they are simply epiphenomenal to our observation of the behavior itself. This view, of course, rejects the idea of culture altogether.

The second dismal theoretical implication of positivism is the polar opposite of the first. When "culture" is described in positivist ways, it is reified or essentialized. In the classic constructivist sociology text *The Social Construction of Reality,* Berger and Luckmann (1967) put it this way:

> Reification is the apprehension of human phenomena as if they were things, that is, in non-human or possibly supra-human terms. . . . Reification implies that men (*human beings*) are capable of forgetting their own authorship of the human world, and further, that the dialectic between man, the producer, and his products is lost to consciousness. . . . Man, the producer of a world, is apprehended as its product, and human activity as an epiphenomenon of non-human processes. . . . That is, man is capable paradoxically of producing a reality that denies him. (p. 89)

This kind of reification is the natural concomitant of a positivist epistemology. Positivism carries the assumption that things exist aside from their description—that there is an objective world that exists independently of our observation of it.

Much of social science continues to emulate the positivism of traditional science in assuming that social phenomena can be discovered and classified in definite and enduring ways. Cross-cultural classification schemes such as those of Hofstede (1991) or Trompenaars (1993), however they might have been intended, are frequently used in this way.

Like other social sciences, intercultural relations too often falls into naïve reifications of "culture" that emerge from our unconscious acceptance of a positivist epistemology. For instance, the popular iceberg metaphor presents "explicit culture" as visible above the waterline, whereas "implicit culture" lurks dangerously out of view underwater. The implication of the metaphor is that culture is a thing that must be known to be successfully circumnavigated. Does this idea of culture lead us to a sophisticated praxis of intercultural adaptation? Or does it more likely fuel the efforts of some entrepreneurs to produce ever more ornate descriptions of implicit culture?

The third dismal implication of positivism for intercultural theory is epitomized by much of the field of cross-cultural psychology. Typically, studies in this field focus on how cultural context does or does not affect the manifestation of certain psychological variables, with the goal of finding those variables that are the most "universal"—that is, the variables that are least affected by culture. These studies are positivist in two ways: in their methodology they reify culture, and in their goals they reify psychological processes. In the first case, by making culture an independent variable, researchers must specify the parameters of the "cultural context" in which the dependent variable will be measured. In doing so, they treat descriptions such as self-reports of "cultural values" or "cultural identification" as indicative of a reality existing outside of the reporter's consciousness. In the second case (and paradoxically), these studies often have the goal of discovering universal psychological processes that are unaffected by cultural context. Hence, having reified culture to create the independent variable, they try to show that the dependent variable (a psychological process such as "tolerance of ambiguity") is not, in fact, dependent on cultural context.

An example of the search for transcultural absolutes can be found in some of the work of the cross-cultural psychologist John Berry (2004). While he argues that studies should look for both similarities and differences across cultures, and that basic psychological processes are likely to manifest differently in different cultural contexts, he nevertheless makes the basic positivist assumption that a reality exists independently of our description of it:

> A working assumption . . . is that such "universal laws" of human behavior can be approached even though they may not be fully reached. That is, I believe that we may eventually discover the underlying psychological processes that are characteristic of the species, *homo sapiens*, as a whole. (p. 167)

Implications for Intercultural Learning

Because positivism specializes in description, it implies for the practice of intercultural relations that descriptive knowledge alone is sufficient for success in intercultural encounters. In its extreme form, this is the assumptive base of traditional study abroad programs that include no preparation at all for the cross-cultural experience. Because reality is what it is, and because all reasonable observers can apprehend that reality, it follows that one needs only to get into the vicinity of the reality to learn about it.

Somewhat less extreme is the employment of "area studies" for study abroad orientation programs. These programs and websites purport to prepare students for the cross-cultural experience by giving them information about the institutions, customs, and mores of the "target" culture. Sometimes this information is even about subjective culture, such as information about nonverbal behavior, communication style, or cultural values. While such information may be a useful concomitant of intercultural competence, it does not in itself constitute competence. One must know what to do with the information to make it useful. A medical doctor who has all the latest information about cancer is not necessarily able to perform a successful cancer surgery. In every other arena, we accept that knowledge is useful only in a more general context of competence. Perhaps it is a special characteristic of ethnocentrism that people often cannot imagine that intercultural learning might demand competence, and so they think information will suffice.

Another distinctly positivist approach to preparing people for cross-cultural contact is the provision of a list of "dos and don'ts." Interculturalists seem to have a kind of approach/withdrawal attitude toward these kind of recipes. On the positive side, they like being able to augment simple information with something that seems more practical, and frequently program participants request or even demand such lists. But on the negative side, intercultural practitioners generally know that lists of dos and don'ts are not very helpful in the long run for intercultural communication. Although not many interculturalists would put it this way, they are experiencing paradigmatic confusion. Behavioral recipes emerge from a positivist paradigm, and, as we will see, concepts of intercultural communication almost always emerge from a constructivist paradigm. The confusion is generated by hoping that a technique based in one paradigm will generate an outcome in another paradigm.

The Relativist (Einsteinian) Paradigm

Einstein's assumption of relativity overturned the Cartesian/Newtonian notion of an objective observer. In Einstein's view, any observation is necessarily restricted by our "frame of reference"—specifically, how we are moving relative to the rest of the universe. All understanding must occur relative to the context of both the observer and the observed. In the social sciences, this idea is most often expressed through systems theory (Watzlawick, Beavin, & Jackson, 1967), in which meaning is defined in the mutual interaction of elements within systems. For instance, to take their well-known example, one cannot determine absolutely whether a husband drinks because his wife nags or his wife nags because her husband drinks; all we can say is that each defines the other as the cause of the behavior. They are, in a profound way, defining each other through their interaction.

In the humanistic application of relativism, postmodernists of the Frankfurt (e.g., Theodor Adorno) and French (e.g., Jean-François Lyotard) schools reject the assumption of objectivity, replacing it with a very Einsteinian assumption of relativity. In its poststructural social form, the assumption of relativity has acquired its own load of reification. If a frame of reference is taken to be a "thing," such as a worldview, it may become an object that imprisons our perception. After an acknowledgment of our differing worldviews, there is nothing much more to be done, except perhaps to decry the efforts of the more powerful to impose their worldview on the less powerful. The tyranny of absolutism is exchanged for the rigidity of relativism.

The anthropologists Boas (1911) and Herskovits (1958) earlier generated this same trade-off. In defining culture in relativistic terms, they attempted to counter the absolutist notions of social Darwinism—the idea that culture is the evolution of civilization. But in so doing, they eliminated any way of comparing and contrasting cultures and implied that the only way to know another culture was to become assimilated or resocialized into it. This assumption continues to hold sway in the assimilationist approach to immigration issues, in which the goal is the immigrants' one-way "adjustment" to the new culture.

Implications for Intercultural Theory

The relativist paradigm lies at the heart of mainstream theories of human communication, including those of intercultural communication, and are based heavily on systems theory. Systems-based research, rather than searching for the universal law with which to predict human behavior, tries to describe how roles and rules interact in complex systems. Communication research in particular seeks to understand how people are influenced by context to create the meanings that they do. So it was natural that culture was defined as a system, and the meanings created by people within the system were classified as "cultural elements." These categories of elements are the typical constituents of intercultural courses, such as language use, nonverbal behavior, communication style, cognitive style, and cultural values. Intercultural theory in this paradigm describes how people who are influenced by one set of elements attempt to understand and be understood by people who are influenced by a different set of elements (cf. Hall, 1959; Stewart & Bennett, 1993).

Unlike the universalist aspirations of cross-cultural psychology, intercultural communication simply describes the discontinuities of meaning that occur when different sets of cultural elements collide. Interculturalists are less likely to seek underlying variables to correlate with outcomes, and more likely to seek systemic explanations of how particular meaning is created in or across cultural context. Like all of relativism, this approach has the strength of maintaining relevance to the particular context under consideration and it avoids the "etic error" of overgeneralizing nomothetic data. On the other hand, a relativistic approach may make the "emic error" of being so particular to context, of being so "thick" (Geertz, 1973), that no generalization at all can be made.

> The major limitation for intercultural theory of the relativistic paradigm is the lack of any assumption of "crossing context." For instance, in the extreme forms of contextualism represented by some poststructuralists, any claim of operating out of one's system is thought to be bogus, it being simply a denial of the inevitable limitation that a system places upon its elements. This claim is made most strongly when the context is one of privilege and power. In this view, not only does one naturally desire to remain in the context of power, but any attempt to understand phenomena outside that context is inevitably tainted by the power perspective of the original context. This view defines culture mostly in terms of institutional dominance, and so tends to miss the idea of subjective culture that is commonly used in intercultural relations. (M. Bennett, 1998a)

Implications for Practice

Practitioners of intercultural relations tend to use the relativist paradigm quite naturally. They are wont to give imprecations such as, "It's not bad or good, it's just different," with the implication that no judgment of phenomena is possible from outside the context. Of course, this is a good protection from the ravages of positivism-based colonialism, but it has its own limitations of being at least simplistic, if not solipsistic.

More sophisticated practitioners of this paradigm use the idea of "perspective" quite well, frequently using the metaphor of "colored glasses" to express the idea that culture colors perspective. However, the idea of perspective is rife with possibilities for paradigmatic confusion. One such confusion is the idea that one could "put one's glasses aside," thus assumedly revealing the true world that underlies the various distortions of culture. This is, of course, a positivist notion with a relativistic overlay, which creates an inherent incoherence. Another confusion is assuming that an awareness of perspective translates into an ability to shift perspective. Not only is this generally untrue, but it is theoretically not possible within the relativistic paradigm. There is nothing wrong with teaching the idea of perspective, but the approach needs to be augmented with some constructivist thinking before it can become sufficiently self-reflexive to allow the actual transformation of context, and thus perspective.

The Constructivist (Quantum) Paradigm

Paradoxically but necessarily, the very idea of "paradigm" exists in a paradigm. Thomas Kuhn (1967) showed that the observer, the observer's theory, and the research apparatus itself were all essentially expressions of a perspective, and, therefore, the results of all experiments conducted with this perspective were also expressions of the same perspective. In other words, our perspective *constructs* the reality that we describe. This is a quite different notion than that of relativistic perspective, which simply describes different views of reality. In this constructivist paradigm, the observer interacts with reality via his or her perspective in such a way that reality is organized according to that perspective.

This interaction of observer and observed has been demonstrated most dramatically by quantum physicists. For instance, Werner Heisenberg famously observed in his "uncertainty principle" that it is impossible to separate the properties of objects from the measurement of them, nor from the measurer who wields the measurement apparatus (Briggs & Peat, 1984). In this view, reality takes on the quality of a self-fulfilling prophecy, in which our perspective is the prophecy and the necessary interaction of our perspective with all that we observe is the mechanism of fulfillment of the prophecy.

The application of the quantum scientific paradigm to social science has yielded the approach of *constructivism*. The idea of constructivism is closely linked with the quantum idea of "organization of reality through observer/ observation/observed interaction." The recent lineage of this notion traces back to Piaget's (1954) work in developmental psychology, George Kelly's (1963) theory of personal constructs, Berger and Luckmann's (1967) work in sociology, Gregory Bateson's (1972) work in anthropology, the Palo Alto school of psychology (Watzlawick, 1984), Heinz Von Foerster's work in neurophysiology (Segal, 1986), the work of neurobiologists Humberto Maturana and Francisco Varela (1992), George Lakoff and Mark Johnson's work in linguistics (1999), and my own work in developmental intercultural sensitivity (M. Bennett, 2004; Bennett & Castiglioni, 2004). Here is a representative constructivist statement by Kelly (1963):

> A person can be a witness to a tremendous parade of episodes and yet, if he fails to keep making something out of them, or if he waits until they have all occurred before he attempts to reconstrue them, he gains little in the way of experience from having been around when they happened. (p. 73)

This quote contains many of the core concepts of constructivism. By using the term *episodes*, Kelly (1963) implies that there is no inherent meaning in the phenomena themselves. People have to "make something out of them"; that is, they need to (and necessarily must) interact with the episodes for them to become meaningful events. Furthermore, Kelly suggests that "experience" occurs not only in context, as do the relativists, but that it may not occur at all without engagement of the phenomena. This is a profoundly nonpositivist notion—one that affects intercultural work dramatically.

Implications for Intercultural Theory

The constructivist paradigm avoids the reification of culture, either in its objective sense of institutions or in its subjective sense of worldview. In this view, "culture" is simply our description of patterns of behavior generated through human interaction within some boundary condition. For instance, "Japanese culture" is a description of patterns of interaction among people (and their products, such as institutions) within the boundary condition of a geographical nation-state grouping. When people both describe a culture and consider themselves as participating in it, the term *culture* may also refer to an identity.

Humberto Maturana and Francisco Varela (1992) offer a brand of constructivism particularly appropriate for understanding the idea of culture: "Those behavioral patterns which have been acquired ontogenically in the communicative dynamics of a social environment and which have been stable through generations, we shall call 'cultural behaviors' " (p. 162). In this view, cultural behavior is the ongoing manifestations of an organization of reality maintained by the interaction within a social environment. This definition of *culture* avoids both the reification of positivism and the contextualism of relativism. Culture is a result of the lived experience (praxis) of participating in social action. Part of our experience is "languaging," including languaging about our experience, which generates the explanations about our lived experience that we can call "culture." In other words, culture is a construction, but culture is not purely a cognitive invention. It is both the explanation and the essence of our lived social experience. Our cultural behavior is an enactment of our collective experience, and, through this enactment, it becomes yet more experience. This is the essence of cultural identity (Bennett & Castiglioni, 2004).

Following this definition of culture, people do not *have* a worldview; rather, they are constantly in the process of interacting with the world in ways that both express the pattern of the history of their interactions and contribute to those patterns (Berger & Luckmann, 1967). They are constructing a view of the world. So, if one wishes to participate in Japanese culture as an Italian, he or she must stop organizing the world in an Italian way and start organizing it in a Japanese way. (This is the theoretical ideal, never achieved, of course.) The ability to use self-reflexive consciousness in such a way as to construct alternative cultures and move into alternative experience is the crux of intercultural adaptation. When two people are doing this, it generates a "virtual third culture"—the interactional space where intercultural learning occurs.

Implications for Practice

For a praxis of intercultural relations, the minimum conceptual requirement is a self-reflexive definition of culture. There are two reasons for this. One is the obvious observation that how we define culture is itself a product of culture. Any definition of culture needs to take into account that it is defining the human activity of defining. When we realize this, we can spend less time arguing over the "best" definition of culture and more time assessing any definition for its usefulness to our purposes.

The second reason for using a self-reflexive definition of culture relates directly to our purpose. When we encourage intercultural learning, we are asking people to engage in a self-reflexive act. Specifically, we are asking them to use the process of defining culture (which is their culture) to redefine culture in a way that is not their culture. Because our different experience is a function of how we organize reality differently, the only way people can have access to the experience of a different culture is by organizing reality more in that way than in their own way. Both positivists and relativists would say that this is impossible. A constructivist would just say it is difficult. But even the constructivist would say it is impossible if we are using a reified definition of culture. With a self-reflexive definition of culture, we can proceed to explore the nature of cultural experience in a paradigmatically coherent way. That is, we are not struggling with trying to join a positivist metaphor such as "culture as iceberg" with a constructivist outcome such as "reframing cultural experience." Instead, we can aptly claim that the dynamic quality of cultural organization can be engaged by our equally dynamic individual consciousness.

The most general practical goal of intercultural learning is to overcome ethnocentrism and to enable successful communication in a multicultural environment. The constructivist paradigm allows us to see that ethnocentrism is simply the inability to experience reality differently than we were originally taught. This paradigm enables us to conceive different realities, to imagine how experience is different in those realities, and to enact to some degree that alien experience. This is the crux of communication—the ability to transcend our own limited experience and embody the world as another is experiencing it.

A Constructivist Model

The Developmental Model of Intercultural Sensitivity (DMIS) (M. Bennett, 1986, 1993, 2004) uses constructivist concepts to describe the process of intercultural learning. The model represents two major paradigmatic departures from many other explanations of cross-cultural behavior. First, the DMIS does not make the positivist assumption commonly made by cross-cultural psychologists that people's behavior is "caused" by any combination of personality, knowledge, attitudes, or skills. From a constructivist perspective, no amount of measurement of those variables will yield an understanding of how or why some people are better than others at intercultural relations. Second, the DMIS does not make the relativist assumption common to intercultural communication that an unprejudiced understanding of one's own and other cultures will automatically yield better intercultural relations. In this sense, the DMIS is neither an affective nor a cognitive model of intercultural communication.

The DMIS does assume, along with cognitive complexity theory (Applegate & Sypher, 1988; Delia, O'Keefe, & O'Keefe, 1982), that expertise in certain kinds of communication is a function of differentiating and integrating constructs in more complex ways. However, by tapping more directly into radical constructivist notions (Watzlawick, 1984), the DMIS further assumes that our experience of reality itself is a function of how we organize our perception—that things become more real as we perceive them in more sensitive (i.e., more highly discriminated, or complex) ways. The model then defines a sequence whereby "cultural difference" becomes more real, which generates more complex intercultural experience, which in turn can be enacted as more interculturally competent behavior.

The DMIS suggests six distinct kinds of experience spread across a continuum that shades from ethnocentrism to ethnorelativism. I use the term *ethnocentrism* to refer to the experience of one's own culture as "central to reality." By this I mean that the beliefs and behaviors that people receive in their primary socialization are unquestioned; they are experienced as "just the way things are." I coined the term *ethnorelativism* to mean the opposite of ethnocentrism—the experience of one's own beliefs and behaviors as just one organization of reality among many viable possibilities. In general, the more ethnocentric positions represent ways of *avoiding the experience of cultural difference,* either by denying its existence (Denial), by raising defenses against it (Defense), or by minimizing its importance (Minimization). The more ethnorelative positions represent ways of *seeking the experience of cultural difference*, either by accepting its importance (Acceptance), by adapting perspective to take it into account (Adaptation), or by integrating the experience into one's personal or organizational identity (Integration). The sequence of these experiences became the stages of the DMIS.

The usage of "stages" in the DMIS is similar to the use of the term in other stage theories (e.g., Erikson, 1959), in that each stage builds from the previous one, and unresolved issues from earlier stages can become problems later in the developmental process. However, "stage" should never be used as a label, as in "he is in/at the Defense stage." To do so would be a form of paradigmatic confusion, because stage theories derive for the most part from constructivist roots, and using them as labels would be distinctly positivist. To avoid this confusion, I have begun to speak of the stages as "positions" along the continuum of development.

While the positions have been shown to be conceptually and experientially distinct and to occur in a developmental sequence (Hammer, Bennett, & Wiseman, 2003), they coexist to some extent in all of us. Therefore, I use the term *predominant experience* (PE) to describe particular positions.

For instance, someone with a PE of Minimization may nevertheless experience Defense in some instances, and Acceptance in others. All of us, no matter how "developed" we are, probably maintain a little Denial in our inability to experience an event occurring in another culture (e.g., a terrorist attack) as having the same intensity as a similar event in our own culture. Development occurs not through stepping from stage to stage, but from moving the peak of our PE along the continuum.

The default condition of a typical, monocultural primary socialization is *Denial* of cultural difference—the experience of one's own culture as the only reality. At the level of this experience, "things are the way they are." From a metalevel, we might say that the beliefs, behaviors, and values that constitute a culture are experienced as unquestionably real or true. Other cultures either are not noticed at all or are construed in rather vague ways. As a result, either cultural difference is not experienced at all, or it is experienced as associated with a kind of undifferentiated *other* such as "foreigner" or "immigrant." In extreme cases, the people of one's own culture may be perceived to be the only real humans and other people viewed as simpler forms in the environment to be tolerated, exploited, or eliminated as necessary.

In facilitating intercultural learning, various issues associated with each developmental position need to be recognized and moved toward resolution. At Denial, the main issue to be resolved is the tendency to avoid noticing or confronting cultural difference. People here need to attend to the simple existence of other cultures, both globally and domestically. Those who facilitate this initial recognition (e.g., study abroad advisors) need to understand that Denial is not a refusal to "confront the facts." It is instead an inability to make the perceptual distinctions that allow cultural events to be recognized as such. When facilitators fail to understand the experience of Denial, they are likely to present cultural information in too complex ways and to become impatient at the aggressive ignorance often displayed at this point of development. In orientations for study abroad, Denial may lead to the "endless logistics" syndrome, in which students resist cultural topics as "irrelevant" or "obvious" and are concerned exclusively with expanding already familiar categories such as money, security, transportation, and partying.

The resolution of Denial issues allows people to create simple categories for particular cultures, which sets up the conditions for the experience of Defense. In study abroad, if the resolution of Denial issues occurs in a minimal pre-departure program, the student enters the cross-cultural context with a PE of Defense. This condition is likely to lead to excessive stress for the student, problems with host families, and huge time demands on program administrators. In the more likely case that Denial issues are resolved only during the initial part of the sojourn, the student returns home with a PE of Defense—on outcome certainly contrary to the goals of study abroad.

Defense against cultural difference is the experience of one's own culture (or an adopted culture) as the only viable one—the most "evolved" form of civilization, or at least the only good way to live. People with a PE of Defense have become more adept at discriminating difference, so they experience cultural differences as more real than do people at Denial. But the Defense experience is not sufficiently complex to generate an equally "human" experience of the other. Although the cultural differences experienced by people with a Defense perspective are stereotypical, they nevertheless seem real by comparison to the Denial condition. Consequently, people at Defense are more openly threatened by cultural differences than are people at Denial. The perception of cultures is polarized into "us and them," where one's own culture is superior and other cultures are inferior.

In study abroad, Defense is the driver of students' exclusivity behavior. When they remain entirely in a bubble or enclave of their compatriots, they are defending themselves against the threat of the host culture. In my experience, discussions within these exclusivity groups tend toward denigrating the host culture and exalting the home culture. In the international domain, Defense is clearly the predominant orientation of "nation building." Like mentoring, nation-building efforts usually are implicit (and sometimes even explicit) attempts to export the builders' assumedly superior cultural values. The polarized worldview is also evident in the statement "You're either with us or against us," uttered by a variety of world leaders. Other incidents of a culturally polarized worldview are evident in the complaints of travelers about unfamiliar food and similar failures of other cultures to not be "like us."

A variation on Defense is *Reversal,* in which an adopted culture is experienced as superior to the culture of one's primary socialization ("going native," or "passing"). Reversal is like Defense in that it maintains a polarized, "us and them" worldview. It is unlike Defense in that one's own culture, rather than another one, is the threat. Reversal is common among full-year exchange students and other long-term sojourners such as missionaries, diplomats, and corporate expatriates. Reversal may masquerade as cultural sensitivity, because it provides a positive experience of a different culture along with seemingly analytical criticisms of one's own culture. However, the positive experience of the other culture is at an unsophisticated stereotypical level, and the criticism of one's own culture is usually an internalization of others' negative stereotypes.

Study abroad orientations and on-site programs can address Defense by emphasizing common humanity, tolerance, and application of the Golden Rule (Bennett, 1979). Facilitators who try to correct the stereotypes of people in Defense are likely to fall prey to the polarized experience themselves, becoming yet another example of the evils of multiculturalism or globalization. The need here is to establish commonality, not to introduce more sophisticated understanding of difference. When this resolution is accomplished, the stage is set for a move into Minimization.

Minimization of cultural difference is the state in which elements of one's own cultural worldview are experienced as universal. The threat associated with cultural differences experienced in Defense is neutralized by subsuming the differences into familiar categories. For instance, cultural differences may be subordinated to the overwhelming similarity of people's biological nature (*human similarity*). The experience of similarity of natural physical processes may then be generalized to other assumedly natural phenomena such as needs and motivations. The assumption that typologies (personality, learning style, etc.) apply equally well in all cultures is an example of Minimization.

The experience of similarity might also be experienced in the assumed cross-cultural applicability of certain religious, economic, political, or philosophical concepts (*universal values*). For instance, the religious assumptions that everyone in the world is a child of God or that everyone has karma are examples of Minimization. It is not intrinsically ethnocentric to have a religious belief; however, it is ethnocentric to assume that people in other cultures share your belief, or at least they would if they could. Similarly, the assumption that people of all cultures would like to live in a democratic society (or in a benevolent dictatorship) if they only could is ethnocentric by this definition. Because these "universal absolutes" obscure deep cultural differences, other cultures may be trivialized or romanticized at Minimization.

People at Minimization expect similarities, and they may become insistent about correcting others' behavior to match their expectations. Many exchange students have reported to me that their host families, despite their kindness, generosity, and sincere curiosity about different customs, do not really want their students to have different basic values from theirs. I have observed that many host families seem to be operating with a PE of Minimization. The families are motivated by sharing the host country's way of life with the student, on the assumption that of course the student will appreciate that way of life once he or she sees what it is. If the student is insufficiently appreciative, it threatens the Minimization assumption that all everyone really wants to be is "like us." This operation of Minimization is far more dangerous, of course, when it is promoted by armed nation builders.

Particularly for people of dominant cultures, Minimization tends to mask recognition of their own culture (ethnicity) and the institutional privilege it affords its members. Because people with a predominant experience of Minimization no longer experience others in a polarized way, they tend to overestimate their racial and ethnic appreciation. Although they may be relatively tolerant, people at Minimization are unable to apprehend other cultures completely because they cannot see their own culture clearly. If, for instance, I cannot see that my communication style is a cultural pattern, I think that everyone does (or would if they could) use the same style. Consequently, I judge the failure to use my style as a lack of social skill or as a choice to be "alternative." Either of these judgments misses the point that other people may be naturally using a culturally different style.

The cross-cultural dimension of study abroad may itself be enough to move students from Defense to Minimization. There is ample evidence that cross-cultural contact in the relatively equal-power situation of international study is sufficient in itself to generate a reduction of stereotypes and an increase in tolerance (Allport, 1954; Amir, 1969; Pettigrew & Tropp, 2000). However, if the goal of the program is to achieve the more ethnorelative experience of intercultural learning, some efforts should be made to resolve Minimization before or during the program. The main issue is the recognition of one's own culture (cultural self-awareness). In more general terms, this is the ability to experience culture as a *context*. Only when one sees that much of one's experience is a function of the particular context in which one was socialized can one fully imagine alternatives to it.

Facilitators of development beyond Minimization need to stress the implementation of cultural self-awareness in contrast to other cultures before they move into too much detail about the other cultures. In study abroad pre-departure programs, this effort involves resisting the demand for more culture-specific information about the destination until sufficient cultural self-awareness has been established. For on-site programs, the implication is that host-culture learning should continually be integrated with own-culture learning. It is likely that such integration is the natural outcome of moving between host culture and home culture environments, thus explaining the finding of greater intercultural learning for partial rather than full immersion study abroad programs (Vande Berg, 2009).

The *Acceptance* of cultural difference is the more ethnorelative experience of one's own culture as just one of a number of equally complex worldviews. By discriminating differences among cultures (including one's own), and by constructing a kind of self-reflexive perspective, people with this PE are able to experience others as different from themselves, but equally human. People at Acceptance can construct culture-general categories that allow them to generate a range of relevant cultural contrasts among many cultures. Thus, they are not necessarily experts in one or more cultures (although they might also be that); rather, they are adept at identifying how cultural differences in general operate in a wide range of human interactions.

In this last regard, it is important to remember that the DMIS is not a model of knowledge, attitude, or skills. Therefore, the fact that one is knowledgeable about a culture may or may not be associated with the ethnorelative experience of Acceptance. Essentially, culture-specific information does not contribute to ethnorelative experience unless basic Minimization issues have been resolved first. People need to be developmentally ready to use culture-specific information in the service of intercultural learning.

In addition to not being just about knowledge, the experience of Acceptance is not the same as "agreement." It is naïve to think that intercultural sensitivity and competence is always associated with liking other cultures. An uncritical agreement with other cultures is more characteristic of the ethnocentric experience of Reversal, particularly if it is accompanied by a critical view of one's own culture.

To accept the relativity of values to cultural context (and thus to attain the potential to experience the world as organized by different values), one needs to figure out how to maintain ethical commitment in the face of such relativity. This is a matter of *contextual relativism*, a term coined by Lee Knefelkamp (1998) in reference to William Perry's (1970) Scheme of Cognitive and Ethical Development. We all need to make value judgments to be functional human beings, but when such judgments are made at early developmental positions—in DMIS terms, as enactments of ethnocentric experience—they explicitly or implicitly support the assumed centrality of our own culture. The more ethnorelative alternative is for judgments to be a commitment to one context over another context that may be equally complex and potentially good—what Perry calls "commitment in relativism" (Moore, 2001).

Like other frameworks useful for intercultural learning, a model of ethical development should be established in study abroad pre-departure, either through coursework or minimally in an orientation program. This provides participants with schemata to organize their experience abroad. From a constructivist perspective, it is not possible for people to have any kind of experience at all without schemata. Therefore, the question is not, Should we guide participants' overseas experience?; it is simply a matter of *what* schemata participants will use to organize their perception. Lacking any alternative, students will use either schemata from their native cultures or, perhaps, schemata that are generated haphazardly in response to the foreign environment. If a study abroad program is claiming that its outcome is intercultural learning, then the program needs to be providing coherent intercultural learning schemata to enable that kind of experience.

Resolution of the issue of value relativity allows people to have a significant experience of a different culture without losing their own cultural worldviews. This is the crux of *Adaptation*. People with a PE of Adaptation can engage in intercultural empathy—the ability to take perspective or shift frame of reference vis-à-vis other cultures. This shift is not merely cognitive; it is a change in the organization of lived experience, which necessarily includes affect and behavior. In other words, people at Adaptation are able to reorganize their perception of events so that it is more like the worldview of the target culture. The alternative experience afforded by that reorganization can then be enacted in culturally appropriate feelings and behavior. If this process of frame shifting and code shifting is deepened and habitualized, it becomes the basis of biculturality or multiculturality.

The idea of Adaptation is firmly lodged in constructivism; it depends on the paradigmatic assumption that reality is not fixed, in either an absolute or a relative way. Rather, much of what we experience as reality is the manifestation of an agreement to organize our perception in a particular way. Our "natural" experience of reality—particularly social reality—is only natural to a particular social/cultural context. Unless we have received bicultural socialization, any systematic experience of an alternative reality demands an act of consciousness—the intentional reorganization of perception. Therefore, if we wish to experience a different culture, we need to intentionally reorganize our perception to be more like that of the target culture worldview. Further, because the experience of one's own culture is embodied (Bennett & Castiglioni, 2004), the new organization of perception must also be embodied for it to generate feelings appropriate to the other culture. At that point, and only then, can we enact those feelings as adaptive behavior in the alternative culture.

The "experience of another culture" has long been one of the goals of study abroad programs. But the definition of what constitutes such an experience has been rooted in either positivist or relativist paradigms. In the former case, experience was thought to be the inevitable outcome of being in the vicinity of events when they occur; all that was necessary for experiencing the other culture was to be there. By this positivist criterion, study abroad programs need only physically place students in the other cultural context for intercultural experience to occur. Switching to a relativist paradigm merely adds the requirement that students be aware of how their own perspective may differ from that of the host culture—at best, an expression of Acceptance in DMIS terms. For a predominant experience of Adaptation to be achieved, the ethnocentric issues of Denial, Defense, and Minimization must have been sufficiently resolved; adequate perceptual frameworks for identifying cultural differences must have been established; and ethical issues must have been addressed. These elements, in this order, seldom occur by chance—and thus the imperative for "interventionist" programs (Vande Berg, 2009).

The major issue to be resolved at Adaptation is that of authenticity. How is it possible to perceive and behave in culturally different ways and still "be yourself"? The successful resolution of this issue generates *Integration*. In the personal form of Integration, the predominant experience of one's self is expanded to include a broader repertoire of cultural worldviews (Bennett & Castiglioni, 2004). In many ways, an expanded intercultural repertoire is simply an extension of contextual shifts that we frequently make in interpersonal relations, such as shifting between appropriate feelings and communication behavior with one's grandparent and one's spouse. Shifting cultural context is not dramatically different from this, although it occurs at a cultural rather than a personal level of abstraction. Where most of us can move in and out of different familial contexts, people with a PE of Integration can move in and out of different cultural worldviews. An important difference is that learning to shift familial context is part of our primary socialization, whereas intercultural shifting is usually consciously acquired later in life— perhaps through a study abroad program! Although we generally do not feel inauthentic at changing our behavior according to family context, some people may feel that the more conscious shifting of cultural context is hypocritical, or at least inconsistent. This feeling is ameliorated by integrating intercultural competence into identity, so that people can experience themselves as having context-shifting abilities in a variety of domains.

In terms of the paradigms discussed in this work, Integration can be seen as the conscious use of constructivism in defining one's identity. In this view, identity is an ongoing process of construing events in a way that generates the experience of "self." This process probably includes the maintenance of a kind of personal historical narrative that habitualizes certain feelings that are connected to one's self (Damasio, 1999). People with a PE of Integration feel that they are continually in the process of deciding what events in a variety of cultural contexts are intrinsic to who they are. They experience themselves as "in process," as opposed to having any set identity. This feeling should not be confused, however, with the feeling of not exercising a cultural worldview. People with feelings of transcendence of culture or alienation from culture are more likely to be experiencing Reversal rather than Integration (Hammer, Bennett, & Wiseman, 2003).

Trying to understand Integration from a positivist or relativist paradigm generates paradigmatic confusion. For instance, the positivist view of "self" is as an object—a thing that may stay hidden or that can be discovered by peeling away onion-like layers of consciousness to reveal the enduring true self. When people experiencing intercultural development carry this positivist view of identity into ethnorelativism, their feeling of an absolute self clashes with new feelings of self defined by context and consciousness. One manifestation of this clash is the ethical confusion generated at Acceptance, where the true self contradicts contextual relativity. Another is the authenticity issue of Adaptation, where a single true self is insufficient to explain dramatic worldview shifts. To avoid this same paradigmatic confusion at Integration, we should not describe an objective self that is "caught" in the margins between cultures, as I and others have done in the past (J. Bennett, 1993; M. Bennett, 1993). Rather, we should assume that people with a PE of Integration are consciously constructing dynamic identities for themselves that acknowledge their primary socialization but that extend who they are into alternative worldviews and cultural bridge building.

I do not think that interculturally sensitive people are generally *better* people. To say so would imply that there were one universally good kind of person and that this particular model just happened to describe that goodness. On the contrary, the DMIS describes what it means to be good at intercultural relations. All we can say about more ethnorelative people is that they are better at experiencing cultural differences than are more ethnocentric people, and therefore they are potentially better at adapting to those differences in interaction. I personally believe that the world would be a better place if intercultural competence were more commonly practiced by ethnorelative people. Insofar as study abroad programs are concerned, they could contribute substantially to this development by examining their paradigmatic assumptions, generating coherent programmatic designs, and facilitating intercultural learning as an intentional educational effort.

References

Albert, R. (1995). The intercultural sensitizer/cultural assimilator as a cross-cultural training method. In S. Fowler & M. Mumford (Eds.), *Intercultural sourcebook: Cross-cultural training methods* (Vol. 1, pp. 157–167). Yarmouth, ME: Intercultural Press.

Allport, G. (1954). *The nature of prejudice*. New York: Addison-Wesley.

Amir, Y. (1969). Contact hypothesis in ethnic relations. *Psychological Bulletin, 71,* 319–343.

Applegate, J. L., & Sypher, H. E. (1988). Constructivist theory and intercultural communication research. In Y. Kim & W. Gudykunst (Eds.), *Theoretical perspectives in intercultural communication* (pp. 41–65). Beverly Hills, CA: Sage.

Bateson, G. (1972). *Steps to an ecology of mind: Collected essays in anthropology, psychiatry, evolution, and epistemology.* San Francisco, CA: Chandler.

Bennett, J. (1993). Cultural marginality: Identity issues in intercultural training. In R. M. Paige (Ed.), *Education for the intercultural experience* (2nd ed., pp. 109–135). Yarmouth, ME: Intercultural Press.

Bennett, M. (1979). Overcoming the Golden Rule: Sympathy and empathy. In D. Nimmo (Ed.), *Communication Yearbook 3* (pp. 406–422). New Brunswick, NJ: Transaction Publishers.

Bennett, M. (1985). *Paradigms.* Class handout from Communication and Consciousness, Portland State University, Portland, OR.

Bennett, M. (1986). A developmental approach to training intercultural sensitivity. *International Journal of Intercultural Relations, 10*(2), 179–186.

Bennett, M. (1993). Towards ethnorelativism: A developmental model of intercultural sensitivity. In R. M. Paige (Ed.), *Education for the intercultural experience* (pp. 21–71). Yarmouth, ME: Intercultural Press.

Bennett, M. (1998a). Intercultural communication: A current perspective. In M. Bennett (Ed.), *Basic concept of intercultural communication: A reader.* Yarmouth, ME: Intercultural Press.

Bennett, M. (1998b). *Paradigmatic assumptions of intercultural communication.* Class handout from Advanced Intercultural Communication, Portland State University, Portland, OR.

Bennett, M. (2004). Becoming interculturally competent. In J. S. Wurzel (Ed.), *Toward multiculturalism: A reader in multicultural education*. Newton, MA: Intercultural Resource.

Bennett, M. (2005). *Paradigmatic assumptions of intercultural communication*. Retrieved from http://www.idrinstitute.org

Bennett, M. (2010). A short conceptual history of intercultural learning in study abroad. In W. Hoffa & S. DePaul (Eds.), *A history of U.S. study abroad: 1965–present*. Special publication of *Frontiers: The Interdisciplinary Journal of Study Abroad*, 419 449.

Bennett, M., & Castiglioni, I. (2004). Embodied ethnocentrism and the feeling of culture: A key to training for intercultural competence. In D. Landis, J. Bennett, & M. Bennett (Eds.), *Handbook of intercultural training* (3rd ed., pp. 249–265). Thousand Oaks, CA: Sage.

Berger, P., & Luckmann, T. (1967). *The social construction of reality*. New York: Doubleday.

Berry, J. (2004). Fundamental psychological processes in intercultural relations. In D. Landis, J. Bennett, & M. Bennett (Eds.), *Handbook of intercultural training* (3rd ed.) (pp. 166–184). Thousand Oaks, CA: Sage.

Boas, F. (1911). *The mind of primitive man*. New York: Collier Books.

Briggs, J., & Peat, F. (1984). *The looking glass universe: The emerging science of wholeness*. New York: Simon & Schuster.

Comte, A. (1966). *System of positive polity*. New York: Ben Franklin.

Damasio, A. (1999). *The feeling of what happens: Body and emotion in the making of consciousness*. New York: Harcourt Brace.

Delia, J. G., O'Keefe, B. J., & O'Keefe, D. J. (1982). The constructivist approach to communication. In F. E. X. Dance (Ed.), *Human communication theory: Comparative essays* (pp. 147–191). New York: Harper & Row.

Erikson, E. H. (1959). *Identity and the Life Cycle*. New York: International Universities Press.

Geertz, C. (1973). Thick description: Toward an interpretative theory of culture. In C. Geertz, *The interpretation of cultures* (pp. 3–30). New York: Basic Books.

Hall, E. (1959). *The silent language*. Garden City, NJ: Anchor.

Hammer, M., Bennett, M., & Wiseman, R. (2003). Measuring intercultural sensitivity: The Intercultural Development Inventory. *International Journal of Intercultural Relations, 27*(4), 421–443.

Herskovits, M. (1958). Some further comments on cultural relativism. *American Anthropologist, 60*(2), 266–273.

Hoffa, W. (2000). *A history of U.S. study abroad: Beginnings to 1965*. Special Publication of *Frontiers: The Interdisciplinary Journal of Study Abroad on Study Abroad*. Carlisle, PA: Forum for Education Abroad, Dickinson College.

Hofstede, G. (1991). *Cultures and organizations*. Berkshire, England: McGraw-Hill Book Company (UK) Ltd.

Intercultural Development Research Institute (IDRInstitute). (2011). IDRAcademy mission statement. Retrieved from www.idrinstitute.org/page.asp?menu1 = 11& menu2 = 13

Kelly, G. (1963). *A theory of personality.* New York: Norton.

Knefelkamp, L. (1998). Introduction. In W. G. Perry, Jr. (Ed.), *Forms of ethical and intellectual development in the college years: A scheme* (pp. xi–xxxviii). San Francisco, CA: Jossey-Bass.

Kuhn, T. (1967). *The structure of scientific revolutions.* Chicago, IL: University of Chicago Press.

Lakoff, G., & Johnson, M. (1999). *Philosophy in the flesh: The embodied mind and its challenge to Western thought.* New York: Basic Books.

Maturana H., & Varela, F. (1992). *The tree of knowledge: The biological roots of human understanding* (Rev. ed.). Boston, MA: Shambhala.

Moore, W. S. (2001). Understanding learning in a postmodern world: Reconsidering the Perry Scheme of Intellectual and Ethical Development. In B. Hofer & P. Pintrich (Eds.), *Personal epistemology: The psychology of beliefs about knowledge and knowing* (pp. 17–36). Mahwah, NJ: Lawrence Erlbaum.

Perry, W. (1970). *Forms of intellectual and ethical development in the college years: A scheme.* New York: Holt, Rinehart & Winston.

Pettigrew, T. F., & Tropp, L. (2000). Does intergroup contact reduce racial and ethnic prejudice throughout the world? In S. Oskamp (Ed.), *Reducing prejudice and discrimination* (pp. 93–114). Mahwah, NJ: Lawrence Erlbaum.

Piaget, J. (1954). *The construction of reality in the child.* New York: Basic Books.

Prigogine, I., & Glansdorff, P. (1971). *Thermodynamic theory of structure, stability and fluctuations.* New York: Wiley.

Segal, L. (1986). *The dream of reality: Heinz Von Foerster's constructivism.* New York: W.W. Norton.

Stewart, E., & Bennett, M. (1993). *American cultural patterns: A cross-cultural approach.* Yarmouth, ME: Intercultural Press.

Trompenaars, F. (1993). *Riding the waves of culture: Understanding cultural diversity in business.* London: Economist Books.

Vande Berg, M. (2009). Intervening in student learning abroad: A research-based inquiry. *International Journal of Intercultural Education,* 20(4), S15–S27.

Watzlawick, P. (Ed.). (1984). *The invented reality.* New York: W.W. Norton.

Watzlawick, P., Beavin, J., & Jackson, D. (1967). *Pragmatics of human communication.* New York: Norton.

5

THE INTERCULTURAL DEVELOPMENT INVENTORY

A New Frontier in Assessment and
Development of Intercultural Competence

Mitchell R. Hammer

I n today's global environment, study abroad is an essential experience for students in universities and secondary schools. As U.S. President Barack Obama recently commented,

> I'd like to find new ways to connect young Americans to young people all around the world, by supporting opportunities to learn new languages, and serve and study, welcoming students from other countries to our shores. . . . Simple exchanges can break down walls between us. (Oaks, 2009, paras. 3 and 4)

Former U.S. President George W. Bush stated similar aspirations in 2001:

> By studying foreign cultures and languages and living abroad, we gain a better understanding of the many similarities that we share and learn to respect our differences. The relationships that are formed between individuals from different countries, as part of international education programs and exchanges, can also foster goodwill that develops into vibrant, mutually beneficial partnerships among nations. (The Center for Global Education, 2001, para. 3)

Building positive relations among cultures, breaking down walls of prejudice and racism, and fostering international goodwill are noble—and critical—goals for universities and K–12 schools in the 21st century. If international education efforts are to consistently achieve such lofty goals, however, it is imperative that intercultural competence development becomes a core mission when students go abroad. Yet this is no easy task. Building intercultural competence involves increasing cultural self-awareness; deepening understanding of the experiences, values, perceptions, and behaviors of people from diverse cultural communities; and expanding the capability to shift cultural perspective and adapt behavior to bridge across cultural differences (Hammer, 2009a, 2010, 2011).

In this chapter, I discuss intercultural competence development within study abroad and how the work others and I are doing with the Intercultural Development Inventory (IDI) and IDI Guided Development is helping students, faculty, and study abroad professionals achieve increased capability in shifting cultural perspective and adapting behavior across cultural differences. More specifically, I review the IDI and the theoretic framework that the IDI measures: the Intercultural Development Continuum (IDC). I then discuss the impact of the "immersion assumption" as a common raison d'être for supporting international education and summarize how IDI findings challenge the veracity of this assumption as it applies to developing intercultural competence during the study abroad sojourn. I conclude with a discussion of two important concerns: (a) how to reconcile students' often reported statements that learning from study abroad is transformational, when IDI results indicate only marginal gains in intercultural competence capability of students enrolled in "immersion-based" exchange programs; and (b) what IDI research reveals to be key IDI Guided Development programmatic learning strategies in international education that substantially increase the capabilities of students abroad to adapt to diverse cultural values and practices.

The Intercultural Development Inventory

The IDI v3 is a 50-item questionnaire, available online and in a paper-and-pencil format, in either an education version or an organization version.[1] The IDI can be completed in 15–20 minutes and, in addition to English, it has to date been back-translated into 13 languages. Back-translation protocols, unlike simple translation, ensure both linguistic and conceptual equivalence of the IDI items (Brislin, 1970, 1976, 1980). The IDI is used by individuals and organizations across academic disciplines as well as a wide range of organizations and industries. In this chapter, I discuss the use of the IDI specifically within international education.

Once individuals complete the IDI, the IDI web-based analytic program scores each person's answers and generates a number of reports. The IDI can be used to assess an individual's level of intercultural competence; in this case, an IDI Individual Profile Report is prepared only for that individual, who could be, for instance, a student participating in study abroad, a faculty member, or a study abroad facilitator or advisor. In addition to the individual IDI Profile Report, a customized, Intercultural Development Plan (IDP) is also prepared. This IDP provides detailed guidance for the individual to further develop his/her intercultural competence. The IDI can also be used to identify a group's (or an organization's) overall approach to dealing with cultural differences and commonalities. In this case, various group and sub-group IDI Profile Reports are produced.

The IDI questionnaire includes contexting questions that allow respondents to describe their intercultural experiences in terms of (a) their cross-cultural goals, (b) the challenges they face navigating cultural differences, (c) critical (intercultural) incidents they encounter around cultural differences during their study abroad sojourn, and (d) ways they navigate those cultural differences. Responses to these questions provide a cultural grounding for relating IDI profile scores to the actual experiences of the individual.

When using the IDI to determine group or organizational levels of intercultural competence, interviews (e.g., individual or focus group interviews) are conducted that assess these same domains of cross-cultural goals, challenges, and critical (intercultural) incidents involving navigation of cultural differences and commonalities. When used with a group, results from the interviews provide valuable information regarding how the group members' IDI profile results are manifest in their intercultural competence strategies while living/studying in a foreign culture. Overall, these qualitative strategies help situate the individual, group, and/or organizational IDI profile results in the cultural experiences of the respondents.

More than 1,400 Qualified Administrators in more than 30 countries have extensively applied the IDI in academic and nonacademic contexts. In addition, IDI-related literature is rapidly expanding and currently consists of more than 60 published articles and book chapters as well as over 42 PhD dissertations.

The IDI has been rigorously tested and has cross-cultural generalizability, both internationally and with domestic diversity. Furthermore, in developing the instrument, psychometric scale construction protocols were followed to ensure that it is not culturally biased or susceptible to social desirability effects (i.e., individuals cannot "figure out" how to answer in order to gain a higher score) (Hammer, 2011; Hammer, Bennett, & Wiseman, 2003).

The IDI possesses strong content and construct validity (Hammer, 2009a, 2011; Hammer et al., 2003; Paige, Jacobs-Cassuto, Yershova, & DeJaeghere, 2003). Recent studies indicate strong predictive validity of the IDI as well (Hammer, 2011). In one study within the corporate sector, higher levels of intercultural competence, as measured by the IDI, were strongly predictive of successful recruitment and staffing of diverse talent in organizations. In another study, higher IDI scores among students were predictive of important study abroad outcomes, including greater knowledge of the host culture, less intercultural anxiety when interacting with culturally diverse individuals, increased intercultural friendships, and higher satisfaction with one's study abroad experience (Hammer, 2005a, 2011).

The Intercultural Development Continuum (IDC)

Results from the IDI are arrayed along the IDC, a theoretical framework that ranges from the more monocultural mindsets of Denial and Polarization through the transitional orientation of Minimization to the intercultural or global mindsets of Acceptance and Adaptation. The capability of deeply shifting cultural perspective and bridging behavior across cultural differences is most fully achieved when one maintains an Adaptation perspective (see Figure 5.1).

The IDC is a model of intercultural competence grounded in the Developmental Model of Intercultural Sensitivity (DMIS) originally proposed by Milton Bennett (1986, 1993). Since the original DMIS was proposed, IDI research findings have both supported the basic tenets of the DMIS and provided a revision of some aspects of its framework (Hammer, 2009a, 2011). The IDC represents this revised theoretic framework, which the IDI in turn measures. Following are some of the revisions to the original DMIS that are incorporated into the IDC:

- The Minimization orientation is identified in the original DMIS formulation as ethnocentric, although IDI research indicates that the Minimization orientation is not ethnocentric (i.e., not monocultural). However, Minimization is also not ethnorelative (i.e., this

FIGURE 5.1
Intercultural Development Continuum

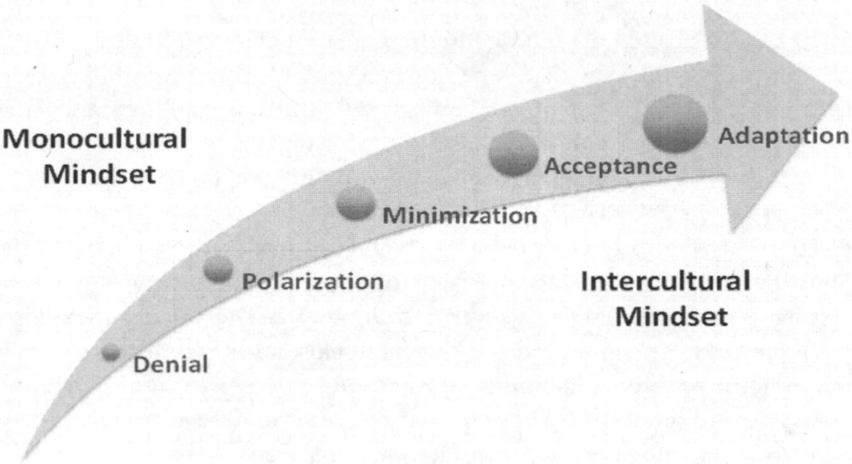

mindset is not intercultural/global); its focus on identifying commonalities among diverse groups tends to mask deeper recognition of cultural differences. Thus, Minimization is now represented as a transitional orientation between monocultural and intercultural mindsets.

- The DMIS identifies Denial, Defense, Reversal, Minimization, Acceptance, Adaptation, and Integration as the primary stages of intercultural development. IDI v3 validation confirms Denial, Polarization (which consists of Defense and Reversal), Minimization, and Adaptation as the primary orientations of intercultural competence. Integration, posited in the DMIS as a stage beyond Adaptation, is not theoretically related to the development of intercultural competence—the focus of the IDI (Bennett, 2004; Hammer, 2011). Rather, Integration, as described in the DMIS, is concerned with the construction of an intercultural identity rather than the development of intercultural competence.

- The IDI assesses Cultural Disengagement, which is the degree to which an individual or group experiences a sense of disconnection from a primary cultural community. IDI research shows that this dimension is conceptually located outside the IDC, is not an orientation or dimension of intercultural competence, and is not a dimension of the "Integration" stage identified in the original DMIS (see Hammer, 2009a, and 2011 for a detailed delineation of these distinctions).

The Denial and Polarization mindsets are monocultural in their orientation and reflect the view that "one's own culture is central to reality" (Bennett, 1993, p. 30). The intercultural/global mindsets of Acceptance and Adaptation represent a greater capability of shifting perspective and adapting behavior to cultural context. Individuals with an Acceptance or Adaptation mindset understand that one's own cultural patterns are "not any more central to reality than any other culture" (Bennett, 1993, p. 46). In between the intercultural/global mindsets of Acceptance and Adaptation and the monocultural perspectives of Denial and Polarization is the transitional orientation of Minimization. Minimization is not monocultural in its capability, yet it is also not fully intercultural in its recognition of deeper patterns of cultural difference and the ability to appropriately respond to these differences (Bennett, 2004; Hammer, 2009a, 2011; Hammer et al., 2003).

Monocultural Mindsets

A Denial mindset reflects less capability for understanding and appropriately responding to cultural differences, what Triandis (1994) terms "subjective culture" (i.e., the values, beliefs, perceptions, emotional responses, and behavior shared by a group of people). Individuals with a Denial orientation often do not recognize differences in perceptions and behavior as "cultural." A Denial orientation is characteristic of individuals who have limited experience with other cultural groups and therefore tend to operate with broad stereotypes and generalizations about the cultural "other." Those at Denial may also maintain a distance from other cultural groups and express little interest in learning about the cultural values and practices of diverse communities. This orientation tends to be associated more with members of a dominant culture, because they may have more opportunity to remain relatively isolated from cultural diversity. By contrast, members of nondominant groups are less likely to maintain a Denial orientation, because they may more often need to engage cultural differences. When Denial is present within an organization, cultural diversity often feels "ignored."

Study abroad students with a Denial mindset may become rapidly overwhelmed upon arrival in a foreign culture, because they typically will have had little if any "other culture" experiences and few intercultural frameworks or lenses to make sense of the host national's behavior. Although they may initially approach their experience in an unknown culture with a sense of naïve optimism, they fairly quickly find that their monocultural skill set is simply insufficient for the challenges of cultural difference that they often face in trying to live and study in a foreign country. Therefore, a Denial orientation can quickly develop into a Polarization mindset if cultural differences are not systematically focused on in ways that are supportive. This support is important, because venturing into the unknown experience of host nationals is quickly seen, from a Denial perspective, as fraught with perils of misunderstanding, confusion, and increasing frustration.

The primary intercultural competence development strategy for Denial is to help the individual or group notice and confront cultural differences (Bennett, 2004; Hammer, 2009a, 2010, 2011). This process begins with working to help them perceive and understand cultural differences in more observable areas of human behavior (e.g., clothing, food, music, art, dance), and then to move to more subtle arenas (e.g., nonverbal behavior, customs, dos and taboos). The individual's or group's development across the continuum is aided through increased interaction with people from different cultures under communicatively supportive conditions, and by having the individual or group closely observe things that are perceived to be both common and different (in terms of perceptions, values, and behaviors).

Polarization is a judgmental mindset that views cultural differences from an "us versus them" perspective. Polarization can take the form of Defense ("My cultural practices are superior to other cultural practices") or Reversal ("Other cultures are better than mine"). Within Defense, cultural differences are often perceived as divisive and threatening to one's own cultural way of doing things, while Reversal is a mindset that values and may idealize other cultural practices while denigrating those of one's own culture group. Reversal may also support the "cause" of an oppressed group, but this is done with little knowledge of what the "cause" means to people from the oppressed community. When Polarization is present, diversity typically feels "uncomfortable."

Host nationals typically see study abroad students who exhibit a Polarization perspective of Defense as possessing a cultural "chip on their shoulder." Students with Defense mindsets often engage in conversations with host nationals that are comparative in nature; that is, they say, "We do things this way in my country," and then expect host nationals to state how things are done in their country. Defense orientation students largely frame their interaction in terms of whether they judge the comparison favorably or unfavorably. Learning in the host culture tends to reinforce preexisting views and/or stereotypes, and interactions in the host country tend to be with like-minded individuals, either those from the student's own country or host nationals who share a favorable view toward the student's country and way of life.

Students with a Reversal form of Polarization mindset express a favorable view toward the host country and the people from that country. Host nationals can perceive this more positive evaluation of their own culture, at least initially, in a favorable light. Students with Reversal may also denigrate their own culture and in this way provide a mental comfort zone for themselves. However, Reversal is grounded in a judgmental platform that interferes with a deeper understanding of the host culture's values and practices. Students with a Reversal orientation tend to gravitate toward groups that may be underrepresented in the host country and may attempt to "help" those groups during their study abroad program. Unfortunately, students with Reversal mindsets often may engage in helping actions with little deep understanding of what the situation means to the underrepresented group.

The primary intercultural competence development strategy for individuals or groups at Polarization is, first, to help them recognize when they are overemphasizing differences without fully understanding them; and, second, to help them search for commonalities and adopt a less evaluative stance toward understanding differences.

Minimization, as a transitional mindset, highlights cultural commonality and universal values and principles that can mask a deeper understanding and consideration of cultural differences. Minimization can take one of two forms: (a) the highlighting of similarities due to limited cultural self-awareness, which is more commonly experienced by dominant group members within a cultural community; or (b) the highlighting of similarities more deliberatively as a *strategy* for navigating the values and practices largely determined by the dominant culture group, which is more commonly experienced by nondominant group members within a larger cultural community. "Minimization as a strategy" may have survival value for nondominant culture members and may be expressed as "go along to get along." When Minimization from a dominant culture perspective exists, diversity often feels "not heard."

Students studying abroad who have a Minimization orientation generally experience a certain degree of success in navigating unfamiliar cultural practices. Students at Minimization are often skillful in identifying commonalities that can be drawn upon to bridge different cultural practices. When the overall goals and challenges in the host culture do not demand accommodation to *different* values or practices, students at Minimization will experience a sense of effectiveness in living and learning in the host country.

The more the educational imperative allows commonality strategies to be functionally sufficient, the more Minimization mindsets will likely be reinforced during the study abroad program and the more reinforcement students will receive for maintaining a Minimization mindset rather than further developing toward Acceptance or Adaptation orientations. However, students at Minimization may find themselves needing to adapt more to the challenging cultural experiences that they encounter, rather than trying to navigate these differences through a commonality strategy.

The intercultural competence developmental strategy for Minimization is to increase cultural self-awareness, including awareness around power and privilege. In addition, increasing understanding about deeper patterns of cultural difference (e.g., conflict resolution styles; Hammer, 2005b, 2009b) and culture-general frameworks (e.g., individualism/collectivism), as well as culture-specific patterns of difference, is essential to gaining a balanced focus on similarities and cultural differences.

Acceptance and Adaptation are intercultural/global mindsets. In Acceptance, individuals recognize and appreciate patterns of cultural difference and commonality in their own and other cultures. An individual with an Acceptance orientation begins to understand how a cultural pattern of behavior makes sense within a different cultural community. Acceptance "involves increased self-reflection in which one is able to experience others as both different from oneself yet equally human" (Hammer, 2009a, p. 209). Although students with an Acceptance mindset are often curious about different cultures, they are not clear about how to appropriately adapt to cultural difference. When Acceptance is present, diversity feels "understood."

Students with an Acceptance orientation experience the foreign culture as a complex maze of differences, with each recognized difference enlarging intercultural understanding. Acceptance orientation students face challenges, however, around ethical or moral dilemmas that may arise while overseas. While a student at Acceptance searches for a deeper understanding of cultural differences, this mindset often leads to the student having difficulty reconciling behavior in the host country that although arising within a cultural context nevertheless is considered unethical or immoral from his or her own cultural viewpoint.

The intercultural competence development strategy for Acceptance is to help individuals or groups engage in intercultural interactions in order to gain more knowledge about cultural differences, including culture-general and culture-specific frameworks, and to gain skills in adapting to these differences. In addition, their focus should be on developing strategies for making ethical judgments by fully considering what a particular practice means from their own cultural perspective, and the meaning and value that a cultural practice represents in a different cultural community.

Adaptation is an orientation that is capable of shifting cultural perspective and changing behavior in culturally appropriate and authentic ways. Adaptation involves both deep cultural bridging across diverse communities and an increased repertoire of cultural frameworks and practices available to draw upon in reconciling cultural commonalities and differences. For those at Adaptation, intercultural competence means adaptation in performance. When an Adaptation mindset is present, diversity feels "valued and involved."

Students with an Adaptation mindset typically engage people from the host culture in deep and meaningful ways while consciously focusing on learning adaptive strategies. Problems can arise when students with an Adaptation mindset express little tolerance toward the "non-adaptive" intercultural competence capability of study abroad counterparts. This can result in students with an Adaptation mindset interactionally distancing themselves from their fellow study abroad students. When this happens, learning from fellow students is compromised.

The intercultural competence development strategy for Adaptation is to continue to build on one's knowledge of cultural differences and to further develop skills for adapting to these differences. Another competence-building strategy is to engage in cultural mediation between two or more cultural groups that are experiencing problems or misunderstandings in order to support more productive relations. The overall task for individuals at Adaptation is to further deepen their understanding of cultural patterns of difference and to incorporate adaptive strategies when interacting across cultural diversity.

The Immersion Assumption

Political, business, and international education leaders often support study abroad opportunities based on the view that immersion in another culture will lead to students increasing their intercultural competence—their capability to shift cultural perspective and adapt behavior to cultural context (see chapter 1 of this volume). This view is a central assumption of many academic study abroad programs as well as college summer programs that are more humanitarian in nature, such as those that ask students to build homes on the Navajo reservation in Arizona or work on water purification projects in Guatemala.

Consistent with this immersion assumption, leaders in international education have established *mechanisms and structures* to increase study abroad programs (see chapter 1 of this volume). As a consequence, colleges have increasingly committed resources to establish international education offices that "send" students abroad to study and "receive" international students to learn on their home campuses. In many cases, the mission of the study abroad and international student professional—if we define this in terms of what often comprises a good part of their work priorities—is to market study programs to their own students or to arrange for international students to study at their university. In short, the focus is on ensuring that efficient mechanisms and structures are in place to fluidly move, situate, and facilitate the departure and return of students to the home campus or the entrance and eventual departure of students from other countries.

One implication of the immersion assumption is that study abroad professionals can simply focus on the mechanics and logistics of ensuring that students are placed—or, better still, "immersed"—within a suitable cross-cultural environment. That is, once educators have taken steps to immerse students in a culturally diverse experience, it is then often assumed that students' intercultural skills will be enhanced, and they will return to their home culture better prepared to navigate complex cultural differences in perceptions, values, and practices among diverse communities.

While the immersion assumption may provide a rationale for increasing study abroad opportunities for students, it has also allowed the study abroad community to ignore whether, in fact, immersing students on study abroad actually increases their intercultural competence.

Challenging the Immersion Assumption

The work others and I have been doing over the past 10 years with the IDI, in examining the impact of study abroad experiences on students' intercultural competence development, directly challenges the veracity of the immersion assumption. First, colleges and universities often claim they are "global," preparing students to function across cultures in the 21st century. This is said to occur through such efforts as the internationalization of the

curriculum; cross-cultural dormitory living arrangements; increased domestic and international diversity in the student body; and across-the-
curriculum international or global courses (e.g., requiring all first-year
undergraduate students to take a course in intercultural communication).
Yet IDI research reveals that students' intercultural competence does not
significantly develop as a result of their on-campus, presumably "global"
education. In other words, immersion in the college experience—even at an
institution with a culturally diverse student body—does not result in
increased intercultural capability (see chapter 2 of this volume; Hammer,
2005a; Pedersen, 2009, 2010; Sample, 2009; Vande Berg et al., 2009).

Second, IDI research findings on the study abroad experience itself, in
examining both shorter-term programs (e.g., three-week sojourns) and
longer study abroad experiences (e.g., semester or full-year programs), reveal
that longer durations overseas tend to result in only slightly higher levels of
intercultural competence. These findings suggest that duration does exert
some marginal influence on intercultural competence development, but
overall, the results are underwhelming in terms of supporting the assumption
that the amount of time students spend abroad is meaningfully associated
with their increased intercultural competence (see chapter 2 of this volume;
Pedersen, 2009, 2010; Sample, 2009; Vande Berg, Connor-Linton, & Paige,
2009).

These results serve to confirm the observation that being in the vicinity
of an event in another culture does not mean that one has an intercultural
experience merely by being exposed to it. For many students, being
immersed in a foreign culture does not necessarily demonstrate that they are
learning how to shift cultural perspective or adapt behavior; even those
enrolling in programs of longer, rather than shorter, duration are on average
showing only marginal gains in intercultural development when left to their
own devices.

Transformation and IDI-Documented Intercultural Competence Gains

Recent research findings are drawing the study abroad community's attention to a serious disconnect regarding the impact of simple immersion study
abroad experiences: Returning students not infrequently report that they
have been "transformed" through their "immersion" study abroad program,
whereas research using the IDI is showing that students are, on average,
not making substantial gains in their intercultural competence development.

Where divergent results are found, battle lines are drawn, and this battle has been largely argued under the guise of the familiar quantitative-qualitative research methods debate.

Those in the quantitative camp typically point out that qualitative self-reports or interview results are less valid and reliable measures than psycho-metrically derived quantitative assessments. Proponents of qualitative methods often reply that quantitative measures simply are not methodologically sensitive enough to capture the kinds of insights and learning that self-reports or interviews identify. Thus, with shields raised, the quantitative versus qualitative war continues on the battlefield of study abroad—at the cost of student learning and intercultural competence development.

Developmental Interviewing

As noted earlier, the IDI incorporates both quantitative assessment protocols (via the 50-item questionnaire) and qualitative methods, depending on whether the assessment is focused on individual development (in which case, contexting questions are included in the IDI questionnaire), or on group or organization development (in which case, individual, developmental interview guides and/or focus group interview guides are used in place of the contexting questions). The kind of qualitative data gathering that we do with the IDI is fundamentally different, however, from student reports, made during reentry interviews or focus groups, about being "transformed."

When the IDI is used in study abroad, we gather qualitative data from students that specifically focus on the ways in which they have engaged cultural differences and commonalities during their study abroad experience. We ask them to provide accounts of specific situations or critical incidents that they encountered overseas and to explain what the cultural differences were that "made a difference" in each situation; what strategies they used to navigate these identified differences; and, finally, what they perceive the outcomes to have been.

This kind of qualitative data gathering is what I term *developmental interviewing*. I have found that developmental interviewing more accurately represents a student's actual experience relevant to a gain (or the lack of any gain) in intercultural competence as assessed by the IDI. When developmental interviewing is used, we find a strong relationship between "what the IDI says" in terms of the students' overall developmental orientation and the ways they have experienced cultural commonalities and differences during the developmental interviews they complete at the end of a program overseas or upon their return to the home campus.

The reason is that developmental interviewing asks student to meta-reflect on their experience from the vantage point of specific situations that demand intercultural competence. Notice that we are *not*, in using the IDI, asking students general, open-ended questions about what they think they learned by studying in another country; we are not, that is, relying on the more non-referent, open-ended qualitative interviewing methods traditionally used in debriefing study abroad returnees.

Traditional Open-Ended Interviewing

In other qualitative assessments of student learning abroad, interviewers often ask open-ended questions regarding what the student has learned while overseas. When such unfocused, non-referential questions are posed, the accounts that emerge are grounded in hypersensory memories—not developmental recollections. Whalen (2009) identifies this important characteristic of study abroad when he observes that education abroad is distinct and memorable, with the study abroad experience recalled more frequently and with more emotion than other college memories.

Precipitating sensory stimuli activate emotion and subsequent cognitive appraisals of an event and are expressed through physiological changes (e.g., heart rate) (Hammer, 2007). The study abroad experience often serves its student participants with what can be characterized as a hypersensory buffet. Upon arrival in the host country, students are typically assaulted by new and unfamiliar sensory stimuli, including more pungent smells, exotic colors and sights, and never before encountered combinations of sounds. These hypersensory perceptions situate study abroad memories as more vivid, real, and impactful than other more mundane sensory memories that students may have stored before, during, or after their extraordinary encounter with a new and largely unknown cultural milieu.

When interviewed (or when their journals are reviewed), it is common to find that students often express strong certainty about and enthusiasm for their study abroad experiences. They readily relate (at least from their self-reported vantage point) that the overseas experience has dramatically increased their awareness, deepened their commitment to working across cultures, allowed them to form international friendships, and helped them achieve a wide assortment of other outcomes. Unfortunately, these reflections are not particularly insightful where their capacity for navigating cultural differences and commonalities is concerned. In other words, traditional open-ended interviewing protocols do not gather developmental information; they simply gather different (i.e., hypersensory memory) data from students about their experiences.

IDI Guided Development: Lessons Learned

IDI research reveals that when educators make use of IDI Guided Development in intervening in their students' learning abroad, they are able to increase substantially their capability to adapt to diverse cultural values and practices. While intercultural competence development is dependent on students' "experiencing another culture," it is equally dependent on their becoming *"interculturally* experienced." That is, while being in a foreign country is the platform in which learning may take place, students also need guided reflection on their "experiences" in another culture in order to learn and develop interculturally (see Hammer, 2009a and chapter 2 of this volume). In this regard, IDI research is identifying key programmatic components of IDI Guided Development that have the greatest impact in increasing intercultural competence development during study abroad.

Engle and Engle (2003) provide a useful framework to discuss essential programmatic elements of study abroad. They originally proposed seven "defining components of overseas programs" (p. 8) but added an eighth in 2004:

1. Duration of the student sojourn
2. Entry target language proficiency
3. Extent of target language use (the extent to which the language is used/required language in class and outside of class)
4. Nature of the teaching faculty (i.e., home institution faculty, local faculty)
5. Type of coursework (e.g., advanced language study, history)
6. Whether students received mentoring or guided cultural reflection   .
7. Experiential learning activities (e.g., community service)
8. Type of housing (e.g., homestay, college dormitory)

IDI research results suggest that some of these factors have a significant impact on the development of intercultural competence among study abroad students (Vande Berg, 2009; Vande Berg et al., 2009).

Cultural Mentoring

Cultural mentoring that involves guided reflection on the students' cultural experience is a foundational developmental strategy of IDI Guided Development. Such mentoring, which facilitates students' reflection on their encounters with cultural difference and commonality, is developmentally grounded in the students' individual IDI and/or group profile results. Of the eight factors identified by Engle and Engle (2004), findings from the Georgetown Consortium study have shown group cultural mentoring to have the greatest impact in increasing students' intercultural competence, as measured by the IDI (chapter 2 of this volume; Vande Berg, 2009; Vande Berg et al., 2009). Findings from Engle and Engle's (2003) study of students enrolling at the American University Center of Provence (AUCP) (chapter 12 of this volume) strongly suggest that immersion in the host culture and cultural mentoring interact to increase the intercultural competence of students; the Georgetown Consortium study reported that AUCP students averaged 12.47 points of IDI gain, compared with average gains of 1.32 points of gain for students at 60 other study abroad programs who were not benefiting from this approach (Vande Berg et al., 2009).

Some study abroad programs are expanding the concept of cultural mentoring to include the provision of individual IDI profile feedback to students prior to departure. Pedersen (2010), for example, incorporates individual IDI mentoring in her pre-departure preparation of students and relies on these IDI profile results to help them continue to develop their intercultural competence afterward. Results from her pre-posttest administration of the IDI reveal that students participating in her pre-departure cultural mentoring program had average gains of 11 points on the IDI, compared with gains of only 1.22 points for students who remained on the home campus.

Vande Berg, Quinn, and Menyhart (see chapter 16 of this volume) describe another approach to cultural mentoring with the IDI. They are using the IDI as an integral part of their training of teachers abroad who will be teaching an intercultural course, the Seminar on Living and Learning Abroad. They coach new seminar teachers extensively during their first two semesters teaching the course, using their individual IDI profiles to tailor the coaching to each teacher's developmental needs. Students enrolled in the seminar also complete pre- and post-IDIs; trained to interpret individual student IDI profiles, the teachers rely on these results while they intervene in the students' intercultural development, individually and as a group, throughout their semester abroad. By the end of the spring 2011 semester, 13 of these seminar classes had improved by an average of 9.0 IDI points—a considerable gain when compared with the 1.32 points of gain that students enrolling in 60 Georgetown Consortium study programs made during their terms abroad (Vande Berg et al., 2009).

In short, research findings are showing that cultural mentoring can produce very substantial gains in intercultural competence among study abroad students. These average gains, ranging from 9 to more than 12 points on the IDI, translate into movement representing nearly a full developmental orientation—that is, movement from, for example, Minimization to Acceptance.

Duration of Study Abroad

IDI research findings show only modest increases in intercultural competence when students abroad complete longer- as opposed to shorter-term sojourns (see chapter 2 of this volume; Medina López Portillo, 2004). However, when there is systematic use of the IDI and IDI Guided Development interventions, duration seems to have an intercultural competence multiplier effect, resulting in substantially greater gains over the same period of time, compared with non–IDI Guided Development efforts (see chapters 2, 8, 12, 14, and 16 of this volume; Pedersen, 2009).

Intercultural Content

IDI research demonstrates that intercultural competence development depends on interventions that help students increase their cultural self-awareness as well as their cultural other-awareness (e.g., differences between their own cultural values and those of other culture groups). This suggests that helping students achieve more general, *non-culturally* grounded personal or even interpersonal awareness does not migrate into the cultural domain. As Paige and Vande Berg comment, "Cultural content anchors the intercultural experience by serving as a foundation for reflection and learning" (see page 54 of this volume).

Reflection on Intercultural Experiences

IDI research shows that *unexamined* cultural experiences do not facilitate intercultural competence development. Rather, experience plus cultural reflection result in greater cultural insights and increase students' intercultural competence. Targeted cultural reflection, grounded in IDI profile results, can be obtained through cultural mentors (discussed earlier) as well as journals, group discussions, and one-on-one dialogue with host nationals and/or other international students (see chapters 4, 10–12, 14, and 16 of this volume). The caveat is that these activities must be framed to elicit inquiry into one's own cultural assumptions, values, and practices vis-à-vis the assumptions, values, and practices of host country nationals or other international students. Cultural reflection is often best gained through in-depth analysis of critical incidents, in which cultural differences emerge through reflection on the students' experiences that "make a difference."

Involvement in the Cultural Setting

Paige and Vande Berg comment that although "immersion in another culture, in and of itself, is not as powerful as immersion plus reflection, engagement with the culture is still at the heart of the study abroad experience" (see page 54 of this volume). Intercultural competence development is aided when students become involved in the day-to-day life of host country nationals rather than isolating themselves within their own cultural group. Living in the host country demands greater intercultural capabilities of students than living in their own cultural island; when they remain in their own cultural bubble, students perceive and respond to the host culture primarily on their own terms.

Pre-Departure and Reentry Preparation

IDI research supports the proposition that intercultural preparation prior to departure and the integration of study abroad learning following the return home facilitate significant gains in intercultural competence. The type of pre-departure and reentry programming that appears to be most beneficial directly focuses on cultural learning as opposed to either "dos and taboos" or noncultural content (e.g., sights to see) (Sample, 2009; chapter 11 of this volume).

Virtual and On-Site Learning Interventions

IDI research suggests that online intercultural learning activities can also aid the development of intercultural competence among study abroad students. One study shows that students abroad whose intercultural learning and development is facilitated online, through courses taught by faculty in the home culture, make considerably higher gains, on average, than students whose learning is not facilitated (see chapter 14 of this volume). Research also shows that students who are enrolled in intercultural courses on-site with faculty members who physically meet with them that facilitate their learning outperform those who are learning online (compare, e.g., the average gains reported by Engle and Engle as well as Vande Berg, Quinn, and Menyhart with those reported by Lou and Bosley in this volume). Both of these results are encouraging insofar as both online and face-to-face formats appear to help students increase their intercultural competence. Presumably, these results would also support "blended" programs that incorporate both online and in-person learning modalities.

Conclusion

Research and practice with the IDI is generating significant insights about the development of intercultural competence during a student's study abroad experience. This body of emerging work has challenged the accuracy of the immersion assumption as a justification for supporting study abroad programs that largely or wholly leave students to their own (cross-cultural learning) devices. IDI research indicates that students who are "immersed" in their institutions' "global" learning initiatives on the home campus do not significantly increase their intercultural competence. Furthermore, students who go abroad through universities and colleges that enroll them in programs that aim simply to "immerse" them in the host culture also fail to significantly increase their intercultural competence.

In contrast to these findings, IDI research indicates that students who participate in programs that take steps to deeply immerse them in the host culture as well as provide expert cultural mentoring that is developmental— that is, mentoring that asks the students to reflect on their experiences, and to reflect on how they characteristically make meaning of their experiences—do succeed in helping their students develop intercultural competence. IDI-based research is showing specifically that interventions based on IDI assessments of students' intercultural competence (i.e., IDI Guided Development) result in significantly greater capability to shift cultural perspective and adapt behavior to cultural differences—the essence of intercultural development. This research has identified the following program components as most influential in building intercultural competence during study abroad: cultural mentoring, learning about patterns of cultural differences, reflection on intercultural experiences, active involvement in the cultural setting, pre-departure and reentry preparation, and onsite intercultural interventions.

As we move further into the second decade of the 21st century, international education has the potential to build dramatically the intercultural competence of the next generation of global leaders. This vision can be realized by recognizing (a) that the immersion assumption cannot support the development of intercultural competence and (b) that intercultural competence is teachable, learnable, and achievable if learning interventions are appropriately designed based on the developmental mindset of the student.

Note

1. IDI v1, v2, and v3 are owned by Mitchell R. Hammer, IDI, LLC. The current IDI v3 and its web-based analytical system were developed by Mitchell Hammer and revised from earlier versions of the IDI developed by Mitchell Hammer and Milton Bennett.

References

Bennett, M. J. (1986). Towards ethnorelativism: A developmental approach to training for intercultural sensitivity. *International Journal of Intercultural Relations, 10*(2), 179–196.

Bennett, M. J. (1993). Towards ethnorelativism: A developmental model of intercultural sensitivity. In R. M. Paige (Ed.), *Education for the intercultural experience* (2nd ed., pp. 21–71). Yarmouth, ME: Intercultural Press.

Bennett, M. J. (2004). Becoming interculturally competent. In J. Wurzel (Ed.), *Towards multiculturalism: A reader in multicultural education* (2nd ed., pp. 62–77). Newton, MA: Intercultural Resource.

Brislin, R. W. (1970). Back-translation for cross-cultural research. *Journal of Cross-cultural Psychology, 1*(3), 185–216.

Brislin, R. W. (1976). Comparative research methodology: Cross-cultural studies. *International Journal of Psychology, 11*(3), 215–229.

Brislin, R. W. (1980). Translation and content analysis of oral and written materials. In H. C. Triandis & J. W. Berry (Eds.), *Handbook of cross-cultural psychology* (Vol. 2, pp. 389–444). Boston, MA: Allyn & Bacon.

The Center for Global Education. (2001). International education week 2001 message. http://globaled.us/now/fullstatementbush.html#3

Engle, L., & Engle, J. (2003). Study abroad levels: Toward a classification of program types. *Frontiers: The Interdisciplinary Journal of Study Abroad, IX*, 1–20.

Engle, L., & Engle, J. (2004). Assessing language acquisition and intercultural sensitivity development in relation to study abroad program design. *Frontiers: The Interdisciplinary Journal of Study Abroad, X*, 219–236.

Hammer, M. R. (2005a). *Assessment of the impact of the AFS study abroad experience: Executive Summary*. New York: AFS, International.

Hammer, M. R. (2005b). The Intercultural Conflict Style Inventory: A conceptual framework and measure of intercultural conflict approaches. *International Journal of Intercultural Research, 29*, 675–695.

Hammer, M. R. (2007). *Saving lives: The S.A.F.E. model for negotiating hostage and crisis incidents*. Westport, CT: Praeger International Security.

Hammer, M. R. (2009a). The Intercultural Development Inventory: An approach for assessing and building intercultural competence. In M. A. Moodian (Ed.), *Contemporary leadership and intercultural competence: Exploring the cross-cultural dynamics within organizations* (pp. 203–217). Thousand Oaks, CA: Sage.

Hammer, M. R. (2009b). Solving problems and resolving conflict using the Intercultural Conflict Style model and Inventory. In M. A. Moodian (Ed.), *Contemporary leadership and intercultural competence: Exploring the cross-cultural dynamics within organizations* (pp. 219–232). Thousand Oaks, CA: Sage.

Hammer, M. R. (2010). *The Intercultural Development Inventory manual*. Berlin, MD: IDI.

Hammer, M. R. (2011). Additional cross-cultural validity testing of the Intercultural Development Inventory. *International Journal of Intercultural Relations, 35*, 474–487.

Hammer, M. R., Bennett, M. J., & Wiseman, R. (2003). The Intercultural Development Inventory: A measure of intercultural sensitivity. *International Journal of Intercultural Relations, 27*, 421–443.

Medina-López-Portillo, A. (2004). Intercultural learning assessment: The link between program duration and the development of intercultural sensitivity. *Frontiers: The Interdisciplinary Journal of Study Abroad, X*, 179–200.

Oaks, U. (2009, April 9). President Obama in Turkey: "Exchanges can break down walls between us" [Web log post]. Retrieved from http://blog.nafsa.org/2009/04/09/president obama in turkey exchanges can break down walls between us/

Paige, R. M., Jacobs-Cassuto, M., Yershova, Y. A., & DeJaeghere, J. (2003). Assessing intercultural sensitivity: An empirical analysis of the Hammer and Bennett Intercultural Development Inventory. *International Journal of Intercultural Relations, 27*, 467–486.

Pedersen, P. J. (2009). Teaching towards an ethnorelative worldview through psychology study abroad. *Intercultural Education, 20* (supplement 1–2), 73–86.

Pedersen, P. J. (2010). Assessing intercultural effectiveness outcomes in a year-long study abroad program. *International Journal of Intercultural Relations, 34*, 70–80.

Sample, S. G. (2009, October). *Intercultural development and the international curriculum*. Paper presented at the IDI Conference, Minneapolis, MN.

Triandis, H. C. (1994). *Culture and social behavior*. New York: McGraw-Hill.

Vande Berg, M. (2009). Intervening in students learning abroad: A research-based inquiry. *Intercultural Education, 20* (supplement 1–2), 15–28.

Vande Berg, M., Connor-Linton, J., & Paige, R. M. (2009). The Georgetown Consortium Project: Interventions for student learning abroad. *Frontiers: The Interdisciplinary Journal of Study Abroad, XVIII,* 1–76.

Whalen, B. (2009). Measuring impact: Learning from evaluations to assess study abroad outcomes. Available from www.iie.org/~/media/Files/Corporate/Membership/Articles-and-Presentations/Measuring-Impact.ashx

6

USING EXPERIENTIAL LEARNING THEORY TO PROMOTE STUDENT LEARNING AND DEVELOPMENT IN PROGRAMS OF EDUCATION ABROAD

Angela M. Passarelli and David A. Kolb

S tudy abroad programs are rich with possibilities for meaningful and transformative learning. By living, studying, and working in an unfamiliar culture, students are challenged to make sense of the novelty and ambiguity with which they are regularly confronted. As a result of this sense-making process, students adopt new ways of thinking, acting, and relating in the world. For students who move mindfully through the study abroad experience, it has the potential to change their worldview, provide a new perspective on their course of study, and yield a network of mind-expanding relationships.

On the other hand, programs that do not adopt a holistic approach to student learning can become little more than a glorified vacation. At best, the students report having fun or being "satisfied" with the experience and return home unchanged. They engage in the experience at a surface level, maintaining distance from the physical, social, or intellectual tensions of the learning endeavor. At worst, carelessness places students in harm because they have engaged in dangerous or high-risk behaviors.

The difference in these two scenarios is a programmatic emphasis on the student's learning and development, and a model of shared responsibility for learning. Attention must be paid to designing a learning experience that helps students fully absorb and integrate their experiences at increasing levels of complexity. Additionally, everyone involved in the study abroad experience—campus administrators, faculty, homestay families, and the students themselves—should understand the learning process and how they can skillfully intervene to maximize learning.

We suggest that Experiential Learning Theory (ELT; D. A. Kolb, 1984) provides a model for educational interventions in study abroad because of its holistic approach to human adaptation through the transformation of experience into knowledge. Accordingly, in this chapter, we focus on *how* students learn and the role of the educator in that process. We begin by providing an overview of ELT and its key concepts: the cycle and spiral of learning from experience, learning styles, learning flexibility, learning spaces, and the ELT of development. We then offer guidance to study abroad educators on the use of these concepts to maximize student learning and development.

Experiential Learning Theory

ELT is a dynamic view of learning based on a learning cycle driven by the resolution of the dual dialectics of action-reflection and experience-conceptualization. ELT draws on the work of prominent 20th-century scholars who gave experience a central role in their theories of human learning and development—notably William James, John Dewey, Kurt Lewin, Jean Piaget, Lev Vygotsky, Carl Jung, Paulo Freire, and Carl Rogers—creating a dynamic, holistic model of the process of learning from experience and a multidimensional model of adult development. Integrating the work of these foundational scholars, Kolb (1984) proposed six characteristics of experiential learning:

1. *Learning is best conceived as a process, not in terms of outcomes.* Although punctuated by knowledge milestones, learning does not end at an outcome, nor is it always evidenced in performance. Rather, learning occurs through the course of connected experiences in which knowledge is modified and re-formed. As Dewey suggests, "Education must be conceived as a continuing reconstruction of experience: . . . the process and goal of education are one and the same thing" (1897, p. 79).

2. *All learning is relearning.* Learning is best facilitated by a process that draws out the learners' beliefs and ideas about a topic so that they can be examined, tested, and integrated with new, more refined ideas. Piaget called this proposition constructivism—individuals construct their knowledge of the world based on their experience (Flavell, 1963).

3. *Learning requires the resolution of conflicts between dialectically opposed modes of adaptation to the world.* Conflict, differences, and disagreement are what drive the learning process. These tensions are resolved in iterations of movement back and forth between opposing modes of reflection and action and feeling and thinking.

4. *Learning is a holistic process of adaptation.* Learning is not just the result of cognition but involves the integrated functioning of the total person—thinking, feeling, perceiving, and behaving. It encompasses other specialized models of adaptation from the scientific method to problem solving, decision making, and creativity.

5. *Learning results from synergetic transactions between the person and the environment.* In Piaget's terms, learning occurs through equilibration of the dialectic processes of assimilating new experiences into existing concepts and accommodating existing concepts to new experience (Flavell, 1963). Following Lewin's (1951) famous formula that behavior is a function of the person and the environment, ELT holds that learning is influenced by characteristics of the learner and the learning space.

6. *Learning is the process of creating knowledge.* In ELT, knowledge is viewed as the transaction between two forms of knowledge: social knowledge, which is coconstructed in a sociohistorical context, and personal knowledge, the subjective experience of the learner. This conceptualization of knowledge stands in contrast to that of the "transmission" model of education in which preexisting, fixed ideas are transmitted to the learner.

The Cycle of Experiential Learning

ELT defines learning as "the process whereby knowledge is created through the transformation of experience. Knowledge results from the combination of grasping and transforming experience" (Kolb, 1984, p. 41). Grasping experience refers to the process of taking in information, and transforming experience is how individuals interpret and act on that information. The ELT model portrays two dialectically related modes of grasping experience—concrete experience (CE) and abstract conceptualization (AC)—and two dialectically related modes of transforming experience—reflective observation (RO) and active experimentation (AE). Learning arises from the resolution of creative tension among these four learning modes. This process is portrayed as an idealized learning cycle or spiral in which the learner "touches all the bases"—experiencing (CE), reflecting (RO), thinking (AC), and acting (AE)—in a recursive process that is sensitive to the learning situation and what is being learned. Immediate or concrete experiences are the basis for observations and reflections. These reflections are assimilated and distilled into abstract concepts from which new implications for action can be drawn. These implications can be actively tested and serve as guides in creating new experiences (Figure 6.1). Evidence from experiential learning research in international contexts supports the cross-cultural applicability of the model (Joy & Kolb, 2009; A. Y. Kolb, & Kolb, 2011a, 2011b).

Learning Style

Learning style describes the unique ways that individuals spiral through the learning cycle based on their preference for the four different learning modes:

FIGURE 6.1
The experiential learning cycle

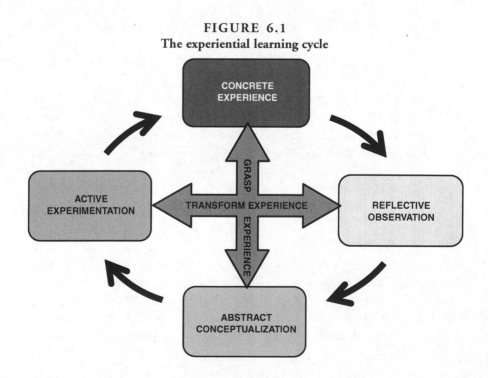

CE, RO, AC, and AE. Because of one's genetic makeup, particular life experiences, and the demands of the present environment, a preferred way of choosing among these four learning modes is developed. The conflict between being concrete or abstract and between being active or reflective is resolved in patterned, characteristic ways. Previous research has shown that learning styles are influenced by culture, personality type, educational specialization, career choice, and current job role and tasks (Kolb, 1984, 2005).

Much of the research on ELT has focused on the concept of learning style using the Kolb Learning Style Inventory (KLSI) to assess individual learning styles (Kolb, 2005). Although individuals who take the KLSI show many different patterns of scores, nine consistent styles have been identified based on individuals' relative preferences for the four learning modes (Boyatzis & Mainemelis, 2000; Eickmann, Kolb, & Kolb, 2004; Kolb, 2005; A. Y. Kolb, & Kolb, 2005). Four of these style types emphasize one of the four learning modes: experiencing (CE), reflecting (RO), thinking (AC), and acting (AE) (Abbey, Hunt, & Weiser, 1985; Hunt, 1987). Four others represent style types that emphasize two learning modes, one from the grasping dimension and one from the transforming dimension of the ELT model: imagining (CE and RO), analyzing (AC and RO), deciding (AC and AE), and initiating (CE and AE). The final style type balances all four modes of the learning cycle: balancing (CE, RO, AC, and AE) (Mainemelis, Boyatzis, & Kolb, 2002).

These learning style types can be systematically arranged on a two-dimensional learning space defined by AC-CE and AE-RO. This space, including a description of the distinguishing characteristics of each style, is depicted in Figure 6.2.

ELT posits that learning style is not a fixed psychological trait but a dynamic state resulting from synergistic transactions between the person and the environment. This dynamic state arises from an individual's preferential resolution of the dual dialectics of experiencing/conceptualizing and acting/reflecting. According to Kolb (1984),

> The stability and endurance of these states in individuals comes not solely from fixed genetic qualities or characteristics of human beings: nor, for that matter, does it come from the stable fixed demands of environmental circumstances. Rather, stable and enduring patterns of human individuality arise from consistent patterns of transaction between the individual and his or her environment. . . . The way we process the possibilities of each new emerging event determines the range of choices and decisions we see.

FIGURE 6.2
Distinguishing Characteristics of Learning Style Types

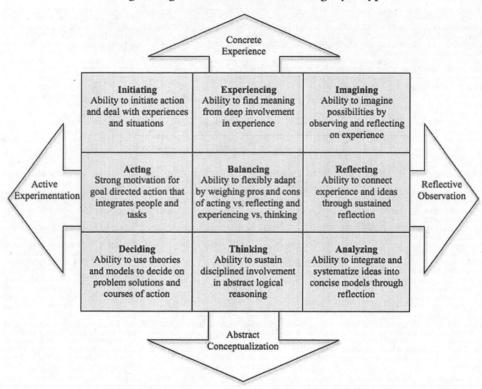

Concrete Experience

Initiating	Experiencing	Imagining
Ability to initiate action and deal with experiences and situations	Ability to find meaning from deep involvement in experience	Ability to imagine possibilities by observing and reflecting on experience

Acting	Balancing	Reflecting
Strong motivation for goal directed action that integrates people and tasks	Ability to flexibly adapt by weighing pros and cons of acting vs. reflecting and experiencing vs. thinking	Ability to connect experience and ideas through sustained reflection

Deciding	Thinking	Analyzing
Ability to use theories and models to decide on problem solutions and courses of action	Ability to sustain disciplined involvement in abstract logical reasoning	Ability to integrate and systematize ideas into concise models through reflection

Active Experimentation

Reflective Observation

Abstract Conceptualization

The choices and decisions we make to some extent determine the events we live through, and these events influence our future choices. Thus, people create themselves through the choice of the actual occasions that they live through. (pp. 63–64)

Learning Flexibility

Another important aspect of learning style is learning flexibility, the extent to which an individual adapts his or her learning style to the demands of the learning situation. As we have just seen, learning style is not a fixed personality trait but more like a habit of learning shaped by experience and choices—it can be an automatic, unconscious mode of adapting or it can be consciously modified and changed. The learning style types that we have described portray how one prefers to learn in general. Many individuals feel that their learning style type accurately describes how they learn most of the time. They are consistent in their approach to learning. Others, however, report that they tend to change their learning approach depending on the situation they are in or what they are learning. They may say, for example, that they use one style in the classroom and another at home with their friends and family. These are flexible learners.

Learning flexibility is the ability to use each of the four learning modes to move freely around the learning cycle and to modify one's approach to learning based on the learning situation. Experiencing, reflecting, thinking, and acting each provide valuable perspectives on the learning task in a way that deepens and enriches knowledge. This can be seen as traveling through each of the regions of the learning space in the process of learning. Learning flexibility can help us move in and out of the learning space regions, capitalizing on the strengths of each learning style. Learning flexibility broadens the learning comfort zone and allows us to operate comfortably and effectively in more regions of the learning space, promoting deep learning and development.

The flexibility to move from one learning mode to another in the learning cycle is important for effective learning. Research on flexibility using the Adaptive Style Inventory (Boyatzis & Kolb, 1993) found that individuals who balance the dialectics of action-reflection and concrete-abstract have greater adaptive flexibility in their learning (Mainemelis et al., 2002). Individuals with high adaptive flexibility are more self-directed, have richer life structures, and experience less conflict in their lives (Kolb, 1984).

Learning Space

If learning is to occur, it requires a space for it to take place. The great potential of study abroad learning experiences is that they offer a rich variety and depth of learning spaces. Although for most the concept of learning space first conjures up the image of the physical classroom environment, it is much broader and multidimensional. Dimensions of learning space include physical, cultural, institutional, social, and psychological aspects. In ELT these dimensions all come together in the experience of the learner. This concept of learning space builds on Kurt Lewin's (1951) field theory and his concept of life space. For Lewin, person and environment are interdependent variables in which behavior is a function of person and environment and the life space is the total psychological environment, which the person experiences subjectively. To take time as an example, in many organizations today employees are so busy doing their work that they feel that there is no time to learn how to do things better. This feeling is shaped by the objective conditions of a hectic work schedule along with the expectation that time spent reflecting will not be rewarded. Teachers objectively create learning spaces by the information and activities that they offer in their course; but this space is also interpreted in the students' subjective experience through the lens of their learning style.

Because a learning space is, in the end, what the learner experiences it to be, it is the psychological and social dimensions of learning spaces that have the most influence on learning. From this perspective learning spaces can be viewed as aggregates of human characteristics. Strange and Banning (2001) argue that learning spaces are transmitted through people such that the main features of any learning environment arise from the characteristics of its members. When the "human aggregate" approach is used, the experiential learning space is defined by the attracting and repelling forces (positive and negative valences) of the poles of the dual dialectics of action/reflection and experiencing/conceptualizing, creating a two-dimensional map of the regions of the learning space like that shown in Figure 6.2. An individual's learning style positions him or her in one of these regions, depending on the equilibrium of forces among action, reflection, experiencing, and conceptualizing. As with the concept of life space, this position is determined by a combination of individual disposition and characteristics of the learning environment.

The KLSI measures an individual's preference for a particular region of the learning space, their home region, so to speak. The regions of the ELT learning space offer a typology of the different types of learning based on the extent to which they require action versus reflection and experiencing versus thinking, thereby emphasizing some stages of the learning cycle over others. A number of studies on learning spaces in higher education have been conducted using the human aggregate approach by showing the percentage of students whose learning style places them in the different learning space regions (Eickmann et al., 2004; Kolb & Kolb, 2005). Figure 6.3, for example, shows the ELT learning space of the MBA program in a major management school. In this particular case, students are predominantly concentrated in the abstract and active regions of the learning space, as are the faculty. This creates a learning space that tends to emphasize the quantitative and technical aspects of management over the human and relationship factors.

The ELT learning space concept emphasizes that learning is not one universal process but a map of learning territories, a frame of reference within which many different ways of learning can flourish and interrelate. It

FIGURE 6.3
The ELT learning space of an MBA program

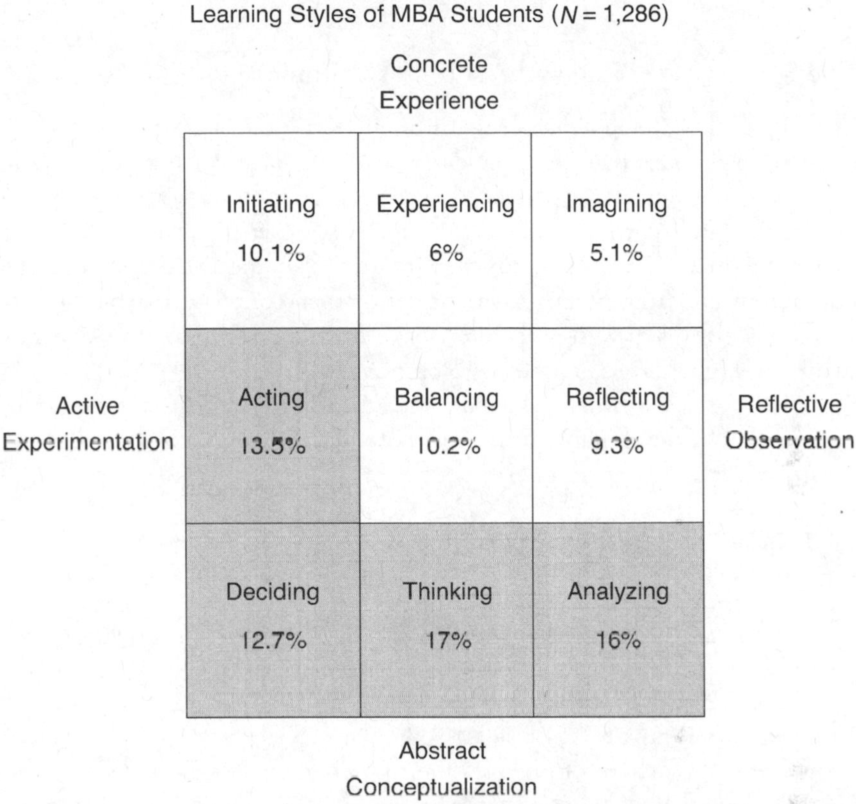

Learning Styles of MBA Students (*N* = 1,286)

Concrete
Experience

	Initiating 10.1%	Experiencing 6%	Imagining 5.1%
Active Experimentation	Acting 13.5%	Balancing 10.2%	Reflecting 9.3%
	Deciding 12.7%	Thinking 17%	Analyzing 16%

Active
Experimentation

Reflective
Observation

Abstract
Conceptualization

is a holistic framework that orients the many different ways of learning to one another. The process of experiential learning can be viewed as a process of locomotion through the learning regions that is influenced by a person's position in the learning space. One's position in the learning space defines his or her experience and thus his or her "reality."

Kolb and Kolb (2005) developed principles for creating spaces that maximize learning and development. For a learner to engage fully in the learning cycle, a space must be provided to engage in the four modes of the cycle: experiencing, reflecting, thinking, and acting. It must be a hospitable, welcoming space that is characterized by respect for all. It must be safe and supportive, but also challenging. And it must allow learners to be in charge of their own learning and allow time for the repetitive practice that develops expertise.

The Spiral of Learning and Adult Development

In ELT, adult development occurs through learning from experience. This is based on the idea that the experiential learning cycle is actually a learning *spiral*. When a concrete experience is enriched by reflection, given meaning by thinking and transformed by action, the new experience created becomes richer, broader, and deeper. Further iterations of the cycle continue the exploration and transfer to experiences in other contexts. In this process learning is integrated with other knowledge and generalized to other contexts leading to higher levels of adult development.

Zull (2002) explained a link between ELT and neuroscience research, suggesting that the spiraling process of experiential learning is related to the process of brain functioning:

> Concrete experiences come through the sensory cortex, reflective observation involves the integrative cortex at the back, creating new abstract concepts occurs in the frontal integrative cortex, and active testing involves the motor brain. In other words, the learning cycle arises from the structure of the brain. (p. 18)

Humberto Maturana (1970) also arrived at the concept of a spiral when he searched for the pattern of organization that characterizes all living systems. He concluded that all living systems are organized in a closed circular process that allows for evolutionary change in a way that circularity is maintained. He called this process *autopoiesis,* which means "self-making," emphasizing the self-referential and self-organizing nature of life. Applying autopoiesis to cognition, he argued that the process of knowing was identical to autopoiesis, the spiraling process of life (Maturana & Varela, 1980).

Progress toward development is seen as increases in the complexity and sophistication of the dimensions associated with the four modes of the learning cycle—affective, perceptual, symbolic, and behavioral complexity—and the integration of these modes in a flexible full cycle of learning. The concept of *deep learning* describes the developmental process of learning that fully integrates the four modes of the experiential learning cycle: experiencing, reflecting, thinking, and acting (Border, 2007; Jensen & Kolb, 1994). Deep learning refers to the kind of learning that leads to development in the ELT model. The ELT developmental model (Kolb, 1984) follows Jung's theory that adult development moves from a specialized way of adapting toward a holistic integrated stage that he calls individuation. The model defines three stages: (a) *acquisition,* from birth to adolescence where basic abilities and cognitive structures develop; (b) *specialization,* from formal schooling through the early work and personal experiences of adulthood where social, educational, and organizational socialization forces shape the development of a particular, specialized learning style; and (c) *integration,* in midcareer and later life where nondominant modes of learning are expressed in work and personal life.

Development through these stages is characterized by increased integration of the dialectic conflicts between the four primary learning modes (AC-CE and AE-RO) and by increasing complexity and relativism in adapting to the world. Each of the learning modes is associated with a form of complexity that is used in conscious experience to transform sensory data into knowledge such that development of CE increases affective complexity, development of RO increases perceptual complexity, development of AC increases symbolic complexity, and development of AE increases behavioral complexity (Figure 6.4). These learning modes and complexities create a multidimensional developmental process that is guided by an individual's particular learning style and life path.

Students have the opportunity to build these complexities abroad, and most of them will benefit from an educator's skilled guidance. Affective complexity arises from increasingly meaningful interactions with diverse people, especially when students are attuned to how they feel in the context of these relationships. Increases in openness to experience, sensitivity to beauty and aesthetics, bodily awareness, and the ability to be fully present in the moment also contribute to the development of affective complexity. Students develop perceptual complexity as they learn to notice detail, attend to multiple stimuli, and embrace a multiplicity of viewpoints. The ability to locate one's self among an array of external data also contributes to perceptual complexity. The classic indication of advances in symbolic complexity is the mastery of a new language. However, symbolic complexity can also be developed as students organize their experience into preexisting knowledge structures and begin to engage in systems thinking, understanding interconnections among stimuli, analysis, and model building. Finally, development of behavioral complexity occurs as students experiment with new, culturally relevant practices. Greater behavioral complexity is associated with increased flexibility in executing actions that match demands of the environment.

FIGURE 6.4
ELT of growth and development

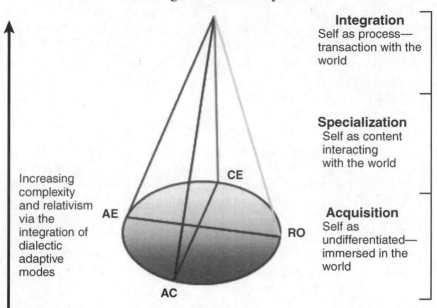

Integration
Self as process—
transaction with the
world

Specialization
Self as content
interacting
with the world

Acquisition
Self as
undifferentiated—
immersed in the
world

Increasing
complexity
and relativism
via the
integration of
dialectic
adaptive
modes

CE

AE

RO

AC

Using Experiential Learning in the Design and Conduct of Education Abroad Programs

Since their emergence in the early 1970s, the principles and concepts of experiential learning that we have outlined have been used to create curricula and conduct educational courses and programs in K–12 education (McCarthy, 1987), undergraduate education (Mentkowski & Associates, 2000), and professional education (Boyatzis, Cowen, & Kolb, 1995; Reese, 1998). Experiential learning approaches have been implemented in virtually every discipline (A. Y. Kolb, & Kolb, 2006). Many of the nontraditional educational innovations that have flowered during this period have used experiential learning as their "educational platform"—college programs for adult learners, service-learning, prior learning assessment, and outdoor adventure education. Similarly, experiential learning principles and concepts provide theoretical grounding to the practice of education abroad. In the following section, we offer some considerations for adopting experiential learning as an educational approach and crafting experiences that promote student ownership of the learning process abroad.

Becoming an Experiential Educator

To apply principles and practices of ELT is to become an experiential educator. For many this requires a reexamination of one's teaching philosophy and teaching practices. Those who think of experiential learning as techniques and games miss the deeper message that the foundational scholars of experiential learning were trying to convey. The practices of experiential learning are most effective when they are expressions of this fundamental philosophy captured in the following four propositions:

1. *Educating is a relationship.* In the midst of the multitude of educational theories, learning technologies, and institutional procedures and constraints, it is easy to lose sight of the most important thing: Teaching is above all a profound human relationship. We can all think of teachers who have had a major impact on our lives and in most cases this involved a special relationship in which we felt recognized, valued, and empowered by the teacher. Palmer (1997) described the courage necessary for a teacher to fully enter into learning relationships with students as a willingness to expose one's inner world; honor students as complex, relational beings; and masterfully weave these worlds together with the course content.

2. *Educating is holistic.* It is about educating the whole person. Educating the whole person means that the goal of education is not solely cognitive knowledge of the facts, but also includes development of social and emotional maturity. In ELT terms it is about facilitating integrated development in affective, perceptual, cognitive, and behavioral realms. Rather than acquiring generalized knowledge stripped of any context, learning is situated to the person's life setting and life path (Lave & Wenger, 1991). Dewey (1897) put it well: "I believe that education which does not occur through forms of life that are worth living for their own sake is always a poor substitute for genuine reality and tends to cramp and to deaden."

3. *Educating is learning-oriented.* The crisis in American education has led to an excessive emphasis on performance and learning outcomes, often resulting in rote memorization and "teaching to the test" while ignoring broader developmental activities such as music and the arts. This is in strong contrast to the experiential learning view stated at the outset of this chapter that it is the process of learning that should be the primary focus. Education should focus on how students are

arriving at answers by focusing on fundamental concepts, the process of inquiry, critical thinking, and choiceful creation of values.

4. *Educating is learner centered.* ELT scholars put forward a constructivist view of knowledge and learning that emphasizes the importance of organizing the educational process around the experience of learners. This entails meeting them "where they are" in their understanding and building their confidence and competence to the point where they become independent, self-directed learners.

The Teacher's Role in Experiential Learning

Adopting an experiential approach to teaching can at first be challenging and a bit unsettling, as was indicated by interviews with faculty members who participated in experiential education training and implemented ELT techniques in their courses. Regarding this, one teacher said, "Actually, teaching was easier before I learned about experiential learning. My main focus was to collect and organize my course material and present it clearly. I had never thought much about how the students were reacting and their thoughts about the material." Another said, "In the beginning I had a lot of concerns about losing control. Using experiential exercises brings up surprising stuff and makes me have to think and react on my feet." Ultimately, however, the experiential approach becomes far more enriching and rewarding. An experienced teacher reported, "I was beginning to get really bored presenting the same material year after year. Experiential learning has opened up conversations with the students about their experience and ideas and now I am actually learning new things along with them."

Teaching around the learning cycle and to different learning styles introduces the need for adjustments in the role that one takes with learners. The Teaching Role Profile (Kolb & Kolb, 2012) was created to help educators understand their preferred teaching role and plan for how they can adapt to teaching around the learning cycle. The self-report instrument is based on the assumption that preferences for teaching roles emerge from a combination of beliefs about teaching and learning, goals for the educational process, preferred teaching style, and instructional practices (see Table 6.1). Although referred to as "teaching" roles, this model is not limited to individuals in a social position of teacher or professor. This framework can be extended to individuals in educational systems who have teaching roles as advisors, administrators, student affairs professionals, peers, tour guides, or homestay parents.

TABLE 6.1

Examples of beliefs, goals, styles, and practices associated with teaching roles

Educator Role	Beliefs: "Learning occurs best when . . ."	Goals: "My students develop . . ."	Style: "As a teacher, I prefer to be . . ."	Practices: "Instructional forms I often use include . . ."
Facilitator	It begins with the learners' experience	Empathy and understanding of others	Creative, warm, affirming	Class discussion, journals, personal stories
Expert	New concepts are integrated into existing mental frameworks	Analytic and conceptual abilities	Logical, authoritative	Lectures, readings, written assignments
Evaluator	Clear standards and feedback are provided	Problem-solving skills	Structured, outcome-oriented, objective	Laboratories, graded homework assignments
Coach	It takes place in a real-life context	Ability to work productively with others	Applied, collaborative, risk-taking	Field projects, role plays, simulations

A teaching role is a patterned set of behaviors that emerge in response to the learning environment, including students and the learning task demands. Each teaching role engages students to learn in a unique manner, using one mode of grasping experience and one mode of transforming experience. In the facilitator role, educators draw on the modes of concrete experience and reflective observation to help learners get in touch with their own experience and reflect on it. Subject matter experts, using the modes of reflective observation and abstract conceptualization, help learners organize and connect their reflection to the knowledge base of the subject matter. They may provide models or theories for learners to use in subsequent analysis. In the standard setting and evaluating role, educators use abstract conceptualization and active experimentation to help students apply knowledge toward performance goals. They closely monitor the quality of student performance toward the standards that they set and provide consistent feedback. Finally, those in the coaching role draw on concrete experience and active experimentation to help learners take action to achieve personally meaningful goals. These roles can also be organized by their relative focus on the student versus the subject and action versus knowledge, as illustrated in Figure 6.5.

Highly effective educators do not rely solely on one role. Rather, they organize their educational activities in such a manner that they address all four learning modes: experiencing, reflecting, thinking, and acting. As they do this, they lead learners around the cycle, shifting the role that they play depending on which stage of the cycle they are addressing. In effect, the role they adopt helps to create a learning space designed to facilitate the transition from one learning mode to another, as was shown in Figure 6.1. Often this is done in a recursive fashion, repeating the cycle many times in a learning program. The cycle then becomes a spiral, with each passage through the cycle deepening and extending learners' understanding of the subject.

Hunt (1987) suggested that a learning spiral is shared between individuals in human interaction. People relate to one another in a pattern of alternating "reading" and "flexing" that mirrors the experiential learning process. When one person is *reading*, receiving feedback (CE) and formulating perceptions (RO), the other person is *flexing*, creating intentions based on those perceptions (AC) and acting on them (AE). As the exchange continues, both parties alternate between reading and flexing. Based on the actions that they take, educators can activate different learning modes in students according to their patterns of reading and flexing (Abbey et al., 1985).

FIGURE 6.5

Teaching Roles

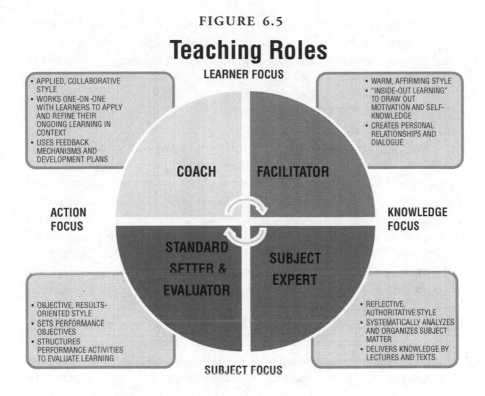

LEARNER FOCUS

- APPLIED, COLLABORATIVE STYLE
- WORKS ONE-ON-ONE WITH LEARNERS TO APPLY AND REFINE THEIR ONGOING LEARNING IN CONTEXT
- USES FEEDBACK MECHANISMS AND DEVELOPMENT PLANS

- WARM, AFFIRMING STYLE
- "INSIDE-OUT LEARNING" TO DRAW OUT MOTIVATION AND SELF-KNOWLEDGE
- CREATES PERSONAL RELATIONSHIPS AND DIALOGUE

COACH   **FACILITATOR**

ACTION FOCUS   **KNOWLEDGE FOCUS**

STANDARD SETTER & EVALUATOR   **SUBJECT EXPERT**

- OBJECTIVE, RESULTS-ORIENTED STYLE
- SETS PERFORMANCE OBJECTIVES
- STRUCTURES PERFORMANCE ACTIVITIES TO EVALUATE LEARNING

- REFLECTIVE, AUTHORITATIVE STYLE
- SYSTEMATICALLY ANALYZES AND ORGANIZES SUBJECT MATTER
- DELIVERS KNOWLEDGE BY LECTURES AND TEXTS

SUBJECT FOCUS

Selecting the appropriate role to enact at the appropriate time is an art. Educators must consider multiple factors in the moment-to-moment choices they make about how to respond to students. Educators must balance the learning mode they intend to elicit with signals that students send about how they expect the educator to behave (Gaff & Gaff, 1981; Kahn, Wolfe, Quinn, & Snoek, 1964). Selection of a teaching role is also affected by role-specific identity—one's self-knowledge specific to certain educational settings—such that educators have a tendency to assume roles that align with their preferred teaching role and learning style (Nicoll-Senft & Seider, 2010). Finally, aspects of the learning space also influence teaching role selection, particularly physical configurations, temporal constraints, and instructional norms associated with various disciplines.

As we have discussed, educators can gain flexibility in enacting the four teaching roles. Just as students can gain proficiency in integrating multiple learning modes, educators can gain flexibility in shifting fluidly among the four teaching roles. First, narrowly defined assumptions about teaching and learning tend to result in an imbalance in teaching role enactment. Challenging one's current beliefs about the purpose and process of education could lead to an expanded philosophy that naturally encapsulates more teaching roles. This also applies to students who have their own beliefs about education. The extent to which students are encouraged to understand the learning process and their own learning styles and teaching role preferences will determine the possible range of effective teaching roles.

Second, empathy is important for responding appropriately to the role requirements of a learning situation (Mead, 1934). Empathy is the ability to sense others' feelings and perspectives, and take an active interest in their concerns (Boyatzis, 2009). In an educational context, this begins with understanding the class composition: age, gender, and learning styles; selected major/minor or concentration; previous exposure to course content; students' previous work experiences; future career goals; and any other variable that might affect academic performance. Empathic responses are even more likely when the teacher gets to know each student as an individual. Information available through these interpersonal relationships allows the teacher to adapt his or her teaching role to the developmental needs of the students, as well as monitor optimal levels of challenge and support (Sanford, 1968).

Third, educators can use mechanisms to facilitate smooth transitions between teaching roles. The first mechanism is to explain the experiential learning cycle and four teaching roles up front so that students understand how to respond when they perceive changes in a teacher's behavior toward them. Another mechanism is to establish predictable patterns of role shifting. This can be accomplished by displaying an agenda for each class so that students can follow along and anticipate role shifts. Class routines also assist with establishing predictability. For example, opening each class with a guided writing exercise or quiz helps students assume the appropriate learning mode. A final mechanism deals with utilizing changes in physical location. Physical movement between different spaces, such as large-group instruction and small-group breakouts or the classroom and the field, often cues a change in learning mode and facilitates smooth teaching role transitions.

Fourth, team teaching is a method to achieve enactment of all four teaching roles. Team teaching must go beyond simply taking turns leading class (such that each faculty member is present for one class per week rather than two). Teaching teammates should work closely together using complementary strengths to perform all of the educator roles. This allows all roles to be present in the learning system. It also provides role modeling for teachers to learn from one another. In the instance that team teaching is not an option, teachers can engage students as teachers and ask them to play these roles in a peer capacity.

In summary, the four teaching roles—facilitator, expert, evaluator, and coach—provide a holistic framework for implementing experiential learning. Selection of teaching role is influenced by desired student learning mode, student signals, one's teaching identity, and demands of the learning space. Because teaching roles are fluid rather than fixed, mechanisms for shifting among the roles can be employed. Effectively shifting between roles offers a relational way to intervene in student learning.

Using ELT to Promote Ownership of the Learning Process

ELT calls for full engagement of students in the learning endeavor. Thus, in addition to the teaching role, consideration must be given to helping students take ownership of the learning process when designing study abroad programs and course activities. One way to do this is to *educate students on the experiential learning cycle and their own learning style preferences*. Surprisingly, many students have not thought about what learning is and do not understand their unique way of learning. Without explicit awareness, unconscious beliefs or "lay theories" govern the way that individuals engage in the learning process (Molden & Dweck, 2006). In particular, Dweck and her colleagues (2008) have examined the differences between those who see their abilities and attributes as fixed and those who believe that they can incrementally learn and change themselves. Those individuals who believe that they can learn and develop have a *learning identity*. The learner faces a difficult challenge with a "mastery response" whereas the person with a fixed identity is more likely to withdraw or quit. Learners embrace challenge, persist in the face of obstacles, learn from criticism, and are inspired by and learn from the success of others. The fixed identity person avoids challenge, gives up easily, avoids criticism, and feels threatened by the success of others. Not surprisingly, students with a learning identity, regardless of their tested intelligence, are more successful in school than those with a fixed identity (Kolb & Kolb, 2009).

Educating students on experiential learning and their learning style helps develop a learning identity. "Learning to learn" interventions have led to increased classroom motivation and a reversal in declining grades (Blackwell, Trzesniewski, & Dweck, 2007), as well as significant improvements in adolescents' achievement test scores (Good, Aronson, & Inzlicht, 2003) and higher grades among college students (Aronson, Fried, & Good, 2002; Hutt, 2007). It is our contention that an understanding of the experiential learning process will empower students to feel more capable and be more effective at maximizing learning opportunities abroad.

A second strategy for empowering involvement in the learning process is to *create engaging learning environments using a variety of instructional methods.* Curricula that emphasize active involvement, a variety of learning activities, and an element of choice tend to engender personal investment in learning. A word of clarification must be offered here. Popular practice suggests that curricula be designed to match the learning style of learners. Although this idea is recommended by many learning style models other than ELT and is the basis for testing the validity of the learning style concept for some researchers (Pashler, McDaniel, Rohrer, & Bjork, 2008), it is *not* the recommended approach in ELT. The ELT approach is to build curricula around the cycle of learning in such a way that all learning modes are used and all styles of learning are engaged. In this way, every program, course, or class session has something to engage and connect with learners of every style. Learners are also encouraged to develop learning style flexibility and to move freely around the learning cycle.

Svinick and Dixon (1987) describe a comprehensive instructional model to deal with the constraints and challenges that instructors and students encounter as they adopt experiential learning as an instructional design framework. They offer an instructional design model that incorporates a broad range of learning activities that lead students through the full cycle of learning, thus giving teachers a rich array of instructional choices, as well as the benefit of offering students a more complete learning experience gained from multiple perspectives. The model is also useful in responding to one of the key challenges of experiential methods: understanding the role of the student in the learning process. As the model in Figure 6.6 suggests, teachers are able to design the learning activities based on how much student involvement would be appropriate given the time constraint that most instructors face. Activities at the outer rim of the learning cycle allow for a greater student involvement, whereas those close to the center involve limited student participation.

A third way for students to take ownership of learning is to *build diverse learning relationships.* ELT defines learning relationships as connections between one or more individuals that promote growth and movement through the learning spiral, ultimately inspiring future learning and relationship building. A connection is constituted by an interaction or series of

FIGURE 6.6
Instructional activities by student involvement

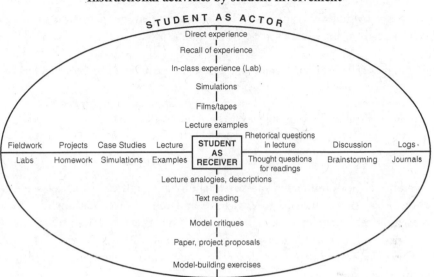

Note: Adapted from Svinick, M. D., & Dixon, N. M. (1987). The Kolb model modified for classroom activities. *College Teaching, 35*(4), 141–146.

interactions that build toward a deeper relationship. Similar to Fletcher and Ragins's (2007) description of the development of a mentoring relationship through a series of small "episodes," learning relationships evolve as learning interactions increase in quality and frequency. Each interaction carries with it a sentiment, or an emotional charge, that sets the tone for learning. Interactions characterized by compassion, mutual respect, and support build the trust and positive emotional resources necessary to create space for learning—even when learning is challenging. Such growth-fostering relationships have been found to cultivate an increased sense of vitality, ability to take action, clarity about self and the relationship, sense of self-worth, and desire to form more connections in both parties (Miller & Stiver, 1997).

In the context of study abroad, possibilities for learning relationships are vast. Professors, staff, peers, homestay families, roommates, internship supervisors and coworkers, tour guides, local citizens, and even tourists represent individuals who might comprise a student's network of learning relationships abroad. Within this network, study abroad educators are uniquely positioned to intervene in student learning through holistic relationships with students that extend beyond the walls of the classroom. In fact, Sanford (1968) suggested that study abroad programs led by faculty from the home campus provide opportunities for students to experience authentic student-faculty relationships that they do not always enjoy at home:

> In those relatively small communities abroad, many [students] learned for the first time what intellectual fellowship is and how rewarding a teacher can be when he is encouraged to reveal himself as a person. Students have an opportunity to see him in a variety of roles—as husband, father, traveling companion, gourmet, connoisseur of the arts, and member of a complex human community. (p. 172)

In addition, both home and site-based faculty and staff can intervene experientially by asking students to engage in and reflect on situations in which they form relationships with culturally different others. Meaningful relationships abroad not only ease the adaptive challenge of living abroad but also facilitate transformative learning and the development of cultural competence.

Conclusion

Study abroad programs are rich with opportunities for growth and development. These learning opportunities are best realized through an intentional process of transforming experience into knowledge. We have illuminated one such process by highlighting the fundamentals of ELT: the cycle of experiential learning, learning styles, learning flexibility, learning space, and the ELT of development or learning spiral. To catalyze the application of theory to practice, we also introduced key propositions for becoming an experiential educator, a discussion of teaching roles, and ideas for inspiring student ownership in the learning experience. It is our hope that these concepts will assist educators in intervening masterfully in the learning process in study abroad experiences, thereby maximizing student learning.

References

Abbey, D. S., Hunt, D. E., & Weiser, J. C. (1985). Variations on a theme by Kolb: A new perspective for understanding counseling and supervision. *The Counseling Psychologist, 13*(3), 477–501.

Aronson, J., Fried, C. B., & Good, C. (2002). Reducing stereotype threat and boosting academic achievement of African-American students: The role of conceptions of intelligence. *Journal of Experimental Social Psychology, 38,* 113–125.

Blackwell, L. S., Trzesniewski, K. H., & Dweck, C. S. (2007). Implicit theories of intelligence predict achievement across an adolescent transition: A longitudinal study and an intervention. *Child Development, 78*(1), 246–263.

Border, L. L. B. (2007). Understanding learning styles: The key to unlocking deep learning and in-depth teaching. *NEA Higher Education Advocate, 24*(5), 5–8.

Boyatzis, R. E. (2009). Competencies as a behavioral approach to emotional intelligence. *Journal of Management Development, 28*(9), 749–770.

Boyatzis, R. E., Cowen, S. S., & Kolb, D. A. (1995). *Innovation in professional education: Steps on a journey from teaching to learning.* San Francisco, CA: Jossey-Bass.

Boyatzis, R. E., & Kolb, D. A. (1993). *Adaptive Style Inventory: Self scored inventory and interpretation booklet.* Boston: TRG Hay/McBer, Training Resources Group.

Boyatzis, R. E., & Mainemelis, C. (2000). *An empirical study of pluralism of learning and adaptive styles in an MBA program* (Working paper 00–1). Cleveland, OH: Department of Organizational Behavior, Weatherhead School of Management, Case Western Reserve University.

Dewey, J. (1897). My pedagogic creed. *The School Journal, LIV*(3), 77–80.

Dweck, C. S. (2008). *Mindset: The new psychology of success.* New York: Ballantine Books.

Eickmann, P., Kolb, A. Y., & Kolb, D. A. (2004). Designing learning. In F. Collopy & R. Boland (Eds.), *Managing as designing: Creating a new vocabulary for management education and research* (pp. 241–247). Palo Alto, CA: Stanford University Press.

Flavell, J. H. (1963). *The developmental psychology of Jean Piaget.* Princeton, NJ: D Van Nostrand.

Fletcher, J. K., & Ragins, B. R. (2007). Stone Center relational cultural theory: A window on relational mentoring. In B. R. Ragins & K. E. Kram (Eds.), *The handbook of mentoring at work: Theory, research, and practice* (pp. 373–399). Thousand Oaks, CA: Sage.

Gaff, J. G., & Gaff, S. S. (1981). Student-faculty relationships. In A. Chickering (Ed.), *The modern American college: Responding to the new realities of diverse students and a changing society.* San Francisco, CA: Jossey-Bass.

Good, C., Aronson, J., & Inzlicht, M. (2003). Improving adolescents' standardized test performance: An intervention to reduce the effects of stereotype threat. *Journal of Applied Developmental Psychology, 24,* 645–662.

Hunt, D. E. (1987). *Beginning with ourselves.* Cambridge, MA: Brookline.

Hutt, G. K. (2007). *Experiential learning spaces: Hermetic transformational leadership for psychological safety, consciousness development and math anxiety related inferiority complex depotentiation* (Unpublished doctoral dissertation). Case Western Reserve University, Cleveland, OH.

Jensen, P., & Kolb, D. (1994). Learning and development. In M. Keeton (Ed.), *Perspective in experiential learning* (pp. 79–83). Chicago, IL: Council for Adult and Experiential Learning.

Joy, S., & Kolb, D. A. (2009). Are there cultural differences in learning style? *International Journal of Intercultural Relations, 33*(1), 69–85.

Kahn, R. L., Wolfe, D. M., Quinn, R. P., & Snoek, J. D. (1964). *Organizational stress: Studies in role conflict and ambiguity.* New York: Wiley & Sons.

Kolb, A. Y., & Kolb, D. A. (2005). Learning styles and learning spaces: Enhancing experiential learning in higher education. *Academy of Management Learning and Education, 4*(2), 193–212.

Kolb, A. Y., & Kolb, D. A. (2006). Learning style and learning spaces: A review of the multidisciplinary application of experiential learning theory in higher education. In R. Sims & S. Sims (Eds.), *Learning styles and learning: A key to meeting the accountability demands in education* (pp. 45–91). Hauppauge, NY: Nova Publishers.

Kolb, A. Y., & Kolb, D. A. (2009). On becoming a learner: The concept of learning identity. In D. Bamford-Rees, B. Doyle, B. Klein-Collins, & J. Wertheim, (Eds.), *Learning never ends: Essays on adult learning inspired by the life and work of David O. Justice* (pp. 5–13). Chicago, IL: CAEL Forum and News.

Kolb, A. Y., & Kolb, D. A. (2011a). *Experiential learning theory bibliography: Volume 1, 1971–2005.* Cleveland, OH: Experience Based Learning Systems. Cleveland, OH. Retrieved from www.learningfromexperience.com

Kolb, A. Y., & Kolb, D. A. (2011b). *Experiential learning theory bibliography: Volume 2, 2006–2011.* Cleveland, OH: Experience Based Learning Systems. Retrieved from http://www.learningfromexperience.com

Kolb, A. Y., & Kolb, D. A. (2011c). *Learning Style Inventory Version 4.0* Hay Resources Direct. 116 Huntington Avenue, Boston, MA 02116. Retrieved from http://www.haygroup.com/leadershipandtalentondemand

Kolb, A. Y., & Kolb, D. A. (2012). The teaching role profile. Cleveland, OH: Experience Based Learning Systems.

Kolb, D. A. (1984). *Experiential learning: Experience as a source of learning and development.* Upper Saddle River, NJ: Prentice-Hall.

Kolb, D. A. (2005). *Learning Style Inventory Version 3.1.* Boston, MA: Hay Resources Direct. Retrieved from http://www.haygroup.com/leadershipandtalentondemand

Lave, J., & Wenger, E. (1991). *Situated learning: Legitimate peripheral participation.* Cambridge, UK: Cambridge University Press.

Lewin, K. (1951). *Field theory in social science: Selected theoretical papers (Edited by Dorwin Cartwright.).* Harpers. Retrieved from http://search.ebscohost.com/login.aspx?direct = true&db = psyh&AN = 1951-06769-000&site = ehost-live

Mainemelis, C., Boyatzis, R., & Kolb, D. A. (2002). Learning styles and adaptive flexibility: Testing experiential learning theory. *Management Learning, 33*(1), 5–33.

Maturana, H. (1970). The biology of cognition. In H. Maturana & F. Varela (Eds., 1980), *Autopoiesis and cognition: The realization of the living* (pp. 5–58). Dordrecht, Holland: D. Reidel Publishing Company.

Maturana, H., & Varela, F. (1980). *Autopoiesis and cognition.* Dordrecht, Holland: D. Reidel Publishing Company.

McCarthy, B. (1987). *The 4MAT System: Teaching to learning styles with right/left mode techniques.* Barrington, IL: Excel.

Mead, G. H. (1934). *Mind, self, and society.* Chicago, IL: University of Chicago Press.

Mentkowski, M., & Associates. (2000). *Learning that lasts: Integrating learning, development, and performance in college and beyond.* San Francisco, CA: Jossey-Bass.

Miller, J. B., & Stiver, I. (1997). *The healing connection.* Boston, MA: Beacon Press.

Molden, D. C., & Dweck, C. S. (2006). Finding "meaning" in psychology: A lay theories approach to self-regulation, social perception and social development. *American Psychologist, 61*(3), 192–203.

Nicoll-Senft, J. M., & Seider, S. N. (2010). Assessing the impact of the 4MAT teaching model across multiple disciplines in higher education. *College Teaching, 58,* 19–27.

Palmer, P. J. (1997). *The heart of a teacher: Identity and integrity in teaching.* Center for Courage & Renewal. Retrieved from http://www.couragerenewal.org/parker/writings/heart-of-a-teacher

Pashler, H., McDaniel, M., Rohrer, D., & Bjork, R. (2008). Learning styles: Concepts and evidence. *Psychological Science in the Public Interest, 9*(3), 106–119.

Reese, J. H. (1998). *Enhancing law students' performance: Learning style interventions.* Saratoga Springs, NY: The National Center on Adult Learning, Empire State College.

Sanford, N. (1968). *Where colleges fail: A study of student as person.* San Francisco, CA: Jossey-Bass.

Strange, C. C., & Banning, J. H. (2001). *Educating by design: Creating campus learning environments that work.* San Francisco, CA: Jossey-Bass.

Svinick, M. D., & Dixon, N. M. (1987). The Kolb model modified for classroom activities. *College Teaching, 35*(4), 141–146.

Zull, J. (2002). *The art of changing the brain.* Sterling, VA: Stylus.

7

THE BRAIN, LEARNING, AND STUDY ABROAD

James E. Zull

I was a senior in high school and needed money. My parents were insisting that I go to college, but it was expensive. I had saved only $200 from my paper route.

"You have to get a job," my parents said. I knew they were right, but I didn't like it. I didn't mind working, in principle, but I also wanted to be on the track team in the spring. A job was sure to throw a monkey wrench into my plans!

But I didn't have a choice. My dad took over. He knew the owner of an appliance store, and they needed someone to help with deliveries. So Dad volunteered me.

My life had been very sheltered up to then. Home, school, and church were all I knew. For the most part, these were positive environments, but things were quite different at my job. I was in a totally new culture, with a new set of behaviors and beliefs. And I began to notice things that confused, disgusted, and even frightened me.

There were two particular individuals who influenced me at the store. The first was Mike. He was the store manager and made decisions about sales, money, and prices. He also specialized in deception. From "bait and switch" to covering up damage, Mike knew a thousand ways to cheat the customer.

Sam was the other new influence. He drove the delivery truck, and I got to know him mostly by listening. Sam talked continually as we drove around town. And he spoke of only one thing—women! He also learned quickly how much he could shock me. He would tell a dirty joke, then look at me and roar with laughter as my face turned pink.

I didn't really like this new culture, but, out of curiosity, I suppose, I did experiment with it. Dirty jokes came first, but I was not well suited for that. I couldn't prevent those unexpected feelings of embarrassment, and sometimes shame, that those jokes elicited in me. Girls were still to be worshiped, as far as I was concerned.

I also experimented with lying when Mike let me meet customers. But that was even worse than dirty jokes. It was just so much hard work. Deceit had to be deliberate, and carefully executed!

I wasn't happy with these experiments, but I still wanted to get back on the track team. So I tried out lying again, utilizing deliberate deceit to escape the store. I told Mike that my parents wanted me to quit, but I told my parents that I wasn't needed anymore.

Neither of these claims was completely true, but the latter bothered me the most. I felt guilty, and worried. I knew that my dad could check out my story anytime. But, strangely, he never mentioned it. Maybe he already knew the story and decided that I had learned my lesson. Or maybe he just decided that I had grown up, and it wasn't his problem.

I never knew.

T his is a story of a culture change and my efforts to adapt to that change. It is not quite the same as moving to a different country, but it does have many features in common with such a change. The story is remarkably similar to ones that are told by immigrants as they struggle in their new environment (Wexler, 2006). A major element in study abroad is a culture change, so I hope that the story will be useful in our discussion.

Our species is quite good at this kind of adaptation, particularly when we are young. In some ways it is what the human brain evolved to do. Survival as a species depended greatly on our ability to respond appropriately to the nature of our environment, and to the changes in it. This is true both for long-term change throughout life and for sudden change when we encounter immediate problems to be solved or opportunities to be seized.

Although we may adapt to culture change, it is highly emotional. That is also clear from the story I told. In fact, the emotional aspect is probably the most important, and it plays a central role in the discussion developed in this chapter. Whereas research may suggest that students in study abroad programs may not study enough, and have not learned enough, I argue that it is the culture change that is most problematic. The challenges of study abroad cannot be met simply by studying more.

Constructivism and the Brain

Let us remind ourselves of the framework that emerged earlier in this book: the learning theory called *constructivism*. It is based on the realization that individuals construct the meaning of new experiences on the foundation that they already have—on what they already know. This individual uniqueness inevitably means that the interpretations that emerge from specific experiences are not absolute. What seem to be "true" understandings are different for each individual, and thus the "truth" that emerges is *our* truth, not *the* truth.

This becomes particularly important when we try to explain learning in neurological terms. The idea that knowledge resides in networks of neurons "constructed" through our experience explains why our knowledge is personal. Each person has his or her own collection of networks, which differs from that of other individuals. And thus individual learning is unique.

The main objective here is to examine the biological machinery that operates in constructivism. The hope is that this will give us insights into learning, which is a physical process, while also providing a helpful view of unique learning experiences, such as study abroad. We may even be able to explore exactly what we mean by "transformation," an issue that Vande Berg, Paige, and Lou raised in chapter 1.

Brain Topic I: Behavior and Emotion

I have divided our discussion of the brain into three parts: (1) behavior and emotion; (2) knowledge and neuronal networks; and (3) cognition and learning. This section of the chapter focuses on the first one of these.

Behavior

Starting with "behavior" may surprise you if you are drawn to the philosophical. It may seem simplistic, applicable to "lower" species, but less so to *Homo sapiens*. But, of course, species are all related. And those relationships do carry over in natural selection and evolution. Further, we should be careful with the terms *lower* and *higher* when thinking about species. We may be higher than fish when it comes to calculus, but lower when it comes to swimming. Neither is "superior" in any absolute way.

Behavior is at the root of evolution through natural selection. Over evolutionary time, living organisms settled on specific behaviors (actions) that were successful in particular environments or experiences. An example is "escape behavior" in animals. Originally, this kind of behavior was not produced by cognition. It was not a response to "thinking," but rather simply a matter of chance. Some individuals were just born "fast," and others were not. The fast individuals survived (by escaping), and their genes were passed on. They came to characterize the entire species.

At this point, this particular behavior may seem irrelevant or at least less important for the human organism because evolution has endowed us with a cognitive brain that allows us to go beyond depending totally on speed. And it may seem even less relevant in a discussion of higher education, or study abroad, which many view as primarily mental. But as we will see, the behavior machinery in the brain is actually very important in educational settings and may very well be central to the challenge of learning abroad.

Behavior and Emotion

Once we begin a discussion of behavior, we find ourselves thinking about emotions. The reason is that behaviors emerge from a drive to do something—to act. Another word for that drive is *emotion*. In fact, psychologists commonly use this connection as an actual definition of emotion (Zhu & Thagard, 2002). We behave according to our wants and our fears; to a desire for more, and a desire for less. For example, mating behavior is driven by attraction and appeal: "Get me closer," "Give me more!" We can call this *positive* emotion. And escape behavior is driven by repulsion and fear: "Get me less," "Get me away!" *Negative* emotion.

Although the emotions provide the drive, the actual physical behaviors themselves are expressed by the body—the "nonbrain" parts of the body. But, again, we must look to the brain for the origin and nature of these behaviors. They are the overt bodily expression of ideas generated in the brain. If we are inclined to believe in nonphysical phenomena (which I am not), we can think of behaviors as a physical form of the nonphysical, the nonphysical being thoughts or ideas.

Negative and Positive

Let us look more into the negative and positive emotion systems, starting with the negative. These systems are possibly the most obvious, both in their origin and in their results. They are typified by the instinct to run away from danger, or to fight against it: flight or fight. It is easy to see the merit of this behavior. It may save our lives in an instant. There is little time for thought or argument. And there is a lot of energy available. In an emergency we become stronger, our heart beats faster, and we do not take time to think. We cannot reason with ourselves, analyze the complexities, or plan ahead. Rather, we take the most direct and obvious actions possible. Although flight may be the most immediate response, if we cannot escape we may turn to resistance—we may fight. And fiercely!

This negative emotion system and its attendant behaviors evolved to save the individual. By contrast, we can think of the positive behaviors as saving groups of individuals—groups as small as two, but also as large as whole species. The unifying concept here is that in order to save anyone other than ourselves, it helps to have cooperation, and often, affection. As we will see, the actions and strategies associated with positive emotion are organized in a broader, more vague but more subtle manner than those associated with negative emotions. Rather than force, we may use seduction. Rather than push or strike, we lure, and persuade.

The Brain and Emotions

It should not surprise us that the structure and functions for these two distinct kinds of behavior (positive and negative) also utilize some distinct regions and structures in the brain. The negative responses and behaviors emerge primarily from the well-known system in the body (the adrenal gland near the kidneys), but that response still is activated by signals from the brain. Those signals originate in ancient brain structures such as the amygdala (LeDoux, 1998), which sends danger signals directly to the body, triggering escape behaviors. This system is relatively subconscious and is not easily controlled by intent. In fact, it has also been shown to play a fundamental role in memory of fearful or traumatic experiences.

It seems likely that a better understanding of this little brain structure, the size of an almond, will be helpful for educators both at home and abroad. Educational experiences and memories are often fearful, and can remain so for years. In general is it likely that better understanding of these powerful emotions ultimately will be helpful in understanding student (and teacher) behaviors.

The positive emotion systems involve different and ancient brain structures called the *basal ganglia*. These regions of the brain have the ability to respond to the well-known internal reward chemical, dopamine (Bozarth, 1994). Thus, the basal ganglia are central in our ability to carry out actions that are motivated by a conscious feeling, a need or desire, by our ability to achieve goals by conscious, voluntary actions. An example would be the purposeful movement of my fingers over the keyboard in order to express my thoughts as I write. I find this satisfying, and I do it in order to experience the intrinsic reward of satisfaction.

Other examples are the behaviors leading to reproduction. Actions of this type generate strong perceptions of control, and reward. And the behaviors are complex and subtle actions of the body such as those that characterize mating "dances" in many species.

Even though they are primitive, the negative and positive emotion systems can be highly complex. In the human brain, both can come into play at the same time and be triggered by the same experiences. For example, when we see a beautiful face we may feel both joy and fear. We may want to get closer but still resist expressing that desire because we fear rejection. Or when we have a new experience, we may be uncertain how to react and show the behavior of *not acting*. The newness means that we cannot be certain what such an experience means, and we can imagine both wonderful and awful outcomes. Best to wait and see!

Emotion, Thought, and Memory

Emotion and thought are often viewed as opposites, even enemies. We warn our students not to be emotional. We believe in "cold reason." But neuroscience tends to support a different perspective. The chemicals most frequently associated with emotion (adrenaline, dopamine, serotonin, etc.) actually flood the regions of the brain most responsible for cognition. Furthermore, the cognitive processes themselves are rewarding. It is satisfying to solve problems, even though it requires energy. We are willing to expend that energy, and often do so continually throughout our waking hours. Without our internal reward system, or our fear of failure—our emotion systems—we may well remain inert, exhibiting the behaviors that lead to such labels as "sloth" or "lazy." Our work ethic may suffer. We may lose motivation.

Memory is also strongly associated with the emotion systems in the primitive regions of the brain, regions that produce the aforementioned chemicals. In fact, the most compelling amnesia ever observed in experimental animals was generated by blocking delivery of these emotion chemicals to mentally higher regions of the brain (Gaffan, 2005).

Brain Topic II: Knowledge and Neuronal Networks

The second brain topic draws attention to the ability of neurons in the brain and elsewhere to connect with other neurons, forming complex and extensive networks. These networks can be as small as two or three neurons, or as large as many thousands. They do not have to be localized in the brain, but most of them are. An example of a small, nonbrain network is a reflex. For example, if we touch something hot, we will spontaneously jerk our hand away. This can be attributed primarily to three types of neuron: one to sense heat; one to stimulate the arm muscle; and one to connect the other two, forming a network. Many brain networks are the same as this reflex in character. They carry out the sequence *sense-connect-act.*

Knowledge as Networks

The network described in the previous section represents knowledge. The content of that knowledge can be simply defined as "What to do when we touch something hot." The elements of that knowledge are very similar to those of a many neuron network in the brain. Those elements are (a) *sensing* something in our environment, (b) *connecting* that knowledge to an action system, and (c) stimulating contraction or relaxation of specific muscles that generate *action* (behavior).

We become aware of experiences through our sensory neurons, such as those we find in the eye or the ear. However, awareness is not the whole of learning, as I have defined it here. For example:

> We are walking down a country road when we hear a vehicle approaching behind us. We sense it and are aware of it. But we need more information, so we look back. We see a motorbike, and it is moving fast toward us. Then we realize that our country road is also a bike path, and we quickly step aside. This action-response engages specialized motor neurons in the brain, so now our sensory neurons are linked to the motor neurons in a "knowledge network." The next time we hear a bike approaching, we may step to the side automatically. We have new knowledge of what we should do when we hear a bike behind us.

This elementary example helps us understand the assertion "learning is physical." It is a process leading to formation (or loss) of connections between physical entities called neurons. It illustrates how forming new connections leads to a new physical entity, a network. If we examine more carefully, we can see other aspects of this concept. The original networks can be physically altered, disrupted, or even silenced. These physical changes are the basis for change in our knowledge.

Neuronal Networks and Emotion

We know that learning is greatly influenced by emotion. This influence can show itself in enhanced memory, motivation, and behaviors such as repetition and mimicry. Biologically, the impact of emotion on learning is best described as the result of physical and chemical modification of the connections between neurons—synapses (Kandel, 2006). This scientific explanation is based on the discovery that the brain chemicals we commonly associate with emotion generate their effects by "modulating" synapses in ways that influence their strength, duration, and sensitivity.

As mentioned earlier, emotion systems change the properties of networks through actions of chemicals that are secreted by neurons in the most ancient parts of the brain (e.g., the brain stem). The actual cell bodies of those neurons send out extensions that reach the most evolutionarily recent brain structure, the *neocortex*, which is the surface coating of the brain. The word *cortex* means "bark" (as in tree bark), and the prefix *neo* or "new" refers to the appearance of the cortex recently in evolutionary time (as recently as millions of years!). It is visible when looking at an isolated brain, and it is by far, physically, the largest part of the brain. The neocortex and brain stem are shown in Figure 7.1.

To repeat, the *ancient* brain stem chemically regulates the *new cortex*—the neocortex. The emotion systems greatly modify neural networks; they influence knowledge.

Brain Topic III: Cognition and Learning

To begin our examination of cognition and learning, let us turn to the experiential learning cycle proposed by David Kolb more than 25 years ago (Kolb, 1984) and discussed in a more recent context in chapters 1, 6, and 16 of this book. This cycle, or spiral, consists of four components, each of which contributes specific cognitive aspects to our experiences. However, each of these cognitive elements also engages the emotions in complex and profound ways. Some of these ideas are described in my prior work (Zull, 2002, 2011), and their application to the topic of study abroad provides an opportunity to extend them further.

The four elements of learning proposed by Kolb are *concrete experience, reflective observation, abstract hypothesis,* and *active testing.* Each represents a segment in the learning cycle. Most often we begin discussion of this cycle

FIGURE 7.1
The neocortex and brain stem

Neocortex

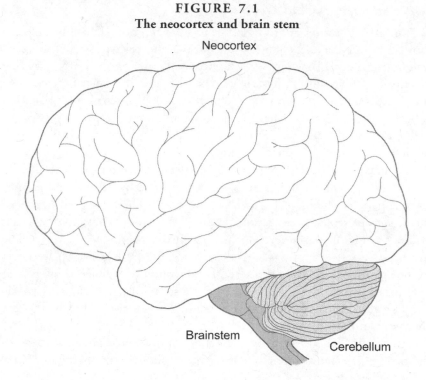

Brainstem

Cerebellum

with concrete experience. Thus, one turn of the cycle is completed with *active testing* (the last element), but that element also produces a new *concrete experience*, which then becomes part of a new cycle consisting of the same four elements (see Figure 7.2).

I have proposed that each of these four elements of the learning cycle heavily, but not exclusively, engages different regions of the neocortex. Each is associated with different functions, so that the cycle engages four different broad functions of cognition and learning. This perspective suggested new terminology that proved useful for discussing learning in both brain research and education. The four brain functions engaged are: *sensing, remembering, theorizing,* and *acting,* in that sequence. I have called these the *four pillars* of learning.

The way these pillars relate to Kolb's terminology is described in the next section of this chapter. First, however, let us look at a direct link between the four pillars and a remarkable experiment in cognitive neuroscience that appeared in the literature (Thorpe & Fabre-Thorpe, 2001) at nearly

FIGURE 7.2
The four elements of the learning cycle proposed by Kolb

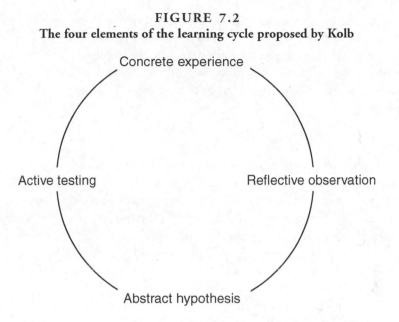

the same time as publication of *The Art of Changing the Brain* (Zull, 2002). In this experiment, researchers asked the question, "Can monkeys distinguish cats from dogs?" Their experiments determined that the answer to this question is yes. But for us, the most compelling aspect of the work is that the monkeys actually utilized the four regions of cortex associated with the four pillars.

Not only did they use these areas, but they used them in the sequence proposed for the learning cycle, which is as follows: (a) sensory (perceiving major aspects of different images—cats and dogs), (b) memory (comparing the perceived image to remembered ones), (c) theorizing (deciding the nature of the perceived image—cat or dog?), and (d) testing that judgment by a specific action (pressing red button if dog, green button if cat).

These results come as close to a direct physical test of our theory as possible. They allow us to peer directly into a process of thought, and in so doing see the cycle of learning.

The Pillars

My objective so far has been to introduce some key ideas in general form, particularly the concept of the pillars. Now, we will consider those ideas in more detail, which will ultimately help us think about the topic of study abroad in the final sections of the chapter. In particular, this more detailed discussion will help us see how different aspects of learning may be influenced by the culture change encountered by students in such programs. Specifically, we will focus on each of the pillars and the impact of emotion on them.

First Pillar: Sensing

Kolb begins with the term *concrete experience*. This is perhaps the most direct link to the concept of "experiential" learning. It does not refer to mental experiences such as reflection or "rumination" but can include many things that are often viewed as mental. For example, listening to music or watching movies can easily be thought of as mental experiences. They are clearly more complex than just passive watching or listening, although they start their journey in the mind via the route of our eyes and ears. They begin as concrete experiences.

We become aware of our experiences by using the sensory systems in, and associated with, the brain. This awareness develops as the brain receives physical information from the environment. In the way we will use this terminology here, the sensory systems give us facts about what is happening, but not evaluation or interpretations. That is, sometimes we will speak of this sensory process as "perception," but when used this way the word simply means "sensing," not understanding or cognition.

Each moment of life is part of an unending list of experiences, and it is impossible to keep track of them. Arguably, most are forgotten, but those that are memorable usually gain that status by further processing and actions (i.e., the learning cycle). However, simply thinking about such concrete experiences does not, in itself, constitute this kind of experience. Neither does intentional recalling or self-analysis. That kind of experience fits more easily into the phenomenon that we call *metacognition*, which I discuss more in the section "Study Abroad and Active Testing."

In education, this sensory route is of great importance in getting information. For a formal class, listening to a lecture qualifies as such a route. But experiential learning does not focus on the information in the lecture as much as on the total experience. Experiences that are concrete to one person may not be to another. Going to class and taking notes has real and immediate meaning to a college student, but not necessarily to a plumber or a kindergartner. A mathematical expression may be concrete for a student of science but not a history student, while the reverse may be true when the subject is political theory. Prior experience and knowledge play an important role in whether something is concrete or not. Thus, concreteness is not an absolute. It is relative, varying both with the learner and with the experience.

Another aspect of concrete experience is seen by considering the emotions. Information about our experiences is gathered by our sensory brain, but the context and meanings emerge via emotions. When we sense emotions, we call them "feelings," and few would argue that our feelings are not real. In our personal experience, our feelings are just as real as something seen. We can sense objects, people, places, processes, shapes, colors, and so forth cognitively. But each of those cognitive aspects can also have emotional meaning. We sense things through the functions of the negative and positive emotion systems described earlier in this chapter. We gain knowledge through feelings that come with the sensory information. There is a wide range of feelings that can emerge when we become aware of what we are sensing, such as confidence, recognition, fear, attraction, and excitement.

We can sense things that do not generate emotions, but if we do they have no meaning, and thus no feelings—they draw a blank. When we hear someone speaking in a foreign language, we may simply shrug our shoulders. The emotion systems are part of the sensory machinery in the brain. Biologically, this means that our brain does not have any networks that represent a "blank" experience. If we have existing networks for an experience, or part of an experience, it can have meaning. If we do not, it will not.

Second Pillar: Remembering

Kolb called the second phase of the cycle *reflective observation*. Often in discussion of this concept, we focus on the *reflective* part. Overall, the term gives a strong feeling of thinking back, recalling experiences, searching for meaning, and mental freedom. There is no time limit on reflection, and no outside control over what we think about. We can reflect on whatever interests us, as long as we please.

Reflection does not exclusively engage any brain function or anatomic area of the cortex. However, *processing* our experiences engages the integrative regions of the cortex, in both the back and front. The processing itself utilizes the memory capabilities of the brain. The back regions are heavily engaged in formation and manipulation of long-term memory, and the front regions in manipulating and using working memory. To reflect, we recall and change our memories in a continuing and dynamic process. Recall and formation are both central in reflection. Ultimately, it seems that memory lies behind all aspects of reflection, thought, reasoning, and creativity—a true pillar of learning.

Emotional memories do not, on their own, guarantee learning. We may recall that an experience was emotional but still forget the details. In fact, some research suggests that the information in a memory may be physically separated from the emotion of the memory. This idea has been utilized in psychotherapy. Inhibition of the fear component of a traumatic memory, thought to involve the amygdala, can be achieved without affecting recall of the actual facts of the memory (Kindt, Soeter, & Verfliet, 2009). These discoveries are of great importance and may ultimately enhance the general effectiveness of psychotherapy.

Our goal in reflection is to discover both the facts and the emotions linked to memory of experiences. Those memories may have been drifting below our level of consciousness, so their discovery can add to our conscious understanding of experiences. One way to view reflection is to think of it as a search for meaning, based on our own experiential life.

This search cannot be forced. Conscious efforts at recall often fail. We are most likely to succeed if we can reduce distractions inherent in the busyness of daily life. One way to achieve that goal is to engage our brain in what we might call "mindless" activity, activity that engages our sensory and/or motor system but leaves the integrative cortex free. Some examples of these kinds of activities are taking a shower, walking the dog, knitting, and humming a tune. In terms of the learning cycle, the most important reflections are those that reveal a specific and meaningful concrete experience. Educators are most likely to succeed when they give their students the right kinds of experiences, those they cannot help thinking about.

When I say that reflection is a "search for meaning," I am claiming that memories emerging from reflection have emotional significance. That is why they are memorable. Their significance is found in how they make us feel. They may include long-forgotten fears or hopes, and discovering them may be comforting or provocative. In addition, the very process of reflection is in itself emotional. There is a feeling of freedom, and even joy, in exploring our own memories and discovering previously unrecognized meanings.

Another emotional aspect of reflective recall is the freedom from time pressure. We can, and do, recall and reflect on our experiences, throughout our life. No one, not even ourselves, can cut off our mental life. This relieves us of time pressures that we encounter in other aspects of the learning cycle, and in learning in general. Our concrete experiences are often specifically limited to a certain amount of time. The opportunity passes, or the conversation is over. The same is true of the later aspects of the cycle. Decisions are required, and things must be done. Only with this second pillar do we find relief from this pressure. This applies not only to specific and conscious reflective recall, but to all our internal and external experience. Revisiting is permitted, and often we find new meaning simply because the pressure is off.

Third Pillar: Theorizing

Reflection is productive when it begins to reveal new and deeper meanings in the purely sensory information of our concrete experiences. We begin to go beyond merely remembering what happened in the past to discovering new insights, ideas, and theories. This clearly differs from recall. It goes beyond the factual and declarative description of the past 'and leads to thoughts and proposals about the future. It is less passive and receptive, and more linked to choice and action. It is decisive and inventive.

This division between past and future, information and ideas, observations and predictions is a central element of learning. It could be a major factor in explaining the difference between the brain of humans and that of other primates. Our survival as a species depended on these capabilities. They allow us to assess our own learning as well as that of others. Consciously moving from simply recording experiences to actively changing and designing them is a major factor in assessing learning, both in experiential and in formal settings. When we can *do* something with our information rather than just repeat it, we come much closer to actually demonstrating learning.

The structure of the brain reflects this division between the receptive and the active. When we utilize the theorizing pillar of learning, we also use regions of the cortex that anatomists define as "frontal." This is in contrast to the regions of the cortex in the back of the head that are more dedicated to sensing and remembering. In fact, the most striking line of functional division in the cortex is the boundary between the somatosensory and the primary motor (sensing the body and moving the body). It divides the cortex into a front half and a back half, and that structural feature is reflected in the functional role of each half.

The emotional aspect of theorizing may be more compelling than that of any of the other pillars. Engaging mental functions such as *choosing, imagining, judging, planning,* and *creating* (among others) has been linked with activity in the front regions of the cortex and often activates the positive emotion systems. We love our ideas. We believe in our choices. We are anxious to try out our plans. We eagerly anticipate the future.

Frontal regions of the cortex in the human brain are thought to be the most recent to emerge in evolution. So it is not surprising to find that the functions most identified with intelligence, and thus with our species, primarily engage this part of the brain. These are the "higher-order" capabilities and are most advanced in the most "highly evolved" parts of the human brain.

However, a collection of much more ancient brain structures is also essential to these advanced human capabilities. As discussed earlier, the "collection" consists of a highly complex aggregate of physically distinct structures, which together are called the *basal ganglia*. There are three somewhat separate parts of the basal ganglia, one of which is most important to this discussion. It is called the *nucleus accumbens.* More than any other brain structure, the nucleus accumbens interacts with our positive emotion chemical, dopamine.

The nucleus accumbens is also involved in control of voluntary actions—movement. It is one area of the brain that malfunctions in Parkinson's disease. In this condition, there is a reduced impact of dopamine, which leads to a loss of control over many motor (movement) functions. Thus, in the nucleus accumbens, we see a link between positive emotion and control of action. The brain system that gives us our ability for purposeful movement (e.g., using a fork to eat our dinner) also gives us the greatest potential for reward. Movement and reward may be linked.

In earlier work, I extended this idea beyond physical control and movement to the concept of "mental movement." It is exciting and rewarding to *imagine* progress and movement toward a mental goal. This is one reason we enjoy stories: A good story sets up a goal. We want justice, we want reconciliation, we want love. The reader wants to see progress, movement toward the goal. If there is none, boredom sets in. In education, learners feel reward when they know that they are making progress. They have a mental goal and a desire to achieve it. If they feel blocked or stagnant, the reward diminishes and we begin to see a lack of interest.

The third pillar is strongly supported by the positive emotion system.

Fourth Pillar: Testing With Action

Mental theories must be tested by "doing." Left to themselves, they ultimately become sterile. They have been called "inert knowledge" (Whitehead, 1929). The third pillar of learning, the hypothesizing aspect, provides ideas and beliefs to test. However, going beyond identifying "what" we will test, and then initiating the testing process, is not automatic. Perhaps more than any of the pillars, testing with action takes awareness and intention. We must identify our theories, which is often difficult. In addition, we must do the work of designing actions that will directly and actively test our theories.

The fourth pillar not only completes one cycle of learning but also triggers the beginning of a second one. Active testing is, in itself, concrete experience. It is something we do, and its results are perceived with our sensory brain. We design and carry out actions that are purposeful and that, when executed, give us new concrete experiences. The testing experiences become part of a new cycle. If testing demonstrates that our theories are flawed, we will create new ones. In so doing, we will experience both the cognitive and emotional aspects of that new experience. On the other hand, if the results of our testing support our original theory, we can build on them and get new insights and ideas. Active testing gives us insight into our original thoughts and also automatically initiates a new cycle. Its impact is in both directions of the cycle; it affects both what has gone before and what will happen next.

Despite its essential and powerful impact on learning, learners often resist the active-testing phase. Because we love our theories, we may object to anything that questions them or suggests that we should modify them. This seems to be especially true of university faculty members. In my experience, it is the most frequent objection to the learning cycle. "I know when my ideas are right," they claim. "I don't need to test them."

This resistance is remarkable, especially when we find it in the "expert." Individuals who have spent their lives building knowledge about a subject may reject what is arguably the most important and valuable aspect of learning. Even when we know that we should be happy to discover error, our ownership of ideas often prevents us from acknowledging it.

The emotional nature of the fourth pillar is compelling. We are strongly attached to the ideas and plans that we ourselves invent. Thus, the possibility that they might be mistaken generates tension and conflict in our mind. If we are going to test our theories, we need to overcome those emotional barriers through determination and committed energy. There are also elements of positive emotion attached to active testing. If it does not conflict with our ideas, it is very satisfying. As we await the outcome of active testing, there is great anticipation as well as second guessing. We find ourselves evaluating our own work, looking for errors, and discovering lessons that we have learned. As I stressed in *From Brain to Mind* (Zull, 2011), the emotions associated with ownership emerge in great force when we actively test our ideas.

My Culture Change

Let us go back to the story at the beginning of this chapter. That story gave some very clear examples of behavior, emotion, and learning in a context of dramatic culture change.

An obvious, but sometimes forgotten, point is the emotional impact of a sudden change in culture. For a novice, this change may be sensed almost unconsciously, creating discomfort without the person actually identifying its cause—a classic amygdala effect. The precise and specific differences in a new culture may not be identified immediately, but the emotional brain will nonetheless begin to process the new environment via its primary sensory systems. The rapid response of the amygdala may then lead to subconscious behaviors such as fight or flight.

In my story, I knew that the environment at the appliance store was very different from that at home. I sensed it right away, but it took a while to realize what some of the differences were. I felt very uncomfortable but did not know exactly why. I attribute my emotions to the power and speed of my sensory brain. I sensed difference almost instantly by its effect on the emotion systems in my brain.

The discomfort of the new culture was the force that drove me to worry about my job and the store. I began to think about it a lot. This was not my normal behavior. To that point, I had been a typical teen, excited and energized by each new day, looking forward to seeing my friends, with no worries or concerns. Now my behavior changed: I became quieter at home and more analytical about my workplace and job. I became more reflective.

My reflections consisted primarily of memories, the second pillar of learning. I remembered experiences from my home life and experiences at the store. Those memories were not accessed immediately, but as I continued to reflect they continued to grow and find their way into my conscious mind. They became material for more thought, which in turn again brought up more memories.

After a period of reflection, inevitably I began to form a theory. I brought in the third pillar of learning. My theory had two parts. First, I theorized that my discomfort was directly related to Mike and Sam. Pinning the problem on them was not hard. Second, I theorized that I would be more comfortable if I mimicked them. That would require me to change my behavior.

Once I had my theory, it was not long before I began to try it out. I brought in the fourth pillar of learning: testing my theory by changing my actions. If I did not test it, it really would have no use at all; it would be just a bit of "inert knowledge." My emotions were driving my behavior, leading me to action. There were both positive and negative emotions at work. One was a hope that I would fit in and be more comfortable. But I was also plagued by doubts and somewhat frightened. I hoped that my theory was correct but what would I do if it was not? These new behaviors really were not me.

Once I began actively testing my theory, I encountered a whole new set of emotions, and those drove me to new ideas, and another turn of the learning cycle. The testing produced new experiences and my awareness of them via my sensory brain led me to new thoughts and new theories. It started a long process of cycling that continues to spin today. I still remember those experiences and invent new theories about them.

Study Abroad: What Are We Looking For?

As discussed by Vande Berg, Paige, and Lou in chapter 1, a great deal of the concern about the value of study abroad is based on student perceptions of change in affective elements of their own mind—their perception was (is) that they were *transformed*.

In my prior work, I discuss the concept of transformation and change. The very title of my first book, *The Art of Changing the Brain* (Zull, 2002), arises from the idea that learning is change, that this change occurs in the brain, and that it is or can be transforming. However, the word *transformation* implies more than change, and it is important to develop a common understanding of its meaning here. We face a key question: What do we mean by transformation?

I suspect that a student's answer to this question may differ from that of a faculty member. It seems likely that the change we, as faculty, are looking for is more profound and more compelling than students imagine, and perhaps more than we ourselves realize. Transformation is deep and abiding change that occurs when we truly grasp something new and use it in our life. That change emerges as we progress through the learning cycle, demonstrating itself in our actions, beliefs, and behaviors. Furthermore, the reality of transformation may not be apparent for years; knowledge of its existence may not ever reach our consciousness.

Study abroad may well be the beginning of such transformation. If this is so, we must be wary of our methods and timing in assessing the impact of study abroad. We should look beyond "cognitive change" and attend to change in emotion and instincts, "affective change." We should also remember and value the centrality of emotion and its role as the foundation of cognition. In study abroad, we may lay this foundation, but the superstructure of actions and behaviors it will eventually support may not become apparent immediately. In assessing whether study abroad is transforming, we must be patient.

Revisiting Study Abroad and the Brain Cycle

Let's examine the learning cycle further in the special case of study abroad, emphasizing the emotional aspects relevant to the four pillars of learning. This may lead us to new insights about experiential learning, as well as ideas about how to improve both study abroad and, perhaps, other such programs in higher education.

Study Abroad and the Sensory Brain

The term *sensory cortex* refers to the regions of the cerebral cortex that first *receive* information about the nature of the environment. That information is gathered via the sense organs, such as the eyes or ears, and is sent to the cortex by internal neuronal pathways. These pathways run parallel to one another, thus providing a very powerful way to gather complex data at high speed. Once this information reaches the cortex, it is integrated into complete images and other patterns that originate in the same fashion. The human brain can be exquisitely sensitive to small changes in the environment, or totally miss them. But, whether or not we pay attention to possible changes, they still may have an impact or record a pattern.

When a student travels to an unfamiliar destination, the student's cortex receives a great deal of information in the way I just described. However, the meaning of the information is determined by the student's prior experiences. If the new information does not match the old, or if it is totally novel, the amygdala may be activated, leading to feelings of uncertainty or even fear. On the other hand, a student can be energized by the new culture, resulting in excitement and positive emotions. However, in that case the student may also experience high levels of distraction, interfering with work and study habits in unpredictable and subconscious ways. This kind of response seems to be the basis for the concern that study abroad may become an extended "vacation."

It is important to recognize that the brain responses to the "home culture" have been developing over a lifetime. The behaviors and emotions associated with it are embedded and will not necessarily change immediately, if at all. If the culture change is significant, this effect may last for unpredictable periods of time. Thus, a student who has developed healthy and productive habits at home may still be adjusting to the new culture at the end of a school term abroad without ever seriously getting back to academic work. In fact, the richer and more diverse the new environment is, the longer and more powerful are the distractions. A one-semester experience may not be long enough for a student to regain footing, no matter how well prepared the student, or his or her mentor, may be.

That possibility suggests that more planning, and *different planning*, may be needed. Some of the possible changes in both student and mentor planning are identified in the last few pages of this chapter.

Study Abroad, Memory, and Reflection

In *From Brain to Mind* (Zull, 2011), I stressed the centrality of memory in cognitive and emotional brain functions. Memory is a major pillar of learning, but it does not equal learning; it is just one of the pillars.

Study abroad may require us to adjust our memories, to form new ones but forget others. Thus, we encounter two barriers: (a) increased awareness of habitual behaviors; and (b) selection of behaviors that we may wish to alter, eliminate, or add. For example, a student who undertakes study abroad in Germany may have the habit of engaging in open discussion during lectures, whereas in the German culture, a professor may not expect or approve of this behavior. Thus, the student may find it necessary to forget that behavior in the classroom, although remembering it in his or her private studying. This challenge is one of *selective* memory formation and/or selective weakening. What to remember, and what to forget.

The value of reflection may rest primarily in leading to relevant memories. Reflection can lead to their discovery. In *The Art of Changing the Brain* (Zull, 2002), I present a model for such discovery. As I mentioned earlier in this chapter, that model depends on engaging both sensory and motor brain with routine or mundane tasks (e.g., looking out a window while knitting).

Under these conditions there is less demand on the integrative cortex, and it can continue to activate existing networks in a quasi-random or purposeless manner. This increases the probability that previously hidden or weak networks will be revealed and become relevant to the learner's experience. This theory of reflection is supported by research that indicates the existence of a "default network" that fires even when not activated by new sensory experience (Mason, Norton, Van Horn, Wegner, Grafton, & Macrae, 2007). The activity may trigger weak firing of entire networks that is not intense enough to reach consciousness, so-called *implicit* memory.

Here, our objective is to help students who travel abroad have both time and method for reflection. Students should be aware of the key role of reflection in learning and develop the habit of thinking about their experiences. Faculty members can provide guidance regarding this pillar of learning. However, if those mentors do not themselves subscribe to the value of reflection, the challenge will be great.

Reflection and discovery of such neuronal networks also get us closer to the actual substance of knowledge. As I argue in *From Brain to Mind* (Zull, 2011), if knowledge is networks and networks generate patterns such as images and melodies, then reflection often brings up the actual pattern for the knowledge or some element of it. This may be one of the reasons that images are so easy to remember (Kosslyn, 1994). Rather than symbols of knowledge such as those that compose language, the initial "raw" image is the most fundamental aspect of representations of the perceived environment.

Study Abroad and the Pillar of Theorizing

If students are able to reflect as discussed in the previous section, they will not only discover relevant and useful memories, they will also begin to develop new ideas and theories about their experience. This is the next step in deeper learning.

Although reflecting and theorizing were separated in our earlier discussion of learning, that separation is artificial in some aspects. These brain processes (reflection, theorizing) are dynamic, fluid, and linked to one another. As I explain in *The Art of Changing the Brain* (Zull, 2002), there is extensive wiring carrying information both forward and backward between the regions of the brain cortex that are heavily engaged by these cognitive functions. Edelman (1992) has stressed this process of "reentry" and its centrality in cognitive mapping. For example, he suggests that processing information in the theorizing regions of the cortex (front regions) may have as much or even more impact than the actual sensory experience itself (back regions). This may be why our theories often seem to be more important than our actual sensory experiences. We may believe our mind more than our eyes.

Without the appearance of such ideas, plans, and theories, reflection is sterile; it leads nowhere. Thus, it is important for students and their mentors to consciously encourage the emergence of *new* "thoughts" and connections as time goes by in study abroad. If this abstraction and theorizing does not emerge in the student's work, direct and conscious efforts to catalyze it can become part of any proposed faculty guidance.

It is also important that students be aware of their own processing and theorizing. This awareness is part of "metacognition," which is discussed in the next section. Awareness of our own mental processes is perhaps the greatest step in developing mental maturity, and thus *transformation*. The human brain seems to be the only place in the universe where such a process occurs. I suggest that its development is key in programs of study abroad.

Study Abroad and Active Testing

In general, students in study abroad programs should know the learning cycle and be metacognitive about it, blending the cycle with their new daily life and experiences. It seems likely that many of the perceived shortcomings of study abroad programs are the result of a shallow experiential base, in which most of the mental attention is paid to new experiences without further reflection or creative effort. Enjoyable, and potentially rich, experience is not adequately processed in a metacognitive way.

One of the best and most powerful ways for students to become more metacognitive is to consciously and actively test their new theories. To achieve this last step in the learning cycle, students must first recognize and analyze their own mental life as it relates to study abroad. Passive recognition is not adequate; it must be connected to action. Preparation for the study abroad experience should include developing the habit of intentional introspection by the student, followed by actions that test new ideas and awareness of this process, both by students and by faculty advisors.

Challenges

The neuroscience approach provides us with some clear-cut challenges in study abroad. Four of them are discussed in the following sections.

Constructivism

Because knowledge is constructed from prior experience, the meanings that people make of specific experiences are highly diverse and individual. The network patterns in individual brains are the product of experience; no two individuals have the same experience, so no two brains have the same networks. This presents a major challenge in study abroad. Behaviors that characterize the home culture are deeply embedded and may be operating at a subconscious level. It may be a challenge even to identify them. It is difficult to construct effective and appropriate new neuronal patterns using such widely different foundations. Add to that the difficulty of comprehending and then beginning to practice what those new patterns are. This in itself may take more time than is normally allotted to study abroad programs.

The Role of Emotion

Our brain perspective makes us vividly aware of the connection between cognition and emotion. On the time scale of evolution, our modern brain has emerged as a combination of some ancient brain structures extensively entangled with emotional behaviors, and more recent ones that endow us with cognition. The ancient ones retain their function of modulating the recent ones. Thus, the cognitive content of experiences is stabilized when those experiences stimulate the emotions. Learning and memory are greatest when cognition and emotion work together. In any educational setting, the goal is to activate this synergistic system.

In terms of study abroad programs, this presents an interesting challenge. It suggests that learning will be best when the experience naturally engages the student. It may not be important whether the experience is positive or negative, as long as it is interesting. In general, the chance for this to occur is greatest in novel environments. It is not necessary that the student be consciously aware of the novelty, or even that it be identified with language. Our sensory systems can influence us in powerful, but still subconscious, ways.

The goal of engaging the emotions presents the challenge of identifying the novel, or the interesting, for the student. This is not trivial because if constructivism is valid the experiential knowledge of each person is different. What is novel for one can be boring for another. This challenge is undoubtedly amplified by technology, because it is more and more common for students to share knowledge about places and people. Thus, part of the "preparation" for study abroad proposed in chapter 1 and earlier in this chapter may well have to include deeper knowledge about past experiences of individual students, and the use of that information to help identify what is novel.

What Has Value?

Another challenge presented by the inclusion of both cognition and emotion in educational experiences is determining what experiences have academic value. Not surprisingly, it is clear that mentors and faculty members almost automatically attribute value to what they consider intellectual rather than experiential. Some topics suit their preferences; others do not. Here are examples:

> Suitable: Language, academic subjects, appreciation of the culture, enrichment of the home curricula
>
> Unsuitable: Parties, play, entertainment, exotic foods, "vacations," romantic activities, travel

Note that, in general, those that suit are hard work and cognitive, whereas those that do not are easy and emotional. Thus, if we accept nature's message that cognition and emotion must come together for learning, we may have work to do. For example, we may need to ask questions such as, "Is anything learned on a vacation?" Or, "What might students learn at a party—academically?"

My own suggestion about what has value is that we consider the whole experience, not just the academic content. As I wrote in *The Art of Changing the Brain* (Zull, 2002), there is a kind of "teaching trap" revealed by our considerations of the brain and learning. Because of his or her unique life experiences, it is difficult to control what catches the attention of any particular person. Our brains all have different networks, and those networks trap new experiences in unknown and unpredictable places, whether we intend it or not. We have relatively little control over what catches the attention of our own mind, let alone that of others. It is a trap to imagine that we know what a person has learned from any experience. This applies whether we study at home or study abroad. Answering the "value" question is not easy.

Preparation

Finally, let me remind you of two challenges in preparing students for study abroad that I discussed earlier in this chapter. First, we should think about the concept of the learning cycle itself, particularly as it emerges when we consider the actual physical process of learning in the brain. My personal experience is that this approach catches the interest of students in a unique way. There is a strong appeal in thinking about learning as a physical process and applying that idea to their own brain. This is illustrated in the following comments from a student in my class a few years ago:

> I never thought that learning is physical. It made all the difference when I realized this. I began to work on school learning the same way I would on any physical skill. I put in more effort, and I was more aware of my effort, just like I did when I was learning a new sport. I used to struggle to get a B average, and now I am getting As.

And for study abroad, I stress the *reflection/memory* aspect of the cycle. It is of particular importance because the time constraints of travel and adaptation to new cultures work against it.

Second, it is particularly appropriate and useful for students to learn about metacognition in preparation for study abroad. This goes under the heading of self-knowledge and is arguably the most remarkable brain function yet identified. Study abroad offers many opportunities for personal growth and understanding of ourselves. What better idea than to study one's self while abroad?

References

Bozarth, M. A. (1994). *Pleasure systems in the brain.* Retrieved from http://wings.buf falo.edu/aru/ARUreport01.htm

Edelman, G. M. (1992). *Bright air, brilliant fire* (pp. 85–90). New York: Basic Books.

Gaffan, D. (2005). Widespread cortical networks underlie memory and attention. *Science, 309,* 2172–2174.

Kandel, E. L. (2006). *In search of memory: A new science of mind* (pp. 165–180). New York: Norton.

Kindt, M., Soeter, M., & Verfliet, B. (2009). Beyond extinction: Erasing human fear responses and preventing the return of fear. *Nature Neuroscience, 12,* 256–260.

Kolb, D. A. (1984). *Experiential learning.* Englewood Cliffs, NJ: Prentice Hall.

Kosslyn, S. M. (1994). *Images and brain.* Boston, MA: MIT Press.

LeDoux, J. E. (1998). *The emotional brain: The mysterious underpinnings of emotional life.* New York: Simon & Schuster.

Mason, M. F., Norton, M. I., Van Horn, M. I., Wegner, D. M., Grafton, S. T., and Macrae, C. N. (2007). Wandering minds: The default network and stimulus-independent thought. *Science, 315,* 393–396.

Thorpe, S. J., & Fabre-Thorpe, M. (2001). Seeking categories in the brain. *Science, 291,* 260.

Wexler, B. E. (2006). *Brain and culture.* Cambridge, MA: MIT Press.

Whitehead, A. N. (1929). *The aims of education and other essays.* New York: The Free Press.

Zhu, J., & Thagard, P. (2002). Emotion and action. *Philosophical Psychology, 15,* 19–36.

Zull, J. E. (2002). *The art of changing the brain: Enriching teaching by exploring the biology of learning.* Sterling, VA: Stylus.

Zull, J. E. (2011). *From brain to mind: Neuroscience as a guide to change in education.* Sterling, VA: Stylus.

8

ANTHROPOLOGY, INTERCULTURAL COMMUNICATION, AND STUDY ABROAD

Bruce La Brack and Laura Bathurst

In this chapter we review the historical development of two schools of thought that inform current beliefs and practices about how to best prepare students to study, live, and work abroad. We also examine their theories that seek to characterize how humans make sense of the world and each other in cross-cultural situations. More specifically, we focus on the related but distinct fields of anthropology and intercultural communication, two disciplines that have had a significant impact on the applied world of international education and training and, by extension, on intercultural learning in study abroad.

Over the past century within the United States two major approaches to study abroad have been established, one derived from anthropology and the other from intercultural communication. The intertwined histories of these two fields, coupled with increasingly easier, faster, more diverse, and cheaper travel opportunities, have combined to influence the worldwide international educational exchange activities known today as "study abroad." As these important but often divergent theories have been applied to cross-cultural training for study abroad, they have given rise to conflicting ideas about how the intercultural explorations of experiential learners can best be supported.

During anthropology's initial formative period in the United States, in the late 1800s and early 1900s, a major ideological shift took place in the field that would significantly influence study abroad decades later: Anthropology abandoned ethnocentric, unilineal evolutionary perspectives in favor of cultural relativist positions. This approach favored sensitive, respectful, cultural exploration enacted through participant observation field research, aspects that eventually found their way into study abroad. In the late 1960s, another major ideological shift began to influence study abroad as some institutions and organizations began to move gradually from a laissez-faire attitude toward the study abroad experience to a much more actively managed process, heavily influenced by intercultural communication. As a result, current training and institutional support have come to stress an integrated and guided approach to the culture-learning process, and study abroad sponsors have increasingly favored delivering "interventionist" training from predeparture through post-reentry. Recent research results from several large-scale and sophisticated assessment projects clearly indicate that better student outcomes in study abroad experiences are achieved when appropriate "interventionist" strategies are employed. The question of how we have arrived at this current state of affairs, and what anthropology and intercultural communication have contributed—collectively and separately—to current approaches, is the topic of this chapter. What we provide here is a brief overview of two distinct disciplines, examining how they became intertwined in the context of developing and providing training for students participating in study abroad activities.

Until recently, little research attention has been paid to the interaction *between* anthropological ideas and methods and those of intercultural communication, or to the corresponding integration of these approaches into the preparation of students for study abroad. Although intercultural communication has borrowed and adapted extensively from vast anthropological, methodological, and theoretical resources, anthropology has not reciprocated to any significant extent. Most anthropologists today are either oblivious about the field of intercultural communication or vaguely critical of it. As a result, those familiar with the intercultural field tend to be familiar with how much it has borrowed from anthropology and to acknowledge that intellectual debt. It is the rare anthropologist, however, who chooses to incorporate intercultural communication theories, conceptual categories, or insights into his or her own teaching, training, or research.

Nevertheless, when one focuses on how undergraduate students are increasingly being prepared to study abroad, at least in North America (and parts of Europe and Asia), a perceptive observer can discern the continuing influences and importance of both anthropology and intercultural theory and practice to pre-departure and reentry courses. It is important to note that we are limiting our discussion here to *outbound* study abroad activities and programs, although concepts and practices derived from both disciplines can easily be adapted to cross-cultural orientations for incoming international students. Our main goal in this chapter is to discuss several of these key theoretical threads and their corresponding approaches, and to outline why using both "tool kits" is likely to result in considerable synergy. Indeed, when combined with a commitment to "interventionist" models and careful critical outcomes assessment, the potential gains in student learning and positive experiences abroad are likely to be substantial.

Early Foundations of Anthropology and the Role of Fieldwork

While all starting points are somewhat arbitrary, when examining the historical development of study abroad theory and practice, the influence of anthropologist Franz Boas and his students is unmistakable and offers a good place to begin. It is clear that a number of fundamental theoretical foundations for anthropology, which were subsequently adopted by intercultural communication theory, were invented or further elaborated by Boas. Widely considered the father of American anthropology, Boas played an important role in establishing a new kind of academic anthropology beginning at the end of the 19th century and continuing during the first four decades of the 20th century (Barth, Gingrich, Parkin, & Silverman, 2005; Harris, 1968). During his distinguished career, Boas established anthropology on both a more scientific and more humanistic basis, advocating a relativist approach to understand how each culture creates its own meanings and is worthy of our understanding. He was an empiricist and an avid ethnographic fieldworker, prescribing a host of ways to observe, record, compare, and understand human beings that were novel in his day. He was also a believer in the malleability and utility of culture and a social activist.

Boas's contributions to anthropology were numerous, but the most relevant to the history of study abroad are his attention to the concept of "culture" and his emphasis on the necessity of anthropological fieldwork. The foundational work of Boas and his students in re-conceptualizing "culture" set the stage for the birth of intercultural communication and the institutionalization of experiential culture-learning through immersion. The roots of contemporary approaches to interventionist study abroad can be seen as reflecting both of these important contributions.

Anthropological Fieldwork as Study Abroad

At the time when Boas was gaining prominence in the study of human societies around the world, many of his colleagues were practicing "armchair anthropology," drawing most of the data on which their anthropological knowledge was constructed from the accounts of travelers (explorers, missionaries, merchants, soldiers, journalists, colonial administrators, etc.). Boas was quite vocal in challenging the validity of a "science" based on such unsystematic and potentially biased data collection techniques, and he advocated for an anthropology based on firsthand data collection in the field. Indeed, his own journey from physicist to anthropologist—he had written his doctoral dissertation on the color of water—stemmed from a transformational "study abroad" year doing fieldwork among the Baffin Island Inuit.

Overtly "anti-theory," Boas believed that the errors of the 19th-century evolutionists were largely due to faulty data, and he advocated a suspension of "grand theory" building in anthropology until sufficient reliable data could be systematically collected by trained researchers in the field. Ironically, at the same time that he was cautioning against extrapolation from data, he was beginning to provide the methodological and philosophical means to generate the ethnographic facts that would eventually provide exactly the kind of data necessary to make more general ethnological statements about how humans view and organize their lives.

Boas founded the first academic anthropology department in the United States in 1888 at Clark University and the first anthropology PhD degree program in 1899 at Columbia University. He remained at Columbia until his retirement in 1936, training a generation of students devoted to anthropological fieldwork who later became leaders in the field. Boas was certainly not the only early anthropologist to recognize the value of learning about a culture firsthand. However, he was key in establishing fieldwork as both a rite of passage and a fundamental element of becoming a cultural anthropologist in the United States.

Boas institutionalized what eventually became a common expectation and practice of *anthropological study* abroad: ethnographic fieldwork. At first, however, he and his students engaged in research among Native American groups within U.S. boundaries. He argued that this "salvage anthropology" was urgent because of the rapid disappearance of native cultures. Numerous anthropologists have documented the strong, complex relationship between anthropology and colonialism, and the American anthropology of Boas and his students was certainly influenced by the internal colonialism and assimilationist policies of the U.S. government.

The emphasis on fieldwork was widely adopted in the early 1900s by anthropologists in the British and French traditions as well, who focused their research on their own colonized populations. Until the 1920s, however, field research was typically limited to a period of months. Long-term ethnographic fieldwork of a year or more became the anthropological ideal after the 1922 publication of Bronislaw Malinowski's *Argonauts of the Western Pacific*. This classic ethnography was based on two years of ethnographic research that Malinowski conducted in the Trobriand Islands during three research trips between 1914 and 1920, when he was essentially stranded in Australia during World War I. The resulting monograph made a compelling case for long-term, highly detailed research and cultural immersion through *participant observation*, setting a new standard for anthropologists everywhere.

The tradition of ethnographic fieldwork has much in common with the development of student study abroad. Anthropologists have spent more than a century developing and refining research methods to enable practitioners to learn a culture while profoundly engaged within it. Much has changed since Boas and Malinowski experimented with ethnographic methods, yet many of their conclusions about the best techniques for learning a foreign culture made their way into the core assumptions that still structure student study abroad. Indeed, it seems almost "common sense" today to state that to learn another culture one should be immersed in it, learn the language, and avoid judging aspects of the other culture by the standards of one's own culture. However, the necessity of trying to understand the "native's point of view" (Malinowski, 1922), which we today consider to be a fundamental part of "intercultural competence," was not generally seen as important by the general public at that time.

Boas's insistence that knowledge of other cultures should be gathered through empirical fieldwork connects to his second major contribution to student study abroad: the concept of "culture." First Boas himself, and then his students, contributed key elements to the notion of culture, laying the groundwork for the emergence of intercultural communication as a distinct field of study. This rethinking and repositioning of the definition of culture represented a fundamental break with prior conceptualizations. The new model provided both anthropology and, eventually, study abroad with a perspective conducive to respectful inquiry.

Reworking the Culture Concept

Perhaps the most widely recognized contribution of Boas to the discipline of anthropology is the idea of "cultural relativity"—a concept that revolutionized the discipline. In the 1800s, anthropology had emerged as a distinct area of study, and evolutionary anthropology provided the dominant perspective. It was widely believed that all human societies passed through the same progression of stages, with the same technologies, kinship systems, religious systems, and so forth at each stage. Cultural difference was explained as the result of some societies existing at earlier stages than others. Early anthropologists spent significant time and energy attempting to classify human societies into a linear progression and arguing over whose classification system was best.

For the evolutionists, "culture" was synonymous with "civilized" and was something that societies gained as they progressed from simple to complex. It is no surprise that the pinnacle of civilization tended to be the society of the one doing the theorizing. Earlier European and American anthropologists (e.g., Lewis Henry Morgan and Edward B. Tyler) had first begun to explore the concept of culture and to popularize it, but it was Boas who effectively delinked it from "stages of evolution" and other theories of racial superiority or inferiority. Boas rejected the systematic racism of his time, specifically the ideas of racial hierarchies, unilineal evolution, and cultural "rankings" of societies from "savage" to "civilized" that dominated public discussions during that era.

Boas argued that the way of life of the people of each society developed as a result of the particular history of that society, a theoretical orientation that became known as "historical particularism." He believed that every society was equally complex—it was the blindness of the researchers, not the backwardness of the natives, that caused this complexity to be missed and misunderstood. Boas called this blindness "ethnocentrism," which meant the tendency of people to understand the world through their own cultural lens, and he introduced the idea of "cultural relativity" to anthropology. According to Boas, anthropologists needed to understand cultural differences from a relative perspective, or as Agar (1994) so succinctly puts it, as "expressions of alternative systems" (p. 57). In a sense, Boas had expanded the concept of "culture" from a singular to a plural form. In familiar terms, he shifted from "Big C" to "little c"—from *Culture* to *cultures* within the discipline of anthropology.

While Boas's introduction of the idea of the relativity of cultures marked a paradigm shift in anthropology, his "anti-theory" stance eschewed attempts to explain the data collected through ethnographic research, or to make culture-general conclusions or applications. However, by the 1930s, Boas's students, who dominated U.S. anthropology, were returning to theory building in force. Their foundational work in neo-evolutionary cultural ecology and culture and personality gained widespread followings in the discipline. It is the work of the latter set of anthropologists, interrogating the relationship between culture and psychology, that is relevant for our present purposes.

Margaret Mead's *Coming of Age in Samoa* (1928) and Ruth Benedict's *Patterns of Culture* (1934) were widely read; both were national best sellers at the time and highly influential. Mead, especially, popularized anthropology and redefined "culture" in general use to accord with anthropologists' understanding of the term, in contrast with previously accepted definitions of culture as "cultivated taste" or "the contents of a petrie [*sic*] dish" (Goldschmidt, 2000, p. 794). Further, these scholars reworked the concept of culture to refer primarily to unconscious cultural patterns shared by members of a group that guide their behavior and their interpretations of experience. This pushed "culture" even more firmly into the mental realm. Culture was no longer considered a collection of traits. It was now conceptualized as a set of "configurations" that could be identified through "national character" studies (e.g., Benedict, 1934, 1946), or the comparative study of language structure (e.g., Sapir, 1929; Whorf, 1941). They also sought to understand how such patterns were transmitted, often focusing on child-rearing techniques as a result of Sigmund Freud's influence. By the 1950s, the culture and personality "school" was essentially discarded in anthropology, and the culture and personality school's core concern with how culture is transmitted has become largely peripheral in anthropology ever since (Goldschmidt, 2000, p. 794).

Unfortunately, anthropology discarded some promising ideas in need of nuance, along with the less useful, when this area of intellectual inquiry was abandoned. But the emerging field of intercultural communication drew upon, developed, and applied similar key theories within a new framework, utilizing ideas such as those on values (e.g., Kluckhohn, 1951; Kluckhohn & Strodtbeck, 1961) and Cora DuBois's (1951) notion of "culture shock." These and other intellectual influences of key anthropologists and scholars from other disciplines found their way into the work of Edward T. Hall.

Emergence of the Field of Intercultural Communication

At the same time that Boas was reinventing aspects of anthropology, the field of study abroad was emerging from the "British Grand Tour" mentality, derived from the 18th-century practice of privileged young Englishmen filling their time between a university education and the beginning of a career with an extended tour of continental Europe. By the late 19th century, the Grand Tour had also become indigenized as an American phenomenon, and during the era between the post–Civil War and the turn of the century many wealthy and even middle-class Americans were taking such trips by ship and train. Essentially, this began the long process of transforming the independent Grand Tour into university-based study abroad programs.

The first student-based overseas travel and study programs that we would recognize today as "study abroad" were a later development, not widely available in the United States until the 1920s, and not common until the 1950s, ushered in as a part of the post–World War II travel and education boom. Although there were some notable early exceptions, until the 1960s there was very little activity that resembled cross-cultural training for study abroad program participants, and absolutely nothing that would qualify today as intercultural communication training (Hoffa, 2007).

Edward T. Hall: The Invention of Intercultural Theory and Training Implications

Perhaps the individual most crucial to the process of applying and adapting anthropological theory and categories beyond disciplinary boundaries is Edward T. Hall. Trained as a traditional anthropologist, Hall retained a preference for descriptive, qualitative research. However, throughout his life he sought to extend the scope and borders of how anthropology was applied, and proposed several major theoretical breakthroughs that changed the way "culture" and "communication" were conceptualized. Although he was also a graduate of Columbia University's PhD program (1942), his earlier life (1933-7) working for the U.S. Indian Bureau with Native American (e.g., Hopi and Navajo) construction crews in the Southwest confirmed a pattern of intense personal interaction with people who were culturally very different from him. Gifted with a contemplative and analytical mind, Hall had already generated insights about how culture was projected and expressed in communicative interactions, only part of which were verbal.

Hall continued his cultural observations during World War II, serving in the U.S. Army as an officer with an African American regiment in Germany and the Philippines, then continued his research throughout Europe, the Middle East, and Asia into the mid-1950s. From 1950 to 1955, he served in the Foreign Service Institute (FSI) of the U.S. State Department to develop intercultural communication skills for Foreign Service personnel (Leeds-Hurwitz, 1999, 2010; Rogers & Hart, 2002; Rogers, Hart, & Miike, 2002).

The combination of Hall's preference for practical and applied intercultural knowledge, and the need for Foreign Service Officers to be able to appropriately communicate with and supervise their international counterparts, led him to develop a whole series of "etic" (external) cultural categories (e.g., high- and low-context cultures, direct and indirect communication styles, polychronic and monochronic time) that have over time proved invaluable to many study abroad students. He is also considered the founder of the field of proxemics, and he wrote extensively about the multiple ways that silence and other nonverbal behaviors communicate important information between individuals.

Before Hall, the field of intercultural communication can be described as being in a pre-paradigmatic era (Martin, Nakayama, & Carbaugh, 2011). Although there were many earlier researchers who made contributions, there are few core concepts of "culture-general" comparative categories related to intercultural communication patterns that Hall did not originate or significantly elaborate. Within the FSI crucible, Hall designed new ways to explain, characterize, compare, and contrast cultural patterns to provide working professionals with simple, understandable, and immediately useful ways to facilitate communication across a wide range of cultures and contexts.

The training techniques and categories developed by Hall have been increasingly adapted by study abroad professionals as guidelines for the type of content essential for anyone intending to work, travel, or study abroad. However, Hall became estranged from the anthropological establishment and found little support for his insights and models among his contemporary professional peers. To this day, the flow of "culture-general" ideas, theories, and categories from the field of intercultural communication back into cultural anthropology has not taken place to any appreciable degree. The only exception might be Hall's work on the anthropology of space (proxemics) and the importance of nonverbal communication (including silence), which is still read and appreciated by anthropologists (e.g., Basso, 1970). Yet the work of Edward T. Hall provided essential conceptual underpinnings for the field of intercultural communication—derived, ironically enough, from an intellectual foundation of Boasian ideas and attitudes, and elaborated upon by Boas's disciples such as Margaret Mead and Ruth Benedict.

Anthropology's Divergence From Intercultural Communication

As Hall was laying the foundations of intercultural communication, key changes were occurring within anthropology that would take it in a different direction. Much of what made the rapidly developing field of intercultural communication especially relevant to study abroad was also what was to make anthropology especially hostile to intercultural theory and practice. In addition, two major shifts in anthropological theories in the second half of the 20th century made some anthropological frameworks challenging to apply, or irrelevant to use, in study abroad contexts. Nevertheless, anthropology continued to make contributions to the rapidly expanding area of international exchange in ways that complemented the approach of intercultural communication theory.

At the end of the 1940s, a new generation of Boasian anthropologists were assuming control of U.S. anthropology, and "salvage ethnography" was no longer the order of the day (Goldschmidt, 2000, p. 795). U.S. anthropology, increasingly drawing on sociological theory, was turning away from theories of cultural homogeneity and interrogating processes of social interaction. Ten years later, as intercultural communication emerged as a unique area of study, three major theoretical approaches dominated the discipline of anthropology: American cultural and psycho-cultural anthropology, British structural functionalism, and American neo-evolutionism (Ortner, 1984). It was through the blending of psychologically oriented U.S. cultural anthropology with sociological attention to social dynamics, or "culture in action," that intercultural communication was spawned. Hall's theories built upon the earlier work of Kluckhohn, Sapir, and others, integrating these ideas within an interactive framework.

Hall's theories were directed primarily toward interaction—"midlevel" social analysis (Bennett, 2010). Notably, although at midcentury U.S. anthropologists increasingly attended to social interaction with the incorporation of sociological theories, this shift did not lead to widespread appreciation of midlevel analyses. Rather, anthropological theory in the 1960s increasingly privileged the work of scholars uniting analyses of "high-level" cultural structures and the "low-level" beliefs and behaviors of individuals, and the primary focus of anthropological theory became the relationship between the two. Social interaction became firmly entrenched as "worthy of theorizing" in anthropology, but such theories were valued for illuminating the relationships between structures and individuals, not as an end in themselves.

Hall's lack of explicit engagement with the prevailing theoretical concerns in anthropology led to the lukewarm reception of his work by anthropologists. When Hall's ideas were well received by contemporaries, even positive reviewers tended to underline his marginal status with labels such as "creative," "provocative," and "maverick." The clash with prevailing theories within anthropology had the overall effect of leading the discipline in different directions, and, as a result, intercultural communication had to find an alternative disciplinary home.

In the second half of the 20th century, anthropological and intercultural theory diverged in other ways as well. Since the 1950s, anthropological theory had been dominated by emphases on meaning and materiality. "Meaning" refers to the ways in which humans make sense of the world, and "materiality" refers to relationships between humans and that world's physical realities. In the 1960s and 1970s, theoretical approaches tended to favor one over the other. The French structuralism of Claude Levi-Strauss, the interpretive anthropology of Clifford Geertz, and the symbolic anthropology of Victor Turner and Mary Douglas shared a primary concern with meaning; the cultural ecology of Leslie White and the political economy of Eric Wolf and Sidney Mintz, among others, emphasized materiality—at least at first.

By the 1970s, a growing number of scholars were intentionally working to collapse this separation through an explicit engagement with the topic of "power." The first version of such efforts was focused inward—"reflexive" anthropology. By the 1980s, anthropological attention to reflexive examination of the discipline of anthropology itself, which had been increasing since the 1960s, intensified. Scholars turned a critical eye to the processes of doing ethnographic fieldwork, writing ethnographies, and producing ethnographic knowledge. Analysis of the role of anthropology in the perpetuation of power structures (e.g., Asad, 1973) contributed to a deepening commitment by many anthropologists to refuse to engage in social science supportive of the status quo. Critiques of ethnographic objectivity and ethnographers' subjectivities (e.g., Clifford & Marcus, 1986; Rosaldo, 1989) set off a dominant strain of reflexive analysis, focused largely on deconstructing texts, which lasted until the end of the 1990s.

Attempts to build theories that attended simultaneously to mental meanings and material realities took an outward-looking form, as well. In the 1980s and 1990s, theories sparked by the ideas of Pierre Bourdieu, Michel Foucault, and others turned anthropologists' attention to the processes through which systems of inequality are produced and reproduced through interrelated material and symbolic means—many of which pass unnoticed in daily life.

Little of this anthropological debate influenced study abroad. Further, the discipline's tendency to value and reward theoreticians more than practitioners left little professional incentive for anthropologists to care about international educational exchange. Individual anthropologists did engage in study abroad activities, and anthropological works, especially ethnographies, were used by interculturalists and some study abroad professionals to facilitate culture learning. But anthropologists, as a group, were not engaged with interculturalists during the period when intercultural communication theory and practice began to come of age, especially in study abroad contexts.

Intercultural Communication Theory Building and Study Abroad: 1975 to the Present

In a sense, intercultural communication theory and the field of study abroad grew, diversified, and matured together. Beginning in the mid-1970s, study abroad activity expanded significantly; destinations proliferated, institutions and providers refined and diversified their programs, nontraditional participants were recruited, and almost everyone increasingly paid attention to some form of cross-cultural training. Emerging intercultural communication concepts, training methods, and research results began to be applied within some study abroad training programs, albeit often unsystematically and/or sporadically. At the outset, the delivery of training was focused on preparing outbound students to adjust to new cultural contexts. However, training related to reentry and fostering post-experience learning slowly gained momentum and is now considered by some practitioners to be as important as, if not more important than, pre-departure activities.

Due to space constraints, we can only provide broad outlines of the development of various strands of intercultural communication theory by decade, and track the incorporation of new concepts and methodologies into study abroad preparation. Although these rough snapshots are unavoidably simplistic, they do capture the general trajectory as well as the interplay of the evolution of intercultural communication theory and its gradual adoption by increasing numbers of international educational exchange professionals.

The 1950s and 1960s, as noted earlier, are generally taken to be the founding decades of intercultural communication as a separate discipline, largely due to the conceptual work of E. T. Hall. Many disparate intellectual threads that coalesced in this period can be traced back almost a half-century. These decades saw the development of foundational definitions of culture shock, "curves of adjustment," and other processes applicable to study abroad.

The first half of the 1960s was a period of relative stasis from a theoretical perspective. Bennett (2010) notes, "Traditionalists and the experientialists were arguing over appropriate learning goals and teaching methods in university study abroad programs, an argument mostly uninformed by awareness" (p. 424). Nevertheless, innovative and integrative cross-cultural training, using intercultural and anthropological perspectives, was being developed in many academic and nonacademic venues including the Peace Corps, the East-West Center, the School for International Training, the U.S. Navy, and the former United States Information Agency. The concept of "re-entry" adjustment was also gaining attention, and the Canadian International Development Agency offered one of the first institutional reentry courses in North America.

In the 1970s, particularly in the last half of the decade, intercultural communication research increased significantly, although, as noted earlier, it is considered today as relatively atheoretical (Martin et al., 2011). Organizations and research groups dedicated to intercultural communication topics were founded (e.g., SIETAR: the Society for International Education, Training and Research), and the first intercultural communication texts, readers, and training manuals were being published. NAFSA (then, the National Association of Foreign Student Advisers) increasingly encouraged and supported training for both study abroad participants and international students and cosponsored the innovative Intercultural Communication Workshops (Bennett, 2010).

Intercultural communication training programs were begun at large (University of Minnesota, Twin Cities), medium (Portland State University, Oregon), and small (University of the Pacific, Stockton, California) institutions. Training was instituted at study abroad provider organizations including the service-learning Volunteers in Asia program at Stanford University (see Bryan, Darrow, Marrow, & Palmquist, 1972, 1975); the high school exchange sponsors American Field Service (AFS) and Youth for Understanding (YFU); and the American Heritage Association (now, AHA International) in Portland, Oregon. Early intercultural communication scholars such as Dean Barnlund and John (Jack) Condon were doing work in Japan that would eventually have an impact in the United States. In 1979, Kohls's *Survival Kit for Overseas Living* was published, and soon became the standard training guide for increasing numbers of U.S. American study abroad students. The first Stanford Institute for Intercultural Communication was held in 1975. It relocated to Portland, Oregon, in 1987 under the auspices of the

Intercultural Communication Institute, and continued to be a crucial training ground for study abroad professionals.

The 1980s proved to be a very productive continuation of the preceding decade. Intercultural communication theory building matured and proliferated, and the first U.S. research compilations related to intercultural communication were created. The first two collections of intercultural theory and an intercultural handbook were published, and were gratefully received by trainers and study abroad professionals as a source of training suggestions and examples of applied theory.

Scholars such as William Gudykunst, Milton Bennett, Richard Bristlin, Janet Bennett, Y. Y. Kim, Hiroko Nishida, Stella Ting-Toomey, and Richard Wiseman in the United States, and Geert Hostede in Europe, were developing theories, categories, and models that were quickly adapted and applied in cross-cultural training contexts, including, to some extent, in study abroad. Overall, interdisciplinary perspectives from anthropology, sociology, psychology, counseling, communication theory, linguistics, and English as a Second Language (ESL) were regularly incorporated into intercultural training throughout the decade, enriching the scope and giving rise to novel points of view and ways to convey them to varied audiences.

The use of "critical incident" methodology became popular during this period (e.g., Brislin, Cushner, Cherrie, & Yong, 1986) and was utilized in some study abroad programs as a way to help outbound students learn from their returning peers how to analyze and avoid similar problems in the future. Such cumulative knowledge was useful in building a "library" of critical incidents, not only for current students but also to store important institutional memory of common cross-cultural problems for later reference.

In academia, there were more than 200 intercultural communication courses offered in U.S. colleges and universities at this time, and study abroad cross-cultural training was becoming more common, although it tended to be largely concentrated in pre-departure orientations. The founding of the Intercultural Press in 1980 resulted in the publication and distribution of a large and useful collection of materials that were quickly utilized by some study abroad professionals as course texts, supplementary readings, and sources of cross-cultural training methodologies and exercises. Films and videos illustrating cross-cultural interactions and offering ways to categorize and understand other cultural patterns began to emerge, including the business-centered *Going International Series*, and *Cold Water*, focused on international student adjustment. They, too, were increasingly incorporated into study abroad training programs.

Other valuable sources of training materials were AFS-International and YFU, organizations whose missions were to promote international youth exchange for secondary students. Although designed for younger audiences, many university study abroad programs found these excellent compilations useful sources for college intercultural training programs (e.g., Grove, 1989). Michael Paige edited the seminal collection *Education for the Intercultural Experience* in 1993, which contains several articles specifically devoted to study abroad preparation and related activities.

In the mid-1980s, Milton Bennett conceptualized the Developmental Model of Intercultural Sensitivity (Bennett, 1986a, 1986b, 1993; see chapter 4 of this volume). He and Mitch Hammer later constructed the Intercultural Development Inventory, which was subsequently adopted by colleges and corporations to gauge orientations toward difference, as a diagnostic tool to ascertain a potential learner's readiness for cross-cultural training, and as a pre- and post-instrument to measure development from ethnocentric to more ethnorelative orientations. Other instruments useful for raising awareness about one's own cultural preferences and giving some indication of how well one might adapt abroad continued to be developed and employed in study abroad training contexts, including the Cross-Cultural Adaptability Inventory (Kelley & Meyers, 1995, 1999).

The 1990s was a decade when intercultural theory building and cross-cultural training, especially in the study abroad area, expanded and diversified exponentially. Ever more sophisticated media dealing with culture-general and intercultural communication topics appeared (e.g., *A Different Place: The Intercultural Classroom,* Wurzel, 1993), and the second edition of the *Handbook of Intercultural Training* (Landis & Bhagat, 1995) was published. The International Academy for Intercultural Research, founded in 1997, continued publishing *The International Journal of Intercultural Relations,* with frequent articles on study abroad topics providing both theoretical perspectives and applied materials.

It was also the first decade in which the problem of not having *enough* materials available for trainers and study abroad providers was transformed into a problem of facing a potentially confusing tidal wave of available resources. Paradoxically, this frequently made it *harder* for those without some prior knowledge and experience in the training field to select materials, sequence training activities, create integrated designs, and evaluate the effectiveness of intercultural training. During this time, concern for building and promoting intercultural competence was growing in importance, albeit slowly, and was being applied across a myriad of new settings—a trend that continued through the following decade. Training related to cultivating intercultural awareness and appropriate cross-cultural behavior began to be more widely adopted as a part of undergraduate college general education requirements, as well as in counseling, health care, corporate assignment preparation, and study abroad preparation.

The first decade of the 21st century saw an unprecedented expansion in activities related to study abroad including

- An increase in both the volume of study abroad activities and the use of an intercultural focus in training for both orientation and reentry
- Institutional support for both intercultural training and its integration into study abroad
- Large-scale, collaborative, mixed-methods research related to study abroad outcomes and effectiveness
- The accelerated production of training materials
- Perhaps most revolutionary, the use of the Internet as a channel for distributing intercultural knowledge, and as a vehicle for delivering intercultural training anywhere, anytime, asynchronously

Basically, the integration of theory-based training into study abroad had come of age.

Issues of domestic and international diversity came to be widely regarded as two sides of the same theoretical coin, and the quest for ways to build intercultural competence became more intense. In the United States, it is probably safe to say that most study abroad programs offer some kind of pre-departure orientation, most of which include at least some discussion of topics related to or central to intercultural theory. The sheer volume of research, scholarship, program creation and evaluation, training models, and resources precludes a comprehensive review here, but many important developments and trends related to the utilization of intercultural theory in study abroad have been highlighted.

Concurrent with the explosive growth and diversification of study abroad was a major change in institutional support for the development of cross-cultural/intercultural training activities, and institutions' increasing commitment to provide both theory and content as part of their educational missions. NAFSA: Association of International Educators did this in a number of ways, including offering more theory-based and application sessions at its regional and national meetings, expanding its Trainer Core to include more intercultural professional courses, and creating additional opportunities for foundational and advanced workshops through its Intercultural Communication and Training Network. The creation of a new Teaching, Learning, and Scholarship (TLS) Knowledge Community within NAFSA focused on promoting theory-to-practice awareness. This led, in 2008, to the creation of the TLS Theory Connections: Intercultural Communication and Training section of NAFSA's online Resource Library, designed to explicitly link intercultural theory and current issues to campus orientation and reentry activities (www.nafsa.org/KnowledgeCommunity/default.aspx). Additionally, NAFSA has undertaken publication and/or distribution of books, pamphlets, and training-related materials to support its members' efforts to provide timely and effective training on intercultural topics.

The Forum on Education Abroad (FEA) was founded in 2001 to promote best practices in study abroad. The journal *Frontiers: The Interdisciplinary Journal of Study Abroad*, which was established in 1995 and later became a strategic partner of FEA, quickly became an essential resource of new theoretical ideas and all manner of research-reporting and cutting-edge discussions. The Forum subsequently published two excellent histories of study abroad in the United States (Hoffa, 2007; Hoffa & DePaul, 2010), created Standards of Good Practice, and developed a Quality Improvement Program (QUIP) for Education Abroad. It also partnered with several universities to advance research projects in an effort to promote understanding of what factors influence positive outcomes in study abroad.

Study abroad providers continued to develop programs and assessment guidelines that promote cultural competence including AFS, Council on International Educational Exchange (CIEE), and IES Abroad. In 1990, IES Abroad debuted the *IES Abroad MAP (Model Assessment Practice) for Study Abroad* (www.iesabroad.org/IES/Advisors_and_Faculty/iesMap.html), a comprehensive educational tool for designing and evaluating study abroad programs. The release of the fifth edition in October 2011 confirmed IES Abroad's ongoing support for holistic student learning, as do its Continuing Orientation and Reentry programs. CIEE and AFS have both developed "interventionist" intercultural training modules and programs to increase intercultural competence throughout their organizations, including materials developed for specific audiences (e.g., student participants, home-stay families, faculty, and in-country program directors and instructors).

Valuable handbooks continued to be published. Among the most useful for study abroad practitioners was the *Handbook of Intercultural Training* (Landis, Bennett, & Bennett, 2004). Included with the many authoritative articles in this collection is Paige's (2004) "Instrumentation in Intercultural Training," a review of 35 instruments that were available to educators. Another useful compendium is *The SAGE Handbook of Intercultural Competence* (Deardorff, 2009), which includes many articles related to study abroad. In addition, training instruments proliferated throughout the decade. One of particular interest to study abroad professionals was Hammer's Intercultural Conflict Style Inventory, an instrument that offers insight into how people respond to conflict. It can also be used by trainers to create awareness of the role of cultural conditioning upon individual responses to conflict (i.e., promoting a shift from "taking things personally" to recognizing "cultural styles").

In this period, program assessment became increasingly common and several large-scale, collaborative, mixed-methods research projects related to study abroad outcomes and effectiveness were undertaken. One of the largest and most interesting was the Georgetown Consortium study. (For a more detailed account of these exemplary research projects, see chapter 2 of this volume.)

Programs and materials continued to be developed, including the University of Minnesota's Maximizing Study Abroad (MAXSA) project, which resulted in publication of the book *Maximizing Study Abroad: A Student's Guide to Strategies for Language and Culture Learning and Use* (Paige, Cohen, Kappler, Chi, & Lassegard, 2002), and two accompanying guides for program professionals and language instructors. Further research was conducted using the MAXSA materials as the basis of a study abroad orientation course at the University of Minnesota (see chapter 13 of this volume).

The ultimate "game changer" in this decade was the rapid growth of online, web-based training, and the almost instant availability and utilization of information technology (Donnatelli, 2010). Free online materials became available such as those at the Peace Corps's "Culture Matters" website (Storti & Bennhold-Samaan, 1998), and the "What's Up With Culture?" website (La Brack, 2003). The latter website offered the first Internet training resource specifically targeting traditional-age U.S.-American study abroad students. This site, based on intercultural principles and theory, contains materials designed to help students from pre-departure orientation through reentry phases of study abroad. Since 2005, hundreds of additional sites have been created and distributed through the Internet (e.g., Rhodes, 2011).

Essentially, this means that materials are available to study abroad students anywhere, anytime. All manner of education and training will be significantly impacted by this new development, in ways that are both novel and challenging. Small study abroad offices that lack resources and/or expertise locally can potentially access and provide materials to their students at little or no cost. Large programs that simply cannot hold face-to-face orientations due to time, space, and schedule restrictions can hold "virtual" orientations whenever and wherever necessary.

It seems likely that the Internet may become the preferred channel for delivery of many kinds of data, feedback forums, journaling sites, knowledge content, self-assessment instruments, media (including audio files for iPods, as well as videos and pictures via smartphones and iPads), and direct "cultural mentoring" via services such as Skype. This is an exciting, evolving realm in education generally, but its implications for study abroad professionals seem limited only by our technical capabilities, computer savvy, and collective imaginations.

Where Are We Now?

The divergent histories of anthropology and intercultural communication that we have outlined in the previous sections have led to equally divergent conceptualizations of the goals of the study abroad experience. In anthropology, the success of a study abroad experience tends to be assessed by the degree to which the student emerges with a *deep understanding of the host culture.* Conversely, intercultural communication, although not neglecting the importance of learning the local culture, considers the acquisition and refinement of *general intercultural skills (competencies) that facilitate interaction* as the primary goal of study abroad. Intercultural communication promotes the acquiring of knowledge and perspectives that facilitate working successfully across cultural difference. This is also increasingly an explicit core goal of some study abroad programs. While both anthropology and intercultural communication place value on strategic intervention *during* the study abroad experience, two distinct approaches to such intervention arise out of their distinct histories and aims.

Training informed by intercultural communication theory seeks to assist students in interacting and functioning effectively in the host culture (a culture-specific goal) as a means to develop their abilities to *quickly function effectively in any intercultural situation* (a culture-general goal). These training interventions have two primary goals: to provide cognitive frameworks that facilitate empathetic interpretations of communication behavior in intercultural interactions, and to assist students in generating culturally appropriate behavior. They typically include topics such as communication and conflict styles; contrasting values sets; and the "D.I.E." model of description, interpretation, and evaluation of behavior. Another function of intercultural training is to provide emotional support to students so that cognitive learning is not blocked by too much emotional challenge. Examples of this type of support are the introduction of models of culture shock, and peer discussions about the experience, to lessen future feelings of isolation. While interculturalists and anthropologists share a desire to help students deepen their culture-specific knowledge and understanding of the host culture, interculturalists generally believe *it is the ability to interact effectively that makes such learning possible.*

Training arising from an anthropological approach to study abroad fosters methods that help students to gain a deep understanding *of a slice of the host culture* (a culture- and context-specific goal), as well as to develop a greater facility to *learn about any culture*, wherever they may find themselves in the future (a culture-general goal). This ability includes cultivating increased cultural awareness, which is meant literally, and refers to increased awareness of elements of human life that are cultural in origin but that are generally understood to be "natural," including, perhaps most important for many anthropologists, the student's view of his or her own culture. The focus is on "understanding" of self and others—not on the nature of the interaction. Anthropological intervention in study abroad tends to follow the model of a "field school," in which students learn and apply ethnographic methods, especially participant observation and formal and informal interviewing techniques. While anthropologists and interculturalists share a desire to help students function effectively in their host cultures, anthropologists generally believe that *an intimate and complex understanding of a culture, including detailed culture-specific knowledge, makes effective interactions in a host culture possible.*

Ethnographic techniques are ideally suited for achieving what Clifford Geertz refers to as "thick" description, a deep understanding of another culture. Indeed, this is exactly the principle that has guided their creation and refinement since Boas's time. Further, anthropologists tend to seek holistic—albeit admittedly partial—understandings of the interrelated workings of cultural systems. In contemporary anthropology, often special attention is paid to the relationships among social, ideological, and economic structures, and to the ways in which these structures shape and are shaped by the actions of individuals—in a word, attention turned to "power." Most anthropologists still expect to gain knowledge of complex cultural systems largely from firsthand interaction *within* the cultural system. Indeed, although anthropologists use a wide variety of methods in research, participant observation remains the gold standard because it is so well suited to produce this kind of knowledge.

In the study abroad context, the underlying assumptions that tend to guide anthropological, ethnographic-based study abroad programs with "field school" components are that longer-term experience in one location is more valuable than shorter-term experiences in multiple locations, and that immersion in a culture other than one's own will necessarily result in increased cross-cultural understanding. The second of these can appear to be a variant of the "contact hypothesis" that has been studied and refined by numerous scholars (and critiqued by others such as Thomas Pettigrew). In the most extreme form, this could produce a "hands-off," noninterventionist approach to study abroad. However, anthropologically oriented study abroad programs in which ethnographic work plays a primary role in structuring the experience for students are indeed interventionist. The anthropological knowledge guiding ethnographic methods, grounded in anthropological theory, is a kind of intervention—whether or not anthropologists recognize it as such. The continued tenacity of the "contact hypothesis" among anthropologists is striking and perhaps related to the conflation, in practice, of ethnographic research with more general immersion experiences, because anthropologists usually do both simultaneously.

Interculturalists, on the other hand, focus on the "interaction" as their preferred level of analysis and tend to understand "culture" as referring to the mental constructs, shared among members of groups, that guide the behavior of individuals as well as their interpretation of the behavior of others. Functioning more effectively in intercultural contexts is the overarching goal, and the knowledge needed to do so is gained through interaction with culture carriers—although it is not as context dependent as the anthropological approach necessitates.

Although many institutions incorporate, to some extent, anthropological perspectives and methods along with intercultural communication theory and practice into their student preparation, rarely are both approaches deeply integrated in the same study abroad program. An early example of such integration began in 1976 when one of the authors (La Brack) initiated a process at the University of the Pacific, Stockton, California, that resulted in the establishment of a longstanding, for-credit, required, cross-cultural training program for study abroad. The program is the oldest example of its type in the United States and continues to this day within the School of International Studies (SIS).

Pacific's cross-cultural training courses were the first to explicitly link together pre-departure orientations and reentry components (La Brack, 1993), and to require completing both as a graduation requirement within SIS. (For a detailed account of the founding and evolution of this program see chapter 11 of this volume.) Because La Brack was an anthropologist by training, it was a natural progression to use both anthropological methods and resources (including ethnographies, field methods, and cultural categories) in these courses, and to incorporate the emerging literature on intercultural communication as it became available. All SIS students take a cultural anthropology course as a part of their core requirements, so an instructor can be sure that at least some of the prospective study abroad participants will have a grasp of its theoretical basics by the time they are preparing to enter the study abroad process. Over time, the emphasis on the more anthropological aspects within the study abroad preparation courses has been reduced and replaced by an increased reliance on intercultural communication theory, concepts, and tools.

In 1995, at Azusa Pacific University in Azusa, California, another innovative program balancing anthropological and intercultural principles began. The faculty and administration, under the leadership of Dr. Richard Slimbach, developed and implemented a unique interdisciplinary academic major: Global Studies. It includes study abroad preparation that extends across a student's entire academic program and integrates fieldwork components beginning domestically in central Los Angeles (L.A. Term), and concluding internationally with an overseas study component (Global Learning Term). Their international study abroad settings are largely situated in non-Western communities within Latin America, Africa, or Asia. Embedded throughout the curriculum over the entire four-year academic program, basic anthropological approaches and tools are continually referenced and applied, as are concepts and models from intercultural communication. Students in the Global Studies Program are continually challenged to apply conceptual knowledge to an interpretation of complex social realities, and to do so while negotiating the stress of living and learning in unfamiliar milieus. This program is certainly one of the most interesting, sophisticated, complex, integrated, and conceptually rich undergraduate majors in the United States and is explicitly interventionist in its approach to study abroad (Slimbach, 2005, 2010, 2011).

Another excellent example of study abroad materials that incorporate exercises drawn from both intercultural and anthropological theory is the resource developed at Penn State (available as a .pdf download—see bibliography) *Embedded Education Abroad Faculty Toolkit: Developing and Implementing Course-Embedded Faculty-Led International Programs* (Morais, Ogden, & Buzinde, 2009). For thoughtful articles about study abroad with anthropological themes, see Ogden (2006, 2007).

Conclusion

Our account here about how anthropology and intercultural communication theory arose, developed, and became incorporated into study abroad preparation is necessarily complicated. We recognize that most international education professionals are so busy performing their duties that, although intellectually interesting, such discussions can seem rather abstract and of marginal relevance. However, the echoes of these two disciplines will continue to reverberate whenever faculty and staff gather to consider ways to provide appropriate instruction and opportunities for their students to increase their cultural competency by participating in study abroad. In other words, education through experiential means requires both planning and support if it is to be maximally effective. Recent research continues to confirm the benefit of appropriate and supportive intervention as students go through their overseas sojourns. No matter how that active role is conceived by those responsible, it will likely be informed, at least in part, by ideas from both anthropology and intercultural communication.

In these arenas, there is relatively little ideological tension between the goals of the trainers, their programs, and their participants. Anthropology supplies mostly a disciplinary worldview that is particularly compatible with study abroad goals. Intercultural communication provides a methodology, a perspective, and conceptual categories that support and promote a concern for how students *interact* with those who are culturally different. Anthropology's philosophical contribution will remain central to study abroad preparation because of its emphasis on participant observation and its concern for culture-specific knowledge, and intercultural communication will continue to provide tools that make communication across cultural borders more efficient, empathetic, and productive.

There has never been a more exciting or challenging time to be in the international education field, and the future will certainly not be a continuation of "business as usual." Past practices and prior models are unlikely to provide the kinds of engagement and training interventions that our students will need to make the most of their time abroad. It is important how we, as study abroad professionals, respond to these new circumstances, new technologies, and evolving theoretical ideas. We also need to pay attention to what research and program assessments are revealing about how we can incrementally improve our students' study abroad cultural learning. We can no longer assume that it is sufficient simply to create opportunities for our students to encounter difference abroad. We need to understand the profound importance and influence that educators can bring to study abroad by paying attention not only to the content of our students' education, but also to the context of the experience. Above all, we should consider delivering developmentally based training across the entire arc of the study abroad experience.

It truly matters how we decide to support and advise our students *while the experience is taking place and upon their return home*. By whatever name we call it (interventionism, cultural mentoring), this more direct and engaged style of providing timely and appropriate support to our students abroad seems destined to be the new standard for study abroad professionals. In a very real sense, the new paradigm for study abroad requires professionals in the field to somehow provide continual engagement throughout the study abroad cycle, ideally one that balances both challenge and support. We will need to continually seek the "teachable moments" that will result in greater intercultural sensitivity and increase the ability of our students to benefit fully from being "in the vicinity of events."

References

Agar, M. (1994). *Language shock*. New York: HarperCollins.

Asad, T. (Ed.). (1973). *Anthropology and the colonial encounter*. London, UK: Ithaca Press.

Barth, F., Gingrich, A., Parkin, R., & Silverman, S. (2005). *One discipline, four ways*. Chicago, IL: University of Chicago Press.

Basso, K. H. (1970). "To give up on words": Silence in western Apache culture. *Southwestern Journal of Anthropology, 26*(3), 213–230.

Benedict, R. (1934). *Patterns of culture*. Boston, MA: Houghton Mifflin.

Benedict, R. (1946). *The chrysanthemum and the sword*. Boston, MA: Houghton Mifflin.

Bennett, M. J. (1986a). A developmental approach to training for intercultural sensitivity. *International Journal of Intercultural Relations, 10*(2), 179–196.

Bennett, M. J. (1986b). Towards ethnorelativism: A developmental model of intercultural sensitivity. In R. M. Paige (Ed.), *Cross-cultural orientation: New conceptualizations and applications* (pp. 27–69). New York: University Press of America.

Bennett, M. J. (1993). Towards ethnorelativism: A developmental model of intercultural sensitivity. In R. M. Paige (Ed.), *Education for the intercultural experience* (pp. 21–71). Yarmouth, ME: Intercultural Press.

Bennett, M. J. (2010). A short conceptual history of intercultural learning in study abroad. In W. Hoffa & S. DePaul (Eds.), *A history of U.S. study abroad: 1965– present. Frontiers: The Interdisciplinary Journal of Study Abroad*, Special Issue, 419– 450. (See: http://www.frontiersjournal.com/FrontiersHstvol2announce.htm.)

Brislin, R. W., Cushner, K., Cherrie, C., & Yong, M. (1986). *Intercultural interactions: A practical guide*. Beverly Hills, CA: Sage.

Bryan, G., Darrow, K., Marrow, D., & Palmquist, B. (Eds). (1975). *Transcultural study guide* (2nd ed.). Washington, DC: Volunteers in Asia.

Clifford, J., & Marcus, G. (Eds.). (1986). *Writing culture: The poetics and politics of ethnography*. Berkeley, CA: University of California Press.

Deardorff, D. K. (Ed.). (2009). *The SAGE handbook of intercultural competence*. Beverly Hills, CA: Sage.

Donnatelli, L. (2010). The impact of technology on study abroad. In W. Hoffa & S. DePaul (Eds.), *A history of U.S. study abroad: 1965–present. Frontiers: The Interdisciplinary Journal of Study Abroad, Special Issue*, 295–320.

DuBois, C. (1951, December). Culture shock. Panel discussion at the Midwest regional meeting of the Institute of International Education in Chicago, November 28, 1951. Retrieved from http://www.smcm.edu/Academics/internationaled/Pdf/cultureshockarticle.pdf

Goldschmidt, W. (2000). A perspective on anthropology. *American Anthropologist, 102*(4), 789–807.

Grove, C. (1989). *Orientation handbook for youth exchange programs*. Yarmouth, ME: Intercultural Press.

Harris, M. (1968). *The rise of anthropological theory*. New York: Thomas Y. Crowell.

Hoffa, W. (Ed.). (2007). *A history of U.S. study abroad: Beginnings to 1965. Frontiers: The Interdisciplinary Journal of Study Abroad*, Special Issue, Lancaster, PA: Whitmore Printing.

Hoffa, W., & DePaul, S. (Eds.). (2010). *A history of U.S. study abroad: 1965–present. Frontiers: The Interdisciplinary Journal of Study Abroad*, Special Issue, Lancaster, PA: Whitmore Printing.

Kelley, C., & Meyers, J. (1995). *Cross-cultural adaptability inventory: Manual*. Minneapolis, MN: NCS Pearson.

Kelley, C., & Meyers, J. (1999). The cross-cultural adaptability inventory. In S. M. Fowler & M. G. Mumford (Eds.), *Intercultural sourcebook: Cross-cultural training methods* (Vol. 2, pp. 53–60). Yarmouth, ME: Intercultural Press.

Kluckhohn, C. (1951). Values and value-orientations in the theory of action. In T. Parsons & E. A. Shils (Eds.), *Toward a general theory of action* (pp. 388–433). Cambridge, MA: Harvard University Press.

Kluckhohn, C., & Strodtbeck, F. (1961). *Variations in value orientation.* Evanston, IL: Row, Peterson.

Kohls, L. R. (1979). *Survival kit for overseas living.* Yarmouth, ME: Intercultural Press.

La Brack, B. (1993). The missing linkage: The process of integrating orientation and reentry. In R. M. Paige (Ed.), *Education for the intercultural experience* (pp. 241–279). Yarmouth, ME: Intercultural Press. Retrieved from http://globaled.us/safeti/vini2000ed_missing_linkage.asp

La Brack, B. (2003). *What's up with culture?* Retrieved from http://www2.pacific.edu/sis/culture/

Landis, D., Bennett, J. M., & Bennett, M. J. (Eds.). (2004). *Handbook of intercultural training* (3rd ed.). Beverly Hills, CA: Sage.

Landis, D., & Bhagat, R. S. (Eds.). (1995). *Handbook of intercultural training* (2nd ed.). Beverly Hills, CA: Sage.

Leeds-Hurwitz, W. (1990). Notes on the history of intercultural communication: The Foreign Service Institute and the mandate for intercultural training. *The Quarterly Journal of Speech, 76,* 262–281.

Leeds-Hurwitz, W. (2010). Writing the intellectual history of intercultural communication. In T. K. Nakayama & R. T. Halualani (Eds.), *Handbook of critical intercultural communication* (pp. 21–33). Malden, MA: Blackwell.

Malinowski, B. (1922). *Argonauts of the western Pacific.* London: G. Routledge.

Martin, J. N., Nakayama, T. K., & Carbaugh, D. (2012). The history and development of the study of intercultural communication and applied linguistics. In J. Jackson (Ed.), *The Routledge handbook of language and intercultural communication* (pp. 17–37). New York: Routledge.

Mead, M. (1928). *Coming of age in Samoa.* New York: Morrow.

Morais, D., Ogden, A., & Buzinde, C. (2009). *Embedded education abroad faculty toolkit: Developing and implementing course-embedded faculty-led international programs.* University Park, PA: The Pennsylvania State University Schreyer Institute for Teaching Excellence and University Office of Global Programs. Retrieved from http://www.global.psu.edu/faculty_staff/pdf/EmbeddedToolkit.pdf

Ogden, A. (2006). Ethnographic inquiry: Reframing the learning core of education abroad. *Frontiers: The Interdisciplinary Journal of Study Abroad, 13,* 87–112.

Ogden, A. (2007). The view from the veranda: Understanding today's colonial student. *Frontiers: The Interdisciplinary Journal of Study Abroad, 15,* 35–56.

Ortner, S. B. (1984). Theory in anthropology since the sixties. *Comparative Studies in Society and History, 26*(1), 126–166.

Paige, R. M. (Ed.). (1993). *Education for the intercultural experience.* Yarmouth, ME: Intercultural Press.

Paige, R. M. (2004). Instrumentation in intercultural training. In D. Landis, J. M. Bennett, & M. J. Bennett (Eds.), *Handbook of intercultural training* (3rd ed., pp. 85–128). Thousand Oaks, CA: Sage.

Paige, R. M., Cohen, A. D., Kappler, B., Chi, J. C., & Lassegard, J. P. (Eds.). (2002). *Maximizing study abroad: A student's guide to strategies for language and culture learning and use.* Minneapolis, MN: Center for Advanced Research on Language Acquisition, University of Minnesota.

Rhodes, G. (2011). *Global scholar: Online learning for study abroad.* Retrieved from http://www.globalscholar.us/

Rogers, E. M., & Hart, W. B. (2002). The histories of intercultural, international, and development communication. In W. B. Gudykunst & B. Mody (Eds.), *Handbook of international and intercultural communication* (2nd ed., pp. 1–18). Thousand Oaks, CA: Sage.

Rogers, E. M., Hart, W. B., & Miike, Y. (2002). Edward T. Hall and the history of intercultural communication: The United States and Japan. *Keio Communication Review, 24,* 3–26.

Rosaldo, R. (1989). *Culture and truth: The remaking of social analysis.* Boston, MA: Beacon Press.

Sapir, E. (1929). The status of linguistics as a science. *Language, 5,* 207–214.

Slimbach, R. (2005). The transcultural journey. *Frontiers: The Interdisciplinary Journal of Study Abroad, 11,* 205–230.

Slimbach, R. (2010). *Becoming world wise: A guide to global learning.* Sterling, VA: Stylus.

Slimbach, R. (2011). *Transcultural journeys: Anthropology for everyday life.* Monrovia, CA: World Wise Books.

Storti, C., & Bennhold-Samaan, L. (1998). *Culture matters: The Peace Corps cross-cultural workbook.* Washington, DC: Peace Corps. Retrieved from http://www.peacecorps.gov/wws/educators/enrichment/culturematters/index.html

Whorf, B. L. (1941). The relation of habitual thought and behavior to language. In L. Spier (Ed.), *Language, culture, and personality: Essays in memory of Edward Sapir* (pp. 75–93). Menasha, WI: Sapir Memorial Publication Fund.

Wurzel, J. S. (Producer). (1993). *A different place: The intercultural classroom (Parts 1 & 2)* [Video, DVD, & online]. Newton, MA: Intercultural Resource.

9

THE PSYCHOLOGY OF
STUDENT LEARNING ABROAD

Victor Savicki

As a field of study psychology is quite broad. The American Psychological Association (APA) gives the following definition:

> Psychology is the study of the mind and behavior. The discipline embraces all aspects of the human experience—from the functions of the brain to the actions of nations, from child development to care for the aged. In every conceivable setting from scientific research centers to mental health care services, "the understanding of behavior" is the enterprise of psychologists. (APA, 2010)

For our purposes—that is, in examining the relationship of psychology to study abroad—the term *psychology* in this chapter generally reflects applied areas such as clinical, counseling, educational, and industrial/organizational psychology. This emphasis attempts to cover conceptual and research areas that are only briefly addressed in other chapters in this volume. Psychology as a discipline incorporates aspects from biology to sociology, from physics to philosophy, from political science to engineering. In the interest of helping individuals, groups, families, and organizations, psychology is both a science and an art. It draws on the science of research findings as well as the art of interpersonal relationships. Over the decades, research in the discipline has been inextricably intertwined with the evolution of its applications. The parallel tracks of science and practice have mutually informed each other, with advances and revelations on one track leading to changes on the other.

In this chapter, I discuss how changes in psychology have paralleled and sometimes encouraged changes in education abroad. I also discuss specific psychological theories and research whose "understanding behavior" goals have been harnessed to illuminate important issues in study abroad.

My goal in tracing the application of psychology to study abroad is to show how the field's psychological findings and practices are being systematically applied to improve study abroad outcomes—that is, to create student learning experiences by intention rather than leaving them to fate and hoping for the best. The evolution of psychology finds common ground with emerging views of study abroad that are learner centered; that hone in on the ways in which students construe events; and that recognize the inherent reciprocity of student thinking, feeling, and behaving. The active, optimistic, interventionist strategy of study abroad program development "by design not chance" is, then, echoed throughout this chapter (Savicki, 2008b).

An Evolution of Ideas in Psychology

Historically, various schools of thought within psychology have emphasized the general themes of affect, behavior, and cognition. Exploration of these themes has sought to understand how humans feel, act, and think under a broad range of conditions. At the beginning of modern psychology, Sigmund Freud (1900/1999), representing practice in the emerging field, emphasized the feelings and emotions underlying human behavior; Wilhelm Wundt (1897), representing the science of psychology, emphasized thinking and learning at the cognitive level; and Ivan P. Pavlov (1897) and B. F. Skinner (1938), using laboratory methods, uncovered psychological links to learning that focused on emotion and behavior. These thinkers and their followers conceived of the world as an orderly, completely knowable set of natural laws that could be broken down into its subunits and then reassembled to provide a greater understanding of behavior. This reductionistic/analytic approach helped to clarify the overwhelming complexity of psychological functioning, on the one hand, yet it oversimplified and overobjectified the intricacy of the human condition, on the other. Even though we have modified or even abandoned many of the ideas and methods in vogue during that era of intense creativity, we have to credit those early psychologists for moving us out of the shackles of superstition and mythology that then surrounded the understandings of human behavior.

As a reaction against the reductionistic/analytic approach, psychologists in various places in the world proposed more holistic and person-centered approaches to research and practice. In Europe, the Gestalt school of psychology emerged (Koffka, 1922), with its focus on the ways that humans and animals make cognitive connections between stimuli. The general theme of person-environment "fit" became important (Lewin, 1935). In the United States, the humanistic psychology wave (Maslow, 1943; Rogers, 1942) focused on the uniqueness of individuals and the impact of interpersonal relationships on the emotional life and cognitive sense of self. These approaches clearly focused on the contribution that the individual made to his or her own psychological processes. Humans were no longer passively buffeted by their base instincts or the external environment alone, but instead contributed to their own growth or maladjustment through cognitive, affective, and behavioral processes. Psychological practice moved away from "experts only" restrictive theories to "giving psychology away" (Miller, 1969), as psychologists acknowledged the centrality of the contribution of the individual to his or her own well-being.

Building on the understanding that the individual contributed to his or her own psychological experience, the constructivist approach has more recently refined and extended the role of the individual as observer/reactor/constructor of his or her experience (Watzlawick, 1984). Theories and approaches such as Kelly's Personal Constructs Theory (Maher, 1969), narrative therapy (White & Epston, 1990), and clinical hypnosis (Haley, 1973) extend the notion of person-environment fit so that the emphasis is on the individual's perceptions and definitions rather than on the characteristics of the environment. Different people react differently to the same environment because they construe the meaning of the environment differently. It is this cognitive and emotional construction that becomes the phenomenon of interest: What would a person have to think in order to feel or behave in a specific way? From this viewpoint, personal reality is flexible, depending on the manner in which the environment is construed. Methods such as positive reinterpretation, cognitive reframing, and changing of one's internal narrative about events may not change the events themselves, but these methods do change the meaning that individuals make about the events, thus changing their personal reality. We will see the power of this approach in the sections "Acculturative Stress" and "Coping" later in this chapter.

The field of psychology has, then, changed since its modern period began at the end of the 19th and beginning of the 20th centuries. Building on the assumptions of the natural laws of science, it has added layers of complexity to the understanding of human behavior. Today, while psychology retains its historical roots, it has evolved to put the learner at the center of the education abroad enterprise. Representing the individual as an active player in how he or she constructs events, psychology has much to say now about how educators can help learners develop beneficial constructions of reality, whether back in their home cultures or abroad.

Levels of Intercultural Adjustment/Adaptation

Some students seem to feel that if they just knew the "rules" of behavior in a host culture they would be able to function quite nicely without really having to understand the host culture itself. These students may feel that understanding the "rules" is equivalent to understanding the culture. They want a cookbook with recipes for different social situations so that they can avoid faux pas and demonstrate their cultural sophistication. Study abroad educators who actively encourage intercultural learning, on the other hand, think it is important for students to understand the underlying differences between cultures in order to develop intercultural competence. When we use the familiar iceberg analogy, we see that students tend to focus on the 10% of cultural difference represented by overt, observable behavior above the waterline, whereas study abroad educators increasingly focus on the other 90%—the mostly covert underlying assumptions and values that lie beneath the waterline, and that make up the most important dimensions of cultural difference.

It may be possible to reconcile these two related but differing strategies for learning about other cultures if we consider two different psychological dimensions with regard to the study abroad sojourner's adjustment/adaptation process. The first dimension, onset/duration, defines whether events affecting a student are acute or chronic. That is, do the demands of the study abroad context arise quickly and last for only a short time, or do demands build up over a longer time and linger? Students tend to focus on distinct, short-term, culture-clash incidents, whereas many educators focus on the longer-term, and more complex, cultural adaptation process.

The second dimension, psychological context, varies depending on the specific psychological factor being considered. Here the distinction concerns how that factor might be construed in "normal" life, back in one's home culture, versus how it might be construed as an indicator of similarity or difference between home and host cultures. For example, we all encounter stresses in our home culture. Most of us do not think about the cultural import of those stressors; we just mobilize ourselves to cope. If someone cuts in line while we are waiting to buy tickets to a movie, we simply act to resolve the situation. In a different national culture, however, stressors may be common, garden variety events that, at the same time, may involve larger, underlying cultural differences. There, cutting in line may be indicative of different assumptions about space, status, the value of time, in-group versus out-group dynamics, and so forth. We cannot presume, in other words, that the same values are in operation in another culture. Students studying in the host culture, focused on the overt and observable, may not be able to use their preferred coping mechanisms because the stress finds its source in the host culture's covert values and worldview. The students' understanding of host culture assumptions and values is, then, imperative if they are to be able to reconstrue events so that these can take on new, intercultural meanings. Understanding such meanings does not necessarily imply acceptance or approval, but rather an awareness that the differences in cultures have effects that we may be able to predict and harness in furthering our own goals. In each of the psychological categories to follow, I examine both the mundane and the culturally significant levels of student experience during the study abroad sojourn.

The ABCs of Acculturation

Ward and her colleagues (Ward, 2001; Ward, Bochner, & Furnham, 2001) have suggested a simple but elegant template for considering important psychological responses of individuals to changes in their cultural experience. This template, what they call "the ABCs of acculturation," addresses the affective, behavioral, and cognitive dimensions of psychological experience. This formulation, a reasonably comprehensive view of the effects of cultural contact, extends to many types of individuals who encounter a different culture: immigrants, refugees, asylum seekers, as well as sojourners (Sam, 2006). Study abroad students fall into the sojourner category: They enter a foreign culture voluntarily for a relatively short period of time and then return to their home culture. Although Ward and her colleagues' template applies to the acculturation of both individuals and groups, our focus here is on psychological acculturation, "the changes an individual experiences as a result of being in contact with other cultures" (Sam, 2006, p. 14).

Affect

The affective component of the ABCs addresses the psychological well-being of individuals. It is inextricably intertwined with the stress and coping literature that has burgeoned in the last three decades, marked by the groundbreaking cognitive mediation theory by Lazarus and his colleagues

(Lazarus & Folkman, 1984). In its simplest form, any environmental event can be a stressor. However, two different people may react to the same event in quite different ways, depending on how they think about the event and their perceived abilities to deal with it. The cognitive appraisal that individuals make in response to the environmental stressor happens in two steps. In the first, individuals determine whether or not the environmental event is a real or potential source of threat, harm, or loss. If the answer is affirmative, then, in the second step, they assess their ability to cope with the stressor. If they appraise the environmental condition as benign or irrelevant, no coping efforts are activated. On the other hand, they may view the environmental condition as a potentially provocative or dangerous stressor and thus mobilize themselves to react.

Depending on a whole host of individual psychological characteristics, individuals may experience the stressor as a challenge, one that they have the wherewithal to overcome; as a threat, one that has the possibility to overwhelm their abilities to cope; or as an actual harm or loss, one that occurs as their coping abilities prove inadequate to deal with the stress. In its broadest sense, coping consists of "the thoughts and behaviors used to manage the internal and external demands of situations that are appraised as stressful" (Folkman & Moskowitz, 2004, p. 745). It is important to note that levels of stress that are manageable might actually increase an individual's sense of well-being by generating opportunities for new learnings, and by increasing a sense of mastery and efficacy. From the point of view of study abroad, interesting questions revolve around which individual characteristics, abilities, and skills help sojourners cope with cultural stressors in ways that preserve and even enhance their sense of psychological well-being.

Behavior

The behavioral component of the ABCs addresses the abilities of the individual student to adapt to "fit in" with the host culture (Ward & Kennedy, 1999). A foreign culture makes demands on sojourners to behave in ways that are different from the norm in their home cultures. Expectations about greetings, formality, dress, use of time, and so on in the host culture require the sojourner to adapt in order to function smoothly when interacting with host culture natives. The challenge for study abroad students is to be able to learn and produce appropriate behavior in response to host culture situational cues. Ward and others (Ward et al., 2001; Ward & Kennedy, 1999) suggest that this learning follows a normal learning curve, with ever-increasing effectiveness of performance until an acceptable repertoire of culturally relevant behaviors is developed. Students demonstrate a wide span of such behavioral learning, and some of this learning may lead to dysfunctional outcomes. Systematic training, rehearsal, and coaching certainly can enhance positive outcomes. Again, psychology as a discipline is interested in differences in characteristics, abilities, and skills that may make the process of learning how to "fit in" more or less difficult.

Cognition

The cognitive component of the ABCs addresses the manner in which the sojourner thinks about himself or herself in relation to both home and host cultures. The subfield of social identification within psychology speaks to this issue (Phinney, 1993; Tajfel, 1981). In a very real sense, students have choices about how they think about themselves, about how they construe their identity. As a social construct, identity is relatively independent from more objective characteristics such as height, weight, race, or gender (Phinney, 1993). For some study abroad students, the exposure to a foreign culture helps throw into high relief the form and substance of their largely unexamined home culture. Values and assumptions that they have taken for granted are called into question, or at least made manifest in contrast to those of the host culture. Ironically, though, many students, even in the face of stark cultural differences, deny such differences, show hostility toward them, or discount their relevance (M. J. Bennett, 1993). Close examination of cultural differences is not a foregone conclusion despite exposure to them (Savicki & Cooley, 2011). Although this exposure to cultural differences can affect all ages, it is especially potent for students in adolescence and young adulthood who, as a normal task of maturing, are struggling to discover and solidify who they are (Erikson, 1968). Again, psychology is interested in individual characteristics, abilities, and skills that may alter the process and outcome of identity development for study abroad students.

Research Findings on the ABCs and Study Abroad

On framing recent study abroad research against Ward and her colleagues' (Ward, 2001; Ward, Bochner, & Furnham, 2001) ABCs of psychological acculturation in this section, I am not suggesting that individual students can be sliced into ABC segments. It is important to bear this in mind, because we do not want to fall into the sorts of reductionist/analytic analyses that have restricted some past psychological research and practice. Affective, behavioral, and cognitive dimensions are clearly related (Masgoret & Ward,

2006); I am continuing to treat them separately here for only heuristic purposes.

Findings on Affect

The psychological well-being of study abroad students depends on many factors, not the least of which are the actual experiences that they encounter during their sojourn. From a stress and coping framework, students are exposed to many events and situations that might be considered stressors. The stress and coping literature identifies large stressors (life changes), such as moving to a new living situation, leaving one's family, starting a new job, or attending a new school (Holmes & Rahe, 1967). Such transitions, when they occur during study abroad, are large, noticeable, and often acute: They emerge rapidly and have very distinct beginnings and endings. Stress can also be chronic, in the sense that the stressors may be relatively low-level irritations or annoyances that can accumulate over time. For example, students may encounter daily hassles, such as people talking too loud in class, people smoking nearby, or difficulty finding a favorite food (Kanner, Coyne, Schaefer, & Lazarus, 1981), or repeated, low-level, problematic interactions at work or school that can lead to burnout (Maslach & Schaufeli, 1993). Both acute and chronic stressors arise during study abroad sojourns. In fact, to varying degrees study abroad is typically designed to put students in contact with stressors that are cultural in nature.

Acculturative Stress

It is also useful to distinguish between common stressors that might occur in a student's home culture—those that occur, for example, when a student chooses to attend a new school or find new roommates—and those stressors that are more obviously related to cultural differences. Such "acculturative stressors" (Berry, 2006b) may arise, for example, when one source of the difficulty/threat/loss caused by the stressor is based on differing values and assumptions between a home and host culture. As Berry (2006b) explains it:

> Acculturative stress is a response by people to life events that are rooted in intercultural contact. Frequently, these reactions include heightened levels of depression (linked to the experience of cultural loss) and of anxiety (linked to uncertainty about how one should live in the new society). (p. 43)

In some circumstances it may of course be impossible to tease apart normal versus acculturative stress; yet it might be helpful for students to recognize that the sources of stress may emerge from the differences of perception fostered by differing cultural assumptions or values. What seems like annoying behavior from one cultural perspective may be perfectly acceptable from another (e.g., differences in comfortable speaking distances, the use of eye contact). Table 9.1 gives a schematic representation of the contrasts discussed so far.

Let us now turn to factors that may contribute to a student's sense of well-being in a study abroad sojourn. We first examine some personality characteristics and abilities that influence students' perceptions of stress, then look at coping styles that may be effective in study abroad settings.

Matsumoto and his colleagues (Matsumoto et al., 2001) have developed a measure of readiness for adjusting to a different culture: the Intercultural Adjustment Potential Scale (ICAPS). This general scale and several of its factor scales (Emotional Regulation, Openness, Flexibility, Creative Thinking) have been used to predict positive psychological adjustment in a foreign culture, both for immigrants (Matsumoto, Hirayama, & Leroux, 2006) and for study abroad students (Savicki, Downing-Burnette, Heller, Binder, & Suntinger, 2004). ICAPS scores and study abroad students' life satisfaction scores from the beginning to the end of a three-month sojourn showed that initial high intercultural adjustment potential was eroded at the same time that satisfaction increased steadily (Savicki et al., 2004). Paradoxically, as students depleted their coping resources during the study abroad sojourn, their satisfaction increased. This result indicates, among other things, that the process of adjusting to a different culture is not easy. Indeed, J. M.

TABLE 9.1
Stressors sorted by type of onset/duration and origin

Onset/Duration	"Normal" Stressors	Acculturative Stressors
Acute	New housing situation, new learning institution	Specific incidents challenging one's worldview, such as cutting in line, having to ask for the bill in a restaurant
Chronic	Communication difficulties, difficulty finding favorite foods, daily hassles	Assumptions about time, gender, personal space

Bennett (2008) posits as one of her five foundation principles for study abroad that "disequilibrium need not lead to dissatisfaction" (p. 17). Dynamic disequilibrium (Joyce, 1984), indicative of some level of distress, may in fact be helpful in motivating students to mobilize their coping abilities and creativity in responding to intercultural demands. In sum, individual students show different potential for intercultural adjustment; that adjustment is not always smooth and difficulty free; and, within bounds, some degree of disequilibrium does not necessarily detract from students' satisfaction during and after their sojourn. Indeed, it may help students to generate effective responses to stressors.

Coping

In the psychological literature, coping is generally divided into two categories: problem focused and emotion focused. Those actions taken to deal with an external source of stress directly illustrate problem-focused coping, and the aim is to remove or defuse the stressor. Emotion-focused coping strategies, by contrast, attempt to soften or avoid the internal reactions and distress associated with exposure to stressors. With these strategies, the stressor is not addressed, only the adverse affective reactions to it. Stress and coping theory and research for the most part has been generated in the United States, and the cultural bias of favoring more active and controlling coping mechanisms is American as well (Wong, Wong, & Scott, 2006). The current literature thus emphasizes the efficacy of problem-focused coping and tends to disparage emotion-focused strategies (Chun, Moos, & Cronkite, 2006). However, even in the United States, recognition is growing that coping strategies that do not directly attack the source of stress might be effective, especially in those situations, such as a study abroad sojourn, in which individuals are unlikely to be able to make changes to the stressful cultural environment in which they find themselves.

Savicki and colleagues (Savicki, 2010a; Savicki et al., 2004) have documented the expected efficacy of problem-focused coping strategies as defined by various subscales of the COPE, a coping strategies inventory, developed by Carver, Scheier, and Weintraub (1989). While Active Coping (directly changing the source of stress) and Planning (developing plans to attack the source of stress) were related to lower psychological symptoms and higher satisfaction, several coping strategies not focused on changing the source of stress were also effective, including Positive Reinterpretation (discovering a positive perspective to the stressful situation), Instrumental Social Support (asking others for advice and help), and Emotional Social Support (soliciting care and concern from others). Several other coping strategies were, however, counterproductive, related to lower psychological adjustment, including Mental Disengagement (distracting oneself from thinking about the stressor), Behavioral Disengagement (reducing one's effort to deal with the stressor, giving up valued goals with which the stressor is interfering), Venting Emotions (complaining without taking any action), and Denial (pretending that the stressor does not exist). These latter ineffective coping strategies are emotion focused.

In summary, both "normal" and acculturative stressors affect study abroad students. Sojourners expend much cognitive and emotional energy in appraising the real or imagined threats and challenges posed by such external stressors. Attempts to cope with the stressors can focus on both the external source of stress and the internal reactions to the stressors. Research has demonstrated that a variety of actions by students have relatively consistent outcomes regarding their psychological well-being. Some coping strategies are effective in reducing deleterious effects of stress, and some are not.

A great advantage to international educators regarding the stress and coping literature is that both the ways that students evaluate stressors (appraisal styles) and the ways that they deal with stress (coping strategies) are teachable. That is, educators may be able to help students reassess a situation so that it is not as threatening, and to teach them the strategy of reframing an event in ways that turn an event into an interesting, exciting, or humorous one, rather than one that is problematic. Student encounters with culturally based stressors provide teaching moments during which it is possible to harness both experiential and transformational learning strategies (Savicki, 2008a).

Findings on Behavior

Research on the development of culturally effective behaviors during the process of sociocultural adaptation has, to a large extent, discredited the conventional U-shaped and W-shaped "culture shock" models (Berry, 2006b; Masgoret & Ward, 2006; Ward et al., 2001). Although there may be several developmental processes operating at once as students come to adapt to their study abroad culture (Savicki, Adams, & Binder, 2008), the most recently advanced theory is that of "cultural learning" (Berry, 2006b). In the cultural learning approach, students arrive at their study abroad sites with behavioral deficits in the sense that the host culture demands different behaviors or different modulations of behavior in order for the student to "fit in," to acquire culturally appropriate skills and to negotiate interactive aspects of the host environment (Ward & Kennedy, 1999, p. 660). Developing these new behaviors follows the usual acquisition curve seen in other forms of psychological learning. It is slow at first, accelerates rapidly, then slows and levels off. Ward and Kennedy (1999) report that sociocultural adaptation difficulties are most prevalent in the first few months of a sojourn, with much of the learning completed after about six months. For most U.S. study abroad students the six-month leveling off in adaptation never materializes because on average these students spend less than eight weeks abroad, with only 4% spending more than a semester (Open Doors, 2009).

In a new culture there is much to learn behaviorally. To measure some of the behaviors that students must learn, Ward and Kennedy (1999) have produced a 29-item Sociocultural Adaptation Scale with two factor-analyzed subscales: Cultural Empathy and Relatedness, and Impersonal Endeavors and Perils. Sample items from the Cultural Empathy and Relatedness scale include "Making yourself understood," "Understanding the local's worldview," and "Being able to see two sides of an intercultural issue." Sample items from the Impersonal Endeavors and Perils scale include "Getting used to the pace of life," "Getting used to the local food/finding food you enjoy," and "Dealing with unsatisfactory service in stores and restaurants" (Ward & Kennedy, 1999, p. 663). In the same manner in which we conceptualized stress and coping to be arrayed across two dimensions, so too can we understand behavioral adaptation through a two-by-two grid with onset/duration of environmental demands on one axis, and "normal" social demands versus demands based on cultural differences on the other (see Table 9.2). Specific, short-term demands that might occur in one's home culture, such as finding a bus stop or cybercafé, can be contrasted with learning how to act in ongoing, longer-term situations with cultural implications, such as using the host culture's proper form of address for teachers and others in authority and getting used to the pace of life.

Recent research suggests that for U.S. study abroad students, the learning curve for behaviors relevant to sociocultural adaptation is neither smooth nor unidimensional (Savicki, 2010b; Savicki, Binder, & Arrúe, in press). In these studies, initial difficulties in adaptation were followed by improved adaptability during the middle of the sojourn only to be followed, at the end, by an increase in difficulties. In other words, over a three-month period, some problems reemerged at the end of the sojourn, especially in the Impersonal Endeavors and Perils factor. It appears that some environmental differences in culture continue to grate—finding favorite foods, for example.

TABLE 9.2
Behavioral adaptation demands sorted by type of onset/duration and origin

Onset/Duration	Social Context	Acculturative
Acute	Specific information and skills, such as finding out how to use public transportation and finding out where to access the Internet	Specific incidents of dealing with persons in authority, using formal versus informal forms of address, waiting to eat until all are served, etc.
Chronic	Differences in behavior in the "student" role, such as less class discussion and less faculty availability	Use of time, space, status, etc.

In addition, different behavioral challenges seemed to emerge at different times during the sojourn (Savicki, Adams, et al., 2008). For example, difficulties with predicting and adapting to public social behavior were strong at first but then grew less frequent, and the ability to notice and explain cross-cultural comparisons grew steadily over time. By contrast, concerns over making social faux pas peaked in the middle of the sojourn but were lower at the beginning and the end. We cannot make the assumption that all behaviors are learned in the same manner or at the same rate.

The research also shows that students who were low and high initial adapters (based on a median split of the Sociocultural Adaptation Scale) retained their relative sociocultural adaptation positions throughout the sojourn, with low initial adapters showing significantly more negative affect, and higher appraisals of threat and loss. The low adapters' adaptation process was fraught with struggle and discomfort even though at the end they were not significantly different from the high adapters in terms of psychological adjustment. These low initial adapters reported more difficulties with everyday Impersonal Endeavors and Perils than they did with abstract understanding of Cultural Empathy and Relatedness. Understanding the culture in general seemed easier than dealing with day-to-day cultural differences. Other issues were, however, as difficult at the end as at the beginning of the sojourn (Savicki, 2010a).

In a comparison of students who participated in programs that required some degree of prior second-language study and those who participated in programs without a language requirement, those who had studied the language prior to departure showed higher early adaptation to the host culture—an advantage for these study abroad students speaking the host culture language. Counterintuitively, however, at the end, study abroad students speaking the host culture language reported significantly more difficulties with sociocultural adaptation. It may be that the more intense exposure to the host culture through language proficiency served to highlight adaptation difficulties in more depth than the less intense cultural immersion for study abroad students who did not speak the language well. Those students who were not required to have prior language proficiency may have blithely assumed that they fit in well because they did not know what they did not know about the culture, thus were blind to potentially distressing cultural differences (Savicki et al., in press).

In summary, adaptation to a new culture encompasses a broad range of relevant behavior. These behaviors, as a general trend, are learned and performed better and better over time. However, the process is not simple; it is fraught with setbacks, and for some students it is burdensome and may not lead to positive outcomes.

International educators can use the research on sociocultural adaptation to help students and faculty recognize that a good deal of learning takes place outside of the classroom. Clearly, there is justification for presenting information on culturally relevant issues. It is also useful to be aware that some seemingly insignificant issues, such as students' ability to find enjoyable food, can loom large over time. Such concerns can and often do form an important part of the adaptation process and should not be forgotten.

Findings on Cognition

The cognitive dimension of the ABCs of acculturation focuses on social identification, specifically on how students incorporate information about their own and others' cultures into their personal identity. In Erikson's (1968) ego identity model, psychological identity refers to a subjective feeling of consistency and continuity of self across situations that provides a sense of stability and serves as a guide for making key life choices. A stable identity develops over time through a process of experimentation, reflection, and observation that peaks in adolescence and may continue into early adulthood. Marcia (1980) has conceptualized identity formation as consisting of both exploration of identity issues and an affective and cognitive commitment to aspects of identity.

The emphasis on social identification may shift from the individual to the group level depending on the social context (Frey & Tropp, 2006). That is, when individuals are placed into cross-cultural context, their group membership (e.g., being an American) may trigger an emphasis on that element of social identification because host culture natives at first perceive them more as "Americans" than as individuals. In general, social identification contains several components: feelings of belonging to a culture, the centrality of cultural membership in one's identity, positive and negative evaluations of one's culture or aspects of culture, and the practice of cultural customs and traditions (Ward, 2001). Table 9.3 organizes social identification demands by onset/duration and whether these demands may be related to acculturation issues. As we have seen with the affective and behavioral dimensions of experience, some events during the study abroad sojourn could just as easily have occurred at home, whereas others find their source in differences between home and host cultures.

Research suggests that study abroad students show a stronger identification with their home culture at the end of a sojourn than they do at the beginning (Savicki & Cooley, 2011; Savicki et al., 2004) and shows that home

TABLE 9.3
Social identification demands sorted by type of onset/duration and origin

Onset/Duration	Normal Identity Process	Acculturation Challenges
Acute	Experiencing a specific event that challenges one's view of one's self, e.g., being treated rudely by a store clerk or being ignored in a foreign social situation	Being viewed as only an "American" rather than an individual (stereotypes, pro- or anti-Americanism, etc.)
Chronic	Being unable to express one's self easily or with high proficiency in a foreign language (feeling dumb), feeling unable to demonstrate one's talents or abilities within the restrictions of the social context ("No one knows how good a singer I am"), etc.	Experiencing symbolic and intergroup contact anxiety; daily confrontation with a viable, alternate worldview that has attractive aspects; etc.

culture identity was significantly higher in study abroad students at the end of their sojourn than in matched students who stayed at home (Savicki, Cooley, & Donnelly, 2008). From the point of view of Berry's (2006a) strategies of acculturation, this high identification with the home culture could be the result of an "integration" strategy in which the student identifies positively with both home and host culture, or a "separation" strategy in which the student identifies positively with the home culture and negatively with the host culture. Berry (2006a) suggests that the integration strategy is preferable, because it has been shown to be correlated with higher psychological adjustment for students. Unfortunately, the separation strategy seems to be more commonly chosen (Savicki, Cooley, et al., 2008). As J. M. Bennett (2008) suggests, cultural contact alone does not guarantee either intercultural competence or reduction in out-group stereotypes.

Higher levels of pre-departure American identity (Meyer-Lee & Evans, 2008) were also predictive of higher self-reported difficulties in adapting to the host culture by the end of the study abroad sojourn (Savicki et al., in press). More specifically, a pre-departure tendency of students to explore and ponder their American identities may be linked to the students feeling threatened and experiencing negative affect and a stronger sense of difficulty with the day-to-day process of fitting into a foreign culture. The very process of thinking about one's national identity while in a foreign culture may induce fearful appraisals and unhappy feelings, as well as a sense of not fitting in. These findings are consistent with recent research in social psychology on the "contact hypothesis" (Pettigrew & Tropp, 2006). Two sources of anxiety may emerge as students make meaningful contact with a new and "strange" culture: symbolic and intergroup contact anxiety (Stephan, Stephan, & Gudykunst, 1999). Symbolic anxiety occurs when the awareness of an alternate view of reality calls into question one's own view. An underlying presupposition is that there is one "right" view; thus, if students accept the other view, then they necessarily reject their own view. Clearly, such thinking limits exploration and may provoke anger and attack on alternate views. It may form part of the basis for the Defense stage of the Developmental Model of Intercultural Sensitivity (M. J. Bennett, 1993; chapter 4 of this volume), in which an individual disparages other cultures while overinflating the importance of his or her own. Intergroup contact anxiety arises when members of two groups encounter one another. There are many concerns represented in this anxiety, including being rejected and evaluated negatively solely on the basis of one's group membership (Voci & Hewstone, 2003).

The psychological task for students, as far as identity is concerned, is to explore who they are and come to a conclusion yielding realistic, positive affirmation. This end result, the combination of exploration and affirmation, Marcia (1980) calls achieved identity. In a recent study, study abroad students had a higher percentage of achieved national identity prior to departure than did students who stayed at home (Savicki & Cooley, 2011). At the end of their sojourn, however, the study abroad students' national identity had been disturbed; they no longer showed achieved identity. The pattern prior to departure was a balance of affirmation and exploration; by the end of the sojourn, affirmation had increased dramatically and exploration had decreased, thus throwing the pre-departure balanced identity out of kilter. The very process of exposure to an alternate worldview had somewhat disrupted their national identity. This awareness of an alternative worldview might in fact be a factor in student reports to the effect that study abroad has "changed my life." The challenge here is to identify how to help students cope with symbolic and intergroup contact anxiety so that they are more likely to employ the integration acculturation strategy than the separation strategy.

In summary, study abroad students suffer a fairly vigorous bombardment of information from the host culture that may lead them to reevaluate some of the home culture ideas that are central to their personal identities. There is no guarantee that they will show enough creativity and flexibility to carry out an integrative acculturation strategy. It is the role of international educators to recognize the anxiety that the cultural information onslaught may generate, and to provide support and clarification.

A theory from the educational psychology literature that may help students understand how learning abroad may affect their identities is transformational learning (Mezirow, 1991), which examines the premises underlying new information in relation to the premises of one's current meaning schema (Hunter, 2008). Within the context of this theory, simply trying to wedge new information into an existing schema is not effective. Learners instead need to examine deeper levels of meaning to be able to transform their meaning perspectives. The good news is that such activities can lead to the expanded worldviews that we hope for when we send our students abroad. The bad news is that this can be difficult, sometimes frightening work for students, because it challenges them to look at their personal identities in a new way.

Conclusion

Much of the theoretical basis for a noninterventionist, or sink-or-swim, approach to study abroad stems from the contact hypothesis (Allport, 1954); the expectation is that immersion leads to ethnorelativism. A major meta-analysis of 50 years' research on Allport's theory does indicate "small to medium" significant reduction of prejudice over a broad variety of inter-group contact situations ($r = -.205$ to $-.214$) (Pettigrew & Tropp, 2006, p. 757). However, this type of contact accounts for only between 4% and 5% of reduction of prejudice. More important, even when key theoretical conditions are met (equal group status, common goals, intergroup coopera-tion, and support from authorities), reduction of prejudice is still not impressive: It is little more than 8%. However, when the ideal conditions are not met, when conditions of anxiety or threat exist, prejudice and avoid-ance can actually increase significantly when individuals come into contact with out-groups (Plant, 2004; Stephan & Stephan, 1985; Voci & Hewstone, 2003). The results of contact with a different culture may, in other words, prove beneficial in a limited way—but in the absence of ideal conditions, the results are not likely to be impressive at all. Where study abroad is con-cerned, this means that international educators will need to intervene in order to deal with the 90%-plus of the variance not accounted for by immer-sion alone. As Ward and her colleagues (2001) put it:

> There is now sufficient evidence, accumulated over several decades, to sug-gest that most people who cross cultures would benefit from some kind of systematic preparation and training to assist them in coping with culture-contact induced stress. Simply dropping culture travellers in at the deep end after some limited introductory information sessions can be costly, both in financial and personal terms. (p. 248)

The "flow" theory from within the positive psychology movement may provide a theoretical framework for intervention (Csikszentmihalyi, Abu-hamdeh, & Nakamura, 2005). The characteristics of flow are consistent with a high degree of engagement with the study abroad situation: "Flow is a subjective state that people report when they are completely involved in something to the point of forgetting time, fatigue, and everything else but the activity itself" (Csikszentmihalyi et al., 2005, p. 600). This state of con-sciousness derives from a balance between the perspectives and skills that an individual brings to an event and the level of environmental challenge that he or she experiences. Too much challenge and insufficient skill lead to anxiety; too much skill and not enough challenge lead to boredom. The optimal condition for individual learners continually adjusts as skills and challenges change; they influence each other reciprocally. Students who value flow seek challenges to test their sense of mastery. Students lacking, or doubtful of, their skills may avoid challenge and retreat.

According to the flow model, international educators may need to "simultaneously provide support and challenge" (Nakamura & Csikszentmihalyi, 2002, p. 99). Each student is likely to have a different level of skill, a different inclination to seek challenge, and a different personal experience with flow. The educator's task is to intervene in a way that builds skills, fosters challenges, and enhances the possibility that students engage in the study abroad environment in ways that enhance their sense of control and mastery. Suggestions from flow research indicate that active, student-centered learning, as promoted in this volume, including "serious play," may be avenues that enhance flow (Nakamura & Csikszentmihalyi, 2002; Schmidt, Shernoff, & Csikszentmihalyi, 2007; cf. Binder, 2008 for examples). The ABCs of acculturation provide a framework through which skills and challenges may be developed. Asking students to focus clearly on their own adjustment, adaptation, and identity offers opportunities for them to deepen their engagement with the culture abroad as well as avenues for balancing challenge and skill. The mission for the international educator, framed in this way, is to assess individual students and to craft flow activities that allow them to balance their individual needs for challenge and support.

Psychology has much to say about student learning abroad. The present state of the field, in both research and practice, strongly supports the notion of student centered learning. Indeed, it goes further: It supports the constructivist notion of students participating in and exercising control over the meaning that they make of various experiences. (Unfortunately, there has been little in the way of systematic training and education for either international educators or their students to help students fulfill their potential in the affect, behavior, and cognition areas that have been discussed in this chapter. Fortuitously, later chapters in this book offer models to remedy this situation.) Students come to their study abroad experiences with a broad range of competencies for understanding and responding appropriately to other cultures, as well as for crafting a meaningful experience for themselves. Research and practice in psychology offer guidance to international educators interested in helping students develop on many different levels through engaging in cultures different from their own.

In short, much of what has been discussed in this chapter can be taught and/or coached. Each student arrives at a different starting place, and the progress each makes in terms of well-being, adaptation, and identity will call upon his or her unique personal resources. Nevertheless, it is not necessary to leave that progress to chance; international educators can design learning opportunities for students rather than relying on the "magic" of intercultural contact (Engle & Engle, 2002). Study abroad outcomes, supported by design rather than left to chance, are as attainable as they are desirable.

References

Allport, G. W. (1954). *The nature of prejudice*. Cambridge, MA: Addison-Wesley.

American Psychological Association (APA). (2010). How does the APA define "psychology"? About APA and Psychology. Retrieved from http://www.apa.org/support/about/apa/

Bennett, J. M. (2008). On becoming a global soul: A path to engagement on study abroad. In V. Savicki (Ed.), *Developing intercultural competence and transformation: Theory, research, and application in international education* (pp. 13–31). Sterling, VA: Stylus.

Bennett, M. J. (1993). Towards ethnorelativism: A developmental model of intercultural sensitivity. In M. Paige (Ed.), *Education for the intercultural experience* (pp. 21–71). Yarmouth, ME: Intercultural Press.

Berry, J. W. (2006a). Contexts of acculturation. In D. L. Sam & J. W. Berry (Eds.), *The Cambridge handbook of acculturation psychology* (pp. 27–42). Cambridge, UK: Cambridge University Press.

Berry, J. W. (2006b). Stress perspectives on acculturation. In D. L. Sam & J. W. Berry (Eds.), *The Cambridge handbook of acculturation psychology* (pp. 43–57). Cambridge, UK: Cambridge University Press.

Binder, F. (2008). Action methods for integration of experience and understanding. In V. Savicki (Ed.), *Developing intercultural competence and transformation: Theory, research, and application in international education* (pp. 195–214). Sterling, VA: Stylus.

Carver, C. S., Scheier, M. F., & Weintraub, J. K. (1989). Assessing coping strategies: A theoretically based approach. *Journal of Personality and Social Psychology, 56*, 267–283.

Chun, C., Moos, R. H., & Cronkite, R. C. (2006). Culture: A fundamental contest for the stress and coping paradigm. In P. T. P. Wong & L. C. J. Wong (Eds.), *Handbook of multicultural perspectives on stress and coping* (pp. 29–53). New York: Springer.

Csikszentmihalyi, M., Abuhamdeh, S., & Nakamura, J. (2005). Flow. In A. J. Elliot & C. S. Dweck (Eds.), *Handbook of competence and motivation* (pp. 598–608). New York: Guilford Press.

Engle, J., & Engle, L. (2002). Neither international nor educative: Study abroad in the time of globalization. In W. Grünsweig & N. Rinehart (Eds.), *Rockin' in Red Square: Critical approaches to international education in the age of cyberculture* (pp. 25–39). Münster, Germany: LIT Verlag.

Erikson, E. (1968). *Identity, youth and crisis*. New York: Norton.

Folkman, S., & Moskowitz, J. T. (2004). Coping: Pitfalls and promise. *Annual Review of Psychology, 55*, 745–774.

Freud, S. (1999). *The interpretation of dreams*. (Joyce Crick, Trans.) New York: Oxford University Press. (Original work published 1900)

Frey, F. E., & Tropp, L. R. (2006). Being seen as individuals versus as group members: Extending research on metaperception to intergroup contexts. *Personality and Social Psychology Review, 10*, 265–280.

Haley, J. (1973). *Uncommon therapy: The psychiatric techniques of Milton H. Erickson, M.D.* New York: Norton.

Holmes, T. H., & Rahe, R. H. (1967). The Social Readjustment Rating Scale. *Journal of Psychosomatic Research, 11*, 213–218.

Hunter, A. (2008). Transformative learning in international education. In V. Savicki (Ed.), *Developing intercultural competence and transformation: Theory, research, and application in international education* (pp. 92–107). Sterling, VA: Stylus.

Joyce, B. R. (1984). Dynamic disequilibrium: The intelligence of growth. *Theory Into Practice, 23*, 26–34.

Kanner, A. D., Coyne, J. C., Schaefer, C., & Lazarus, R. S. (1981). Comparison of two modes of stress measurement: Daily hassles and uplifts versus major life events. *Journal of Behavioral Medicine, 4*, 1–39.

Koffka, K. (1922). Perception: An introduction to Gestalt Theorie. *Psychological Bulletin, 19*, 531–585.

Lazarus, R. S., & Folkman, S. (1984). *Stress, appraisal, and coping*. New York: Springer.

Lewin, K. (1935). *A dynamic theory of personality: Selected papers*. New York: McGraw-Hill.

Maher, B. A. (1969). *Clinical psychology and personality: The selected papers of George Kelly*. New York: Wiley.

Marcia, J. (1980). Identity in adolescence. In J. Addison (Ed.), *Handbook of adolescent psychology* (pp. 159–187). New York: Wiley.

Masgoret, A., & Ward, C. (2006). Culture learning approach to acculturation. In D. L. Sam & J. W. Berry (Eds.), *The Cambridge handbook of acculturation psychology* (pp. 58–77). Cambridge, UK: Cambridge University Press.

Maslach, C., & Schaufeli, W. B. (1993). Historical and conceptual development of burnout. In W. B. Schaufeli, C. Maslach, & T. Marek (Eds.), *Professional burnout: Recent developments in theory and research* (pp. 1–16). Washington, DC: Taylor & Francis.

Maslow, A. H. (1943). A theory of human motivation. *Psychological Review, 50*, 370–396.

Matsumoto, D., Hirayama, S., & Leroux, J. A. (2006). Psychological skills related to intercultural adjustment. In P. T. P. Wong & L. C. J. Wong (Eds.), *Handbook of multicultural perspectives on stress and coping* (pp. 387–405). New York: Springer Science.

Matsumoto, D., Leroux, J. A., Ratzlaff, C., Tatani, H., Uchida, H., Kim, C., & Araki, S. (2001). Development and validation of a measure of intercultural adjustment potential in Japanese sojourners: The Intercultural Adjustment Potential Scale (ICAPS). *International Journal of Intercultural Relations, 25*, 483–510.

Meyer-Lee, E., & Evans, J. (2008, May). New tools for intercultural outcomes learning assessment. In D. Deardorff (Chair), *Assessment toolbox for international educators.* Symposium presented at the NAFSA Annual Conference, Washington, DC.

Mezirow, J. (1991). *Transformative dimensions of adult learning.* San Francisco, CA: Jossey-Bass.

Miller, G. A. (1969). Psychology as a means of promoting human welfare. *American Psychologist, 24*, 1063–1075.

Nakamura, J., & Csikszentmihalyi, M. (2002). The concept of flow. In C. R. Snyder & S. J. Lopez (Eds.), *Handbook of positive psychology* (pp. 89–105). New York: Oxford University Press.

Open Doors. (2009). *Americans study abroad in increasing numbers.* Retrieved from http://www.iie.org/en/Research-and-Publications/Open-Doors

Pavlov, I. P. (1897). *Work of the principle digestive glands.* St. Petersburg, Russia: Kushneroff.

Pettigrew, R. F., & Tropp, L. R. (2006). A meta-analytic test of intergroup contact theory. *Journal of Personality and Social Psychology, 90*, 751–783.

Phinney, J. S. (1993). A three stage model of ethnic identity development in adolescence. In M. E. Bernal & G. P. Knight (Eds.), *Ethnic identity* (pp. 61–79). Albany, NY: State University of New York Press.

Plant, E. A. (2004). Responses to interracial interactions over time. *Personality and Social Psychology Bulletin, 30*, 1458–1471.

Rogers, C. R. (1942). *Counseling and psychotherapy: Newer concepts in practice.* Boston, MA: Houghton-Mifflin.

Sam, D. L. (2006). Acculturation: Conceptual background and core components. In D. L. Sam & J. W. Berry (Eds.), *The Cambridge handbook of acculturation psychology* (pp. 11–26). Cambridge, UK: Cambridge University Press.

Savicki, V. (2008a). Experiential and affective education for international educators. In V. Savicki (Ed.), *Developing intercultural competence and transformation: Theory, research, and application in international education* (pp. 74–91). Sterling, VA: Stylus.

Savicki, V. (2008b). Preface. In V. Savicki (Ed.), *Developing intercultural competence and transformation: Theory, research, and application in international education* (pp. ii–vi). Sterling, VA: Stylus.

Savicki, V. (2010a). An analysis of the contact types of study abroad students: The peer cohort, the host culture, and the electronic presence of the home culture in relationship to readiness and outcomes. *Frontiers: The Interdisciplinary Journal of Study Abroad, 19*, 61–86.

Savicki, V. (2010b). Implications of early sociocultural adaptation for study abroad students. *Frontiers: The Interdisciplinary Journal of Study Abroad, 19*, 205–223.

Savicki, V., Adams, I., & Binder, F. (2008). Intercultural development: Topics and sequences. In V. Savicki (Ed.), *Developing intercultural competence and transformation: Theory, research, and application in international education* (pp. 154–172). Sterling, VA: Stylus.

Savicki, V., Binder, F., & Arrúe, C. (in press). Language fluency and study abroad adaptation. *Frontiers: The Interdisciplinary Journal of Study Abroad.*

Savicki, V., & Cooley, E. (2011). American identity in study abroad students: Contrasts and changes. *Journal of College Student Development, 52*, 339–349.

Savicki, V., Cooley, E., & Donnelly, R. (2008). Acculturative stress, appraisal, coping and intercultural adjustment. In V. Savicki (Ed.), *Developing intercultural competence and transformation: Theory, research, and application in international education* (pp. 173–192). Sterling, VA: Stylus.

Savicki, V., Downing-Burnette, R., Heller, L., Binder, F., & Suntinger, W. (2004). Contrasts, changes, and correlates in actual and potential intercultural adjustment. *International Journal of Intercultural Relations, 28*, 311–329.

Schmidt, J. A., Shernoff, D. J., & Csikszentmihalyi, M. (2007). Individual and situational factors related to the experience of flow in adolescence: A multilevel approach. In A. D. Ong & M. H. M. van Dulmen (Eds.), *Oxford handbook of methods in positive psychology* (pp. 542–558). New York: Oxford University Press.

Skinner, B. F. (1938). *The behavior of organisms: An experimental analysis.* New York: Appleton-Century.

Stephan, W. G., & Stephan, C. W. (1985). Intergroup anxiety. *Journal of Social Issues, 41*, 157–176.

Stephan, W. G., Stephan, C. W., & Gudykunst, W. B. (1999). Anxiety in intergroup relations: A comparison of anxiety/uncertainty management theory and integrated threat theory. *International Journal of Intercultural Relations, 23*, 613–628.

Tajfel, H. (1981). *Human groups and social categories.* Cambridge, UK: Cambridge University Press.

Voci, A., & Hewstone, M. (2003). Intergroup contact and prejudice toward immigrants in Italy: The mediational role of anxiety and the moderational role of group salience. *Group Processes and Intergroup Relations, 6*, 37–54.

Ward, C. (2001). The A, B, Cs of acculturation. In D. Matsumoto (Ed.), *Handbook of culture and psychology* (pp. 411–446). New York: Oxford University Press.

Ward, C., Bochner, S., & Furnham, A. (2001). *The psychology of culture shock* (2nd ed.). London, UK: Routledge.

Ward, C., & Kennedy, A. (1999). The measurement of sociocultural adaptation. *International Journal of Intercultural Relations, 23*, 659–677.

Watzlawick, P. (1984). *Invented reality: How do we know what we believe we know? (Contributions to constructivism).* New York: W. W. Norton.

White, M., & Epston, D. (1990). *Narrative means to therapeutic ends.* New York: W. W. Norton.

Wong, P. T. P., Wong, L. C. J., & Scott, C. (2006). Beyond stress and coping: The positive psychology of transformation. In P. T. P. Wong & L. C. J. Wong (Eds.), *Handbook of multicultural perspectives on stress and coping* (pp. 1–26). New York: Springer.

Wundt, W. (1897). *Outlines of psychology* (C. H. Judd, Trans.) Leipzig, Germany: Engelmann.

10

LEARNING ABROAD AND THE SCHOLARSHIP OF TEACHING AND LEARNING

Jennifer Meta Robinson

The recent critiques of study abroad described in the first chapter of this volume suggest that the pedagogy of immersion, long considered a gold standard for learning in study abroad programs, now joins a host of other educational initiatives coming under both skeptical scrutiny and friendly reconsideration. Across the educational spectrum, legislators, accrediting bodies, administrators, parents, students, and learning abroad faculty and staff are taking a closer look at what students are actually learning and how. The new intervention paradigm that is emerging for the design of study abroad programs has characteristics very similar to those of the Scholarship of Teaching and Learning (SOTL), most notably in that they share a commitment to conducting research into instruction practices that can improve teaching and learning. The purpose of this chapter is to examine the contributions that the SOTL movement can make to study abroad. Such an analysis may be particularly useful at this critical juncture for study abroad programming. SOTL can provide insights regarding teaching and learning, learning environments, empowered educators, and intentional learning opportunities that have all been informed by learning theory and research findings.

SOTL Defined

SOTL in the broadest sense refers to *practitioner scholarship into the relationship between teaching and learning*. It can also be defined by the complementary concept of *scholarly teaching*: practice informed by educational research.

SOTL follows Dewey's (1904) assumption that preparation for teaching requires both practical and theoretical training. His proposition is that practicing one's "command of the necessary tools" of teaching allows "real and vital theoretical instruction, the knowledge of subject-matter and of principles of education" (p. 9). The practice of teaching, then, yields insights into broader principles of instruction that can be tested through processes of validation (Dewey). From this foundation, SOTL proceeds on the assumption that instructors are content experts in their fields of study and thus are uniquely well-positioned to evaluate student learning in those subject areas and, based on those evaluations, to design and revise learning activities in order to enhance learning (Shulman, 1987). Although instructors have the capacity for such iterative and evidence-based teaching, they do not necessarily practice this approach. What SOTL has contributed is a methodology for reflective and inquisitive practice that helps activate the potential of faculty.

The Principles of SOTL

SOTL emphasizes building knowledge about the relationship between pedagogical decisions and student learning. Faculty, staff, and students from every discipline are engaged in this practice, using an inquiry approach to better understand that relationship in order to redesign teaching to be more effective. Myriad theories are in play—learning, pedagogical, subject domain, assessment, political, and critical—in SOTL investigations, depending on the disciplinary specialization of particular scholars and the research focus of particular projects. The field by and large acknowledges the importance of context for learning and teaching; in efforts to understand fully what influences learning, SOTL scholars have investigated many salient factors, including expectations for disciplinary competency, students' affective responses to course topics and learning activities, faculty members' reasoning for their pedagogical choices, institutional mission, student demographics and career goals, teaching assistant training, and employers' needs. SOTL embraces not only the practical and theoretical interweavings of the profession of teaching but also the ethical responsibility for teachers to facilitate learning and redress learning gaps and shortfalls. Moreover, consistent with the mission of education to build and disseminate knowledge, SOTL encourages practitioners to value what they can learn from their own contexts and generalize these as appropriate. In this way, they can share findings with a critical but supportive SOTL community that reviews ideas and disseminates the best of them.

As Dewey's foundational work indicates, reflection on teaching methods is not new. Even apart from philosophies of education, reflection is usually prompted whenever a class meeting does not go as expected—when students ask questions about something just explained, when essays miss their mark, or when laboratory processes fail. Most conscientious teachers cannot help but consider what explains the gap between what she or he thought the students were learning and what they have just demonstrated their learning to be. What SOTL has done is provide a methodology for examining that gap.

Developments in SOTL

The credibility of reflection coupled with investigative scholarship about teaching was enhanced when Ernest Boyer (1990), then president of the Carnegie Foundation for the Advancement of Teaching, described the "scholarship of teaching" as the responsibility of ethical faculty work and teaching as a "communal act" with learners that "must be carefully planned, continuously examined, and relate directly to the subject taught" (pp. 23–24). Taking this theory into the practical realm, the Carnegie Foundation launched the influential Carnegie Academy for the Scholarship of Teaching and Learning, which in 1998 sparked conversations at more than 120 campuses throughout the United States that were willing "to undertake a public process of stock-taking and planning for ways they can support knowledge-building about teaching and learning" with the aim of creating new "support systems, sanctuaries, and learning centers for scholars across the disciplines, interdisciplines, and professions pursuing the scholarship of teaching seriously" (Hutchings & Shulman, 1999). From 1998 to 2005, Carnegie sponsored a program for developing scholars of teaching and from 2004 to 2012 sponsored networks of campuses to "cultivate the conditions necessary to support the scholarship of teaching and learning" (Carnegie Foundation, 2011). The Carnegie programs were focused primarily but not exclusively on higher education in the United States, with the institutional leadership program in particular expanding to include colleges and universities from the United Kingdom, Ireland, and Australia. In the United States, SOTL continues to grow as an area of study in higher education, with many longstanding teaching conferences and journals making reference to the "scholarship of teaching and learning" and benefiting from the work of SOTL scholars. In addition, new SOTL journals and conferences continue to proliferate regionally and nationally. Examples include the *Journal of the Scholarship of Teaching and Learning*; *InSight: A Journal of Scholarly Teaching*, published annually by the Center for Excellence in Teaching and Learning (CETL) at Park University; Eastern Michigan University's annual SOTL Academy, which began in 2009; the International Institute for SoTL Scholars and Mentors, sponsored in 2012 by the Center for Teaching Excellence at Loyola Marymount University; and the Center for Excellence in Teaching at Georgia Southern University's *International Journal for the Scholarship of Teaching and Learning* and its SOTL Commons Conference, annual since 2008.

Begun as a U.S. initiative, SOTL soon went international, and in 2004, the International Society for the Scholarship of Teaching and Learning (ISSOTL) was founded for professionals from around the world to share, review, and disseminate their work. Currently, the annual ISSOTL conference draws 400–800 participants, with significant participation from Japan, the United Kingdom, Australia, Canada, Ireland, Sweden, and the United States. A brief overview of developments in SOTL in the nations most involved in ISSOTL illustrates the momentum building in this area of study even as approaches to that development differ according to context.

In Japan, a movement led by the Kyoto University has focused on "Mutual FD," faculty development that includes reflection, cooperation, and interaction. Nationwide symposia in Japan, drawing more than 500 participants each year, have sought to create a theoretical basis for generative, collegial approaches to improving everyday teaching activities in that educational system (Matsushita, 2011).

In the United Kingdom, the London SOTL International Conference brought more than 100 participants to each of its meetings from 2001 to 2010. These U.K. conferences focused on "enhancing and making public HE [higher education] teaching practices" while also moving beyond "techniques or cognitive processes aimed at analysing and improving practice" to include field-building discussions on theory and educational roles (Fanghanel, Colet, & Bernstein, 2009). Also in the United Kingdom, the Higher Education Academy (2011), funded by the British government, has been supporting academic staff and institutions to provide "the best possible learning experience for all students" through identification and dissemination of effective practices in teaching. The academy has been sponsoring 24 "subject centres" that network teaching professionals across the United Kingdom and help them develop discipline-specific best practices. In the present climate of significant reduced funding throughout the higher education sector in the United Kingdom, this initiative is now in peril and likely to be significantly curtailed (J. Fanghanel, personal communication, November 22, 2011).

Australia, with its relatively centralized educational system, has effectively dovetailed its SOTL efforts with national policies and organizations. The regionwide Higher Education Research and Development Society of Australasia "promotes the development of higher education policy, practice and the study of teaching and learning" while universities in Australia support SOTL through a variety of institutional, disciplinary, and national programs that advocate learning assessment (Higher Education Research and Development Society of Australasia, 2011; International Society for the Scholarship of Teaching and Learning, 2009). Most significantly, some major Australian institutions, including the University of Sydney and the University of New South Wales, have now made it possible for academic staff to be promoted through the ranks, up to and including professor, along a research track focused on SOTL.

In Canada, SOTL is an area of study widely recognized by faculty, with especially strong institutional programs at the University of British Columbia, Mt. Royal College, and McMaster University. Arising from a "grass-roots" movement of faculty that has spread mostly independent of official rewards, unlike the Australian and U.K. models, SOTL has found important support in the Society for Teaching and Learning in Higher Education, whose board in 2002–3 identified SOTL as one of four primary strategic directions for the society (Hughes, 2006; G. Poole, personal communication, November 9, 2011). At that time, a vice president for scholarship was created "to further stimulate member and educational developer SOTL work" (G. Poole, personal communication, November 9, 2011). In 2010, the society launched *The Canadian Journal for the Scholarship of Teaching and Learning*.

In Ireland, University College Cork has been a leader in SOTL since securing 3 million euros to found the National Academy for the Integration of Research, Teaching and Learning and the Irish Integrative Learning Project, launching "an unprecedented level of collaboration within Ireland" (Higgs, 2009).

In Sweden, a 2002 ordinance mandated that lecturers in higher education complete formal training in teaching, though the content and duration of such training was not specified (Lindberg-Sand & Sonesson, 2008). In 2011, ISSOTL's membership elected its regional vice president for Europe from Sweden, and since 2004, a biennial Swedish national conference for the development of university teaching and SOTL has drawn 500 participants.

Sweden's largest higher education institution, Lund University, is particularly notable for how it supports SOTL with a "quality culture" (Mårtensson, Roxå, & Olsson, 2011).

In the United States and abroad, teaching centers have been notably important for their support of both scholarly teaching and SOTL. In general, teaching centers have seen SOTL as a way to engage faculty in reflecting about and assessing what works in their teaching, developing new approaches that are based on evidence of student achievement and framed in theory, and sharing those findings with colleagues. Whether advancing or applying what we know about how people learn, faculty engaged in SOTL seek real improvements in educational environments—not in the laboratory or in theory alone but also in the complex, real-world settings of teaching and learning. Study abroad, too, in its shift from unscripted immersion to intentional design, can make use of campus teaching centers and other public opportunities to describe, revise, and spread useful approaches to this complex, context-sensitive, and potentially powerful educational endeavor. The Global Identity course described by Paige, Harvey, and McCleary in chapter 13 of this volume benefited from a consultation about online instruction with the University of Minnesota's Teaching and Learning Center.

An Inquiry Stance

The invitation at the heart of SOTL is for educators to use the critical and inquisitive habits of mind that they have developed through disciplinary training to understand and design learning environments that best foster student success (Cambridge, 2001; Martin, Benjamin, Prosser, & Trigwell, 1999). To accomplish this charge, they take up questions that they believe will make important differences in student learning. For example, they may consider such cross-curricular competencies as writing, numerical, visual, and environmental literacy (e.g., Faculty Center for Innovative Teaching, 2011; Hattwig, 2011; Illinois State University, 2011; Reynolds, Brondizio, & Robinson, 2010). They may try new ways to support students who are unlikely to flourish in particular subjects (e.g., Jacobs, 2000). Or they may redesign instruction to address discipline-specific misconceptions or threshold concepts that students must negotiate before they can succeed in a particular course of study (e.g., Diaz, Middendorf, Pace, & Shopkow, 2008; Meyer & Land, 2005; Redish, 1999). In each of these examples, the common thread is that the decisions about who is involved, which innovations to make and how, and evaluations of success are all motivated by genuine questions that faculty and staff have about what students are learning and how to enhance it.

For study abroad, three main implications of SOTL's inquiry stance merit consideration: asking questions, gathering evidence, and revising practice accordingly. To begin the process, faculty and staff need to examine areas that they consider successful in current practice, those that seem less successful, and those that perhaps have been largely overlooked or are less integrated into the central educational program.

Asking Questions

In their recommendations for new scholars of teaching, Savory, Burnett, Nelson, and Goodburn (2007) identify general "types of inquiry" that can be adapted slightly to apply to the study of student learning abroad (p. 10). These areas of inquiry and related questions include the following:

- *Idea development*: How does student understanding of a particular concept or topic develop or change during the learning abroad experience?
- *Range of understanding*: To what degree and in what ways is student learning different for various subsets of students? One could compare, for example, majors versus nonmajors, males versus females, and undergraduate students versus graduate students.
- *Depth of understanding*: How much knowledge and understanding are students gaining from the course in comparison with their knowledge before the study abroad experience? Can students analyze and apply concepts to a situation or merely restate earlier, less informed understandings and surface descriptions?
- *Misconceptions*: What misconceptions are students bringing to the study abroad experience and how do these misconceptions change as a result of the learning abroad?
- *Long-term learning*: What knowledge or long-term skills will students carry from having studied abroad into subsequent courses and their careers?
- *Transfer of learning*: Are students able to apply what they have learned in one study abroad program to quite different sites and situations?
- *Measure of critical thinking*: Can students interpret, understand, process, and apply the course concepts to new situations?

- *Progressive dialogue*: Is there discernable development in students' understanding (e.g., of intercultural or disciplinary concepts) during study abroad?
- *Instructional practice*: What is the impact of a specific teaching method, activity, or course material on students' learning?

Additional topics and questions that may assist in the reflection and assessment of study abroad are as follows:

- *Intercultural preparation*: How does the intercultural preparation that students bring from their personal lives, prior educational experiences, or orientation programs intersect with and support their learning abroad experience?
- *Expectations*: How do their expectations, for example, of the target culture or the upcoming residential experience, interact with their actual experiences and learning?
- *Attitudes and preferences*: How does student confidence about learning in particular situations bear on students' success in the study abroad environment? What about their attitudes toward cultural difference?
- *Academic context*: In what ways do particular disciplinary majors prepare students for learning abroad; integrate study abroad into the curriculum; or, alternatively, present particular obstacles to study abroad?
- *Cultural diversity*: Do host countries present certain learning opportunities or obstacles?

Such questions allow faculty and staff members to reflect on the goals that they have for student learning abroad, exercise their own critical abilities in ways that respond to student realities, and revise programming in targeted ways.

Gathering Evidence

How would evidence be gathered to determine progress or success in these areas of inquiry? The answer might begin with rich descriptions of the educational environment—the people, texts, contexts, tasks, opportunities, constraints, histories, traditions, and/or trends. Interviews and surveys of staff, hosts, students, and faculty members would provide insights about what each group contributes, what each group thinks works, and what improvements each group's experiences suggest. The affective responses of students might be relevant to learning: Did they like the host city, feel confident using the appropriate language, or think they learned a lot? Educators should also consider what direct indicators of student learning can be found in existing assignments, such as class papers, journals, or oral proficiency exams. New assignments might be added that allow students to exercise, integrate, and reflect on their new skills and knowledge. Examples would include a capstone creative essay, short video, or photographic montage about a site that they found personally memorable or culturally illuminating.

Some factors can be used as both indicators of the progress of individual students and evidence of program success. In addition, formative assessments that are short, frequent, and low stakes serve as good monitors of progress—for students themselves and for faculty and staff evaluating those students and the programs in which they are participating (Angelo & Cross, 1993; Bransford, Brown, & Cocking, 1999). Research on learning indicates that frequent feedback is important and is most effective when occurring "continuously, but not intrusively, as a part of instruction" (Bransford et al., p. 140). Thus, such assessments can promote learning while also providing indications for small, midstream corrections and just-in-time interventions that can redirect a student or suggest revisions for a study abroad program. For example, a quick check-in can identify students who are struggling with an unfamiliar instructional style at a foreign university or isolating themselves in American enclaves.

In the United States, active and collaborative learning techniques have taken hold in many universities, and many professors now provide typed class notes and extensive slide presentations. U.S. students used to such methods may benefit from help orienting to foreign universities that rely on the traditional lecture method. They may struggle with different expectations for student participation and faculty authority in class. Or they may have a difficult time moving safely beyond familiar American friends and establishments. Electronic journals or public-access blogs can be a good way for students to document their experience in these new learning environments. Staff can introduce students to these differences, help them make the transition to different methods of instruction, and also provide timely and constructive feedback to them. Moreover, quick written assignments give students a chance to practice core skills (reflection, critical thinking, application, analysis, evaluation) and give staff useful information about how students are doing. Questions can be as simple as: What is one surprising thing you observed this week? What similar phenomena have you observed in the United States? What is one thing that the study abroad program is doing to help you learn, and what is one thing that the study abroad program could do to help you learn more?

In study abroad, such assessments can prove particularly important for helping staff monitor and sustain students' discovery and adjustment processes. Transformative learning theory (Mezirow, 1991) suggests that the supporting of significant changes occurs through three main stages:

> [becoming] critically aware of how and why our assumptions have come to constrain the way we perceive, understand, and feel about our world; changing these structures of habitual expectation to make possible a more inclusive, discriminating, and integrating perspective; and finally, making choices or otherwise acting upon these new understandings. (p. 167)

Short, formative assessments with feedback can help move students forward developmentally in a manner that supports transformative learning: identifying and discussing an activating event that highlights the limitations of a student's current knowledge, reflecting critically about why the student might hold these assumptions, discussing alternative approaches with others, and testing new perspectives. These prompts could be given as written, oral, or electronically mediated assignments encouraging students to become more reflective, experimental, and intercultural. This process allows program staff and instructors to keep tabs on student development and foster student growth.

Revising Practice Accordingly

After instructors and staff gather evidence to determine progress and success in student learning abroad, it is not uncommon for them to revise what they do. What those changes are, of course, depends on many factors. Perhaps the evidence calls for better coordination among elements of the curriculum; greater use of existing resources; more finely tuned orientation activities for students or instructors; better alignment of assignments with learning goals; more fruitful use of staff time; or enhanced responsiveness to political, cultural, or environmental factors. Indeed, education is so dynamic that only in rare cases can no improvements be imagined. Without the gathering of evidence, however, revising practice is much more challenging.

Fortunately, researchers now have strong theories of learning and good recommendations for how to employ them in instructional design. Although few faculty and staff members outside teacher education programs have read the educational research literature in depth, literature reviews and meta-analyses provide useful shortcuts. For example, an excellent and frequently referenced text is *How People Learn: Brain, Mind, Experience, and School* (Bransford et al., 1999), which reviews the literature on learning as the basis for recommending evidence-based principles for good teaching or, as the authors put it in a chapter title, moving the state of the art in education "from speculation to science" (p. 3). They review what distinguishes experts from novices, what factors matter in learning transfer, and what possibilities technology offers, among other topics. They also review the design of learning environments and their implications for "what is taught, how it is taught, and how it is assessed" (p. 131). The authors describe four major characteristics around which to organize learning environments: the *learners* and what they bring to the educational setting; the *knowledge* that they are poised to acquire, make sense of, and transfer; the *assessment* practices provided for feedback and revision; and the multiple *community* contexts that set norms and expectations. These "perspectives" on design are not discrete in practice. Rather, they provide useful frames of reference reflecting on and revising current practice. In particular, they can clarify the coordination, or *alignment*, between the goals for learning and the assignments that students undertake to achieve those goals. Study abroad programs emphasizing a learner-centered perspective, for example, would "pay careful attention to the knowledge, skills, attitudes, and beliefs that learners bring to the educational setting" (p. 133). Program and course design, then, would build on that foundation of personal, disciplinary, and cultural experience and assumptions with knowledge-centered activities. These activities would be designed to be relevant and responsive to the students' experience. Assessments of student performance on those activities would provide opportunity for feedback that incrementally supports, or *scaffolds*, their learning in a new culture. And their achievements would be warranted based on their sense of belonging to a community of learners with shared standards and attitudes. As analytical tools, these four perspectives can aid those who facilitate study abroad experiences to analyze the emphasis of their current design and revise it with intentionality.

Examples specific to student learning and development abroad can be found in Part Four of this volume, which provides six examples of courses and programs that intentionally intervene in learning. They show how various activities and assignments can help to uncover students' misconceptions or prompt them "to make predictions about various situations and explain the reasons for their predictions" (Bransford et al., 1999, p. 134). Instructors and program staff who engage in the serious business of designing such interventions benefit from having more information to act on. However, that the information is sourced from individuals does not mean that programs need to be customized for every participant. Instead, administrators and instructors can see prevailing trends, growth, and gaps in learning and make purposeful and efficient interventions in the design of the learning experience. With better understanding of the student experience, study abroad educators can intervene in the learning process so that it unfolds more "by design" than "by chance" (see chapter 9 of this volume).

In redesigning teaching practices, effective revisions must take into account the issue of "alignment," which means *coordinating* learning opportunities with learning goals in order to increase the likelihood that students will reach desired learning outcomes (Bransford et al., 1999). Study abroad resident directors and on-site staff are in a very good position for this work. The core planning of which courses and experiential learning opportunities to offer will occur before a group of students is even identified. Study abroad professionals will do their best to help students achieve the program's learning goals by providing types of housing, excursions, and community engagement activities that will complement these academic and intercultural outcomes. Other parts of the planning occur midstream, as other opportunities and challenges for students become apparent. Throughout the program, the central question is: What learning outcomes will students likely achieve through each of these programming decisions? Thinking through the best ways to align learning and teaching will take an up-front investment of time but will result in the greatest impact.

Supporting Learning by Teachers

One of the most important findings of the SOTL movement since 1990 is that a rich social context fosters the development, review, adoption, and spread of teaching innovations. Because educators in higher education are rarely trained as teachers, instead having made their successes in literature, history, archaeology, computer science, and other specialized fields, they often benefit from and appreciate opportunities to learn about good practices. They also often feel more confident about making changes when they are part of a collegial culture that supports teaching innovations. A great deal of attention in SOTL thus far has been on the challenge of creating social support structures within which educational innovation and institutional change can flourish. This emphasis has been bolstered by SOTL's commitment to the public nature of scholarship, that is, as information intended for public availability. The notion is that an instructor or administrator may become increasingly skilled in his or her work with students in the privacy of a classroom but not necessarily share that with others. Scholars oriented to SOTL are by definition committed to sharing their processes and results; getting feedback from their colleagues; seeking to improve their practice further; and, it is hoped, striving to advance knowledge about teaching and learning. Although SOTL, like traditional scholarship, organizes and shares knowledge through formal, written publications, the field has also recognized that where teaching is concerned, other forums may get the word out more quickly, to more relevant audiences, and in forms that will make it more useful than traditional journal publication. As a result, SOTL has seen numerous types of communities develop to support people as they share and review their practice, often through the contributions of teaching centers and other instructional service offices. Study abroad can build on these ways of developing and spreading good ideas about teaching and learning.

Instructional Workshops

Instructional workshops offer one obvious approach to bringing people together to spread ideas. On many U.S. campuses, the teaching center offers structured, short duration, and skill-based meetings designed to allow individual instructors to make quick adjustments to particular facets of their teaching, such as in-class discussions, multiple-choice test questions, and improved lecturing. People who attend frequently may become acquainted with each other, but these workshops are often open to all comers and thus have a changing roster of participants from many disciplines. Teaching center staff typically welcome suggestions for new workshop topics that will speak to new audiences; the chances are very good that U.S.-based study abroad professionals would find that colleagues in their institution's teaching center would be interested in working with them to develop workshops that address issues in the training of teachers at study center sites abroad, in internationalizing the curriculum, and so on.

Communities of Practice

Less common than one-off instructional workshops but rapidly taking hold across the United States are communities of practice: ongoing meetings of people who seek to address similar problems and share best practices (Wenger, 1998). Normally consisting of small, informal, and cross-organizational groups, communities of practice have emerged among faculty and staff who value the input of peers who are interested in exploring, developing, and disseminating innovations over the longer term. A good part of the appeal of these communities lies in their ability to "create connections for isolated teachers, establish networks for those pursuing pedagogical issues, meet early-career faculty expectations for community, foster multidisciplinary curricula, and begin to bring community to higher education" (Cox, 2004, p. 5). Variations on teacher communities developed for the K–12 world (Grossman, Wineburg, & Woolworth, 2001), faculty learning communities in higher education are typically initiated or administered by a campus teaching center to engage in a structured curriculum "with frequent seminars and activities that provide learning, development, the scholarship of teaching, and community building" (Cox, 2004, p. 8). The process that they follow is typically cooperative and is often inquiry based. These learning communities usually operate at the local level, although some are multi-institutional and even multinational. For example, Fincher and Tenenberg's (2006) "Bootstrapping" communities, funded by the National Science Foundation, bring together computer science faculty from different institutions and different countries into communities of practice, where they use processes familiar to their field to engage in shared teaching and learning enterprises.

Many college and university teaching centers across the United States now support faculty learning communities as focused, cost-effective, and long-term means to advance teaching practices that benefit student learning. Teaching centers often function as an ideal hub for learning communities. Teaching center staff members have the organizational skills, educational knowledge, and institutional mandate to allow them to actively and expertly support and cooperate in the development of effective innovations in teaching. Their knowledge of and access to internal grant funds, their charge to stay current with the literature on teaching, their skills in organizing and disseminating information, their access to models of pedagogy and assessment, their connections with clerical and other support staff, and their charge to work with any discipline as constructively critical outsiders all mean that they can be invaluable partners. Teaching center staff members know the people, teaching issues, and special contexts of their particular institution. Thus, they can assemble resources relevant to the faculty: connections with other support centers, possibilities for funding and equipment, colleagues with complementary skills and interests, and conversations beyond those in which they already participate. At Indiana University (2011), for example, the teaching center supports learning communities on such subjects as teaching and learning in the field of history, innovative teaching with iPads, teaching large classes, adopting new pedagogies in informatics, and internationalizing the curriculum. A learning community of study abroad faculty and staff could be an invaluable structure within which to develop innovative pedagogies and new standards of practice.

Networking

A variation on the faculty learning community theme is to use networking principles to support innovation within and across unit lines. The collegium model brings together small cohorts of people who share an orientation to issues in teaching and learning into a more complex and multidisciplinary network of related practitioners (Robinson et al., 2012). In this sort of forum, teaching innovations benefit from multiple critiques and spread in unpredictable, context-responsive ways. The Teagle Collegium on Inquiry in Action at Indiana University brings together graduate students and their faculty mentors from three departments, each based in different knowledge domains and in diverse teaching traditions, for a yearlong seminar during which they read about learning theory and then design teaching innovations that are appropriate to their disciplinary and course goals. A fourth team—composed of a professor and a graduate student from the learning sciences and a teaching consultant from the campus teaching center—guides the rest of the group in the assessment of their innovations. The networked design of the collegium means that participants have the support of colleagues from their home department with whom they can examine their practices and try new techniques while also having the advantage of colleagues from other fields with different goals and assumptions who can serve as outside reviewers and critical resources. The result is that teachers become more informed, intentional, and accomplished.

Particularly appropriate to the geographical distribution of study abroad programs, a number of asynchronous electronic communities of practice have emerged in recent years that connect people with knowledgeable peers who may be at other institutions and in other time zones. For example, MERLOT: Multimedia Educational Resource for Learning and Online Teaching (www.merlot.org), offers user-generated learning materials, exercises, and web resources on every subject, including study abroad and international education, in a searchable and reviewable format. More interactive, problem-based social networking communities include the Professional and Organizational Development Network in Higher Education (www.pod network.org), which runs an active LISTSERV electronic mailing list of academic development professionals who readily share their advice on teaching and teacher development. Similarly, a "higher education teaching and learning" subgroup is active on LinkedIn (www.linkedin.com), a social networking platform intended for professional communication.

Fortunately, international education professionals have recognized the value of learning communities and networks. Specialized workshops and seminars offered by organizations such as NAFSA: Association of International Educators, The Forum on Education Abroad, and the Council on International Educational Exchange provide communities and materials especially designed to improve learning abroad. NAFSA: Association of International Educators, for example, has five knowledge communities, including the Education Abroad knowledge community and the Teaching, Learning, and Scholarship knowledge community. Here, professionals can take on real challenges and propose changes in a collaborative atmosphere. These communities can and do include both experienced and new participants in study abroad programming. And they can take advantage of both the commonalities and the diversity of their members.

Further means of learning and sharing information about educational practice include pedagogical conferences and the instructional sections of disciplinary conferences. ISSOTL (www.issotl.org) convenes an annual conference for tertiary educators from around the world to share their scholarship. The organization's website also lists regional and national conferences around the world at which scholars of teaching may find others of like mind.

Conclusion

In the long run, a culture of inquiry may be more effective than trying to disseminate any particular set of good practices to already busy people who are deeply embedded in particular contexts. Learning communities, teaching center events, and other sites of public exchange can help to spread this fresh approach to learning abroad while preserving its emphasis on context, responsiveness, and opportunity.

In a paradigm shift from positivism through relativism to experiential constructivism, described by Vande Berg, Paige, and Lou in chapter 1, study abroad professionals will need to reframe their approach to teaching. Experience from the SOTL shows that although concrete examples of how to make this shift may seem to be few in the early days genuinely engaged practitioners will quickly generate new ones that can be assessed, adapted, and transferred in unexpectedly generative ways. Disseminating the most promising of those ideas along collegial networks can help to create opportunities for students to do their best learning. Experience from SOTL shows that supporting study abroad staff and faculty members as they formalize and assess their wisdom of practice can help them to make informed revisions and intervene productively in learning environments in ways that rely more on design than chance.

References

Angelo, T. A., & Cross, K. P. (1993). *Classroom assessment techniques.* San Francisco, CA: Jossey-Bass.

Boyer, E. L. (1990). *Scholarship reconsidered: Priorities of the professoriate.* Princeton, NJ: Carnegie Foundation for the Advancement of Teaching.

Bransford, J. D., Brown, A. L., & Cocking, R. R. (Eds.). (1999). *How people learn: Brain, mind, experience, and school.* Washington, DC: National Academy Press.

Cambridge, B. (2001). Fostering the scholarship of teaching and learning: Communities of practice. In D. Lieberman & C. Wehlburg (Eds.), *To improve the academy* (pp. 3–16). Bolton, MA: Anker.

Carnegie Foundation. (2011). Carnegie Academy for the Scholarship of Teaching and Learning (CASTL). Retrieved from http://www.carnegiefoundation.org/scholarship-teaching-learning

Cox, M. D. (2004, Spring). Introduction to faculty learning communities. *New Directions for Teaching and Learning, 97,* 5–23.

Dewey, J. (1904). The relation of theory to practice in education. In C. A. McMurry (Ed.), *The third yearbook of the National Society for the Scientific Study of Education* (pp. 9–30). Chicago, IL: University of Chicago Press.

Diaz, A., Middendorf, J., Pace, D., & Shopkow, L. (2008). The History Learning Project: A department "decodes" its students. *The Journal of American History, 94*(4), 1211–1224.

Faculty Center for Innovative Teaching. (2011). 2011–2012 Faculty Learning Communities at CMU. Central Michigan University. Retrieved from http://facit.cmich.edu/tag/flc/

Fanghanel, J., Colet, N. R., & Bernstein, D. (2009). Foreword. [Electronic version]. In J. Fanghanel, N. R. Colet, & D. Bernstein (Eds.), *The London Scholarship of Teaching and Learning 7th International Conference Proceedings 2008, 4,* 3–4. London, UK: City University. Retrieved from http://www.heacademy.ac.uk/assets/documents/EvidenceNet/sotl_proceedings/sotl_proceedings_jfthree.pdf

Fincher, S., & Tenenberg, J. (2006). Using theory to inform capacity-building: Bootstrapping communities of practice in computer science education research. *Journal of Engineering Education, 95,* 265–278.

Grossman, P., Wineburg, S., & Woolworth, S. (2001). Toward a theory of teacher community. *The Teachers College Record, 103,* 942–1012.

Hattwig, D. (2011). Interdisciplinary visual literacy learning outcomes: New ideas for developing student competencies around visual materials [Electronic version]. University of Washington. Retrieved from http://depts.washington.edu/sotl/sym posium/2011/

Higgs, B. (2009). The Carnegie catalyst: A case study in internationalisation of SoTL [Electronic version]. *International Journal for the Scholarship of Teaching and Learning, 3*(2). Retrieved from http://academics.georgiasouthern.edu/ijsotl/ v3n2/invited_essays/PDFs/InvitedEssay_Higgs.pdf

Higher Education Academy. (2011). About us. Retrieved from http://www.heacade my.ac.uk/about

Higher Education Research and Development Society of Australasia. (2011). About HERDSA. Retrieved from http://www.herdsa.org.au

Hughes, J.C. (2006). The scholarship of teaching and learning: A Canadian perspective [Electronic version]. Hamilton, ON: Society for Teaching and Learning in Higher Education. Retrieved from http://www.stlhe.ca/wp-content/uploads/ 2011/09/SoTLCanadianPerspectiveJan06.pdf

Hutchings, P., & Shulman, L. (1999). The scholarship of teaching: New elaborations, new developments. *Change, 31*(5), 10–15. Retrieved from http://www.car negiefoundation.org/elibrary/scholarship-teaching-new-elaborations-new-devel opments

Illinois State University. (2011). SoTL Resource Group. Retrieved from http://sotl.il linoisstate.edu/resource/index.shtml

Indiana University. (2011). Faculty Learning Communities. Retrieved from http:// citl.indiana.edu/programs/sotl/flc.php#pfp

International Society for the Scholarship of Teaching & Learning. (2009). Regional SOTL links. Retrieved from http://www.issotl.org/sotl.html

Jacobs, D. (2000). A chemical mixture of methods. In P. Hutchings (Ed.), *Opening lines: Approaches to the scholarship of teaching and learning* (pp. 41–52). Menlo Park, CA: Carnegie Foundation for the Advancement of Teaching.

Lindberg-Sand, A., & Sonesson, A. (2008). Compulsory higher education teacher training in Sweden: Development of a national standards framework based on the Scholarship of Teaching and Learning. *Tertiary Education and Management, 14*, 123–139.

Mårtensson, K., Roxå, T., & Olsson, T. (2011). Developing a quality culture through the Scholarship of Teaching and Learning. *Higher Education Research & Development, 30*(1), 51–62.

Martin, E., Benjamin, J., Prosser, M., & Trigwell, K. (1999). Scholarship of teaching: A study of the approaches of academic staff. In C. Rust (Ed.), *Improving student learning: Improving student learning outcomes* (pp. 326–331). Oxford, UK: Oxford Brookes University.

Matsushita, K. (2011). Foreword: The generative approach and the standards approach. In K. Matsushita (Ed.), *Building networks in higher education: Towards the future of faculty development* (pp. x–xiv). Tokyo: Maruzen Planet.

Meyer, J. H. F., & Land, R. (2005). Threshold concepts and troublesome knowledge: Epistemological considerations and a conceptual framework for teaching and learning. *Higher Education, 49*, 373–388.

Mezirow, J. (1991). *Transformative dimensions of adult learning.* San Francisco, CA: Jossey-Bass.

Redish, E. F. (1999). Diagnosing student problems using the results and methods of physics education research [Electronic version]. International Conference on Physics Teaching, Guilin, People's Republic of China. Retrieved from http://www2.physics.umd.edu/~redish/Papers/Guilin.pdf

Reynolds, H., Brondizio, E., & Robinson, J. M. (Eds.). (2010). *Teaching environmental literacy: Across campus and across the curriculum.* Bloomington, IN: Indiana University Press.

Robinson, J. M., Gresalfi, M., Sievert, A. K., Christensen, T. B., Kearns, K. D., & Zolan, M. E. (2012). Talking across the disciplines: Building communicative competence in a multidisciplinary graduate-student seminar on inquiry in teaching and learning. In K. McKinney (Ed.), *The scholarship of teaching and learning in and across the disciplines.* Bloomington, IN: Indiana University Press.

Savory, P., Burnett, P., Nelson, A., & Goodburn, A. M. (2007). *Inquiry into the college classroom: A journey toward scholarly teaching.* Bolton, MA: Anker.

Shulman, L. S. (1987). Knowledge and teaching: Foundations of the new reform. *Harvard Educational Review, 57*(1), 1–22.

Wenger, E. (1998). *Communities of practice: Learning, meaning, and identity.* Cambridge, UK: Cambridge University Press.

PART THREE

PROGRAM APPLICATIONS: INTERVENING IN STUDENT LEARNING

SHIFTING THE LOCUS OF INTERCULTURAL LEARNING

Intervening Prior to and After Student Experiences Abroad

Laura Bathurst and Bruce La Brack

Over the years of teaching cross-cultural training at the University of the Pacific, Stockton, California, our conceptualizations of how best to prepare students to encounter "the other," as well as how to appropriately facilitate their continued learning once they have returned home, have undergone fundamental philosophic and pragmatic changes. In the past, students were considered primarily responsible for their own intercultural learning while abroad, as well as for the integration and application of that knowledge after their return. Our present view is that a carefully guided, interventionist approach facilitates significant intercultural learning prior to, during, and after the study abroad experience.

In 2010, cross-cultural training to support students studying abroad marked its 35th anniversary at Pacific.[1] To the best of our knowledge, our orientation and reentry courses are the oldest continuous, conceptually linked, credit-bearing courses of this type in the United States. Since their inception in 1975, these courses have gone through many phases of development, experimentation, and revision. First offered as informal, noncredit, voluntary seminars, then upgraded to two-unit, credit-bearing courses, both evolved from informal discussions initiated by students trying to understand "what their international experience meant." By 1977, every student intending to study abroad from Pacific's Callison College was required to take an orientation seminar prior to departure, as well as a reentry seminar upon return. Since 1986, all students in Pacific's School of International Studies (SIS) have been required to take both courses as part of their study abroad experience.

The purpose of this chapter is twofold. Our first goal is to provide an overview of Pacific's program in sufficient detail to enable others wishing to set up similar training programs to benefit from lessons that we have learned over decades. Our second goal, which arises from the most profound of these lessons, is to demonstrate that intervention prior to and after study abroad is *just as critical* to students' intercultural learning as the study abroad experience itself.

To these ends, we provide a detailed description of Pacific's training for study abroad as it exists today. We then contextualize current realities by reviewing our program's history, exploring how and why it evolved as it did. Next we turn to assessment, presenting evidence that our approach does, in fact, contribute to deeper intercultural learning by our students. Finally, we highlight reoccurring challenges that we have encountered, and provide suggestions for the implementation of similar programs elsewhere.

Cross-Cultural Training at Pacific: The Program Today

Currently, the University of the Pacific's SIS offers academic courses for students both prior to and immediately after their return from study abroad. These courses are conceptually designed and pedagogically sequenced to facilitate intercultural competence by introducing students to key intercultural concepts and skills prior to departure, which students then apply while living and studying in the new culture. Following their reentry, students reflect on how they employed these concepts and skills while abroad, and then use them in order to make sense of what they are experiencing at home and on campus.

All students who plan to study abroad through the University of the Pacific are required to take INTL 151: Cross Cultural Training I (CCT I) the semester prior to their departure. They are not permitted to study abroad unless they receive a grade of C or above (73.0%) in this two-semester-unit course. Close coordination is required between the SIS, responsible for cross-cultural training at Pacific, and the Office of International Programs and Services, responsible for shepherding students through the logistical aspects of study abroad.

INTL 161: Cross Cultural Training II (CCT II) is required of all students in Pacific's SIS, all of whom are required to study abroad as part of their curriculum. Although the course is not required of students in Pacific's other academic units, some do take the course voluntarily upon their return. In addition, international students and "global nomads" sometimes take CCT I and/or CCT II and find it helpful in their adjustment to studying in the United States.

Instructors of the cross-cultural training courses are tenured or tenure-track professors who have completed their doctorates, and who have at least partial appointments in the SIS. SIS houses Pacific's cross-cultural training program, as well as its anthropology program. All anthropologists hired by Pacific are expected to teach the cross-cultural training courses, although it is recognized that the field of intercultural communication is distinct from anthropology in its methods, assumptions, and core body of knowledge.

Whether other SIS faculty members are appropriate as instructors for these courses is determined on a case-by-case basis, and instructors have also included political scientists and historians. Prior to teaching cross-cultural training courses, all faculty members are required to undergo a minimum of one week of formal instruction in intercultural training design at the Intercultural Communication Institute's Summer Institute for Intercultural Communication in Portland, Oregon. They are also required to audit each course at Pacific prior to teaching it. More experienced colleagues provide further support, as needed, in the form of mentoring while the course is being taught, especially during the first semester.

The training at the Summer Institute, the auditing of the course prior to teaching it, and the peer mentoring are all considered essential to preparing faculty for their teaching duties in the cross-cultural program. This substantial initial investment in faculty is considered key to the success of the program precisely because it allows for continual improvement of the course through responsive innovation. While instructors have responsibility for delivering core course content, they also have the flexibility to experiment and to respond creatively to changing student needs. In addition, because the program is housed in an academic unit and the courses are taught by tenured or tenure-track faculty as part of their regular teaching assignment, faculty are required to view the course as a "serious" one, a view that is then transmitted to the students both explicitly and implicitly.

Cross-Cultural Training in the SIS Curriculum

It is worth noting the special role of cross-cultural training in the SIS. All SIS undergraduates are required to study abroad for a minimum of one semester, and to complete a core set of interdisciplinary classes, including CCT I and CCT II. Beyond increasing students' knowledge of the world, cross-cultural training makes an additional important contribution to the SIS curriculum that arises from the school's unique mission.

SIS was founded with the aim of achieving a truly interdisciplinary undergraduate education. The goal was to create a learning community in which students would not only be exposed to multiple disciplines by taking classes in them, but also be required to actively explore how different disciplines approach understanding the world. SIS students learn to identify similarities and differences in the basic assumptions, methods, and core questions of the disciplines that they study.

From their first semester in the program, SIS students take interdisciplinary courses taught by professors from multiple disciplines who explicitly train students to bridge disciplinary perspectives. In short, SIS takes an *intercultural* approach to *interdisciplinary* education, and cross-cultural training is expected to assist the students in understanding academic disciplines as well as parts of the world. This perspective, integrated throughout their education, includes the study of cultural anthropology, world history, and comparative political systems. This approach likely contributes to the effectiveness of the orientation course, with roughly half of the students from SIS, as well as the reentry course, which consists almost exclusively of SIS students.

INTL 151: Cross-Cultural Training I Course Design

CCT I is an orientation course designed to be taken by students just prior to their experience abroad. The class is held once a week, for three hours, during the last eight weeks of Pacific's 15-week semester. The deadline for applying for study abroad is just prior to the beginning of the course, and as previously mentioned, students are required to obtain a grade of C or better in order to be permitted to study abroad. The intent is to communicate clearly that studying abroad at Pacific is a privilege, not a right.

Decades of experience watching students prioritize other activities over class has resulted in a stringent course attendance policy, approved by the entire faculty of SIS. Students who miss even one class without the prior approval of their instructor fail the course. Even those who secure the approval of their instructor for an absence are penalized one letter grade, because they have missed 3 of the 24 instructional hours, or one eighth of the course content. This attendance policy can be quite painful to enforce, but it is our experience that the nature of cross-cultural training is that students do not "know what they do not know," or often, even know what they are learning. Indeed, instructors have received many e-mails and comments from former students in the class saying that they did not realize the value of the course until they were actually abroad. The strict attendance policy helps ensure that students learn the material—whether or not they recognize its value.

The content and instructional exercises of the course have evolved significantly over its history and are highly informed by scholarship from the field of intercultural communication, as well as our own experience at Pacific. The sequencing of course material is designed to build toward increasing complexity and challenge while simultaneously increasing students' comfort with each other in order to facilitate productive classroom interaction. This also necessitates the stringent attendance policy; it is our experience that later learning is lessened significantly when students miss class.

The following is a week-by-week overview of the topics covered in the course; instructors are free to modify lesson plans and assignments to improve the course. A perennial challenge is the lack of time to do all we would like to do, in class and out. It is important to be alert for "syllabus creep," in which little exercises or readings are added one by one, eventually resulting in a dramatic increase to the course workload. Thus, we are periodically forced to prune to ensure that the work required is consistent with the two units of academic credit offered.

In the first week, we focus on introducing students to the course and to each other, including explaining the syllabus, key assignments, attendance policy, and key concepts. In the second week, we introduce several useful ways to think about the concept of "culture" and show students how the same events can be experienced quite differently by groups of people with different values and interaction styles. We do this by eliciting, directly from the students, diverse perspectives that are also clearly patterned and predictable using Kolb's Learning Style Inventory. In the third week, we delve deeper into how to learn culture using "A Matter of Honor," an episode of *Star Trek: Next Generation,* in which an exchange of officers occurs among three quite different cultural groups. We also introduce the intercultural tool known to many as "D.I.E." (description, interpretation, evaluation), along with the idea that culture shapes our perceptions.

While we include learning about U.S. culture in each class and assigned readings, this topic is the focus of the fourth week. Classroom exercises are directed toward externalizing aspects of U.S. culture (such as a high value placed on informality), and exploring situations abroad in which acting "normally" as one would in the United States might get the students into trouble. A variety of methods are used, including written descriptions and video dramatizations of cross-cultural misunderstandings or "critical incidents."

During week five, we focus on intercultural communication styles and the predictable misunderstandings that arise from differences between them. During week six, we examine "culture shock"—the difficulty of adjusting to a new culture. We devote the seventh week entirely to a simulation of study abroad using *BaFá BaFá*, and an extensive discussion of the experience. The final week includes visits from campus offices (e.g., financial aid, registrar, and housing) to talk with students about logistical issues, and we spend the remainder of the class focusing on the experience of reentry.

It is worth noting that in several class sessions we include panels of students who have returned from study abroad. We find that students are more likely to take the course seriously if they sometimes hear about study abroad directly from their returning peers, especially when the instructor has helped the returnees identify the most useful stories to share prior to the panel.

INTL 161: Cross-Cultural Training II Course Design

CCT II is designed for students to take as soon as possible following their experience abroad. The class is held once a week, for three hours, during the first seven weeks of the semester. It is our experience that on the first day of class most students do not think they need the course, nor do they wish to take it. Within a few weeks, most find it an extremely welcome addition to their week; instructors regularly receive e-mails and comments from students that make this dramatic shift in attitude explicit. However, this recurring pattern of students not recognizing the need to integrate their reentry experience into their ongoing lives has the obvious and unfortunate consequence of reducing the number of students who choose to take the course voluntarily. The few who take it as an elective usually do so based on the enthusiastic recommendation of a close friend for whom it had previously been required. As with the orientation course, the attendance policy is strict, although the penalty for missing class is not as severe.

In CCT II, materials and exercises revisit the same themes examined in CCT I, but in increased depth. Topics that were dealt with theoretically in the orientation course are revisited, and students are guided in applying and comparing previously introduced ideas and concepts with their actual experience abroad. Ample time is provided for students to share stories and experiences, and we simultaneously encourage them to *analyze* their experiences using the intercultural tools provided in class in order to extract additional educational value. Students continue to learn about their host cultures, their home cultures, and the process of culture learning more generally.

Because students who have returned from diverse study abroad experiences are working through their experiences collectively, they also learn about additional areas of the world. This mixed group, however, has a more important function: to destabilize any facile, dualistic conceptions of cross-cultural phenomena that students might have acquired abroad. For example, students often return from Latin America believing that U.S. Americans are "schedule conscious" and Latin Americans are not. Comments from U.S. students returning from Japan suggest that they saw their Japanese friends as "schedule conscious" in contrast to themselves.

Continuities and Discontinuities With the Past: How We Got Here

The development of Pacific's program parallels, to a great extent, the evolution of the field of intercultural communication. Over the years, experiential learning theory, especially David Kolb's model of the experiential learning cycle (Kolb, 1984), and intercultural theory, especially Milton Bennett's (1986) Developmental Model of Intercultural Sensitivity, have been influential in shaping our program. In addition, there was a growing body of literature on intercultural training and an increasing availability of culture-specific training materials. The program's history also reflects changing institutional realities at Pacific, as well as the cumulative results of ongoing experimentation.

There were six fundamental changes in the program since its inception, and these reflect four major phases of development. In the first phase of the program, a series of informal sessions emerged in response to student requests. During the second phase, these informal sessions became formal courses taken for academic credit, and the orientation and reentry components became linked with content shared between the two. In the third phase, voluntary participation shifted to required participation, and the culture-specific focus became a culture-general focus. The fourth phase began when a permanent home for the program was established in an academic unit. It was during this period that we gradually came to understand that the primary intercultural learning from study abroad did not necessarily occur abroad, but rather as a result of particular kinds of reflection on the experience abroad—and that the frequency and depth of those reflections could be increased by structured interventions both before and after the study abroad experience.

Phase 1: Informal Sessions by Student Request

Cross-cultural training at Pacific has its roots in Callison College, one of Pacific's experimental cluster colleges, established in 1967. While Callison existed, its entire sophomore class studied abroad as a group, accompanied by Pacific professors, first in India (1968–72), then in Japan (1973–80). Prior to 1975, there was no systematic cross-cultural training, nor were orientation or reentry courses offered. The impetus for developing such training came, fittingly enough, from returning students themselves.

In the fall of 1975, students who had recently returned from Japan began to talk to anthropologist Bruce La Brack about how difficult they were finding their readjustment at home and on campus. Over the next year, it became clear that there were psychological and cultural patterns present among the returnees that might be better dealt with on a more systematic basis, and as a group. What evolved into a complex, collective, and interlinked process began as an informal response to a student-generated, student-felt need: an initial attempt to assist individuals in making a smooth transition after returning from study abroad. Within six months, student requests led to a series of informal, voluntary, reentry seminars. Within a year, both orientation and reentry seminars were established, in part, to shift to a more efficient intervention model.

Not surprisingly, these seminars initially had a culture-specific focus because all returning and outbound students were studying abroad in the same location. It did not take long for both students and professors to note that the work completed in these still-voluntary seminars deserved academic credit. By 1977, both seminars were approved as regular Pacific courses worth two semester units each, ushering in the second phase of cross-cultural training at Pacific.

Phase 2: Linked, Culture-Specific Orientation and Reentry Courses

From their creation, the orientation and reentry courses were conceptualized as linked courses, a fact reflected in their titles: Cross Cultural Training I and

Cross Cultural Training II. Material introduced in the orientation course was revisited in the reentry course, and students were encouraged to deepen their reflection on their experience abroad as a mechanism for extracting even more value from the experience. For several years, both pre- and post-experience courses continued to have a culture-specific focus; however, by 1979, a gradual shift toward a culture-general focus began. It was not until the collapse of the cluster college system at Pacific in 1980, and the beginning of the third phase of cross-cultural training at Pacific, that this shift truly gained momentum.

Phase 3: Required Culture-General Orientation Course for All Study Abroad Students

After the dissolution of Pacific's cluster colleges, cross-cultural training courses continued to be taught but without a formal academic home. In 1980, because of the success of the courses as part of Callison's study abroad program, a requirement that all Pacific students departing for study abroad take the orientation course was successfully implemented.

Another significant change occurred as well. No longer were all students in each course going to the same country; thus, the culture-specific content of the course continued to diminish. The increasing focus on culture-general content was also the result of growing clarity by the cross-cultural professors as to what type of material was important to address in the courses. Further, new comparative theoretical and intercultural paradigms were being created specifically for study abroad contexts.

As we shifted from a significant emphasis on culture-specific knowledge to focus more on culture-general principles, we never neglected country- or group-specific knowledge. However, students may acquire culture-specific information fairly easily from a variety of sources outside of the classroom, including interviews, articles, and Internet sites, and that knowledge can be integrated into homework assignments. In addition, program providers, host universities, and international students and staff often include culture-specific information in post-arrival, in-country orientations.

Phase 4: SIS-Based Cross-Cultural Training Program

In the 1985–1986 academic year, the recently founded SIS became the formal home of cross-cultural training at Pacific. Culture-general training was the dominant operating philosophy of the program. Although never truly laissez-faire, Pacific's approach from 1975 to 1986 reflected, to some extent, attitudes of the time holding that the study abroad experience itself was the most important locus of learning. After joining SIS, Pacific's cross-cultural training became more codified and used a developmentally sequenced and directive approach. This paralleled the further maturation of the intercultural field and the emergence of important new theories, coupled with more sophisticated training methods and research on the assessment of study abroad outcomes.

A variety of factors have contributed to the stability of the linked cross-cultural training courses as they now exist. Perhaps most important is the commitment, beginning a decade ago, to develop the cross-cultural training component into an academically respectable and sustainable program—one that would be carried forward by a team of professors, and not be dependent on any single individual. We integrated the courses into the curriculum, trained and supported faculty to deliver the training, and made these activities part of faculty hiring and performance evaluation. In other words, we made cross-cultural training an integral part of the curriculum and faculty workload.

We believe that we now know what works well to accomplish the goals of SIS, the study abroad students, and the cross-cultural training program. Over the years, we have been able to fine-tune the syllabi and include readings from an increasingly more sophisticated body of literature on study abroad, international educational exchange, and student accounts of their experiences overseas. We can now select from a wealth of intercultural communication theories and from hundreds of training exercises, case studies, simulations, and other skill-building resources.

Why Link Orientation and Reentry Courses?

Although many study abroad programs offer some sort of orientation, few offer any significant opportunities to understand the reentry process. This leaves the students to struggle through the process of integrating their overseas experience on their own—often not gaining all they could from their time abroad.

However, the value of teaching reentry extends far beyond the course itself. By design, it generates cultural information and health and safety data that are invaluable—not only for planning future reentry trainings, but for subsequent orientations. In other words, both courses constitute opportunities to evaluate the effectiveness of our program, respond to changing contexts in study abroad, and produce materials that can be used in either course. To accomplish this, we designed a set of assignments for the reentry course, the results of which can be utilized in both courses with appropriate modifications.

In the following sections we provide three examples of this type of "dual purpose" exercise: writing a critical, reflective capstone paper of approximately 20 pages; creating "Critical Incidents" derived from the study abroad experience; and completing a Safety Incident Survey to give SIS some idea of safety-related issues that students have experienced while overseas.

Course Paper

Beginning in 1976, as part of the CCT II course, students were assigned reflective papers to explore the impact of their overseas sojourn and their responses to the return home. These papers have been collected over the years and stored in annual volumes; to date, there are more than 700 papers containing irreplaceable data on student experiences, attitudes, and analyses. It is perhaps the largest collection of student-generated materials related to reentry in the United States.

Current students in the CCT II course can consult this archive to explore the expressive range of past work before they begin writing their own papers. These papers are valuable not only as reflective and analytical accounts of students' overseas experiences but also as a useful resource for students planning to go abroad. Outbound students can browse the past few years to get a general idea of recent student reactions to being abroad and coming home, or they can target only those papers from the country and/or program in which they are intending to study. Thus, the collection can serve two different purposes, depending on whether it is used by a student during orientation or during reentry.

After a few years of gathering these papers, we began to have alumni write and ask for a copy of theirs—either for their own use or, in some cases, to share with friends and family. Although this may be partly motivated by nostalgia, it may also be a way to revisit the person they were, and to share their experience with people interested in that part of their cultural and intellectual development. Thus, the collection may have personal value to alumni long after they have begun their professional lives.

Critical Incidents

We use the term *critical incidents* to describe short examples illustrating some cultural *faux pas* (behavioral, linguistic, or assumption based) that actually happened to a student while abroad. The casual use of critical incidents in the reentry classes was begun in the early 1980s. It was not until 1999 that the exercise was formalized, and we began to assign and collect them in every CCT II class.

Each semester, every reentry class student is required to write and discuss at least two critical incidents from his or her direct personal experience. As part of the assignment, the student constructs a "mini-quiz" for others to see if they can guess the cause of the misunderstanding. The answers also contain the student's perceived reasons for, and explanations of, the incident for the reader.

As part of the process, we compile, organize, and make available to all Pacific study abroad students the critical incidents generated by former study abroad participants. The files are identified by country, gender, program, city, and date. The collection expands by 30 to 40 incidents every semester, as returning students in the reentry class contribute their own critical incidents. Therefore, the collection remains relatively current and useful for anyone contemplating study abroad. Students taking CCT I are encouraged to use this file to examine actual intercultural encounters that their peers have recently experienced in situations and locations similar to those that they are about to face. As of 2012, approximately 1,000 critical incidents were available to Pacific study abroad students.

This collection of student-generated incidents also serves as an "institutional memory" that allows us to see trends and track evolving cultural changes by country, city, and program. Because the critical incidents are derived from the experiences of students just like those who are about to study abroad, they have the added credibility of being peer-based accounts. In turn, this helps to validate the classroom advice given by instructors on how to avoid or minimize intercultural miscommunication and/or conflicts. Like the capstone reentry papers, the critical incidents form a very pragmatic and useful record of student experiences that can be used in both the orientation and reentry.

The FIPSE/SAFETI Research Project and Its Ongoing Impact on CCT

Beginning in the fall of 1998, Pacific joined a group of universities, led by the Center for Global Education, that were concerned with health and safety issues in study abroad. For years we had been concerned about things that we had heard in CCT II regarding risky student behavior and/or deteriorating conditions in some areas where we were sending students (e.g., Russia, Africa). Moreover, because much information about safety-related issues in study abroad is anecdotal, and much that occurs is not officially reported by students for a variety of reasons, we used a small grant to conduct a "safety incident survey" at Pacific. We wanted to determine exactly what was going on overseas with our students, both to gain a better idea of the actual nature and frequency of such events, and to determine whether we could do something more in CCT I to prepare our students for the realities already encountered by their peers.

By December 1999, we had created, pre-tested, distributed, and analyzed questionnaires from nearly 100 former Pacific study abroad students. To our dismay, we found that there were 2.5 safety incidents per student, including robbery, theft, and physical and sexual assault. An earlier account of preliminary results of our initial survey is available online at The Center for Global Education SAFETI Clearinghouse website (http://globaled.us/safeti/).[2] We do not address the liability issues here, nor the moral questions of knowing, or not knowing, what is happening to our students on our programs. What we do discuss are the programmatic changes that we made as a result of having survey results that raised a number of red flags for faculty and staff dealing with study abroad.

Pacific's International Programs and Services (IPS) had assisted in the original pilot survey. IPS agreed to take on the added responsibility of continued data collection beginning fall of 1999, requiring every student who participates in a Pacific study abroad program to complete a Safety Incident Survey as part of the required exit interview. The survey is confidential, untraceable, and unsigned—and destroyed as soon as that semester's data are tabulated. We are so serious about gathering and utilizing this information that it was agreed that a student's overseas grade would not be released to the registrar until this survey was completed.

One of the lessons of our initial survey was the need for 100% compliance to keep IPS and SIS informed of what our students are experiencing. With each semester's data collated, analyzed, and added to the past semester's profile we can track the what, where, and when of safety-related incidents over time. This survey gives us a fairly clear idea of what is going on around the world in terms of the safety of our students.

The survey also gives us data that we can cite in CCT I to alert students about specific things to be aware of in various locations and to provide suggestions on how to avoid negative consequences and situations. The ability to gather reliable, accurate, and current data during the reentry process provides us with practical knowledge about overseas conditions, which we can pass along during the next orientation.

There are other activities that may be used to link orientation and reentry, but these three examples illustrate how the principle can work if those designing and delivering the cross-cultural training courses coordinate their efforts and share information. The synergy is often amazing and mutually reinforces the educational messages in both reentry and orientation.

Assessment: What Works and How We Know It[3]

The SIS at Pacific has used the Intercultural Development Inventory (IDI) for assessment purposes for several years. For SIS students, study abroad coupled with CCT I and CCT II is a key component of a four-year interdisciplinary social science education. One overall goal of that education is the advancement of students' intercultural development, and the IDI is used for assessing that educational objective. We administer the IDI to all incoming first-year students within a few weeks of their arrival on campus, and, again, in a student's senior year prior to graduation. We now administer it in the CCT II class and, recently, in a sample of CCT I classes as well. In this way, we hope to track change not only over the entire undergraduate degree program, but before and after study abroad as well.

We hypothesized that SIS students would demonstrate significant change in their intercultural sensitivity as measured by the IDI, and the data support this hypothesis. In their first semester, the mean IDI score of students is 92.13. In the semester after studying abroad, the average score is 17.46 points higher.[4] This change is highly significant ($t = 8.954; p = .000$). There is no question that SIS students' attitudes are changing considerably throughout this period of their education.[5]

Although the IDI shows that the intercultural sensitivity of SIS students increases, it is important to consider their scores in comparison with those of other groups to understand the potential causes of the change. We compared SIS students' scores with the scores of a smaller control group of Pacific's study abroad returnees ($n = 13$) who were not SIS students and who did not, therefore, take the reentry course, and with the scores of a random sample of Pacific seniors ($n = 35$) who were not SIS students and who had not studied abroad. Those who had studied abroad outside of SIS had a mean IDI score of 95.90 after returning, significantly lower than the scores of the SIS students ($t = 2.92; p = .004$), and not significantly higher than the scores of other Pacific seniors ($t = .99; p = .33$).

This basic comparison suggests that it is not simply the study abroad experience itself that is leading to the substantial change that we see in SIS students. It is difficult to disentangle exactly which curricular influences are most significant, not to mention to account for students' natural maturation that frequently takes place during college. However, we believe that by taking multiple measures over time, we will be better able to understand the intellectual and emotional trajectories that result. We expect that this kind of ongoing, cumulative assessment will allow us to accurately target our training and to better assist our students in their intercultural development.

Recurring Challenges

The challenges inherent in establishing credit-bearing, substantive, and academically respectable cross-cultural orientation and reentry courses can seem formidable. Yet, the reality is that even after this has been accomplished, such programs must be continually monitored, staffed, updated, and adapted to both internal and external changes. Essentially, the level of effort required to create and deliver such training continues to be necessary for as long as the program is in existence. This speaks to the necessity of developing a collaborative team approach, and of seeking critical partnerships within and outside of the sponsoring institution.

If programs are to have a long-term impact and be sustainable, they have to face the same issues as any new enterprise. It is critical to move beyond a single founder, or a few key individuals, to establish a capable and committed team that not only shares the educational philosophy upon which the program is based, but has the necessary academic, political, and training skills to carry out the mission of the program over time. Thus, the shift from "a person to a program" should ideally occur as quickly as possible.

At Pacific, pooling the collective wisdom, international experiences, and academic perspectives of such a team has frequently strengthened the overall program. We have all benefited from the diversity of opinions and approaches. Having a core of cross-cultural trainers also helps to deal with the inevitable rough spots that occur when dealing with difficult internal issues, continuing administrative dialogues, and responding to external changes in the larger world that periodically affect the global study abroad context.

An example of a continuing internal debate is the requirement that every Pacific student who chooses to go abroad on one of our sponsored programs take CCT I. It is extremely rare that we allow exceptions to this rule regardless of student major, extracurricular activities (including participation on intercollegiate athletic teams), part-time job commitments, or public performance requirements (mostly theater and music related). We feel strongly that the information gained by the student will be of sufficient benefit to outweigh the temporary scheduling conflicts and additional work of adding a two-unit course for half a semester. Needless to say, some students, coaches, and even some academic advisors have not, from time to time, seen it that way.

We schedule multiple sections of the courses at what we hope will be relatively convenient times, including late afternoon and early evening sections. We occasionally allow a student to take a class at another time slot in a particular week if an unforeseeable and valid event arises, and/or if there is a reasonable explanation why the temporary shift is necessary. Our policy has always been that a student cannot "make up" a missed class. Depending on the student's attitude and his or her prior class participation, missing a class without an appropriate, verifiable reason can result in failing the course.

Although it is rare that we need to exercise the no-pass option, it does happen. We then find ourselves in the position of having to defend the policy—not only to the student, but to his or her parents and academic advisors as well. Occasionally, a student will petition the Academic Standards Committee in an attempt to gain re-admittance to the class or to have the decision overturned. This action has never resulted in the committee overturning the decision, and the requirement continues to be a source of tension and frustration for a few students.

On the other hand, although all SIS students are required to take CCT II, we have not yet been able to require it for all Pacific students who return from study abroad. Although the reentry course is open to any student who wants to sign up, and we strongly encourage all students in the orientation course to consider taking it, there are seldom more than a handful of non-SIS students who enroll post-sojourn.

The most frequent reason for not taking the course is that the returnees, mostly second-semester juniors or seniors, feel that their schedules are already too heavy to add another course, even if it only meets for seven weeks at the beginning of the semester. Some students express regret that they cannot take what is essentially the second part of an obviously integrated sequence. Because their learning in CCT I proved sufficiently useful, interesting, and practical, they came to appreciate it during their sojourn. However, perceived time pressure almost always trumps intercultural curiosity.

Thus, even at Pacific, we have limits as to how much cross-cultural training we can require. We continue to believe that the true and lasting gains of self-knowledge, the benefits of post-experience analysis and exploration of "what it all means," and the ability to apply the new skills and knowledge are immeasurably enhanced by participating in a serious reentry seminar. Nevertheless, we still cannot get enough support to require CCT II for all returning non-SIS study abroad students. Our continuing experiences with SIS returnees and their positive responses to the reentry course confirm its importance, and its immediate and future benefits to students.

There are many examples of situations that require the cross-cultural training team to reexamine the curriculum, including major shifts in the context of study abroad, such as the post-9/11 safety and security realities related to international travel. Other situations that may affect study abroad are events such as natural disasters, including earthquakes, tsunamis, and volcanic eruptions; health concerns such as potential epidemic flu outbreaks, resurgent and disease-resistant tuberculosis, or high rates of AIDS among local populations; and political unrest and potential terrorist activities.

Although most universities and third-party providers have coherent and practical risk management policies and procedures in place, often external issues are, reasonably, brought into the cross-cultural classroom by students who are anxious, fearful, or just concerned about events or circumstances in their intended study abroad site. Time must be allocated to deal with these issues, and instructors must be ready, willing, and sufficiently knowledgeable to provide reliable information and advice to students. Given almost continual global political unrest and the possibility of disease-related issues, cross-cultural trainers must be sensitive to and have a good understanding of current events and circumstances in the areas their students will visit. Based on the information and advice provided by faculty, students can then choose which location is best for them. Whether to make these issues part of a general class discussion, or to offer individual or small-group briefings to those most affected, is a decision that rests with the instructor.

Of course, orientation courses are not the only source of information and support for students intending to study abroad. Nearly all institutions have some type of Study Abroad/International Education Office that oversees the administrative side of international educational exchange. Such offices have their own health and safety regulations, protocols, and sources of timely information. They also have the ability to contact students electronically and provide authoritative advice and information. If this contact is related to an emergency and/or travel advisory issue, the students in CCT I will always raise the issue in class, and faculty must be prepared to respond.

There are myriad additional internal and external pressures that provide ongoing challenges for faculty delivering study abroad orientation courses. Once again, we believe that the effort necessary to keep an integrated and complex set of courses up and running, and to respond to continuing changes of circumstances, is well worth the effort. However, we also offer a cautionary note that getting such training established can seem a daunting task and does require great time, coordination, and cooperation. Once in place, the training must be maintained, adapted as necessary, and continually evaluated to ensure its relevance, quality, and continuity.

Overcoming Resistance: Suggestions for Implementation of Cross-Cultural Training Elsewhere

Viewed from the outside as a total system, the Pacific cross-cultural training courses can seem too complex, and the variables too difficult, to replicate elsewhere. Granted, adopting Pacific's entire existing design, and implementing it successfully, is highly unlikely given differing academic structures and strictures. However, one should not overlook or devalue a more incremental approach in which adopting some of the policy features and course structures of the Pacific program might prove feasible. After all, the Pacific program began as a series of simple, informal conversations between returning students and a sympathetic instructor.

Resistance is frequently encountered in university settings when individuals attempt to design and deliver cross-cultural training for study abroad, even when the training programs are developed incrementally. One of the most common barriers is the lack of understanding and the dismissive attitude toward the value of intercultural training. Current literature supports direct interventionist training, and the overwhelming preponderance of evidence and research evaluations show that students provided with good pre-departure training, reinforced by in-country orientations and pre-reentry training, perform better overseas. They also experience more satisfaction with their study abroad experience.

Often the staff members of a unit that wants to do training have no academic standing at their institution, for example, the staff of Study Abroad Offices. Frequently, although these staff members may lack advanced degrees, they do have extensive foreign experience and are culturally adept and knowledgeable. The purpose of establishing even an informal orientation course would be to deliver intercultural training at a group level, rather than in individual sessions. Often it can be appropriate to have study abroad staff be the ones to initially offer intercultural training; some thoughtful training is better than none.

Other obstacles may stand in the way of easy adoption of cross-cultural training programs. Small one- or two-person offices often do not have the time, expertise, or funding to take on new projects, no matter how worthy. On the other hand, large programs may claim that there are too many students involved to provide direct instruction, that there are not enough trained instructors available, or that there is not enough time or space to gather.

All of these situations (too few trainers, too many students, not enough time or space) can be at least partially offset through the creative use of the Internet. There are numerous open-access, web-based intercultural training resources. One example is the "What's Up With Culture?" website (www2 .pacific.edu/sis/culture/) developed by Bruce La Brack with the aid of a Department of Education FIPSE (Fund for the Improvement of Postsecondary Education) grant. The content of this free, online training resource grew directly from Pacific's two cross-cultural training courses.

Some face-to-face instruction is, in our opinion, always preferable to employing a wholly electronic curriculum. However, when faced with too many students or too few staff to deliver direct instruction, a thoughtful adaptation of curriculum using readily available Internet resources can go a long way to alleviating those constraints. Students can gain enough culture-general and skills-based training to make a difference in the success of their overseas experience. Of course, students need to be monitored to ensure that the work is actually done, but many institutions have developed ways to accomplish this.

Individual academic departments often wish to offer their own separate orientations for their specialized programs. There can be a tendency for culture-general approaches to be devalued as preparation for study abroad in such situations. There are good pedagogical reasons why certain disciplines and programs might wish to provide their own targeted technical instruction related to study abroad programs (e.g., art history, environmental studies, or engineering). There are equally compelling reasons why all U.S. students who study abroad, regardless of their academic specialty and interests, should learn about intercultural communication theory and practice. Acquiring a basic intercultural vocabulary, understanding contrast-culture values and behaviors, and learning to analyze situations from a nonjudgmental standpoint will allow students to be successful culture learners, as well as to become more proficient in their chosen fields.

It should be noted that, in addition to the traditional social science and liberal arts student orientations, technical programs are beginning to recognize the value of study abroad orientations. STEM (science, technology, engineering, mathematics) programs are increasingly integrating culture-general training into their pre-departure preparations for students pursuing technical instruction in classroom and/or laboratory settings abroad. Some are also adding a reentry component to the study abroad experience in which "cultural lessons learned" can be added to the topics discussed post-sojourn.

An example of one such program is within the School of Engineering at the University of California, San Diego. The school initially enlisted Bruce La Brack (one of this chapter's authors) as an outside consultant on how to incorporate cross-cultural instruction into its curriculum. The subsequent collaboration between the university's Engineering Department and the Education Abroad Program Office led to the adoption of an innovative cross-cultural training component, one that includes pre- and post-experience instruction. More important, since 2006 cross-cultural training has been embedded within the engineering curriculum with the support of, and under the guidance of, the engineering department itself. Student satisfaction with this cross-cultural training remains high, and post-experience student evaluations of its usefulness are overwhelmingly positive.

At most institutions, faculty cannot count intercultural training activities as a normal part of their academic load, nor can they count them toward promotion and tenure. Many faculty understand the benefits of teaching students how to interact and communicate appropriately with their international hosts, teachers, and country nationals. Yet they find themselves having to provide this information or instruction *ad hoc*, and they get little credit for doing so. However motivated faculty may be, such additional teaching/training is difficult to build into existing courses. Their colleagues may not actively oppose their doing this type of activity—as long as it is on their own time and at their own expense. Traditional academic scholarly achievement is frequently evaluated on rather narrow disciplinary criteria related primarily to research and/or teaching. Interdisciplinary work, although becoming more common and accepted, is seldom given the same level of respect as core disciplinary topics.

Many of these resistances have been alleviated to some extent at Pacific through the forging of strategic partnerships. Other campuses could do the same by having key individuals in departments or schools partner with other campus units to help design and deliver cross-cultural training, and to share the expenses. For example, an International Educational Exchange Office could partner with an academic department such as Anthropology or Intercultural Communication. Often these endeavors can begin with small developmental grants to fund pilot programs or be built into grant applications that more generally support undergraduate education abroad and foreign travel.

Conclusion

Despite increasing agreement on the importance of intervening in the study abroad process in both the pre- and post-experience phases, the existence of integrated, structured, and linked orientation and reentry courses remains relatively rare. Although many see the need for a pre-departure orientation, the need for a mandatory reentry course may be less obvious to a casual observer. After all, the student is simply going back home—right? A final brief anecdote illustrates why we continue to believe that post-experience intervention can be as important to intercultural learning as the study abroad experience itself.

An SIS student returning from spending a year studying in Japan was required to enroll in CCT II, despite his protests that he did not need the course. "I'm not experiencing reverse culture shock," he claimed. "In fact, I didn't have culture shock in Japan either." Nevertheless, in spite of his protestations and somewhat negative attitude, he joined the class. Two months later, in the period between the end of the classroom portion of CCT II and the due date of the final term paper for the course, he visited the instructor, Laura Bathurst (one of this chapter's authors), in her office. "What I've realized," he said, "is that I wasn't really in Japan, even though I lived there. That is, I didn't really learn anything about Japanese culture." While certainly an overstatement, this student's reaction set the stage for a positive outcome. Since he now realized that he had not taken full advantage of his international setting and had failed to maximize his potential for culture learning in Japan, he was able to use his final paper to work through the personal and cultural factors that shaped his experience abroad. In addition, the student and faculty member were able to leverage the reentry course activities to promote a great deal of reflective intercultural learning post-experience, including learning from his peers' experiences. Indeed, his IDI results, supporting the observations of his instructor, showed a marked increase in intercultural sensitivity from the first to the eighth week of the reentry course.

Based on our collective experience working with students over the last three decades, we doubt that significant intercultural learning would have resulted from this student's experience abroad if he had not participated in the structured reflection required by CCT II and benefited from learning about the experiences of the other students. This student's case, although thankfully one of the more extreme, illustrates why we put such high value at Pacific on shifting a significant portion of the locus of intercultural learning to the students' return home. Otherwise, it is too easy to "shoebox" the study abroad experience. Our goal is for students to integrate their study abroad experience—from pre-departure planning, to utilizing their intercultural skills abroad, to integrating and applying their learning once back home. We are committed to finding ways to accomplish this goal, while at the same time adapting to constantly changing global conditions and dealing with internal administrative challenges. We believe that we can do this best by continuing to assess how to intervene effectively and appropriately in the study abroad process.

Notes

1. Over the years, the cross-cultural training program has received recognition for its quality and duration (e.g., Vande Berg & Paige, 2009), and in November 2010, the Institute of International Education (http://www.iie.org/en/Research-and-Publications/Open-Doors) recognized Pacific's study abroad program as 14th in the country.

2. Materials available on the SAFETI website include cross-cultural course syllabi; SAFETI survey forms and information; and articles on the historic evolution of the program, including La Brack 2000a, 2000b, and 2000c.

3. The IDI data included in this section were generated and analyzed by Dr. Susan Sample, University of the Pacific, as part of an ongoing assessment of cross-cultural training outcomes. Additional analysis of the program can be found in Sample 2010. Dr. Sample is a member of the SIS cross-cultural training team and regularly teaches Pacific's orientation and reentry courses.

4. The IDI is typically given to students in their fifth week of CCT II. Because some students take the course in the fall semester (after being abroad in the spring), and others take it in the spring, the time between actual return and taking the IDI varies from about six weeks to about five months. No significant difference can be found between those taking it in different semesters.

5. The reported results are those from independent sample t tests. Another small test ($n = 53$), reported in Sample 2010, was done with dependent samples (pre- and post-testing specific students). The conclusions were virtually identical. For those students, the mean change was 19.78 points ($t = 8.249$; $p = .000$).

References

Bennett, M. J. (1986). Towards ethnorelativism: A developmental model of intercultural sensitivity. In R. M. Paige (Ed.), *Cross-cultural orientation: New conceptualizations and applications* (pp. 27–70). New York: University Press of America.

Kolb, D. A. (1984). *Experiential learning: Experience as the source of learning and development.* Englewood Cliffs, NJ: Prentice Hall.

La Brack, B. W. (2000a). The evolution continues: The UOP Cross-Cultural Training Courses. Published online in the *SAFETI (Safety Abroad First—Educational Travel Information) Online Newsletter, 1*(1) (Fall 1999–Winter 2000), a project of the University of Southern California Center for Global Education. Retrieved from http://globaled.us/safeti/v1n12000ed_evolution_continues.asp

La Brack, B. W. (2000b). How do we really know what happens to our students overseas? The University of the Pacific SAFETI survey and its relation to cross-cultural training courses. Published online in the *SAFETI (Safety Abroad First—Educational Travel Information) Online Newsletter, 1*(2) (Spring–Summer 2000), a project of the University of Southern California Center for Global Education. Retrieved from http://globaled.us/safeti/v1n22000ed_how_do_we_really_know_what_happens.asp

La Brack, B. W. (2000c). The missing linkage: The process of integrating orientation and reentry. Reprint of 1993 article, published online in the *SAFETI (Safety Abroad First—Educational Travel Information) Online Newsletter, 1*(1) (Fall 1999–Winter 2000), a project of the University of Southern California Center for Global Education. Retrieved from http://globaled.us/safeti/v1n12000ed_missing_linkage.asp

Sample, S. G. (2010). Study abroad and the international curriculum: Assessing changes in intercultural competence. Conference Proceedings, Intercultural Development Inventory Conference, Minneapolis, MN, October 28–30, 2010.

Vande Berg, M., & Paige, R. M. (2009). The evolution of intercultural competence in U.S. study abroad. In D. K. Deardorff (Ed.), *The SAGE handbook of intercultural competence* (pp. 419–437). Newbury Park, CA: Sage.

12

BEYOND IMMERSION

The American University Center of Provence
Experiment in Holistic Intervention

Lilli Engle and John Engle

C reated as a proactive experiment in optimizing student learning abroad, the American University Center of Provence (AUCP) began operation in Aix-en-Provence in January 1994 and in Marseille in January 2004. The AUCP, recognized by the French Education Ministry as an institution of higher learning, offers semester, academic year, and six-week summer programs to students from more than 120 U.S. colleges and universities. Enrollments vary between 25 and 40 students per semester in Aix, and 15 and 25 students in Marseille.

What has brought increasing attention to the AUCP in the last decade and a half have been a number of distinctive and intentionally orchestrated program features that have proven to be remarkably successful in developing student intercultural competence. In addition to its commitment to pre- and post-semester outcomes assessment since 2001, the AUCP was one of 61 programs abroad that participated in the 2003–5 Georgetown Consortium study (Vande Berg, Connor-Linton, & Paige, 2009). Empirical findings from that study, which tested some 1,300 students using the Intercultural Development Inventory (IDI), show that the 109 participating AUCP students significantly outperformed students enrolled in the other 60 programs. With entry-level scores consistently around 96 points for all groups, AUCP students gained, on average, 12.47 points on the IDI's 90-point scale, compared with the other students' average gains of 1.32 points (Vande Berg, 2011).

Such quantifiable results have, in essence, validated a dream. We launched the AUCP in Aix in 1992, believing we could offer a very different sort of program than those we had seen in operation—international education programs that were "neither international nor educative" (Engle & Engle, 2002, p. 25). We imagined a program designed in ways that would allow qualified U.S. undergraduates to engage with host nationals and, through that engagement, to improve significantly their abilities to speak French and to interact effectively in a new cultural context. We thus set out to make the encounter with cultural difference as enriching a learning experience as possible.

The first step was unconventional in that we implemented a form of "reverse engineering." We identified what we wanted our students to know, understand, and be able to do by semester's end. Then we did our best to design and deliver a program in which *all elements* would combine in support of those goals. The AUCP thus gradually became a holistic (whole program) endeavor that aims actively to challenge students to "immerse" themselves in local French culture while also providing them with the support and analytical tools necessary to be able to learn and develop through that immersion. The process of moving our students toward intercultural competence placed us at the center of the profound paradigm shifts that frame this book (see chapter 1): from assuming that study abroad is primarily a matter of immersion to understanding that, for students to learn and develop interculturally, we must go beyond immersion and intervene in ways that will allow them to make meaning out of the new cultural and linguistic interface that they experience, with the culturally different Other and within themselves. This shift in emphasis amounted to something very new and different in the study abroad landscape of the early 1990s, when we began.

The process of fine-tuning AUCP program design gradually led us to implement what many professionals now understand to be the cutting-edge developmental and educational theories and instruments most pertinent to study abroad: David Kolb's experiential learning cycle (Kolb, 1984; chapter 6 of this volume), the Nevitt Sanford/Janet Bennett model of challenge and support (J. M. Bennett, 2009), James Zull's biological clues to effective teaching (Zull, 2002; chapter 7 of this volume), Milton Bennett's Developmental Model of Intercultural Sensitivity (DMIS) (M. J. Bennett, 1993; chapter 4 of this volume), and Mitchell Hammer's IDI (Hammer, 2009; Hammer, Bennett, & Wiseman, 2003; chapter 5 of this volume). Meanwhile, what we learned about what worked or not in terms of desired learning outcomes came from our students, who guided our every move.

Program Structure

In a brief overview, the AUCP is what our field conventionally calls, sometimes dismissively, an "island program," because of its in-house classes. Focused primarily on semester-long study, the program in Aix-en-Provence specializes in language, literature, civilization, and the arts, while the political science orientation of the Marseille branch emphasizes Mediterranean studies, questions of immigrant identities, and the integration of Islam into secular France. Classes are taught entirely in French by local university professors. The Marseille program includes, as a required course, instruction in Arabic for all levels and incorporates a one-week study term and homestay in Fez, Morocco. For both programs, students arrive with four prior semesters of college-level French. Qualified students in Aix may also enroll for one or more courses at a French university or *grande école*, alongside local students.

In addition, all students participate weekly in a series of community-based, experiential learning activities and attend a required course designed to support intercultural learning. The students' on-site experience is further shaped by a series of program policies designed to advance their learning. These policies include a rigorously enforced French-only speaking pledge and a number of administrative measures that make students responsible for engaging in their own learning process, while limiting the use of e-mail and other electronic communication.

In short, the AUCP program structure provides for a multifaceted learning experience whose all-French-language academic platform rests on three complementary pillars of experiential learning: a synergistic link between course offerings and the local environment, required immersion activities, and training in intercultural communication.

What follows is the story of key lessons learned from the program's steady evolution beyond a pure immersion design.

Cultural Immersion: Challenge and Support

Our goals in launching the AUCP looked beyond U.S. institutional motivations to "internationalize" the curriculum and campus, create ideal "global citizens," or increase raw participant numbers; we intentionally set out to improve the quality and complexity of the *individual student's lived experience abroad*. We did not believe—and the Georgetown Consortium and other studies have since confirmed—that the students we had observed and worked with before the founding of the AUCP were in fact returning home "transformed" through the experience of studying abroad.

Even in terms of simple engagement with the host culture, our observations revealed contrasting tendencies in student behavior abroad. Stimulated by the challenge of the unfamiliar, a small minority of curious and adventurous students spontaneously open themselves to experiencing the new places and people offered by a culturally different environment. Unfortunately, a large majority, accustomed through life on their home campuses to being catered to as student-clients in a carefully maintained comfort zone, never fully risk discovering that fertile learning space where familiar cultural codes give way to the new and different. Instead, they recoil in the face of scarily real opportunities to engage with local people and events, clinging to the security of their own language, habits, and beliefs, and complaining adamantly when things in the host culture are not as they should be by home standards.

Pedagogically, our concern was how to expand the cognitive perspective and adaptive ability of that larger, reticent group. Observing the more adventurous students in action revealed transformational learning to be a gradual process of edging toward the limits of the comfortable and familiar, then tapping the capacity to go beyond. Determined to cultivate such "elasticity" in all AUCP students, we aimed not only to structure cross-cultural encounters capable of taking students *out* of their comfort zone, but also to *expand* the students' ability to discern, understand, and appreciate a greater range of what is possible and acceptable in human thought and behavior. The difference was subtle but fundamental to our developing design. Environmental change offered by cultural immersion was certainly an essential catalyst to intercultural learning but, in itself, not enough. Intercultural learning meant keeping the challenge of the culturally new as high as students could handle, while dosing cultural and academic support to prevent student "flight" in the face of disconcerting difference.

To ensure the gathering of a student group willing and able to rise to the challenge of the targeted level of integration into French culture, our promotional materials set the tone. We clearly communicated rigorous program admission requirements: advanced or at least high intermediate entry-level French, a minimum 3.0 GPA, and serious motivation toward integration and fluency. In addition to detailed course offerings, we underlined our larger goals of French-language proficiency and intercultural competence with the enticement of "living with and like the French."

Promotional materials, the application process, housing, course content and instruction, and administrative services conspired, in word and deed, to bring reality to an initial promotional lure: "If being in a little America is not for you, we invite you to discover the AUCP difference." Clearly, we would not be catering to home-inspired expectations or to the re-creation of the American campus abroad.

To maintain the challenge of cultural difference—and to avoid the all too common scenario of student demands imposing change on the host environment (Citron, 1996, 2002)—we sensitized key players in France and in Morocco to the cultural propensities of our students. Local faculty, host families, administrative staff, and language partners met with the director for orientation sessions at least once per semester in an effort to cultivate good-will and temper expectations, not only in the students but in their hosts as well.

One of the most important decisions concerned the academic program itself. In an effort to respect the cultural integrity and traditional pedagogy of the French university while ensuring a balance of challenge and support for our students, we broke from the traditional immersion model to call upon French faculty to teach for us "in-house" instead of enrolling our students full-time directly at the French university.

"Direct enrollment" still retains a mystique in study abroad, and many of our would-be U.S. partner universities continue to see our choice of in-house courses as limiting, if not controversial. Yet, as corroborated by findings of the Georgetown Consortium study, simply placing American students physically next to host nationals in class and on campus is not in itself a pedagogical magic wand. In that study, the 349 students who were enrolled in classes alongside host nationals showed only a fraction of a point gain (0.7) on the IDI (Vande Berg et al., 2009), in contrast with the 12.47-point gain achieved by AUCP students. Such findings offer quantifiable validation of what we had been observing for years: that the challenge of real direct enrollment is often too unrealistically high to be pedagogically sound. Those who know both the French and the U.S. American university systems from the inside understand that there are daunting differences in such things as student-professor relations, classroom conduct, assignments, grading, and assumed background knowledge. In our own experience in the realm of sink or swim (see chapter 1 of this volume), we saw direct enrollment normally lead to one of two outcomes: Either the students sank (complainingly), or the host university implemented a number of accommodating measures (reversing the adaptation process) to create a special shallow pool for these students, most of whom were badly in need of syllabi, programmed reading assignments, regular testing and corrected coursework, more student/teacher contact, and rescheduled final exams adapted to a U.S. university calendar.

By contrast, the organization of in-house courses gave us a free hand to determine course content; create interdisciplinary synergy among a number of course offerings; avoid the disruption of teachers' strikes; introduce students gradually to a shift in teaching style; and, perhaps most important, introduce sound French-language instruction methodologies into all content courses. We could also implement an appropriate level of academic rigor, supported by clearly defined attendance and grading policies, which set standards of excellence that serious students could meet. In other words, in-house academics allowed us a level of creative control that we judged more effective in furthering program goals than the more facile catering to accepted notions of the academic desirability of blanket direct enrollment.

In parallel, we offered direct enrollment (as a complement to the AUCP's two required courses) to those students who could benefit from a real French classroom. As evidenced by the results of our IDI testing, the balance has proven appropriate for even the strongest students.

Our in-house course offerings thus provided a centerpiece for the assorted integration strategies called "French Practicum," which constituted a core curricular/extracurricular experience designed to introduce our students into local rhythms of life and to reduce their reliance on the too familiar company of their AUCP classmates (Engle & Engle, 1999). French Practicum structured opportunities for students to spend a significant amount of their time in direct, unbuffered contact with the French. Student integration into French life thus took on the shape of a five-pointed star, with individual engagement in French family life, weekly community service, a local sports team or club, weekly conversation exchange with a French peer, and optional direct enrollment. In our conception of the program, as in the narratives of former students, the French Practicum integration measures marked the AUCP difference.

In keeping with the program's ambitions, we saw target-language competence as central to the students' development of intercultural communication skills. Their learning of French benefited, then, from a program-wide effort both in and outside the classroom. In class, language instruction focused on precision of comprehension and expression (often sorely lacking) and aimed to increase the students' French proficiency to advanced and superior levels, as measured by the standards of the American Council on the Teaching of Foreign Languages (ACTFL). Extending beyond specific

French-language classes, language-learning strategies infused all content-based courses. An AUCP art history teacher would thus also assume the role of language instructor, emphasizing the specialized French vocabulary of her subject and requiring its active and appropriate use in class discussions, papers, and final exams. Class work called for regular writing assignments; ample readings; oral presentations; and, whenever possible, interview-based research, which favored the journalistic gathering of knowledge from the lives and roles of local personalities. Without any *one* element being ground-breaking in itself, the language classroom goals were reinforced by all other program aspects in a synergistic effort to make French-language competence and its pleasures an integral part of each student's evolving identity.

From the beginning, enthusiastic application letters suggested that students were drawn to the AUCP in search of "fluency," presumably eager to practice their French in real-life situations. Pledging to speak the host language at all times, even with other AUCP students, both on and off campus—a pledge backed by the sanction of program dismissal—students came to the program for the "enforced" opportunity to cultivate relationships in French. Despite the temptations of speaking English with classmates and in online social networks, students largely succeeded in cultivating the French-language habit, thanks to the supportive efforts of the entire student group, the staff, and host families, as well as that of friends and family at home.

In support of French-language bonding, the program front-loaded heavy doses of *français pratique* in the first week of orientation. Involving students in the mental exercise of anticipating their language needs, the small-group classes highlighted the vocabulary and idioms immediately pertinent to their forthcoming exchanges with their host families and their encounters with selected French-language partners, with whom they had a scheduled *rendez-vous* on the Friday evening of their first week. Throughout the semester, students were encouraged to internally "rehearse" anecdotes about the day that they might then share at the dinner table, and to keep a *petit cahier*, or handy notebook, in which they would actively record words and expressions they wished to include in their own expanding vocabulary.

In recognition of the students' extracurricular commitment to perfecting their French, we went beyond the validation of student performance by way of mere course grades and included pre- and post-semester testing in French-language acquisition using an independent and widely respected assessment instrument. Since the fall of 2000, all AUCP students in Aix, and later in Marseille, have twice taken the TEF (*Test d'évaluation de français*), a testing instrument developed by the Paris Chamber of Commerce and used by many prestigious institutions in France and Canada (including the Canadian government) to measure French-language competence in the three basic areas of written comprehension, listening comprehension, and vocabulary and syntax. The outcomes assessment effort (which included 775 semester-long AUCP students from the fall of 2000 through the spring of 2011) quantifiably confirmed that, on average, our students were indeed progressing as hoped from their entry level of high intermediate to achieve advanced or advanced-plus levels—B1 to B2 or B2 to C1 according to the CEFR, or Common European Framework of Reference for Languages (Council of Europe, 2001).

Successful in providing students with real-life opportunities to develop their language skills, the immersion strategies that we have detailed (integrated housing, language partner, community service, etc.) happened also to be particularly effective in helping participants with their initial adaptation to life away from home and campus, for the simple reason that they gave students *a lot to do*. Only recently arrived in France, our students had *appointments*—language partners to meet, a choir to sing in, a soccer team to practice with, children to tutor, an elderly person awaiting their weekly visit, dinner at eight sharp, Sunday lunch with French host family relatives. The scheduled variety of roles and activities harmonized with the predictable rhythms of French life and together helped provide a sense of security and organized purpose.

Thus, French Practicum fulfilled its mission in that it orchestrated multiple occasions for students to interact directly with host nationals on a daily basis, making available the sticky complexity of intercultural exchange. And, as a result, a few weeks into each semester, the real problems of cultural adaptation began.

Victims of the yet uncontrolled dynamic of challenge and support, we found that our first semesters were the hardest, and full of surprises. French-language partners dropped out of the exchanges. When questioned, they reported that our students knew so little about life in France that they could talk only about themselves; they were "boring." In their homestays, our casual young Americans were put off by their more formal French hosts, whom they could not figure out how to please, and vice versa—a culture clash that elicited in the students easily provoked crying, increased shyness, and uncontrolled fondness for Nutella or big pots of *fromage blanc*. Unprepared to deal with bouts of depression and anxiety, we hired a psychologist to do the housing placements and oversee student progress (a superficial measure that lasted one semester). In class, French professors dismissed students from their classrooms for the "disrespectful" way that they sat in their chairs or resisted even the slightest form of criticism. In short, we fielded daily incidents of bruised egos and piqued insecurities, all clearly engendered by the very cross-cultural encounter that we were trying so hard to induce.

Holistic Program Design

In its evolving design, the AUCP program considered that no one integration strategy or orientation method could weigh heavily enough to tip the balance of student interaction away from the comfort of American peers and computer screens toward sustainable engagement in the host culture. Isolated integration efforts were too easily undermined by contradictory measures, diluted, or lost. Attempts to increase intercultural awareness and adaptive skills thus had to be reinforced by many other measures, each informed by the same vision and purpose. If the AUCP was to be successful in cultivating French-language proficiency and intercultural competence, it would be thanks to the holistic coherence of its design. While the coordination of each student's community service requirement and the language partner exchange required their own form of supportive maintenance, our program-wide endeavor to center all policies and players around a unified collaborative purpose is best illustrated by our management of Internet use and of the homestay.

The Internet Factor

Our determined attempts to ensure a foundational immersion environment obliged us to look closely at our students' growing addiction to the home-based comforts offered by the Internet. Most study abroad programs consider unlimited Internet use to be inevitable and even promote its ready availability. By contrast, we felt the importance of considering carefully and critically the impact of readily available e-mailing and, more recently, social networking on the student experience abroad.

As e-mailing, the Internet, Facebook, smartphones, and webcams infiltrated student life, simple on-site observation of student behavior supported the hypothesis that ready access to electronic communication was offering students yet another way to take refuge in familiar (online) environments and to avoid engagement in the riskier business of forming meaningful relationships with host nationals. Whereas some members of the study abroad community saw online social networking as a modern, valuable way to inter-act cross-culturally, we were wary. In fact, we were fearful that the seductive lure of electronic "connectedness" would undermine the life-enhancing process of exploring face-to-face the mystery of the culturally different Other. Observing, over the years, our students' diminishing interpersonal skills, we saw marked evidence of the concerns addressed by French sociolo-gist and intercultural communications specialist Dominique Wolton (2009). Calling attention to the ironic decline of communication skills in our so-called communication age, Wolton insists that the exchange of information with the anonymous or the like-minded, albeit across continents, does not require or cultivate the skills of perception, understanding, negotiation, and discernment solicited by a true multisensory, interpersonal relationship. Along the same lines, emotional intelligence specialist Daniel Goleman (McKeever, 2011) warns that the lack of sensory feedback from online com-munication "may be fraying social connections" and leading to "emotional numbing, some deadening of empathy."

Accordingly, we instituted a considered policy restricting e-mail and Internet use on the AUCP campus. And while we created an all-French Facebook space for our students and their French-language partners, we attempted as well to bring awareness to the addictive use of laptops, web-cams, or cybercafés. We argued that the more students chose to maintain nonstop electronic relationships with friends and family at home, the more these would dilute the very intensity of the relationships that they reportedly sought to cultivate abroad. By semester's end, many students got it and attributed their newfound friendships to the containment of Internet access and the subsequent liberation of their emotional space for engagement in French life.

If anecdotal evidence were not enough, a marked contrast in measurable assessment results spoke loudly to our concerns. After years of intentionally restricting e-mail and Internet use to the computer lab, in spring 2007 we finally gave in to the growing availability of WiFi and allowed students cam-puswide, at-will connection. Surpassing our worst fears, CNN replaced *Le Monde*, webcams and headsets appeared in the garden, and U.S. American TV series filled free time. Student learning outcomes suffered dramatically as a result. With other program variables relatively constant from the prior fall 2006 semester to spring 2007, quantitative assessment scores in both French-language acquisition (using the TEF) and intercultural competence (using the IDI) dropped, respectively, 47% and 44.5%.

Obliged once again to reconsider our Internet policy, we shared the results of the prior semester's experiment with the incoming fall students and offered them the choice of either signing up for WiFi at the center or doing without it. Happily—and surprisingly—all of them, having weighed the likely impact of unrestricted Internet access on their language and intercultural learning, decided to do without WiFi. And as Table 12.1 shows, outcomes assessment scores for that fall 2007 semester bounced right back up.

Although learning outcomes had previously been impacted by other traceable variables, these particular quantitative results provided eloquent findings in support of the students' curbing of their Internet use and the resulting increase in their active engagement in French life. These informative results also underlined the importance of assessment in the monitoring of program design.

The Homestay

For obvious reasons, the individual homestay provided the first and, generally, the most consistent cultural interface for AUCP students. Nests for sticky problems of cultural adaptation, French homes are also where students potentially forge their deepest relationships and experientially learn the most about themselves and their host culture. The AUCP decision to house all its students individually with French host families provided what amounted to boot camp training in the value of diverse and tightly coordinated intervention in all aspects of the program.

To be sure, integrating the rhythms and habits, rules and regulations, emotional hyperbole and passionate debates of even a semi-traditional French family can be a hefty challenge for young Americans, raised to come and go as they please, to eat when it is convenient (often alone and on the run), and to believe that surface harmony is the sign of solid interpersonal

TABLE 12.1
Learning gains from fall 2006 to fall 2007

	Fall 2006	*Spring 2007*	*Fall 2007*
TEF average point gain	232	123 (-47%)	240
IDI average point gain	18.4	10.2 (-44.5%)	17.1

ties. In short, our students were generally raised to be casually "independent," when respectful "interdependence" is, by contrast, the key to successful bonding in France (as in much of the rest of the world). We, of course, paid attention to special affinities, as well as the standard allergy and dietary restrictions and so forth, when placing students with host families. But this was just the skeleton of the effort. Aware of the potential sticking points, we implemented five synergistic measures to facilitate close student/family relations, which produced observably positive results.

One: We considered housing an integral part of the academic program.

Applying clearly established criteria for recruitment, we screened and selected families for their desire to interact with their students. We turned away offers for room rentals and flatly forbade the presence of other English-speaking students in the host home. Families accepted a loosely pedagogical role with an emphasis on conversation and the sharing of activities, ideas, and concerns, as well as the monitoring of consistent French-language use and Internet habits. Each semester began with a ritual meeting with the resident director, which provided the opportunity to share assessment results and collect and debrief the lived experience of the families themselves—precious occasions for fine tuning personal expectations and reinforcing learning goals.

Two: We eliminated the incoming group flight.

It took us one semester to realize that group travel irrevocably "soldered together" students during the shared stress and giddy enthusiasm of the trans-Atlantic voyage. So our students began traveling independently, knowing that their very own French family would welcome them at the airport or train station on the first Saturday of the program. The French families, proud to assume the role of welcoming hosts, whisked the students off to family weddings or treks in the countryside before bags were even unpacked. By the time the students showed up for orientation on Monday, they could already congratulate themselves for traveling alone, arriving in France at the designated time and place, and integrating into a French family. The policy measure reinforced an essentially important message communicated to the incoming students in a variety of ways: You are coming to the AUCP for a very personal and culturally challenging *French* experience.

Three: We established clear behavioral guidelines.

Aware of the numerous faux pas inherent in French etiquette, we compiled a clear list of the dos and don'ts of French living, as a short, pointed introduction to the more complex considerations of cultural difference to come. Covering a range of daily concerns from refrigerator access to morning greetings to sleeping out, the guidelines were regularly updated by the families, reviewed point by point with the students during orientation, and then signed by the students as being accepted and understood. Clear behavioral guidelines, we found, headed off predictable problems and reassured students, who are often inadvertently torn between their sincere desire to do the right thing and the habitual, often "inappropriate" ritual-free easygoingness of American life. The mutually accepted rules provided students and families with a clear terrain on which to construct, on French terms, their own nuanced and personal relationships.

Four: We emphasized student responsibility in the building of relationships.

First-week exploration of the students' goals and fears regarding their term abroad invariably revealed the desire to make friends with and to be affectionately welcomed by their French hosts. They desired fulfilling relationships, which, unfortunately, no study abroad program can simply *provide*. To counter any consumerist tendency in this vein, we presented the quality of experience as hinging on a responsibility shared between the program and the student-learner—a message reinforced in many ways throughout the semester. Under the terms of this shared responsibility, the open door of a French homestay thus became an opportunity for, not a guarantee of, warm and enriching relations. Learning to see themselves as the co-creators of their experience, the students collectively formulated lists of the many things that they could do to enhance their learning of French and to cultivate local friendships. What could they most constructively *do* in support of their goals? Would they come home with anecdotes to share? Would they accept host family invitations, or favor time with their American peers? Would they engage in dialogue with host family members or withdraw to the safety of their rooms? With the keys to building relationships in France or Morocco clearly defined and discussed in class, students were provided with the information necessary to make conscious choices in light of likely ensuing results.

Five: We collected regular feedback about the housing experience.

Every week students provided written accounts of their engagement in all aspects of the French Practicum integration requirements so that potential problems of adaptation could be detected and treated in their early, benign stages. At semester's end, students filled out a two-part account of their housing experience. In part one, they simply described the characteristics and habits of the host family members, and in part two, they recorded what they personally did to make their homestay a success. Here is a typical self-reflective student account:

> From the start, I tried to participate as much as I could in daily activities, and show interest in the things she [the host mother] was doing. Little things like asking if I could help with dinner or learn her recipe for something made her really proud and helped us bond. She really loved that I took interest in going to the market with her once in a while, and especially when I asked to go with her to visit her mom in the nursing home a few times.

These accounts, made available to students subsequently assigned to the same family, provided a precious resource; they emphasized student accountability in the building of relationships, while offering concrete, peer-inspired guidance.

*   *   *

In summary, the intervention strategies inherent in our holistic program design urged students forward toward intercultural engagement, striving first to clear the way toward deepening relationships with host nationals by smoothing out the foreseeable big bumps in the road. Our goal, however, was never to flatten out the highs and lows of cultural difference, but to keep them within the range of the students' evolving abilities and motivations. We need to emphasize the importance of *ongoing* intervention. When challenged by the hazards of cultural misunderstandings, the students' budding intercultural ability—to suspend judgment, to discern appropriate action, and to adapt to cultural "logics" other than their own—needs continual reinforcement. Often struggling to understand and to accept what they see around them—behavior they, for example, judge as "sexist" or "racist" or "unprofessional" or "rude" or simply "inappropriate"—students clearly need a specialized vocabulary of concepts and considerations to shape their understanding and inform their behavior. In short, our students did not demonstrate the learning that we strove to inspire until we developed the Cultural Patterns course, which we discuss next.

Mentoring for Intercultural Competence

Our early reliance on pre-arrival information packets, incoming orientation sessions, individual counseling, and occasional gatherings around cultural themes gradually and necessarily evolved into a formal credit-bearing course in intercultural communication. In Aix, French Cultural Patterns and (later) in Marseille, French and North African Cultural Patterns provided the missing keystone for a fully constructed intercultural learning experience. Conducted in French, the course addressed "the differences that make a difference to effective intercultural communication": language use, nonverbal behavior, communication style, cognitive style, and cultural values (J. M. Bennett, 2009). Designed to provide pertinent cultural information and theoretical frameworks while acting as a forum for self-reflection and the analysis of real-life events, the class lent new coherence to the program as a whole. It also allowed students to make sense of their lived experience, finding meaning within a newly understood cultural context. In light of the challenges offered by the program's immersion components, the course's multifaceted, hands-on approach to cultural learning proved far more satisfying and effective than simply watching the sink-or-swim phenomenon play itself out. In short, within the experiential context of French Practicum, the course supplied the reflective observation and abstract conceptualization necessary to complete an effective learning cycle as elaborated by Kolb (1984); see Table 12.2.

"Front loaded" during orientation week, the Cultural Patterns class continued throughout the semester, meeting twice a week for a total of three

TABLE 12.2
AUCP's implementation of Kolb's experiential learning cycle

Active Experimentation *Concrete Experience*	*Reflective Observation* *Abstract Conceptualization*
Practicum Components with opportunities for: • Interacting with host nationals on a regular basis • Repositioning the self in society • Trying new ways of interacting • Exercising empathy	Cultural Patterns Class with opportunities for: • Objectively recording and sharing feelings and events • Noticing cultural differences and one's personal reaction to them • Engaging in theoretical discussion and analysis • Cataloguing/schematizing cultural values and assumptions

hours. The syllabus defined the course as "conceived to accompany the students' adaptation process to life in France, as well as to cultivate the development of their intercultural communication skills both in France and elsewhere in the world." Course content explored the values and assumptions underlying language use, behavior, and institutions. Lectures and discussions complemented readings in intercultural communication theory, examination of relevant cultural documents, and the guided development of the students' analytical skills and intercultural perspective.

Urging students beyond neatly structured encounters with host nationals, we created circumstances that would allow them to build relationships. In those uncharted zones of interpersonal give-and-take, empathy, and compromise, students entered the arenas of intercultural learning. It followed that they receive the tools to make sense of their budding intercultural relationships and of their role in that dynamic exchange. Thus, the Cultural Patterns course acknowledged the necessity of addressing the cognitive, emotional, and physical dimensions of the encounter with difference. Above all, through its regular debriefing of the student experience, the course offered powerful opportunities to teach to the emotions elicited by the cross-cultural encounter, the precious moments when students are moved by a heartfelt desire to understand (Zull, 2002; chapter 7 of this volume).

The movement toward intercultural competence engaged students in curricular investigation that we might divide into three central categories: the hidden culture of institutions and events, theoretical frameworks and their limits, and cultural self-awareness and perspective shifting.

The Hidden Culture of Institutions and Events

On its most accessible level, the Cultural Patterns course provided a body of information relevant to the students' lived experience, a context for the considerations that they would hear from their host families, French peers, or national media. Why the constant strikes? What is a *grande école,* as opposed to a university? What does the *Front National* represent? What about retirement, health care, parent-child relationships, dating, marriage, fidelity, unemployment, social services, taxes, upward mobility, or national identity?

Going beyond the explanations offered by a traditional course in French civilization, the Cultural Patterns approach encouraged an investigation of the values and assumptions below the surface representations of culture—

style of dress, eating habits, media, language use, gender relations, dance styles, and so forth. Working with information gathered from class discussions, readings, and their own firsthand observations, students gradually learned to decode cultural clues and patterns, inductively and deductively. Questions and theoretical frameworks guided them to see the values and assumptions that inform the French system of nationalized public health care, for example, and to discern the same values as expressed in other examples of French institutions or behavior. Aligned, in part, with the relativist stance that characterizes much of the work of Edward T. Hall (1959, 1966, 1976, 1983), the course emphasized the ability to discern cultural patterns with respect for the inherent logic in every culture. Focusing on both feelings and events, instructors consistently defused all debate around judgmental notions of right or wrong. Not surprisingly, the students' strong attachment to their own culturally conditioned beliefs about the ways that institutions should be organized or interpersonal relations conducted repeatedly clashed with alternative ways of being and doing. But within the open, informed space of the Cultural Patterns classroom, students were often able to engage in an exciting, developmental process. As Raymonde Carroll (1988) notes, "Indeed, one of the greatest advantages of cultural analysis, aside from that of expanding our horizons, is that of transforming our cultural misunderstandings from a source of occasionally deep wounds into a fascinating and inexhaustible exploration of the other" (p. 11).

Theoretical Frameworks and Their Limits

The intercultural field offers a wealth of theory and research, which serves to support and inform students' growing ability to take a calming and stabilizing analytical distance on their own experience. We cannot understate the importance of a theoretical underpinning to help students take their own often emotionally charged experience out of the subjectively personal into the objectively cultural realm.

The Cultural Patterns classroom experience confirmed that matters of culture were, according to Sanford's terms, "high-challenge content" (J. M. Bennett, 2009; M. J. Bennett, 1993) for most American students, who are— with fine irony—culturally conditioned to dismiss the very notion of cultural difference (Engle, 2007). Products of U.S. American mythic individualism, they believe firmly in the uniqueness of each individual and (in its ironic corollary) the universal commonality of all human beings. Neither belief allows much room for the recognition of cultural conditioning. Interpreting behavior as primarily individual in motivation, they are often reticent to see themselves and others as cultural beings under the influence of a pervasive force rooted in the past, which largely influences actions, tastes, and beliefs.

Countering that tendency, we introduced Bennett's DMIS (this volume)—later to evolve into the Intercultural Development Continuum (IDC) (Hammer, 2009; chapter 5 of this volume)—to couch the course's emphasis on perceiving and experiencing cultural difference within the framework of an increasing complexity in worldview, from a monocultural to a multicultural perspective. Students encountered the IDC in class, most often just before spring or winter break, so that they could listen attentively for the signature statements that travelers (in this case visiting family and friends) most predictably make at the various developmental stages.

In addition, the course found ballast in the theories and concepts advanced by Hall (1983) and others, which provided a refined working vocabulary of cultural analysis. Notably, the cultural dimensions of Geert Hofstede and the value orientations of Kluckhohn, Kluckhohn, and Strodtbeck (Samovar, Porter, & McDaniel, 2009) offered useful scales of reference and pertinent entry points into cultural considerations.

Nonetheless, we discovered early on that intercultural training goes well beyond the ability to explain the whys and wherefores of personal and societal behavior. The pointed Spanish proverb "It is not the same to talk of bulls as to be in the bull ring" reminds us where true learning takes place. For those exposed to a new environment, the intellectual understanding of cultural frameworks will not in itself lead to intercultural competence. That set of skills must be tested and refined in the emotionally engaged bull ring encounter with disturbing cultural difference. The goal of the holistic instructor becomes, then, either to provoke the emotional engagement of a cross-cultural encounter by way of an in-class simulation or to harvest for debriefing the material gleaned from the students' direct, on-site life experience.

Cultural Self-Awareness and Perspective Shifting

As Thiagi (Thiagarajan, 2004), the master of learning games, reaffirms, "People don't learn from experience; they learn from reflecting on their experience." Actively participating in the game of French life, AUCP students provided weekly cultural observations based on their own lived experience, ample material for in-class reflection and debrief. Course instructors adopted Carroll's effective methodology for cultural analysis, which encourages the curious observer to look for the "bizarre" and then to try to imagine a world in which this "bizarre" becomes "normal," or logically acceptable, within its own cultural context (Carroll, 1988). The method opened doors to the notion, central to a constructivist approach, that an *event* does not engender experience; rather, it is the *personal interpretation* of the event that determines the nature of experience. In keeping with this notion, students learned to examine both external events and their own interpretation or emotional response to those events and gradually learned to write their cultural observations with close attention to the use of neutrally descriptive (versus judgmental or evaluative) language.

After a number of weeks of writing, discussing, and debriefing cultural observations, students learned to place a potentially hurtful word, action, or event within its cultural context. In an attempt to foster adaptive response-ability, the methodology of the Cultural Patterns class expanded to include a process that we termed *Creative Inquiry*—the use of a self-reflective series of questions that call attention to the very human tendency to project culturally conditioned judgments and assumptions into ambiguous situations. Guided by the questions, the students gradually learned to be the detached observers of their own emotional reactivity. With that emotional distance achieved, they became *freer* to shift perspective—freer *to choose* to respond to people and situations outside the box of their own cultural conditioning.

What follows are condensations of a few of many memorable student observations, submitted in French, as part of the Cultural Patterns' weekly assignment:

> French fairy tales don't end with "and they lived happily ever after." Instead they say, "and they got married and had many children." I guess the French think that happiness is not an ideal; what's idealized instead is the role of the family in society.
> French couples seem to enjoy arguing. At first I thought it meant that my host parents were dysfunctional, but now I think it's just part of the fun of their relationship.
> I told my French friends that my friend at home had died. I was in tears, but instead of hugging me they all started to talk about their experiences with death. At first I thought that was so egotistical, but now I realize that it was their way of showing me that they were with me and understood what I was feeling, a kind of intellectual hug.

Extending the AUCP Experiment

The ambition of the Cultural Patterns class, indeed of French Practicum and of the program as a whole, has been to help students acquire knowledge and self-awareness in order to position themselves effectively in (and preserve) a world of fascinating difference. As more and more AUCP students bonded with their host families, accepted the pledge to speak only French (even among themselves), adapted to a new learning style, weaned themselves off the safe refuge of their computer screens, and ventured out to social events exclusively with French friends, we were rewarded with the gratifying signs that they were developing intercultural skills and personal growth.

In addition, regular quantitative assessment efforts confirmed subjective observation of our students' achievements. Most recently, in pre- and post-semester testing of the 411 AUCP students enrolled in the Aix and Marseille programs from spring 2006 through spring 2011, gains along the IDI scale averaged 13.43 points, with 39.4% of the students crossing the 115-point bar—that is, shifting in their developmental worldview from Minimization to Acceptance on the IDC scale (Hammer, 2009). Nonetheless, the arrival of each new semester's group inspires a reexamination of how best to place students at the center of the complexly human process of learning abroad.

Although the autobiographical parts of this narrative are important, most relevant to our field is the extent to which the AUCP model can apply to other study abroad contexts and circumstances. There is, of course, no one-size-fits-all, standard recipe for successful program design. That said, we do believe—and empirical research provides important confirmation—that our experimentation has allowed us to identify some of the fundamental elements, structural and pedagogical, that other study programs may wish to incorporate into their own efforts to facilitate intercultural learning. What follows is condensed, practical advice in the eight domains that we have found to have the most impact on the quality of student learning abroad:

1. *Clarity of purpose.* A basic but vital first step is nothing less than to identify what your institution truly believes about the pedagogical and developmental benefits of the envisioned study abroad program. If you are not absolutely clear on this point, no one—including your students—will be. Formulate a concise, program-specific mission statement that is grounded in that belief and present it on all promotional materials, whether destined for potential student-participants, faculty, or administrators.

2. *Clarity of learning goals.* Within the larger umbrella of a clearly defined purpose, identify the skills that you imagine students developing during their time abroad. Move from abstract terms such as *intercultural competence* or *language proficiency* to action verbs such as

"*go* to a French film with pleasure," "*make* local friends," "*navigate* a new city with ease." Once again, articulate this active vision of growing skills in promotional materials, discussions, personal observations, and qualitative assessment questionnaires. Among other things, this will offer direction to students and help them to discern and to take ownership of the concrete goals of their experience abroad.

3. *Cultural immersion.* Identify the level of immersion (exposure, contact, or involvement with the host culture) most appropriate to your students' learning goals, and orchestrate cross-cultural encounters accordingly. When possible, connect immersion activities to credit-bearing coursework in order to make them mandatory. Recognize immersion as a foundation on which to build, instead of as an end in itself.

4. *Holistic design.* Identify what each program component or administrative policy is intended to do in terms of fostering student learning, and examine each one for pedagogical coherence. How do the pieces fit? For example, does the program urge integration into local culture and then implement a no-class-on-Friday policy to encourage weekend travel? Be consistent, economize energy, and create a synergistic flow by harmonizing specific actions with the program's overriding mission.

5. *Challenge and support.* Identify the level of challenge that each activity or encounter will likely represent for your students. Students arrive abroad with "baggage"—a personal set of skills and predispositions. Consider how these will likely interface with the envisioned program components. Plan to offer the necessary inoculations, cultural information, and guidance, while aiming to keep the learning dynamic on the cusp between challenge and support, risk and reassurance.

6. *Reflection and analysis.* Provide students with the time and space to reflect on their intercultural experience and the information to make sense of it. Address both the cognitive and emotional aspects of the study abroad experience using a developmental approach grounded in intercultural theory. In most cases, this will involve significant teacher training in facilitation methods that go beyond the explanation of cultural habits, history, or artifacts to include a range of experiential learning techniques.

7. *Student accountability.* Emphasize the role that students have in their own learning by guiding the collective formulation of lists of things that they can actually do to advance learning goals. Feature the list as part of a midterm assessment initiative, providing the students with an opportunity for self-evaluation. Detail the actions that lead to learning, as well as those that do not, and guide students to see that the quality of their experience will ultimately result from the *choices they make* every day.

8. *Assessment.* Identify valid and reliable testing instruments and commit to the regular pre- and post-term assessment of targeted learning outcomes, both quantitative and qualitative (Engle, 2012). Watch for the lines of correlation that appear between program design and quantifiable outcomes, and make program adjustments accordingly.

A Final Word

Directing the AUCP has been a stimulating adventure of two decades whose ultimate reward has come from the visits and testimonials of former students who recognize, sometimes years after their time abroad, the quality of their experience in Aix or Marseille. Targeting learning goals while experimenting with strategies to achieve them has been a gratifying and empowering process as well, especially now, as the assumptions and convictions that guided our actions have begun to resonate strongly with certain emerging priorities in the field. We hope that, as systems develop to handle growing numbers of participants and programs, the lessons learned from alert proximity to the student experience may find application in service to the highest ambitions of study abroad.

References

Bennett, M. J. (1993). Towards ethnorelativism: A developmental model of intercultural sensitivity. In R. M. Paige (Ed.), *Education for the intercultural experience* (2nd ed., pp. 21–71). Yarmouth, ME: Intercultural Press.

Bennett, J. M. (2009). Transformative training: Designing programs for culture learning. In M. A. Moodian (Ed.), *Contemporary leadership and intercultural competence: Exploring the cross-cultural dynamics within organizations* (pp. 95–110). Thousand Oaks, CA: Sage.

Carroll, R. (1988). *Cultural misunderstandings: The French-American Experience* (C. Volk, Trans.). Chicago, IL: University of Chicago Press.

Citron, J. L. (1996). *Short-term study abroad: Integration, third culture formation, and re-entry.* Washington, DC: NAFSA Association of International Educators.

Citron, J. L. (2002). U.S. students abroad: Host culture integration or third culture formation? In W. Grünzweig & N. Rinehart (Eds.), *Rockin' in Red Square: Critical approaches to international education in the age of cyberculture* (pp. 41–56). Piscataway, NJ: Transaction.

Council of Europe. (2001). *Common European framework of reference for languages.* Cambridge, UK: Cambridge University Press.

Engle, J. (2007, February 2). Culture's unacknowledged iron grip. *The Chronicle of Higher Education, 53,* The Chronicle Review, B16.

Engle, L. (2012). The rewards of designing qualitative assessment questionnaires appropriate to study abroad. *Frontiers: The Interdisciplinary Journal of Study Abroad.*

Engle, L., & Engle, J. (1999). Program intervention in the process of cultural integration: The example of French practicum. *Frontiers: The Interdisciplinary Journal of Study Abroad, 5,* 39–59.

Engle, L., & Engle, J. (2002). Neither international nor educative: Study abroad in the age of globalization. In W. Grünzweig & N. Rinehart (Eds.), *Rockin' in Red Square: Critical approaches to international education in the age of cyberculture* (pp. 25–39). Piscataway, NJ: Transaction.

Engle, L., & Engle, J. (2004). Assessing language acquisition and intercultural sensitivity development in relation to study abroad program design. *Frontiers: The Interdisciplinary Journal of Study Abroad, 10,* 219–236.

Hall, E. T. (1959). *The silent language.* Garden City, NY: Doubleday.

Hall, E. T. (1966). *The hidden dimension.* New York: Doubleday.

Hall, E. T. (1976). *Beyond culture.* New York: Doubleday.

Hall, E. T. (1983). *The dance of life: The other dimension of time.* New York: Doubleday.

Hammer, M. R. (2009). The intercultural development inventory: An approach for assessing and building intercultural competence. In M. A. Moodian (Ed.), *Contemporary leadership and intercultural competence: Exploring the cross-cultural dynamics within organizations* (pp. 203–217). Thousand Oaks, CA: Sage.

Hammer, M. R., Bennett, M. J., & Wiseman, R. (2003). The Intercultural Development Inventory: A measure of intercultural sensitivity. *International Journal of Intercultural Relations, 27,* 421–443.

Kolb, D. A. (1984). *Experiential learning: Experience as the source of learning and development.* Englewood Cliffs, NJ: Prentice Hall.

McKeever, M. (2011, May 18). The brain and emotional intelligence: An interview with Daniel Goleman [Web log post]. Retrieved from http://www.tricycle.com/blog/brain-and-emotional-intelligence-interview-danielgoleman

Samovar, L., Porter, R., & McDaniel, E. (2009). *Communication between cultures* (7th ed., pp. 198–214). Stamford, CT: Cengage Learning.

Thiagarajan, S. (2004). *Six phases of debriefing.* Retrieved from http://www.thiagi
.com/pfp/IE4H/february2004.html#Debriefing

Vande Berg, M. (2011, July). Immersion, transformation and intervention in learner
centered study abroad. Paper presented at the Summer Institute for Intercultural
Communication, Portland, OR.

Vande Berg, M., Connor-Linton, J., & Paige, R. M. (2009). The Georgetown Consortium project: Intervening in student learning abroad. *Frontiers: The Interdisciplinary Journal of Study Abroad, 18,* 1–75.

Wolton, D. (2009). *Informer n'est pas communiquer.* Paris: CNRS Editions.

Zull, J. E. (2002). *The art of changing the brain: Enriching the practice of teaching by
exploring the biology of learning* (pp. 237–238). Sterling, VA: Stylus.

13

THE MAXIMIZING STUDY ABROAD PROJECT

Toward a Pedagogy for Culture and Language Learning

R. Michael Paige, Tara A. Harvey, and Kate S. McCleary

G lobal Identity: Connecting Your International Experience to Your Future is a semester-long, online course currently offered through the Department of Organizational Leadership, Policy, and Development at the University of Minnesota–Twin Cities (UMN), in affiliation with UMN's Learning Abroad Center. It is an elective, one-credit course that students may enroll in while they are participating in a study abroad program. The course in its current form is the result of more than 15 years of curriculum development, research, and practice stemming from UMN's Maximizing Study Abroad (MAXSA) project. In this chapter, we examine that project in detail: the theory building, the textbook development, the research programs, and various courses, all of which contributed to the student learning being supported by the Global Identity course as we know it

We wish to thank Andrew Cohen for reviewing and making helpful suggestions for this chapter. He has been involved with the project from the beginning, was the co–principal investigator with Michael Paige for the MAXSA textbook and research projects, and served as lead author with Paige of the original three textbooks (*Students' Guide*, *Program Professionals' Guide*, and *Language Instructors' Guide*). We also wish to acknowledge the textbook coauthors—Barbara Kappler Mikk, James Lassegard, Julie Chi, Margaret Meagher, and Susan Weaver—all of whom made significant contributions to the original three volumes as well as the revision of the *Students' Guide*. In addition, Barbara Kappler Mikk served as lead author of the new *Instructional Guide*. Finally, we wish to express our appreciation to our research associates—Holly Emert, Joe Hoff, and Rachel Shively—for their excellent work. They were involved in the three-year MAXSA research project from the very beginning and provided invaluable assistance throughout the course of the project.

today. It has been a journey of discovery, challenges, and substantial accomplishments. Most important, for the purposes of this volume, the MAXSA project has provided us with numerous insights into student learning abroad.

The purpose of the MAXSA project, from its inception, has been to identify and develop ways to enhance intercultural development and language acquisition above and beyond what could be accomplished through immersion alone in another culture and language community. The three original MAXSA guides (for students, program professionals, and language instructors) were developed as a means to this end; that is, they were meant to be a stand-alone study abroad intervention. However, extensive use of these guides with students and related research has taught those of us involved that while a solid curriculum is imperative for a study abroad intervention of this type to succeed, it is not enough. One of the major lessons learned from the MAXSA project is the importance of engaging skilled instructors to guide the learning process actively. In other words, a rigorous intercultural curriculum is a necessary but insufficient condition for fostering student learning and development during study abroad. Skilled facilitation is the key.

In this chapter we provide a detailed account of the MAXSA project, discuss the transition to the current form of the course entitled Global Identity: Connecting Your International Experience to Your Future, and describe the format of that course. We also highlight some of the major lessons learned along the way.

Overview of the MAXSA Project

The MAXSA project has its origins in the Culture and Language Learning program sponsored by UMN's Center for Advanced Research in Language Acquisition (CARLA). CARLA was established in 1993 as a National Language Resource Center with funding from the U.S. Department of Education. Its mission has been to build a knowledge base relevant to language learning and acquisition. From the very beginning, there has been a strong interest in how culture could be taught and learned in a language education context, and to that end, the Culture and Language Learning project was initiated in 1993. Throughout its history, 1993 to the present, MAXSA has gone through six phases:

1. Building the Knowledge Foundation (1993–6)
2. Research on Culture Learning (1996–9)

3. Maximizing Study Abroad Textbook Project (1999–2009)
4. Maximizing Study Abroad Research Program (2002–5)
5. Maximizing Study Abroad Course (Fall 2006–Spring 2008)
6. Global Identity Course (Fall 2008–Present)

Building the Knowledge Foundation (1993–6)

The first three years of the Culture and Language Learning project were devoted to building a knowledge foundation regarding culture learning. This was accomplished through extensive literature reviews, three commissioned papers, and two conferences in 1994 and 1996. The three papers address perspectives of the disciplines on culture learning, integration of culture learning and language learning, and application of culture-learning ideas in the language classroom. They were presented at the second conference in 1996, entitled "Culture as the Core: Transforming the Language Curriculum." The conference papers were first published as CARLA working papers and later revised and republished as *Culture as the Core: Perspectives on Culture in Second Language Learning* (Lange & Paige, 2003).

Research on Culture Learning (1996–9)

Three research projects were conducted during the second phase, one of which focused on the assessment of intercultural sensitivity among secondary and tertiary foreign language students. The study utilized a new instrument, the Intercultural Development Inventory (IDI) (Hammer & Bennett, 1998), and tested it in 1997 and 1998 with a group of 353 high school and college students. The results (Paige, Jacobs-Cassuto, Yershova, & DeJaeghere, 2003) showed that the IDI was a valid and reliable measure of intercultural sensitivity (M. J. Bennett, 1993) that could provide important information about students' orientations toward cultural difference. Along with Hammer, Bennett, and Wiseman (2003), the study by Paige and colleagues helped establish the value of the IDI as a major intercultural development instrument, one that continues to be used extensively in intercultural research.

Maximizing Study Abroad Textbook Project (1999–2009)

The goal of the MAXSA textbook project, conducted between 1999 and 2009, was to produce written materials for students, study abroad program professionals, and instructors that could support culture and language learning abroad. To date, the project has produced the following texts:

- Paige, R. M., Cohen, A. D., Kappler, B., Chi, J. C., & Lassegard, J. P. (2002). *Maximizing study abroad: A students' guide to strategies for language and culture learning and use.* Minneapolis, MN: Center for Advanced Research on Language Acquisition, University of Minnesota.
- Paige, R. M., Cohen, A. D., Kappler, B., Chi, J. C., & Lassegard, J. P. (2002). *Maximizing study abroad: A program professionals' guide to strategies for language and culture learning and use.* Minneapolis, MN: Center for Advanced Research on Language Acquisition, University of Minnesota.
- Cohen, A. D., Paige, R. M., Kappler, B., Demmessie, M., Weaver, S. J., Chi, J.C., & Lassegard, J. P. (2003). *Maximizing study abroad: A language instructors' guide to strategies for language and culture learning and use.* Minneapolis, MN: Center for Advanced Research on Language Acquisition, University of Minnesota.
- Paige, R. M., Cohen, A. D., Kappler, B., Chi, J. C., & Lassegard, J. P. (2006). *Maximizing study abroad: A students' guide to strategies for language and culture learning and use* (2nd ed.). Minneapolis, MN: Center for Advanced Research on Language Acquisition, University of Minnesota.
- Mikk, B. K., Cohen, A. D., & Paige, R. M., with Chi, J. C., Lassegard, J. P., Meagher, M., & Weaver, S. (2009). *Maximizing study abroad: An instructional guide to strategies for language and culture learning and use.* Minneapolis, MN: Center for Advanced Research on Language Acquisition, University of Minnesota.

Our discussion of content draws from the second edition of the *Students' Guide,* and that of the research program refers to the first edition.

Authors

The co–principal investigators, Andrew Cohen and R. Michael Paige, are experts in their respective fields of language education and intercultural education, and both had a longstanding interest in study abroad. The idea of writing textbooks to support intercultural development and language acquisition during a study abroad program was stimulated by Cohen's prior work on language-learning strategies and Paige's work in intercultural training.

They were convinced that study abroad programs, by themselves, were doing little to enhance student learning in these areas. Moreover, there was a distinct shortage of texts that could be used by students or by study abroad professionals and instructors. The MAXSA project sought to fill this gap.

Learning Principles

Literature reviews were conducted that built on the earlier work but focused more specifically on the language pedagogy and intercultural training literature (Cohen, Paige, Shively, Emert, & Hoff, 2005). Out of these reviews came four key learning principles that are central to the MAXSA approach (Cohen et al., 2005, p. 30):

1. *The principle of learning strategies.* Learning strategies would be introduced to students with the intention that they (and their study abroad professionals and instructors) could employ them to enhance learning.
2. *The principle of the learning cycle.* Student learning would be addressed throughout the study abroad cycle (prior to departure, during the in-country phase, and after return home).
3. *The principle of interactive learning.* Students would use their everyday interactions with the new language and culture as "authentic material" for learning.
4. *The principle of guided reflection.* The learning process would be informed by providing students with key culture and language concepts to help them make better sense of their experiences.

Design Criteria

To incorporate the four learning principles into the texts, the authors followed six design criteria for writing the *Guides* (Cohen et al., 2005, pp. 17–18). First, they would be *generalizable*, written so that they could be used in different cultural settings and with different languages. Second, they would be *strategies based*, emphasizing the use of strategies for learning and using language and culture. Third, they would be *oriented to the learning cycle,* addressing learning across the pre-departure, in-country, and reentry phases of study abroad. Fourth, they would be *audience specific*, supporting student learning directly as well as through the guidance provided by study abroad professionals and instructors. Fifth, they would be *theory and research based*, with the contents and the sequencing of the *Guides* drawn from theories and research on language acquisition and intercultural development.

Sixth, they would be *flexible in application*, with the intention that they could be used in a wide variety of ways including student self-study, pre-departure and on-site orientations, and formal courses.

MAXSA Content

In this section, the content discussed is from the second edition of the *Students' Guide* so as to provide the reader with the most up-to-date information. The *Students' Guide* is organized into an introduction and two main sections: culture-learning strategies and language-learning strategies. The introduction discusses the purpose of the *Guide*, presents general departure tips, and prepares students for the stress factors (Paige, 1993) that they might encounter. Most important, students are familiarized with the learning strategies approach that is at the heart of MAXSA. The authors assumed that students would not necessarily be consciously aware of how they learn. Therefore, to introduce students to learning styles and learning strategies, three inventories are made available to them at the beginning of the book.

The Inventories

The first inventory, the Learning Style Survey (Cohen, Oxford, & Chi, 2002), "is intended to raise students' awareness about how they learn best, and also to encourage students to 'style-stretch,' that is, to use a variety of learning styles to become a more effective language learner" (Cohen et al., 2005, p. 18). Students can then explore the idea of learning strategies by taking the Culture-Learning Strategies Inventory (Paige, Rong, Zheng, & Kappler, 2002) and the Language Strategy Use Survey (Cohen & Chi, 2002). The culture-learning inventory consists of 60 statements and the language-learning inventory has 90 statements. For both inventories, students have four response choices: (a) "I use this strategy and like it," (b) "I have tried this strategy and would use it again," (c) "I've never used this strategy but am interested in it," and (d) "This strategy doesn't fit for me." These inventories bring to light for the students the fact that they already have a set of learning strategies that they use and that there are others that they might consider using abroad. The inventories begin the process of students becoming self-directed, more empowered, and more capable culture and language learners.

The 60 strategy statements in the Culture-Learning Strategies Inventory are organized around 10 themes. The first theme, being in surroundings that are culturally different from what I am used to, orients students to the culture adaptation process. This is very important for the many students who have had no prior international experiences and lack frameworks for thinking about study abroad in intercultural terms. It is also helpful for more experienced students to reassess their assumptions as they prepare for a new and different study abroad sojourn. The next eight categories address key culture concepts that students will consider in much greater detail while they are in country:

- Adjusting to a new culture and coping with culture shock
- Dealing with difficult times in the new culture
- Making judgments about another culture
- Communicating with people from another culture
- Dealing with different communication styles
- Understanding nonverbal communication in another culture
- Interacting with people in the host culture
- Engaging with my homestay family

The 10th strategies theme, returning home, helps students think in advance about their reentry to their home country and how they can continue the culture and language learning after they return.

The 90 strategy statements in the Language Strategy Use Survey are organized around six themes:

1. Listening
2. Vocabulary learning
3. Speaking
4. Reading
5. Writing
6. Translation

The 26 listening strategies are grouped into strategies for increasing exposure to the target language, becoming more familiar with the sounds in the target language, preparing to listen to target language conversations, listening to conversations in the target language, and knowing what to do when there is little or no comprehension of what is being said. There are 18 vocabulary learning strategies grouped according to learning new words, reviewing vocabulary, recalling vocabulary, and making use of new vocabulary. The three speaking strategies are practicing, engaging in conversations, and figuring out approaches to use when one cannot think of a word or an expression.

The 12 reading strategies relate to improving reading ability and understanding what to do when words and grammatical structures are not understood. The 10 writing strategies address three areas: basic writing, writing an essay or academic paper, and writing a draft of an essay or paper. Finally, there are six specific strategies that address translation and working directly in the target language.

Culture-Learning Strategies

The culture-learning strategies section of the *Student's Guide* is very similar in content to the inventory, but there are some differences because the focus here is on cultural concepts. The introduction, for example, presents the five dimensions of culture learning to encourage students to see the great potential of study abroad in personal learning terms. These dimensions are learning about the self as a culture being, learning about the elements of culture, culture-specific learning, culture-general learning, and learning about learning. The Pre-Departure unit consists of two parts: What Is Culture, Anyway? and Understanding the Ways Cultures Can Differ in Values. The In-Country unit has eight sections: Strategies for Social Relations, Adjusting, Strategies for Developing Intercultural Competence, Strategies for Making Cultural Inferences, Strategies for Keeping a Journal, Strategies for Intercultural Communication, Non-Verbal Communication, and Preparing to Return Home. The Post–Study Abroad Unit contains one component: Continue the Learning. The culture-learning strategies section includes 28 different self-study activities that students can complete. The idea behind these activities is to prompt further thinking about the concepts, make the learning enjoyable, and anchor the learning in student self-reflection.

Language-Learning Strategies

The language-learning strategies section of the *Student's Guide* starts with an introduction that focuses on the student's motivation to learn another language. It continues with the following sections: Listening, Learning Vocabulary, Speaking to Communicate, Reading for Comprehension, Writing, and Translation Strategies. Nine different activities are included in the language-learning strategies section.

The Student Voice

When the original edition of the *Student's Guide* was being written, draft copies were given to three UMN undergraduate students who were on the

Undergraduate Research Opportunities Program (UROP). Under the auspices of UROP, they took the *Guide* with them and reviewed it while they were studying abroad. In addition, more than 70 other students on campus read the *Guide* and were brought together in a series of focus group meetings to share their views with the authors. One of the major recommendations was that the student voice was needed; in its draft form, the *Guide* was coming across as too academically oriented. Accordingly, study abroad returnees including the authors were asked to prepare quotes addressing different parts of the book. As a result, the presence of the student voice through the many quotes from former study abroad participants in both the first and second editions brings many of the concepts to life and also serves as a motivation for students to use the *Guide*.

Maximizing Study Abroad Research Program (2002–5)

The research phase of the MAXSA program was designed to test the efficacy of the materials that had been developed. Whereas the *Guides* had been a response to the need for written culture- and language-learning materials, the research program was "a response to a lack of research assessing the effects of curricular interventions in study abroad—especially those emphasizing language and culture strategies" (Cohen et al., 2005, p. 35).

Overview of the Program

The MAXSA research program consisted of three separate studies, each of which was focused on a particular audience: students, study abroad professionals, or language instructors. This arrangement permitted the researchers to examine the impact of the MAXSA materials on student learning as well as different ways in which the materials could be used by study abroad professionals, such as in orientations and on-site programs, and language instructors in their courses. More on the second and third studies can be found in Cohen et al. (2005). In this chapter, the focus is on student learning.

Research Questions

The student-learning study was principally designed to answer three central research questions (Paige, Cohen, & Shively, 2004, p. 257):

1. How can strategies for learning and using culture and language be conceptualized and measured?

2. How do students compare on intercultural development, second language development, culture strategy use, and language strategy use before and after a study abroad experience?

3. How do study abroad students receiving a language and culture strategy intervention compare to those who do not with respect to intercultural development, second language development, culture strategy use, and language strategy use?

Research Design

The researchers wanted the study to be as rigorous as possible for the questions being posed and therefore elected to use a pretest-posttest experimental design with random assignment of subjects to the experimental, MAXSA intervention (E) group or the nonintervention control (C) group. The participating students studied abroad in the spring and fall of 2003, with 44 students in each group. Later, two E group students dropped out, leaving the final numbers at 42 (E group) and 44 (C group). The four instruments described in the next section were administered before and at the conclusion of their study abroad sojourns. In addition, 16 students were interviewed after the program in order to gain greater insight into the uses and perceived value of the *Guide*.

Research Instruments

Intercultural sensitivity, as conceptualized by M. J. Bennett' (1993) in his Developmental Model of Intercultural Sensitivity (DMIS), was assessed using the well-known Intercultural Development Inventory (IDI) (Hammer & Bennett, 1998). The DMIS is a developmental representation of the respondent's orientation toward cultural difference on a continuum ranging from the three ethnocentric or monocultural orientations of Denial, Defense/Reversal, and Minimization to the three ethnorelative or intercultural orientations of Acceptance, Adaptation, and Integration. This study used version two of the IDI, which consists of five subscales: Denial and Defense combined (DD), Reversal (R), Minimization, (M), Acceptance and Adaptation combined (AA), and Encapsulated Marginality (EM).

The Speech Act Measure of Language Gain (Cohen & Shively, 2002) was specifically developed for the project to serve as the measure of language development. It is important to note that the Speech Act Measure assesses language competence in a cultural context. Ten vignettes were developed pertaining to apologies and requests. For each vignette, students were evaluated on their "overall success" in handling the situation linguistically and culturally as well as on six discrete criteria such as "appropriate level of politeness" and "fit between choice of vocabulary and formality level."

The Strategies Inventory for Learning Culture (Paige, Rong, Zheng, Kappler, Hoff, & Emert, 2002) consisted of 52 items based on nine of the culture-learning categories used in the first edition of the *Students' Guide*. It was the research version of the original Culture-Learning Strategies Inventory. The Language Strategy Survey (Cohen et al., 2002) was the research version of the earlier Language Strategy Use Survey and had 89 items related to the six language skill areas. The major difference from the book version of the inventories was that frequency was measured instead of familiarity with and interest in the strategies. The four response choices were "very often," "often," "sometimes," and "seldom."

All students also completed a background questionnaire at the beginning of the study and an Exit Language Contact Profile based on the work of Freed, Dewey, Segalowitz, and Halter (2004) at the conclusion of the study. Finally, a subset of E group students was interviewed after the program and asked to comment on their impressions of the *Students' Guide*, their experiences with the online course, and their assessment of the impact the course had on their learning.

The Intervention: The MAXSA Online Course

The intervention for the E group students took the form primarily of an online course. The course was organized around three foundational elements: a strategies-based approach to language and culture learning (Cohen et al., 2005), a developmental approach to intercultural competence (Bennett, M. J., 1993), and a constructivist perspective of intercultural encounters (M. J. Bennett, 1993; Kelly, 1963). The readings introduced students to (a) learning strategies, (b) the processes and stages of intercultural development, and (c) the idea of constructing meaning about cultural differences in an increasingly ethnorelative as opposed to ethnocentric manner.

A major feature of the intervention was that the key drivers of learning would be the students themselves. The online instructors were specifically told to maintain a low profile so that their interactions with the students would not in themselves become part of the intervention. Setting up the course in this manner allowed us to test the efficacy of a learning model in which students, supported by the *Students' Guide* and reflective writing assignments, would essentially be responsible for their own language and culture learning.

There was an initial orientation at which time all students were administered the four research instruments and were told about their responsibilities as research subjects. Separately, the E group students were given the *Students' Guide* and an orientation to it. Key concepts such as learning strategies and speech acts were introduced.

There were two major components of the online course. First, there were weekly assigned readings and activities from the culture-learning and language-learning sections of the *Students' Guide* (see pages 321–322 of Cohen et al., 2005, for the complete list of assignments). These were done at orientation, then just prior to departure, and for 11 weeks in-country. Second, students were required to submit "E-journals" every other week (*n* = 7 papers total) to their online instructors. In their E-journal submissions, they answered the following questions (Cohen et al., 2005, pp. 52–53):

1. What were your impressions of the readings in the assigned section?
2. What were your impressions of the activities? Please comment on each of the activities.
3. What types of language and culture strategies are you using in order to deal with the host country language and culture? . . .
4. What are the contexts and situations in which you use these language and culture strategies? . . .
5. How have the readings and activities related to your study abroad experience? Please give examples with explanations. Is there anything else you would like to tell us?

Findings for Research Question One: How can strategies for learning and using culture and language be conceptualized and measured?

As previously mentioned, the researchers developed three instruments for the study. Here, we discuss the work that was done to establish their validity and reliability.

Speech Act Measure of Language Gain (Cohen & Shively, 2002)

As reported by Cohen and Shively (2002/2003), the draft instrument consisting of 18 vignettes (about apologies and requests) was reviewed by native French and Spanish speakers during pilot testing; based on their feedback, the number of vignettes was reduced to 10. Those vignettes were then piloted with six French- and Spanish-language learners to make sure that they were understandable and worked as intended (Cohen et al., 2005, p. 50). For the final version used in the study, native speakers of French and Spanish scored student speech act data.

Strategies Inventory for Learning Culture (Paige et al., 2002)

The 52 items in the research instrument were administered to a non–study abroad sample (N = 277) and subjected to exploratory factor analysis, a process that reduced the nine culture themes to five factors (interpreting culture, nonverbal communication, homestay strategies, culture shock/coping strategies, and reentry strategies). Confirmatory factor analysis demonstrated that the five-factor model represented a "good fit" with the data (Paige et al., 2004).

Language Strategy Survey (Cohen, Oxford, & Chi, 2002)

The Language Strategy Survey was administered to a non–study abroad sample of language learners (N = 300) and then factor analyzed in the same manner as the Strategies Inventory for Learning Culture. This produced a five-factor model (learning structure and vocabulary, speaking, listening, reading, and asking for clarification). Confirmatory factor analysis showed that this model had a "fair" fit with the data. Paige et al. (2004) conclude, "In our estimation, these measures can be used fruitfully in future research studies, as well as in language and culture education. We have found both the *LSS* . . . and the *SILC* . . . to be reliable and valid measures" (p. 271).

Findings for Research Question Two: How do students compare on intercultural development, second language development, culture strategy use, and language strategy use before and after a study abroad experience?

Intercultural Development

For the group as a whole (N = 86), intercultural sensitivity increased 4.47 points on the IDI, from 99.07 to 103.54 (p = .001), Reversal decreased (p = .01), and Acceptance-Adaptation increased (p = .001). Viewed developmentally, these students began very near the midpoint of Minimization and clearly showed a gain, although they were still in Minimization at the conclusion of the study abroad program. Compared to the Georgetown study finding of a 1.32 pretest-posttest gain, this is encouraging. But it is nowhere close to the gains being seen in the American University Center of Provence, University of the Pacific, University of Minnesota–Duluth, or

Council on International Educational Exchange programs that utilize culture-learning interventions.

Second Language Development

Students' speech act performance increased significantly during the period of the study abroad program. On the "overall success" score for the 10 vignettes combined, students gained 3.13 points, which was statistically significant at $p = .000$. Moreover, the gains on 9 of the 10 vignettes were at the $p = .05$ level or better (Cohen et al., 2005).

Culture-Learning Strategies

The findings for the Strategies Inventory for Learning Culture showed, as predicted, that the use of culture-learning strategies increased. At time two, students were using 41 of 52 strategies with greater frequency than at time one, and these changes were statistically significant for 26 of 41 strategies. Of the five culture-learning strategy factors, three showed statistically significant gains: interpreting culture ($p = .05$), nonverbal communication ($p = .001$), and culture shock/coping ($p = .001$).

Language-Learning Strategies

For the language-learning strategies, the results were similar if less dramatic. Students used 44 of 89 strategies more frequently at time two than time one and for 14 of those the increase was statistically significant. An examination of the five factors showed an interesting pattern. There were statistically significant gains in the areas of listening and speaking, but statistically significant declines in reading and structure/vocabulary. Paige et al. (2004) explain, "While abroad, students are likely to have more frequent opportunities than they would have at home to interact with native speakers. As such, strategies for speaking and listening effectively may become more important—and more frequently used—in the study abroad context" (p. 267).

Findings for Research Question Three: How do study abroad students receiving a language and culture strategy intervention compare to those who do not with respect to intercultural development, second language development, culture strategy use, and language strategy use?

Intercultural Development

The results showed that there were no statistically significant differences between the E and C groups on their overall intercultural sensitivity or on any of the IDI subscales. However, in their E-journals and their interviews, the students provided narratives of intercultural engagement that was clearly being informed by the text. In their attempt to understand the null finding on the IDI, the authors (Cohen et al., 2005) speculated that the duration of the study abroad program was perhaps not sufficiently long, that the impact of the intervention may have been overwhelmed by the study abroad experience itself, or that the IDI was not "nuanced enough to pick up the subtle differences between the two groups that are reflected in the E group's journal entries" (p. 59).

In light of the research evidence that is now available to us (but that was not at the time), the more likely interpretation is that the MAXSA intervention, as it was delivered, lacked certain characteristics that could have resulted in a more powerful impact on intercultural sensitivity. Two of the most important would be the presence of a skilled instructor to actively guide the learning process (see chapter 14 of this volume) and the availability of cultural mentoring on-site (see chapter 12). In light of those findings, the MAXSA intervention might have relied too heavily on the students themselves to direct their own learning. We can also rule out the duration factor because it is now known that major changes in intercultural sensitivity can occur over the course of a semester abroad, given the appropriate interventions (chapters 2, 11, 12, 14–16 in this volume). And it is unlikely that the intervention was overwhelmed by the study abroad experience itself. Other study abroad programs reported in this volume demonstrate that the most effective interventions make a difference substantially above and beyond that accounted for by study abroad alone (see chapter 2). Finally, the IDI results and student self-reports via e-journals and interviews are not comparable, so using the results of one to make a statement about the other is inappropriate. As Hammer (see chapter 5) points out, such self-reports of intercultural experiences are "sensory impressions" of those experiences and thus are quite different in nature from valid and reliable instruments measuring a specific construct. Moreover, in their narratives, learners can overestimate the impact of their intercultural experiences. Given that the validity of the IDI has been well established (Hammer, 2011), it is highly unlikely that the IDI was missing something being picked up in the journals and interviews. Rather, the IDI was measuring something different from what the students were discussing in their personal accounts.

Second Language Development

In the first analysis of the language data, the results showed that the E group students gained more than the C group members on criterion 3B, "appropriate level of directness," for all of the apology vignettes, as well as on two criteria for the "meeting professor" vignette (overall success of the apology or request and fit between choice of vocabulary and formality level). These differences were statistically significant at $p = .05$. In the second analysis, the E and C group students were formed into three clusters (overall success increase, overall success decrease, no change). Here, on the overall success measure, the E group outperformed the C group ($p = .05$). This is explained by the fact that only 4 of 42 E group students decreased in speech act performance over time compared with 12 of 44 C group students. The E and C groups were very similar in the number of those who gained and those showing no change. These findings provide modest support for the intervention with respect to language learning.

Culture-Learning Strategies

There were a few statistically significant differences between the E and C groups on the frequency with which they used specific strategies, but no differences on any of the five Strategies Inventory for Learning Culture subscales. The E group students used the generalization versus stereotype strategy (Interpreting Culture category) and the strategy of building relations with local people by spending time with them (Communication category).

Language-Learning Strategies

Again, there were few statistically significant differences between the E and C groups regarding language-learning strategies. Whether the data were analyzed using the original six-factor conceptual model or the statistically generated five factor model, there were no differences between the two groups. When the data were analyzed by individual item, there were eight statistically significant differences. The E group students were more likely to use two listening and two speaking strategies, less likely to translate word for word (a positive finding), and less likely to use three of the vocabulary strategies, although C group students also reduced their use of vocabulary strategies. Regarding vocabulary, Paige et al. (2004) concluded that "the increased exposure to language in the study abroad environment, where words were being acquired more naturally in a rich context, meant that there was less need to use word attack skills in learning vocabulary" (p. 269).

Maximizing Study Abroad Course (Fall 2006–Spring 2008)

Based on the extensive research outlined in the previous sections, in fall 2006 the EdPA 3103: Maximizing Study Abroad (MAXSA) course was launched as a required component for all students studying on semester or academic year programs sponsored or cosponsored by the UMN Learning Abroad Center. For academic year programs the students took the course their first semester overseas. The Learning Abroad Center was committed to ensuring that students received the utmost level of intercultural and language strategy training while abroad. The implementation and facilitation of the course was based on a collaboration between the former Educational Policy and Administration Department (EdPA), now the Department of Organizational Leadership, Policy, and Development, and the UMN Learning Abroad Center.

The one-credit, pass/fail course was overseen by the instructor of record in collaboration with a program director from the Learning Abroad Center. EdPA hired a course coordinator and, depending on enrollment, up to 18 teaching assistants to serve as course instructors from the EdPA graduate program in Comparative and International Development Education and the Educational Psychology program. Two to three staff members from the Learning Abroad Center holding a master's degree or above in comparative and international education fields were also hired as part of the teaching team. Each teaching assistant went through training to teach MAXSA, was assigned a region of the world where they held citizenship and/or expertise, and served as the primary instructor for a section of approximately 25 students.

While retaining the three foundational elements of the research version of the course (strategies-based, developmental, constructivist), there was a major shift in the pedagogy to a substantially stronger role for the course instructors. As part of the research study, students in the experimental group completed assigned readings from the *Maximizing Study Abroad Students' Guide* and submitted related assignments to instructors via e-mail. These instructors intentionally engaged only minimally with students so as not to become part of the intervention. The study, however, found no statistically significant differences between the experimental and control groups on their overall intercultural sensitivity or any of the IDI subscales. Accordingly, the role of the instructor was expanded significantly to serve not only as a sounding board for student assignments but also as a "cultural mentor" from afar (see Vande Berg, Connor-Linton, & Paige, 2009) during their academic semester overseas. When the course was officially launched in fall 2006, the instructors' role was to respond to student assignments with detailed, individualized feedback that was meant to push students to actively engage in reflection, encourage them to think critically, and help them to relate their personal experiences to the intercultural theories and concepts that they were learning through the *Maximizing Study Abroad Guide* readings.

Lessons From the MAXSA Course

The MAXSA course was taught for four semesters between fall 2006 and spring 2008, during which time the authors of this chapter served as the instructor of record (Paige), course instructor (Harvey), and course coordinator and instructor (McCleary). In consultation with Learning Abroad Center professionals and other course instructors, we made several key observations about the course during those first two years, which we discuss next.

The Influential Role of Instructors

Regardless of what students' opinions of the course were, course evaluations from spring 2007, fall 2007, and spring 2008 showed an overwhelming approval for the course instructors. This was documented in the open-ended comments section regarding students' feedback from their instructors. Students responded that they liked their instructors and the feedback that they provided. Instructors were seen as a resource in debriefing cross-cultural snafus, promoting multiple perspectives of an intercultural exchange, encouraging new language-learning techniques, and providing "food for thought" type of questions that carried sojourners through to the next assignment.

The Online Course as a Safeguard

The MAXSA course served as an additional safeguard in monitoring student mental health and safety issues. In a handful of cases, students raised issues and concerns that enabled the instructors to reach out to the Learning Abroad Center staff to notify them of those issues. The information provided by the instructors enabled the Learning Abroad Center and on-site staff to coordinate appropriate responses to students' issues. While this happened in only a few cases, it demonstrated the value of having instructors who were active and involved in their students' learning and who could thus serve as confidants when appropriate and assist them in getting the help that they needed.

Critiques Leading Up to Course Redesign

Although the students had quite positive views of their instructors and some aspects of the course, they also voiced a number of concerns. First, there was considerable opposition to the mandatory nature of the course, regardless of how it was taught (there had been pilot versions with student learning groups, teaching on-site, and a hybrid on-site/online version). Thus, the course was shifted to elective status beginning in fall 2008. Second, many students felt the course content was not sufficiently relevant to their own experiences. Some of the *Maximizing Study Abroad Guide* activities, for example, ask students to analyze the culture- and language-learning experiences of others as a way of putting key concepts into practice without being directly involved in them. However, for a number of students reading about other people's experiences made culture and language learning seem too prescriptive and abstract. It was not about what was happening to them. Third, we had learned anecdotally and through the students' assignments that they were not very adept at explaining the value of their study abroad experiences to others, including faculty and prospective employers.

Global Identity Course (Fall 2008–Present)

This section describes the latest iteration of the course, Global Identity: Connecting Your International Experience to Your Future, and the review process that led up to the changes in the title, course structure (content and sequencing), readings, assignments, and instructional approaches.

Rethinking Course Structure

In response to student concerns about the MAXSA course (being mandated and lacking a connection to the students' specific interests), in spring and summer 2008, Kate McCleary, the course coordinator and an instructor at the time, collaborated with Connie Tzenis of the Center for Teaching and Learning, Christine Anderson in the Learning Abroad Center, and Michael Paige to investigate new approaches to the course content, process, and sequencing while retaining the intercultural learning focus of the *Maximizing Study Abroad Guide*. The result was a substantially revised course: Global Identity: Connecting Your International Experience to Your Future. The new course sought to enhance learning by making the material more relevant to the students' own experiences abroad at different points in time. This meant a major reframing of the course in a way that helped students understand its benefit to *them*. This student-centered orientation is reflected in the new course title, the revised syllabus, and course marketing materials, all of which now emphasize the fact that the course not only will facilitate students' intercultural learning abroad, but also will help them articulate what they have learned to family and friends as well as to potential employers or graduate schools upon their return.

Additional Theoretical Perspectives and Readings That Frame the Course

The course also sought to strengthen the learning process by (a) resequencing the assignments to make them even more developmentally relevant to the students' experiences while abroad, (b) expanding the literature for the reading assignments, (c) more actively supporting and guiding the reflection process, and (d) helping students connect their study abroad experiences to their future. Using Kolb's (1984) experiential learning theory, Moon's (1999, 2004) work on reflection and experiential learning, Hatton and Smith's (1995) operational aspects of reflection, and M. J. Bennett's (1986) work with the DMIS, the assignments for the Global Identity course now build more effectively on one another and require increasingly more complex thought and analysis as the course progresses. New readings were incorporated with existing sections of the *Maximizing Study Abroad Guide* to provide students with greater access to the literature and ensure that students were both challenged by the readings and supported in their intercultural growth. Readings were added to promote deeper understanding of how students' overseas experiences tie into post-undergraduate college life; these include Gupta's (2009) chapter "Beyond Borders: Leading in Today's Multicultural World" and Troobott, Vande Berg, and Rayman's (2008) article "Employer Attitudes Toward Study Abroad." Instructors met with the UMN Career Center to ensure that the information they were sharing with students about marketing their international experience, for instance, in a job interview or graduate school application, was accurate and relevant.

Roles of the Students and Instructor

As part of the course restructuring, the roles of the students as learners and the instructors as teachers and mentors were reviewed. The new Global Identity course utilized an enhanced constructivist pedagogy that asked students to draw from and rely on their own thoughts and experiences within their host culture as part of the course content. This pedagogical approach was intended to enhance learning above and beyond the first iteration of the course by more systematically connecting experience with reflection. The instructors' role was further strengthened; instructors were now responsible for providing students with in-depth feedback and engaging in ongoing dialogue with them about their experiences abroad. It became the role and responsibility of the instructor to infuse language-learning ideas as well as intercultural concepts and vocabulary in their responses to students. In many ways the students' experiences served as the case examples through which the instructors taught key concepts and prompted students to reflect more deeply on the connections among their own experiences, the way that they thought about those experiences, and the intercultural development theories and concepts from the readings.

Students sent their assignments to their designated instructor, who then responded with detailed feedback meant to encourage further reflection and critical thinking, as well as help students relate their own experiences to the materials covered in the course readings. It was not uncommon for an instructor's response to rival the length of a student's original assignment. Although not expected, students sometimes responded to the feedback, engaging in a continued dialogue between student and instructor.

Global Identity Today

Global Identity: Connecting Your International Experience to Your Future continues as an online, one-credit, pass/fail, elective course. The Department of Organizational Leadership, Policy, and Development provides instruction. The course description (Learning Abroad Center, 2011a) addresses students directly by pointing out what Global Identity can do for them. It tells potential participants that they will be able to

- Articulate the value of your experience to future employers, graduate or professional schools, and scholarship committees.
- Demonstrate your intercultural development and skills that can be used as part of a professional portfolio in a job search or application for graduate/professional school by preparing key essays/documents.
- Understand intercultural theories and interactions with cultural difference, as well as language-learning and intercultural communication strategies. These skills help you to start to make connections between your study abroad experience and the broader range of skills connected with this experience, to become a competitive member of a global workforce.

Course Objectives and Learning Outcomes

The course objectives and learning outcomes, as stated in the online syllabus (Learning Abroad Center, 2011b), are reflective of the student-centered orientation of the course. They are as follows:

- To support the learning of intercultural knowledge
- To provide individual feedback to you as a learner to help promote deeper understanding of your experiences in the host culture
- To help you understand the value of the intercultural skill-set you acquire overseas
- To assist in finding ways your new intercultural skill-set can be marketed for future jobs or graduate and professional school
- To promote reflection on how you can integrate your new perspective(s) and skill-sets into life back home

The desired learning outcomes (Learning Abroad Center, 2011b), as set forth to students in the syllabus, are as follows:

- You will be familiar with intercultural literature, models, frameworks, and concepts used in intercultural development and training
- You will be able to recognize and explain the multiple layers of an overseas experience
- You will be able to articulate important intercultural skills and perspectives you have acquired/developed
- You will have the beginning of a study abroad component for a professional portfolio

Assignments

Students have regularly assigned readings, which are accessible through the course website. There are five assignments throughout the semester, beginning just before students depart for their study abroad program. Students submit these assignments via e-mail to their designated course instructor, who then responds in detail with individualized feedback that is meant to encourage further reflection and facilitate intercultural development.

The assignments are sequenced developmentally. Instructors know and students learn that this sequence is designed to support their learning needs, which change over time, and that their assignments build on one another in relation to where they are in the study abroad cycle (pre-departure, early in-country, late in-country, reentry). This was explained in the 2011 Global Identity course syllabus as follows:

This course is a building process and is highly dependent on your willingness to reflect on your experience and the intercultural skills you are developing in order to market this experience once you return. You will have a total of five assignments. Pedagogically, each assignment builds on the previous assignment in some way. (Learning Abroad Center, 2011b)

The following is a short summary of each of the five assignments:

1. *Establishing expectations.* In the first assignment, submitted a week before they depart, the students write about their expectations about the host culture, how they will be viewed and treated there, and their own personal growth during their time abroad.
2. *Seeing and responding.* For the second assignment, students are given a variety of readings on cultural adaptation and culture learning. Then they must write about a picture or song that captures their feelings about the study abroad experience. By using these media, they are able to think creatively about their experiences, thus beginning a process of frame shifting.
3. *Lens shifting and comparative thinking.* The students are given a set of readings, then asked to write an essay comparing an aspect of their home and host cultures. One significant dimension of the paper as stated in the course syllabus is that it should "demonstrate [the students'] ability to make ethnorelative cross-country and/or cross-cultural comparisons on significant issues that are of importance to [them]" (Learning Abroad Center, 2011b).
4. *Identifying job skills and making connections with overseas experience.* Through this three-part assignment, students begin the process of articulating the value of their study abroad experiences to future employees. First, they are asked to list skills that are important in their field of interest and to identify specific experiences they have had overseas that demonstrate how they have developed or honed those skills. Second, they respond to the following prompt: "I see from your resume you studied abroad in _____. Tell me how that experience made you a better candidate for this job/graduate program" (Learning Abroad Center, 2011b). Third, students write two to three bullet points that highlight what they have done, learned, or gotten out of their experience abroad that they would like to include on their resume.
5. *Going beyond "It was awesome."* The final reflection assignment differs for those who are returning home after a semester and those who will remain abroad for the full academic year. Students returning home are asked to make sense of their experience by reviewing and

commenting on their original expectations and answering a series of questions posed in the reentry section of the *Maximizing Study Abroad Students' Guide*. Students who are continuing their study abroad experience have two options. They may choose to reflect on their pre-departure expectations in light of their experience during the first semester and look ahead to their remaining time abroad. Or they can instead reflect on and respond to a thought-provoking article by a former study abroad student—Zemach-Bersin's (2008) "American Students Abroad Can't Be 'Global Citizens.'"

Responses to and Expansion of Global Identity

Course evaluations from fall 2008 through spring 2011 semesters indicated greater student satisfaction with the course. Because the redesign of the course and the change from a required to an elective course happened simultaneously, it is difficult to distinguish which factor affected student approval of the course. However, the positive feedback on the course evaluations over the past two years has strengthened the UMN Learning Abroad Center's commitment to offering this course on its programs and has convinced third party providers to offer this online course to their students. As of spring 2011, two outside institutions were offering the Global Identity course to their students through UMN.

Conclusion

After more than 15 years of curriculum development, research, and practice, much has been learned from UMN's MAXSA project. The *Maximizing Study Abroad Guides*, the Maximizing Study Abroad and current Global Identity online courses, and the research programs are notable accomplishments of the project. Through our own involvement with the project as a whole and the course in particular, we have learned several lessons relevant to promoting student learning abroad.

First, and most significantly, we have come to recognize the importance of engaging skilled instructors to actively guide the learning process during a study abroad intervention. This finding is consistent with what many fellow authors in this volume have discovered about the importance of the instructor or mentor. The thought when the *Maximizing Study Abroad Guides* were being developed was that *they* would be the primary intervention, that is, that sound language and culture content combined with a self-directed strategies-based approach to learning would be sufficient. But that did not prove to be the case. The Maximizing Study Abroad course, now Global Identity, became much more effective when skilled instructors actively engaged with and provided insightful feedback to students. They were able to build upon and reinforce what was provided in the *Students' Guide* through their interactions with students. As a result, we have learned that a solid intercultural curriculum is a definitely necessary but insufficient condition for fostering student learning and development during study abroad. Key concepts can anchor the insights gained by reflecting upon experiences; instructors can help students gain a command of those concepts by means of dialogue and interaction.

Second, we have learned that to promote student participation in a course such as Global Identity we need to address student needs and interests more directly. This can be done by combining the practical (e.g., what the course can mean to them in the future) and the theoretical. As practitioners, it is important to understand what makes intercultural learning relevant to a broad array of students from differing backgrounds and academic majors, and combine what is important to them with the intercultural and language-learning outcomes that we want them to gain from such a course.

Third, we have come to know much more about the multiple ways that instructors can support student learning abroad. These include cultivating critical thinking, curiosity, and reflection; challenging and supporting students to advance their learning; and helping ensure the well-being of the students in their host environment.

As we conclude this chapter, we return to the constructivist foundation of our work. In his classic text *A Theory of Personality: The Psychology of Personal Constructs,* psychologist George Kelly (1963) writes, "A person can be a witness to a tremendous parade of episodes and yet, if he fails to keep making something out of them . . . he gains little in the way of experience from having been around when they happened" (p. 73). Reflecting further on Kelly's work, J. M. Bennett and Salonen (2007) put forward the idea that "learning from experience requires more than being in the vicinity of events when they occur. Learning emerges from our capacity to construe those events and then to reconstrue them in transformative ways" (p. 46). The materials developed over the years by the MAXSA program, in particular, the *Guides* and the Global Identity course, have been designed to promote students' abilities to construe and make sense of the intercultural events that they are experiencing while studying abroad. It is our hope and expectation that what we are learning from these ongoing efforts will indeed contribute to increasingly more effective study abroad programming and enhanced student learning.

References

Bennett, J. M., & Salonen, R. (2007). Intercultural communication and the new American campus. *Change: The Magazine of Higher Learning*, March–April, 46–50.

Bennett, M. J. (1986). A developmental approach to training for intercultural sensitivity. *International Journal of Intercultural Relations, 10*, 179–196.

Bennett, M. J. (1993). Towards ethnorelativism: A developmental model of intercultural sensitivity. In R. M. Paige (Ed.), *Education for the intercultural experience* (pp. 21–71). Yarmouth, ME: Intercultural Press.

Cohen, A. D., & Chi, J. C. (2002). *Language Strategy Use Survey*. Minneapolis, MN: Center for Advanced Research in Language Acquisition, University of Minnesota.

Cohen, A. D., Oxford, R. L., & Chi, J. C. (2002). *Language Strategy Survey*. Minneapolis, MN: Center for Advanced Research in Language Acquisition, University of Minnesota.

Cohen, A. D., Paige, R. M., Shively, R. L., Emert, H. A., & Hoff, J. G. (2005). *Maximizing study abroad through language and culture strategies: Research on students, study abroad program professionals, and language instructors*. Minneapolis, MN: Center for Advanced Research on Language Acquisition, Office of International Programs, University of Minnesota. Retrieved from http://www.carla.umn.edu/maxsa/index.html

Cohen, A. D., & Shively, R. L. (2002). *Speech Act Measure of Language Gain*. Minneapolis, MN: Center for Advanced Research in Language Acquisition, University of Minnesota.

Cohen, A. D., & Shively, R. L. (2002/2003). Measuring speech acts with multiple rejoinder DCTs. *Language Testing Update, 32*, 39–42.

Freed, B. F., Dewey, D. P., Segalowitz, N. S., & Halter, R. H. (2004). The Language Contact Profile. *Studies in Second Language Acquisition, 26*, 349–356.

Gupta, S. R. (2009). Beyond borders: Leading in today's multicultural world. In M. A. Moodian (Ed.), *Contemporary leadership and intercultural competence: Exploring the cross-cultural dynamics within organizations* (pp. 145–158). Thousand Oaks, CA: Sage.

Hammer, M. R. (2011). Additional cross-cultural validity testing of the Intercultural Development Inventory. *International Journal of Intercultural Relations, 35*, 474–487.

Hammer, M. R., & Bennett, M. J. (1998). *The Intercultural Development Inventory*. Portland, OR: Intercultural Communication Institute.

Hammer, M. R., Bennett, M. J., & Wiseman, R. (2003). Measuring intercultural sensitivity: The Intercultural Development Inventory. *International Journal of Intercultural Relations, 27,* 421–443.

Hatton, N., & Smith, D. (1995). Reflection in teacher education: Towards definition and implementation. *Teaching and Teacher Education, 11,* 33–49.

Kelly, G. A. (1963). *A theory of personality: The psychology of personal constructs.* New York: Norton.

Kolb, D. A. (1984). *Experiential learning.* Englewood Cliffs, NJ: Prentice Hall.

Lange, D. L., & Paige, R. M. (Eds.). (2003). *Culture as the core: Perspectives on culture in second language learning.* Greenwich, CT: Information Age Publishing.

Learning Abroad Center. (2011a). *Global Identity: Connecting Your International Experience to Your Future.* Minneapolis, MN: University of Minnesota. Retrieved from http://www.umabroad.umn.edu/students/academics/globalidentity.php

Learning Abroad Center. (2011b). *Global Identity course syllabus.* Minneapolis, MN: University of Minnesota. Retrieved from https://docs.google.com/a/umn.edu/document/d/1wJUK8zvH1xfiI2l65mHx89iUbBSWEon5IXPtxFlqfAI/edit?auth key=CNnuuCo&pli=1

Moon, J. (1999). *Reflection in learning and professional development.* Abingdon, UK: RoutledgeFalmer.

Moon, J. (2004). *A handbook of reflective and experiential learning: Theory and practice.* London, UK: RoutledgeFalmer.

Paige, R. M. (1993). On the nature of intercultural experiences and intercultural education. In R. M. Paige (Ed.), *Education for the intercultural experience* (pp. 1–19). Yarmouth, ME: Intercultural Press.

Paige, R. M., Cohen, A. D., & Shively, R. (2004). Assessing the impact of a strategies-based curriculum on language and culture learning abroad. *Frontiers: The Interdisciplinary Journal of Study Abroad, 10,* 253–276.

Paige, R. M., Jacobs-Cassuto, M., Yershova, Y. A., & DeJaeghere, J. (2003). Assessing intercultural sensitivity: A psychometric analysis of the Hammer and Bennett Intercultural Development Inventory. *International Journal of Intercultural Relations, 27,* 467–486.

Paige, R. M., Rong, J., Zheng, W., & Kappler, B. (2002). *Culture-Learning Strategies Inventory.* Minneapolis, MN: Center for Advanced Research on Language Acquisition, University of Minnesota.

Paige, R. M., Rong, J., Zheng, W., Kappler, B., Hoff, J. G., & Emert, H. (2002). *Strategies Inventory for Learning Culture.* Minneapolis, MN: Center for Advanced Research on Language Acquisition, University of Minnesota.

Trooboff, S., Vande Berg, M., & Rayman, J. (2008). Employer attitudes toward study abroad. *Frontiers: The Interdisciplinary Journal of Study Abroad, 15,* 17–33.

Vande Berg, M., Connor-Linton, J., & Paige, R. M. (2009). The Georgetown Consortium Project: Intervening in student learning abroad. *Frontiers: The Interdisciplinary Journal of Education Abroad, 17,* 1–75.

Zemach-Bersin, T. (2008, March 7). American students abroad can't be "global citizens." *The Chronicle of Higher Education,* A55.

14

FACILITATING INTERCULTURAL LEARNING ABROAD

The Intentional, Targeted Intervention Model

Kris Hemming Lou and Gabriele Weber Bosley

O ur aim in this chapter is to address the question, What can we do about our students' intercultural learning abroad? We present a learning model (the Bosley/Lou Intentional, Targeted Intervention [ITI] model) that is grounded in theories of student learning and intercultural development, informed by recent research on learning outcomes of study abroad, and reverse engineered to allow the learning outcome of intercultural development to drive the model's design. The chapters in the *Foundations of Teaching and Learning* section of this volume represent a wide-ranging discussion of the theoretical strands that inform our rationale behind intentionally intervening in student learning abroad. This experiential/constructivist approach forms the basis for the development of the ITI model. We begin with a brief review of these basic theoretical constructs before devoting our attention to the recent research that confirms the theoretical predictions regarding intercultural learning abroad. We then present the ITI model together with an empirical assessment of how our students fare under this guided facilitation. Of particular note, we include data on international student learning in the United States because the ITI model integrates international students on U.S. campuses with U.S. students abroad in asynchronous learning communities, which empower the participant to function as both learner and teacher.

The Intentional, Targeted Intervention model is held under copyright of Bosley and Lou, 2012.

Throughout we offer guidance and pedagogical strategies that highlight the role of the instructor/facilitator and underscore the various impact opportunities to which the instructor must be attuned. It should go without saying that the instructor must occupy a position of advanced intercultural development in order to facilitate the students' intercultural growth effectively. That said, effective facilitation is a skill like any other that improves with practice. In this spirit, the teaching strategies taken up here are intended to maximize the impact of intercultural facilitation.

Theoretical Basis for Intervention to Promote Intercultural Learning

The *Foundations of Teaching and Learning* section of this volume presents a compelling case for the experiential-constructivist framework of intercultural learning abroad and for the role of intervention within it. Since 2003 our efforts in creating and improving the ITI model have reflected this experiential-constructivist approach.

We take to heart George Kelly's (1963) oft-quoted excerpt from *A Theory of Personality* regarding the necessity of construing and reconstruing events and experiences to "make meaning" (see chapter 4 of this volume). The key factor in Kelly's insight is the *process* of assigning meaning to an event or experience. This process is at once both a function of what the individual brings to bear and the manner and degree to which the individual's interlocutors contribute to the meaning making. What is clearly necessary in both instances is the need to pause to consider the meaning, to reflect on what was experienced, to discuss with oneself and others what happened. Absent this intentional act, the assigned meaning, if any, remains superficial and limited to unexamined frames of reference. In the intercultural context, the deliberate construing and reconstruing of experience is best informed by the multiple lenses of the individual's home culture, those of the host culture, and if possible those of other non–host/non–home culture individuals. Moreover, the process is most effectively achieved through the intervention of a cultural mentor or instructor/facilitator who can stop the flow of experience and initiate a sustained process of reflection.

We draw as well on another seminal work of the 1960s, *The Social Construction of Reality*, by Peter Berger and Thomas Luckmann. Here we find a constructivist approach to an understanding of reality and man's interaction within it that emphasizes the interrelationship of the natural environment

and the social/cultural environment, the latter of which is of primary importance: "The reality of everyday life further presents itself to me as an inter-
subjective world, a world that I share with others" (Berger & Luckmann,
1967, p. 23). It is important to note that while the developing human interre-
lates both with a natural environment and with a specific cultural and social
order, it is the latter that directs his organismic development in a socially
determined manner. The intercultural challenge is clear. Reality, as appre-
hended by our students who have developed within a set social order with
prevailing and dominant frameworks for values, beliefs, attitudes, and behaviors, must somehow develop the capability to alternate among cultural
frameworks to function effectively and appropriately with culturally different
others. Chief among the potential avenues of instruction, then, is a focus on
the impact that the social construction of reality has on one's identity, more
specifically on one's values, beliefs, attitudes, and behaviors.

Here we refer to Berger and Luckmann's notion of reification. The fundamental process is that the dialectic between man, the producer, and his
products is lost to consciousness. One is simply not aware of this limitation
within the confines of a primary cultural framework. The proverbs "The
frog in the well knows nothing of the ocean" and "We see what is behind
our eyes" together capture the essence of our task. Put simply, if the student
is not exposed to the new and different, the chances of grasping this dialectic
and how it impacts her thoughts, feelings, choices, behaviors, and so forth
are indeed slim. If we immerse our student in another culture she is likely to
feel this dialectic quite sharply, but we cannot expect her, on her own (especially if we think in terms of a mere semester or even a year), to take advantage of the immersion opportunity to develop her orientation to this
difference, such that she can effectively and appropriately frame shift on a
cognitive level and code shift on the behavioral level. She must learn to read
herself and how her perception constructs the reality that she sees.

In consequence of these insights, we concluded that the task of intercultural learning within a cultural immersion context is a developmental one
and therefore we turned to Milton Bennett's Developmental Model of Intercultural Sensitivity as the organizing framework for the ITI model. Additionally, Bennett's developmental model mirrors Perry's (1970) model of
intellectual development, which posits a progression from dualistic thinking
(for Bennett the ethnocentric stage of Denial and Defense), through multiplicity and contextual relativism, to finally committed relativism (for Bennett the ethnorelative stage of Adaptation and Integration) (J. M. Bennett,
1993). Notably, reaching the advanced stages of committed relativism for

Perry and adaptation for Bennett requires an ability not only to recognize the validity of other perspectives and to be open to alternatives, but also to act based on reasoning that draws on multiple points of view. More important, both argue that the path along their developmental continua is not paved by experience alone. Education and training must accompany the experiences that fuel the learning.

In this context we turn further to Kolb's Experiential Learning Theory (ELT), wherein learning is "the process whereby knowledge is created through the transformation of experience. Knowledge results from the combination of grasping and transforming experience" (Kolb, 1984, p. 41; chapter 6 of this volume). The key element for our purposes is that ELT gives subjective experience a central role in learning, unlike other learning theories that emphasize cognition and intentional learning behaviors. As we saw in chapter 6, Passarelli and Kolb identify six propositions that characterize ELT, each of which echoes the theoretical principles that we have addressed:

1. Learning is best viewed as a process, rather than as a set of outcomes.
2. All learning is relearning.
3. Learning requires the resolution of conflicts between different ways of seeing and adapting to the world.
4. Learning is a holistic process of adaptation to the world.
5. Learning results from synergetic transactions between the person and the environment.
6. Learning is the process of creating knowledge.

We find ourselves much better equipped now with a theoretical basis for intervening to develop intercultural competence. Moreover, we see the direct relevance of an approach that is developmental and utilizes Kolb's (1984) ELT, in particular his four-stage cycle, which posits that learning starts with (a) concrete experiences that form the basis for (b) reflective observations that are absorbed and refined into (c) abstract concepts, which are then (d) actively tested in the learner's environment in order to transform the experience into new knowledge. Finally, we add to this approach the notion of "Deep Learning":

> Deep learning is represented by a personal commitment to understand the material which is reflected in using various strategies such as reading widely, combining a variety of resources, discussing ideas with others, reflecting on how individual pieces of information relate to larger constructs or patterns, and applying knowledge in real world situations. Also

characteristic of deep learning is integrating and synthesizing information with prior learning in ways that become part of one's thinking and approaching new phenomena and efforts to see things from different perspectives. As Tagg put it, "Deep learning is learning that takes root in our apparatus of understanding, in the embedded meanings that define us and that we use to define the world." (Nelson Laird, Shoup, & Kuh, 2005, p. 4)

These theoretical foundations instruct us to develop curricula that create the learning space for students to reflect on their experiences, to experiment with conclusions reached through guided discussions with their own culture peers and their "other culture" hosts, and to manage their own learning as both subjective learners and teachers. That said, we must first check these theoretical imperatives against the "reality" of empirical data on student learning abroad before moving forward with intervention models designed to accomplish these tasks.

Recent Research on Intercultural Learning Abroad

Research on intercultural learning abroad has been focused heavily on U.S. students in varying cultural "immersion" contexts. One of the more influential studies of immersion practices, the Georgetown Consortium study, examined the impact of study abroad on the development of intercultural competence of U.S. students enrolled in 61 different programs abroad (Vande Berg, Connor-Linton, & Paige, 2009; Paige & Vande Berg, this volume). A central question of the study was to determine whether a long-held axiom of international education—that the experience of studying abroad produces intercultural learning—actually holds up when administering a pre- and posttest that measures one's intercultural development. The study utilized the Intercultural Development Inventory (IDI) for this purpose, and the researchers were able to assess various program components for differences in results that might be related to a variety of cultural immersion and engagement factors. For many, the surprising result was that the average gain in intercultural development for a group of 1,050 students, who did not receive intervention in the form of intercultural instruction, was a mere 1.32 points on the IDI's 90-point continuum (55 through 145).

These results were startling to anyone who had been developing and implementing study abroad programs of any type (e.g., direct enrollment, faculty-led group, third party provider) under the assumption and expectation that students were developing their intercultural competence by virtue of participation in study abroad alone. In our case, because we had been delivering an intercultural learning course to our students abroad since 1995 in its original form, and since 2004 in its current form, we realized the necessity of assessing our programs and the course itself to determine whether the same held true for our students as for those in the Georgetown Consortium study. Indeed, we found that our students, who were not receiving intercultural learning intervention, were underperforming in the same fashion as the students in the large group study.

By contrast, those Willamette and Bellarmine university students over the last seven years ($N = 144$) who were enrolled in our ITI intercultural course, which has components delivered pre-departure, while abroad, and upon return, have achieved an average gain of 8.08 points on the IDI scale (see Figure 14.1).

Aside from the obvious numerical improvement (more than six times the gain measured in the Georgetown study), a movement of this magnitude along the developmental continuum represents fundamental changes in one's orientation to cultural difference. In other words, a gain of one to two points would not be interpreted as signaling a development in orientation that is fundamentally different from when one began the program. Gains in

FIGURE 14.1
**Study abroad supported by ITI Model versus
study abroad without intervention.**

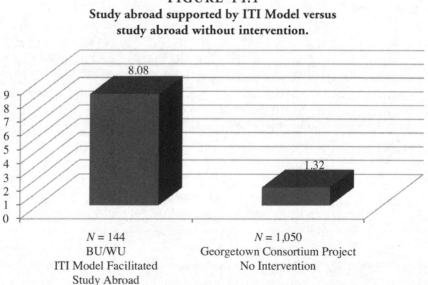

Abbreviations: BU, Bellarmine University; WU, Willamette University.

the range of eight points, however, reflect more significant changes in one's cognitive understanding and behavioral practice. For example, a student who enters a study abroad program at the midrange of an ethnocentric, defensive/ polarizing orientation to the cultural "other" (somewhere between 75 and 79), and who develops this orientation only one to two points, will not have resolved the fundamental issues related to the defensive orientation. On the other hand, if this same student registers a gain of eight points, he or she will have moved into a position of low minimization, which requires resolution of fundamental defensive, polarizing issues. In short, gains in the range of eight points signal either significant development within a scale or development from one fundamental scale to the next, whereas gains limited to one to two points accomplish neither. Finally, and perhaps most sobering, is the fact that our students can be expected to achieve gains in their intercultural competence of one to two points simply by attending, for example, a course on intercultural communication on the home campus. We do not need study abroad if we are satisfied with such minimal developmental gains. On the other hand, we find that to achieve significant gains of five or more points, the most effective mode is to combine intercultural intervention with cultural immersion. Thus, study abroad without focused, intentional intervention can be a powerful, but insufficient, condition for the intercultural development of our students.

The Intercultural Development of International Students in the United States

We now shift our attention to the international students whom we host on our campuses. Are they equally underperforming when it comes to intercultural learning? Are there any significant differences in their intercultural development when they arrive? When they depart? What happens if we intervene with international students to take advantage of their study abroad with us by intentionally facilitating the development of their intercultural competence? And what happens when we include them in the same intercultural course with our study abroad students who are situated in different cultural contexts around the world?

From fall semester 2004 to spring semester 2008, Willamette and Bellarmine universities administered pre and post-IDI assessments of their international exchange and degree-seeking students. The total number of students surveyed was 168, of which 128 (76%) were European. The remaining students (24%) were visiting from 21 countries representing all other habitable continents. The sample included both undergraduate (106) and graduate students (62). When we compared U.S. students and their international peers, the first striking finding was that they started from roughly the same developmental point. In the preassessment of our U.S. Bellarmine and Willamette students ($N = 298$), the average IDI score was 92.31. The average for the international students ($N = 168$) was 91.68, as shown in Figure 14.2.

To some, this result might at first appear counterintuitive. Typically, European students (76% of our sample) have a great deal more exposure to cultural difference in the form of second- and third-language acquisition, including spending significantly more time in other cultures where other languages are spoken. U.S. students are far less likely to have spent as much time visiting or living in another culture than their European counterparts, and they are far less likely to have spent as much time learning second and third languages. These conditions suggest that European students are more experienced in encountering difference. Assuming that this is actually the case, the IDI results would indicate that greater exposure to difference alone does not translate into greater intercultural development. As the theoretical

FIGURE 14.2

IDI scores prior to study abroad for U.S. undergraduate and international graduate and undergraduate students at Bellarmine University (BU) and Willamette University (WU)

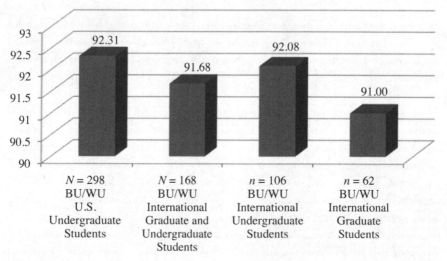

arguments suggest and the research noted here and in chapter 2 has shown, studying abroad without intercultural intervention results in only marginal gains in intercultural development. We would expect the same would hold true of any type of cultural immersion experience.

What are the intercultural challenges that the average student faces on a U.S. campus? The average score of 91.68 occupies the space on the developmental continuum referred to as low Minimization. This means the student has, for the most part, resolved issues related to an ethnocentric posture of defensiveness about his or her own culture or, alternatively, a defense posture about other cultures vis-à-vis one's own. The student has reached a developmental stage that

> Reflect[s] a tendency to highlight commonalities across cultures that can mask important cultural differences in values, perceptions and behaviors. This can often take one of two forms: (1) highlighting commonality that masks equal recognition of cultural differences due to less cultural self-awareness, more commonly experienced among dominant group members within a cultural community, or (2) highlighting commonalities that masks recognition of cultural differences that functions as a strategy for navigating values and practices largely determined by the dominant culture group, more commonly experienced among non-dominant group members within a larger cultural community. (M. Hammer, 2011, p. 6)

The latter form is a very common strategy employed by students studying abroad. Naturally, they are eager to meet others, make friends, and get along as comfortably as possible, all in the context of a university environment with its inherent stresses and challenges. Thus, students focus on commonalities as a means of interacting "productively" with the dominant culture group. This orientation, however, comes at the expense of missing crucial differences in values, perceptions, and behaviors, sometimes resulting in cultural bumps, misunderstandings, discomfort, confusing ambiguity, and so forth. Moreover, when these bumps in the road are serious enough to trigger intense emotional reactions, students will more readily fall into strategies reflecting their "trailing orientation" (Defense):

> As a Trailing Orientation, there are certain times, topics, or situations that Defense may arise (an uncritical orientation that views cultural differences in terms of "us" and "them" in which an uncritical orientation toward one's own cultural values and practices and an overly critical view toward

other cultural values and practices becomes the mode of interaction). (Hammer, 2011, p. 8)

In these instances, students will quite naturally seek out home culture peers (or where there are none, peers who are also "cultural outsiders," such as other international students) and vent their frustrations as a coping strategy. Without diminishing the potential psychological benefits of this venting strategy, this type of unguided processing can prove to be highly unproductive to the intercultural learning experience. These are moments when intervention is most needed, and perhaps most effective.

But when intervention is not forthcoming, when the international students receive neither intercultural coursework nor explicit guidance designed to develop their intercultural skills, what happens to the development of their intercultural competence? Put differently, is the expense and effort behind sending ever greater numbers of students abroad, presumably with the objective of developing intercultural skills with which they can apply themselves more successfully as socioeconomic-politico agents in an increasingly interconnected global community, actually producing the desired result?

A random sample of 30 international students from the 168 who took the IDI pretest was administered a post-IDI at the end of their one-semester stay. The students were selected from five different semesters between fall 2005 and fall 2007. The individual-specific pre- and postassessments revealed that the group averaged a decline in intercultural competence of –1.91. From this random sample it appears that our visiting international students, like our outbound students abroad, are not developing intercultural competence by virtue of studying abroad alone. The results of a second random pre- and postsample of 12 international students who had studied with us for one year (two semesters) revealed an average gain in intercultural competence of just 1.2. We further tested another smaller random sample of 5 international transfer students who had been with us for two full years. In this case, the average gain increased to 4.29, suggesting that something more fundamental might be occurring over an extended period of two years or more, compared with just one or two semesters. We might speculate—recognizing that the size of these samples can only support suggestions rather than assertions— that over the space of two years, students will tend to identify, utilize, and value cultural mentors more than those students who are more transient.

We were also curious whether there might be a significant difference between international undergraduates and graduate students. Remember here that the starting point for these two groups was very similar (see Figure 14.2). The results of a random sample of 9 international graduate students who studied with us for two semesters showed an average gain of just 0.17. Further, for a second sample of 16 students over a two-year span, the average gain was 3.75. Again, although the results for the undergraduate and graduate groups were not identical, they were quite close, and the apparent "mentor effect" of the two-year sojourn was reproduced. For a comparison of these results see Figure 14.3.

Curricular Intervention for Intercultural Learning: The ITI Model

Initially, qualitative assessment of our students' intercultural learning (writings, conversations, observations) led us to the conclusion that it was necessary to intervene in the students' cultural immersion experience. The early

FIGURE 14.3
IDI gains for international undergraduate versus graduate students according to duration of study

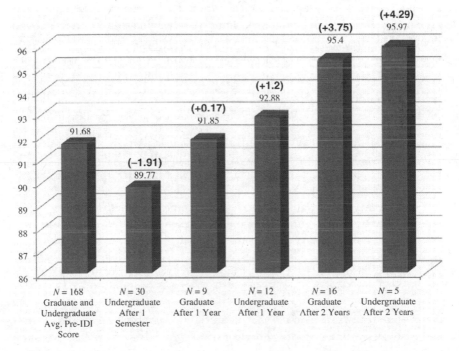

versions of the course (roughly from 1995 to 2003) were undertaken without the benefit of empirical assessment tools and without the advantages of current computer technology that connects students, professors, and staff in virtual platforms with synchronous and asynchronous applications. As a result, our efforts were either group based (i.e., one class equaled one group of students at a single study site) or individual based (i.e., one student taking an independent study). This understandably resulted in student work that concentrated almost exclusively on culture-specific issues. These earlier iterations also focused only on outbound U.S. students until we recognized that the lack of intercultural development pertained to both outbound and inbound students. Thus, the challenge arose to design and implement a means of intervention that would address the needs of both groups.

The development of software platforms that allow synchronous and asynchronous instruction and discussion within discrete learning communities, along with our initial research results using the IDI with outbound and inbound students, gave us the ability and the rationale to restructure the course, beginning in the fall of 2004. We implemented two vital changes. First, we created learning communities of students and instructor(s) who were individually situated in different cultural contexts around the world. Second, we included the international students who were experiencing their own study abroad on our campuses. These two insights led to a course design that focuses much more effectively on culture-general issues. By necessity, the students in the course must advance their analysis from the specific cultural phenomena that they encounter in their host country to culture-general, or metalevel, analyses of similar phenomena in varying cultural contexts:

> Advancing discussion of intercultural concepts with peers in other cultures as opposed to discussion with peers in the same host culture avoids the common pitfall of soothing one another's discomforts with judgmental references. It forces each student to focus on the essence of each situation because they cannot fall back on supposed common understandings. . . . This feature enables the students and instructor to examine how similar cultural processes are at work in different settings with dissimilar outcomes. . . . In the process, the students begin to develop intercultural skills by raising the level of discussion from mere description to cross-cultural comparative analysis. (Lou & Bosley, 2008, p. 280)

The general course design is a blend of ethnographic and interculturalist/constructivist methods, together constituting what we now refer to as the experiential/constructivist approach. It focuses on a progression of critical analysis moving from the examination of the "self" (one's own identity, values, and behaviors) to the "other" and then to the "synthesis" of the two. As mentioned, the course spans the period before departure, the period in country, and the return phase of the study abroad experience. The greater the degree to which each of these phases can be incorporated into a comprehensive whole, the greater the impact will be. Each phase is critical to a holistic and rich intercultural learning experience.

Pre-Departure Phase: Workshop

Students meet as a group for the first time in a pre-departure workshop. We must repeat this workshop for the international students when they arrive, usually well after our outbound students have already departed. The purpose of this workshop is to familiarize students with intercultural concepts as well as issues of perception, interpretation, and evaluation. We conduct student-centered group activities involving interviews, analyses, reflections, essays, questionnaires, role plays, and so on that lay the groundwork for ethnographic assignments to follow in the in-country phase of the course. We assign exercises that examine the students' core and supporting values, which establish a baseline for comparative purposes later in the semester and during the postprogram workshop. Students take the pre-IDI online before the pre-workshop, and then the post-IDI after the postworkshop.

The IDI assessment is not only an assessment tool to determine whether we achieve our learning outcomes. It also serves to educate the instructor on where each individual student stands in the developmental range. It informs us what the learning curve is for each student and allows for targeted instruction that can be tailored to the individual. The pre-IDI assessment might indicate, for example, that student A has placed herself in the Defense stage of intercultural development. The instructor can therefore expect that student A will attempt to protect her worldview structure with steadfast categorical and "us/them" thinking. Her experiences will be polarized into judgmental alignments, and her behavior will retrench into same-culture segregation:

> With this pre-program knowledge, the instructor can look for manifestations of this developmental stage in the student's writings and attempt to mitigate the polarization tendencies by pointing and directing the student

to examples of similarity or "common humanity." (Lou & Bosley, 2008, p. 289)

The critical point here is that the appropriate instruction for a student at this stage of development is to look for similarity in the host culture. This would not be effective instruction for a student who has already resolved Defense issues and is working her way through Minimization. In this case, the student needs to focus on identifying difference and practice relating to host culture individuals on the basis of difference, rather than similarity. This leads us to the next critical course component, which we discuss next.

Immersion Phase: Learning Abroad

Students are matched in groups of three to five on the basis of their pre-IDI assessments. Note that the students are not made aware of their results or why they are grouped as they are. Only after the course is over, and after they have taken the post-IDI, do we offer to discuss their individual results. These IDI-based groupings are important because the course requires that each student provide feedback to each group member each week. If the small group consists of students occupying significantly different stages of the developmental spectrum, the effectiveness of the peer-to-peer feedback will suffer because the students will be talking past each other. It would be akin to a student in algebra giving feedback to a student in calculus. The former would either not comprehend the issues of the latter or focus on issues the latter has long resolved. Further, the instructor can provide relevant feedback to the group as a whole if the members all occupy relatively the same developmental position.

Students are provided with a series of assignments each week that are designed to stimulate engagement with the host culture. Notably, students frequently comment on how beneficial they found the assignments for forcing them into activities that they would not normally have done on their own. Students are required to complete these activities, reflect on a series of prompts that accompany the instructions, and post their responses and reflections on the course site. Further, they must provide feedback to their group members each week. As a result, each student each week should receive feedback from two to four other students and the instructor. The process is asynchronous, and often a student is completing an assignment for the given week, still receiving feedback from the previous week, and perhaps providing feedback for the present week. These asynchronous elements are not disruptive, however, because the relevance of each element is transferable week to week. Our aim is to cultivate a habit of employing the learning cycle of reflecting on an experience, formulating explanations and generalizations, and testing or applying those generalizations, which in turn creates new experiences to reflect on. The process is ongoing, just as each week of the semester blends into the next.

Sample Assignment: The Interactive Learning Process

To underscore how the interactive learning process functions, we offer one example of an assignment (Cultural Bump) from early in the semester abroad. This particular assignment sets the task of selecting an event or experience that produced ambivalent, uncomfortable thoughts or feelings and then considering different perspectives on the issue. During this early phase of the semester, students are focusing on their own identity (values, behaviors, emotional reactions) as it is affected by the cultural immersion. It is important to note that students are prepped for this activity (as they are for most) during the pre-departure workshop. At that time we introduce and discuss typical "cultural bumps" in the abstract and discuss strategies to manage and learn from such situations. Naturally, in the pre-departure stage, students are not emotionally charged by such issues and can only imagine themselves in the situation. This is important, however, in that they are able to first consider the value of practicing a nonjudgmental approach that seeks to consider alternative perspectives or explanations. Once the students are abroad and actually stumbling over real cultural bumps, they have their initial efforts to fall back on when working their way through uncomfortable challenges. Depending on the severity of the emotional challenge, the students will at least make the effort to describe the event or experience as neutrally as possible. The following interchange illustrates this effort:

ERIKA (GERMAN EXCHANGE STUDENT)

I do not really know if you can describe it as a cultural bump, but when I was first confronted with the American college system of fraternities and sororities I was kind of shocked or did not know what to think about it. . . . They have to obey certain rules to be able to be a member of the group and there are certain rules for the recruitment. Almost every student wants to be part of this group and seems to gain a better reputation on campus when they are able to make it in the group.

In Germany, we also have certain clubs or associations who can be compared to a sorority or fraternity. But it can be described as a more open and fun thing. People in those associations are in these to have fun and to meet other people and not to have to obey certain rules. Here in the United States, everything seems to be more serious. I heard from some members of a sorority that there are strict rules like for example that you are not allowed to bring your boyfriend with you or that there are weeks where you are not even allowed to talk to boys. This was very shocking for me and I had the feeling that a sorority excludes other people a lot.

But when I got deeper into the subject and got to know some members of a sorority or fraternity I learned how it is actually supposed to be. Being a member of a sorority or fraternity gives you certain job opportunities later. Moreover, they do not exclude people on purpose, it is just a traditional system that they have to obey and this expects people to go through this certain recruitment. I learned that it is just supposed to be a help for students to get to know new people and to be in a kind of family that protects you and gives you certain opportunities for your later career.

RESPONSE TO ERIKA FROM U.S. STUDENT MARY STUDYING IN IRELAND

I'm glad you are taking a deeper look at the Greek life, it is not all what it looks like in movies. As a member of the Greek community I appreciate your willingness to take a deeper look and am happy that you are not the typical student who judges this group of students based on the media's presentation of their lives. Good job taking a closer look and deciding what is accurate for yourself!

RESPONSE TO ERIKA FROM PEKKA (FINNISH EXCHANGE STUDENT)

I think we have stereotypes about many aspects of American college life because of TV and movies. Then when we actually encounter those things here, we might easily look for stereotypical things and when we find them, we're satisfied and conclude that the stereotype is correct. But as you noticed, learning about e.g., the Greek organisations thoroughly take[s] more than just a superficial glance at their direction. When you got to know people who are actually involved with the organisations you saw something more than the stereotype and learned something real about them, you learned about the reasons behind the things we see on the surface.

RESPONSE TO ERIKA FROM U.S. STUDENT JOHN IN ECUADOR

Yes, the frats and sororities are certainly . . . odd. They do give you future opportunities later in life, and a steady group of people who generally accept you and hang out with you. I think those things are great.

A lot about these systems are [is] very questionable, though. Initially excluding based on gender doesn't seem like the best way to start an organization, and I have found a lot of the sexist attitudes associated with the Greek life to not be stereotypes, but actually the general feelings of a lot of the members.

On the other hand, some of my best friends are in frats, and I have been over to their houses and have hung out with them, and everyone has been very welcoming. I think, like any group, there are the good people and the bad.

Response to Erika from the instructor

You have generated a good conversation on this topic. As the others noted, it was productive to look deeper into the issue to try and understand it from the "American lens" and get a better sense of its value to the actual members. Your description of the German equivalent is interesting in that you suggest it "can be described as a more open and fun thing. People in those associations are in these to have fun." Consider how "having fun" might be constructed differently in the U.S. and Germany, that is, investigate whether the members of these fraternities and sororities are having fun as they define it. You also comment: "Here in the United States, everything seems to be more serious." Do you mean to say "everything"? During the next few weeks make an effort to identify situations, which are not so serious, perhaps even less serious in comparison to the same situation in Germany.

There are a few noteworthy items in this interchange. First, discussing the issue within the framework of the course already serves to challenge the students to consider the topic, feelings, and interpretations in an objective, detached manner. A conversation in a cafe on the same topic, although useful in its own right, might well take a turn away from the learning goal of intercultural development. One hopes as well that the practice of paying attention to "red flag" words such as *stupid, rude*, and *weird* will carry over into everyday interactions. Second, although the feedback from the other students was rather limited (the assignment appears in just the third week of the semester), it should not be underestimated. The learning here works both ways. Erika is benefiting from the perspectives of the U.S. students looking in from abroad. Moreover, the U.S. students are benefiting from Erika's and Pekka's perspectives on the issue because of their ability to represent U.S. culture unfettered by U.S. cultural lenses. These small-group learning communities function best when the students are in control of their own learning and operating as both learners and teachers simultaneously.

The instructor's input is also very important, as we will see later in the review of the assessment data on the actual intercultural development that takes place in the course. Students will tend to skim the surface of analysis and limit themselves to description. It is important to continually push them to dig deeper into the underlying values that give rise to beliefs, which in turn spur action. Put differently, the instructor can serve as a continual check on the students' tendency to interpret and evaluate events and experiences without enough attention to the values and beliefs that one brings to the situation. Finally, although there are many prompts the instructor could give, it is important not to overload the student with too many. One should move slowly, recognizing that each week flows into the next, and focus on elements that surface with regularity, because these will likely reflect the intercultural issues that are the most salient for the particular student.

Postprogram Phase: Workshop

It is difficult to overstate the learning potential when students return to the once familiar home culture. Paramount among the lessons is the notion of transferability of the newly acquired intercultural skills to understanding one's own home culture and how one's identity is not limited to home culture constructions. Further, the students' adaptation back into home culture norms and practices is made easier and more productive when the students recognize the transferability of what they have been doing all semester. Again, the focus on culture-general analysis facilitates the navigation of the return challenges, with which students commonly struggle. The postworkshop is designed to extract these lessons and promote activities and opportunities for the students to continue applying and developing their intercultural skills at home, in particular with nonmainstream culture groups within the home country.

For the instructor this dimension of the course is a delight. The energy and enthusiasm, infused by the common bond forged by a semester of intermittent yet regular sharing of struggles, insights, and growth, finds its culmination in this forum. And yet this very same bond of adventuresome heroes, returning to share their treasures with the wider community, stands also as a framework to be deconstructed. Like the mythical hero who slays the dragon and captures the gold only to have it turn to ashes upon return home, the students' transformation (their golden growth) becomes the central focus of the postimmersion workshop.

One of the most promising results of our course is the observation that due to its ongoing reflective and analytical focus, the students return with the predisposition and skills to meet the challenge of bringing home the gold. The discomfort or disorientation of reentry, while still applicable, is neither a surprise nor a frustration. They have been trained to identify and analyze dispassionately, or at least they will recognize that our regular lecturing and urging throughout the semester also applies here. This challenge—understanding and communicating the developmental growth one has achieved—is often not met by the typical study abroad student. (Lou & Bosley, 2008, p. 293)

Outcomes of Curricular Intervention for Intercultural Learning Abroad

As stated earlier, the U.S. and international students are, on average, beginning their studies abroad at essentially the same stage of intercultural development. We noted as well that both types of students are underperforming roughly at the same rates when it comes to intercultural development on study abroad if they receive no curricular intervention designed to facilitate such learning. What happens, however, to the students who are enrolled in the ITI intercultural course described previously?

Figure 14.4 illustrates the comprehensive results of a total of 200 students who have taken the course since the fall of 2004. The course has been delivered at two separate universities (Bellarmine and Willamette) and has steadily grown in terms of enrollment. Of the total 200 students, 136 were Willamette students (either degree-seeking U.S. nationals or international exchange students) and 64 were Bellarmine U.S. degree-seeking and international exchange students. In addition, 139 were U.S. degree-seeking (Bellarmine and Willamette) and 61 were exchange students (44 Europeans). As shown in Figure 14.4, the average IDI gain for the 144 students (U.S. and international) who received *facilitated instruction* throughout the course was 8.08 points. When we break out the results of U.S. versus international students we find an average gain of 7.55 points for the U.S. students ($n = 115$) and 10.17 for the international students ($n = 29$).

The remaining 56 students of the total 200 represent two semesters of students who guided themselves through the course without instructor facilitation. During the numerous presentations of the course that we have given over the years we have heard the refrain, "How can I deliver this curriculum to the many hundreds of students who study abroad at my institution? It

FIGURE 14.4

ITI Model–supported study abroad: Facilitated and unfacilitated versus study abroad without intercultural intervention

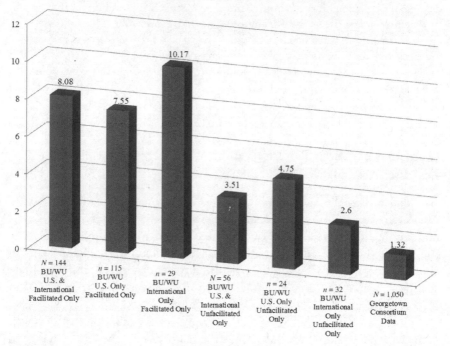

Abbreviations: BU, Bellarmine University; WU, Willamette University.

appears to be too labor intensive to the teaching staff!" As a result, we decided to experiment with the course by allowing the students to "self-guide" through the assignments. The course was constructed in exactly the same way as before, with pre- and postworkshops, IDI pre- and postassessment, small groups of students working together, and so on. The difference was that the instructor's role was reduced to a bare minimum, a level at which the course could have been delivered very broadly to large numbers of students but, as shown in Figure 14.4, with less impressive results. Accordingly, this group of 56 students (U.S. and international) achieved an average IDI gain of only 3.51 points. When we break out the results of U.S. versus international students, we find an average gain of 4.75 points for the U.S. students ($n = 24$) and 2.60 for the international students ($n = 32$).

In Figure 14.4 we see that when the international students received regular and consistent guidance from the instructor throughout the semester they advanced their intercultural competence at an average rate of 10.17 points on the developmental scale. By contrast, the international students without instructor facilitation but who nevertheless received all other elements of the intercultural course performed at a much lower average rate of 2.60. It is important, however, to recall Figure 14.3, in which we noted an average negative decline (-1.91) in the intercultural competence of the 30 international students who received no intercultural intervention at all. This result, together with the positive 2.60 shown in Figure 14.4, suggests a difference of 4.5 points between those who are left to their own devices and those who receive a framework (including peer-to-peer interaction) for intercultural learning, but without the benefit of instructor facilitation.

The result for the U.S. students ($n = 24$) who self-guided through the course (average gain of 4.75 points) is encouraging in that it clearly exceeds the average gain of 1.32 points reported in the Georgetown Consortium study for students enrolling in 60 different programs abroad who received no intercultural intervention. Although the result is still markedly less than the average of 8.08 reported for all students who received facilitated intervention, it indicates that even unfacilitated frameworks of intervention bring important gains in intercultural development. The most important lesson that we take from these results concerns the role of the instructor/facilitator. Although the number of students measured in this experiment with no facilitation is quite low, thereby limiting the generalizability of the findings, we can suggest that the key element in an intervention strategy is the instructor/facilitator. It is fair to say that even without facilitation, we can expect improvement in the intercultural learning of our students abroad if they are given a framework of assignments requiring reflection and processing of their experiences. That said, we also emphasize the importance of an intercultural facilitator to guide the reflection and processing to improve the results significantly. In short, the more facilitation each student receives, the better.

Conclusion

With the intensifying focus on the internationalization of higher education across the globe, we need first to lay to rest the notion that our task is merely to move ever increasing numbers of students across borders. If the purpose of studying abroad is to develop intercultural competence—a task much more complex than simply throwing our students into the deep end of the cultural immersion pool—we need to devise methods to optimize the learning potential of the experience.

We have presented here one such method, the Bosley/Lou ITI Model, which can be adjusted in intensity (more facilitation or less) with corresponding results in intercultural development. We have seen that young adults the world over who are embarking on study abroad sojourns have, on average, roughly the same intercultural challenges and learning tasks to confront. We have also examined how the experience of studying abroad alone does not, on average, translate into significant intercultural learning. We have shown that intervention in the experience is an effective method to achieve significant intercultural development. We have also shown how combining U.S. students abroad with the international exchange students in the United States in a peer-to-peer learning community significantly enhances the learning experience for all.

Here are some steps that international education administrators and educators can take in response to these findings:

- *Establish learning outcomes.* The first order of business is to determine whether one of the objectives (the main objective?) of study abroad at your institution is the development of intercultural competence. If so, this needs to be defined and stated explicitly for everyone (students, parents, trustees, faculty, administrators, coaches, etc.). Remember, most constituencies are assuming that this is already occurring within the study abroad context. Consider further whether the learning goal of intercultural competence is so central to your institution's mission and strategic plan that it would possibly fit within the general education framework.

- *Identify resources and challenges.* Investigate sources for curricular development, faculty professional development, as well as assessment tools. To some degree the availability of funds will be a function of the desirability of the learning outcome, that is, to what degree your institution embraces the overall goal. A vital resource is your teaching faculty. Can you identify one or two people to lead the curricular effort from advancing an intercultural course proposal through the proper academic committees, all the way to implementation and actual teaching/delivery of the course? The answer to this question will determine the scale of your initial efforts and how much you can grow and expand (one, two, or three credits; instructor taught; instructor facilitated; peer facilitated; self-guided; etc.).

- *Evaluate the types of study abroad programs that you operate, or utilize, and determine which types of intervention are most appropriate.* It may be that some programs that your students are attending are already offering intercultural coursework. In this case consider making such courses mandatory. Alternatively, you might have a number of short-term, faculty-led programs, in which case a possible strategy would be to commit to a professional development program for your faculty that provides training to incorporate intercultural material in existing courses that are delivered abroad or to develop full-scale courses that faculty could then deliver. A third consideration is the hiring of adjunct faculty to deliver the intercultural courses, either on-site or in a more virtual format such as the ITI Model. Your institution might also (or only) be sending students to partner universities for direct enrollment. In this case, the ITI Model is well suited to "gather together" individual students in diverse locations into one learning community. This situation is also well suited to incorporate international students in the intercultural learning endeavor. In sum, there is no one right way to intervene. Each cultural immersion program will have its own unique opportunities and challenges.

- *Consider what segment of the student population will receive intercultural coursework.* Do you wish to limit the target group to study abroad students? All of them? It may be that your number of study abroad participants is so large that implementing an "intervention lite" version that is cost-effective and not time-consuming for teaching and administrative staff is the best place to start. This initiative might be accompanied by a full, elective intervention course, which could represent a cornerstone upon which to build. Are there local experiential opportunities in which your students are already engaging that lend themselves to introducing intercultural work? Do you have a steady stream of international students who could be integrated in the courses during their first semester at your institution? If so, do you wish to integrate both outbound and inbound students in one course?

- *Consider engaging your partners abroad in the intervention effort.* Possible partners might include site directors and staff and/or the teaching and international office staff of a partner university. Program staff abroad might be trained to support your efforts by helping facilitate intercultural learning. If your partner university offers intercultural communication courses, engage the teaching faculty of these courses by mutually designing assignments for your students (and theirs) that require them to interact, reflect, and process.

- *Identify a quantitative instrument for pre- and postassessment and to use as a teaching tool.* Use this instrument to accompany the qualitative data that you can gather in the form of student writings, portfolios, digital narratives, and so on. If you are convinced that the quantitative data adequately and appropriately capture your students' intercultural learning—perhaps through cross-referencing the results against the qualitative data—then use the data to move the decision makers at your institution. Further, can your quantitative instrument also be used as a teaching tool—for example, to identify your students' intercultural starting points and then guide the learning curves?

International education has evolved to the point where providing the opportunities for experiential learning within cultural immersion contexts is only the first step. The increasing focus on learning outcomes, and the assessment of those outcomes within higher education in general, extends as well to the international education field. If the research on those learning outcomes reveals a deficit in intercultural learning, as it has so far, it is incumbent on us to devise methods to address the issue. Hand in hand with the focus on learning outcomes, assessment and research is the development of experiential learning theory and its application to the study abroad context. This is of particular importance to intercultural learning because it is fundamentally a developmental proposition that involves the cognitive, affective, and behavioral realms. Accordingly, more than ever, we need to blend the classroom with the experience in a manner that enables student-centered, peer-interactive, instructor-facilitated intercultural learning. Happily, this challenge invites many diverse applications in a field that depends on and emphasizes difference.

References

Bennett, J. M. (1993). Cultural marginality: Identity issues in intercultural training. In M. R. Paige (Ed.), *Education for the intercultural experience* (pp. 109–135). Yarmouth, ME: Intercultural Press.

Bennett, J. M. (2008). On becoming a global soul: A path to engagement during study abroad. In V. Savicki (Ed.), *Developing intercultural competence and transformation: Theory, research, and application in international education* (pp. 13–31). Sterling, VA: Stylus.

Bennett, M. J. (1993). Towards ethnorelativism: A developmental model of intercultural sensitivity. In R. M. Paige (Ed.), *Education for the intercultural experience* (2nd ed., pp. 21–71). Yarmouth, ME: Intercultural Press.

Bennett, M. J. (2001). Radical constructivism: The assumptive base of intercultural communication, statements of (radical) constructivism and implications for intercultural communication. In M. Bennett & M. Hammer (Eds.), *The Intercultural Development Inventory (IDI) manual* (pp. 2–3). Portland, OR: Intercultural Communication Institute.

Bennett, M. J. (2004). Becoming interculturally competent. In J. Wurzel (Ed.), *Towards multiculturalism: A reader in multicultural education* (2nd ed., pp. 62–77). Newton, MA. Intercultural Resource.

Berger, P., & Luckmann, T. (1967). *The social construction of reality.* New York: Doubleday.

Hammer, M. R. (2011). *The Intercultural Development Inventory* V.3 (IDI). Education Profile Report. Ocean Pines, MD: IDI.

Kelly, G. (1963). *A theory of personality.* New York: Norton.

Kolb, A.Y., & Kolb, D. A. (2005). Learning styles and learning spaces: Enhancing experiential learning in higher education. *Academy of Management Learning & Education, 4*(2), 193–212.

Kolb, D. A. (1984). *Experiential learning: Experience as the source of learning and development.* Upper Saddle River, NJ: Prentice Hall.

Lou, K. H., & Bosley, G. W. (2008). Dynamics of cultural contexts: Meta-level intervention in the study abroad experience. In V. Savicki (Ed.), *Developing intercultural competence and transformation* (pp. 276–296). Sterling, VA: Stylus.

Nelson Laird, T. F., Shoup, R., & Kuh, G. D. (2005). *Measuring deep approaches to learning using the National Survey of Student Engagement.* Paper presented at the annual meeting of the Association for Institutional Research, Chicago, IL.

Paige, R. M. (2004). Instrumentation in intercultural training. In D. Landis, J. M. Bennett, & M. J. Bennett (Eds.), *Handbook of intercultural training* (3rd ed., pp. 85–128). Thousand Oaks, CA: Sage.

Paige, R. M., Cohen, A. D., & Shively, R. (2004). Assessing the impact of a strategies-based curriculum on language and culture learning abroad. *Frontiers: The Interdisciplinary Journal of Study Abroad, 10,* 253–276.

Perry, W. G. (1970). *Forms of intellectual and ethical development in the college years.* New York: Rinehart & Winston.

Ramsden, P. (2003). *Learning to teach in higher education.* London: Routledge-Falmer.

Tagg, J. (2003). *The learning paradigm college.* Boston, MA: Anker.

Vande Berg, M., Connor-Linton, J., & Paige, R. M. (2009). The Georgetown Consortium Project: Intervening for student learning abroad. *Frontiers: The Interdisciplinary Journal of Study Abroad, 18,* 1–75.

15

DEVELOPING A GLOBAL LEARNING AND LIVING COMMUNITY

A Case Study of Intercultural Experiences on The Scholar Ship

Adriana Medina-López-Portillo and Riikka Salonen

In the Seychelles, we rented a car, and got a flat tire. The owner tried to convince us that a part of the car is broken but he based his argument on a sound that the car was making and that we could not hear. He had an engagement conflict style and we had a discussion conflict style, which made the conflict get worse. (The Scholar Ship student)

From the convergence of integrative learning, experiential learning theory (ELT), and developmental theories resulted The Scholar Ship (TSS), a transnational academic program for undergraduate and graduate students from around the world. Like other shipboard programs, including Semester at Sea, Peace Boat, and Sea Semester, TSS offered classes during voyages with focused port stops around the world. Its academic design and goals were unique, however, featuring (a) guided learning outcomes; (b) the intentional alignment of all aspects of the program with the desired learning outcomes; (c) an emphasis on experiential learning in which reflection and processing were key elements; (d) an emphasis on attending to students developmentally—that is, working with them at the point where they were in their intercultural development; and (e) the cultural diversity of the student body, faculty, and staff. Unfortunately, because of budget cuts resulting from the global financial crisis, the program was short-lived. It was offered only for two semesters, in fall 2007 and spring 2008.

In this chapter, we introduce the reader to TSS, identify the variables that made it a unique and effective study abroad program, discuss key elements of the program's approach, and analyze key components that were related to the students' development of intercultural competence.

Goals and Learning Outcomes

The TSS program was the realization of a vision: an academic program that would, during a 16-week semester, bring together students and faculty from around the world to form a transnational learning community. The program's lingua franca was English, and it was developed in collaboration with a consortium of leading institutions: Al Akhawayn University; Cardiff University; Fudan University; Macquarie University; the Instituto Tecnológico de Monterrey in Mexico; the University of California, Berkeley; and the University of Ghana. Macquarie University awarded academic credit on behalf of the consortium.

The program's main goals were (a) to support student efforts to achieve globally relevant learning outcomes, (b) to offer them experiential opportunities both on board and onshore, (c) to provide them an intercultural "immersion" experience, and (d) to create opportunities for them to develop a global network of contacts.

The first goal was especially important. The world our students are inheriting owes much of its complexity to globalization (Newell, 2010), with individuals increasingly exposed to cultural differences in their communities, in their schools, and at work. TSS was committed to the belief that higher education needs to play a leading role in preparing students for living in a world that will require them to deal with cultural differences effectively and appropriately. The second and third goals went hand in hand. TSS did not simply offer intercultural immersion experiences that would expose students, faculty, and staff to differences—these participants represented more than 50 nationalities from around the world. More important, the program also provided the individual student with the tools to become aware of "the things that a learner 'brings to' an event—habitual ways of perceiving and behaving that have been informed by genetic makeup, prior experience, and present needs and requirements" (see page 18 of this volume). TSS provided participants with the means to achieve the fourth goal by helping students, faculty, and staff create global networks at personal, professional, and institutionalized levels so that they could continue building relationships long after their engagement with TSS.

In addition to these program goals, TSS was designed to support student efforts to meet six broad learning outcomes. It was expected that by the end of each voyage, students would have

1. achieved greater competence in their chosen academic disciplines;
2. enhanced their competence in intercultural skills associated with success in the workplace;
3. experienced, understood, and learned from a variety of transnational perspectives;
4. navigated the complexities of a diverse global environment with creativity and confidence;
5. understood the background and various perspectives of major global issues, thus developing a compassionate and cooperative attitude toward culturally different others; and as a result
6. serve as effective and appropriate leaders of local, national, or global communities (The Scholar Ship Prospectus, 2007–2008).

We focus in the remainder of this chapter on the ways that TSS targeted the development of the students' intercultural competence.

Frameworks

We have noted that TSS offered students much more than knowledge about culture and a superficial exposure to cultural differences. The program was intentionally committed to the development of the students' intercultural competence. Working with intercultural consultants, including the authors, TSS relied on a combination of familiar educational frameworks and the results of several assessment instruments that were administered to students, faculty, and staff.

The Intercultural Development Continuum

The revised version of Bennett's (M. J. Bennett, 1986, 1993) developmental model of intercultural sensitivity (DMIS), the intercultural development continuum (IDC) (Hammer 2009, 2011; chapter 5 of this volume), describes two broad mindsets that inform five distinct orientations or ways of experiencing and constructing cultural differences. "In the first [monocultural] mindset, those who see culture as a barrier tend to deny, resist, or minimize differences. In the second [the intercultural mindset], those who see culture as a resource tend to accept and appreciate the differences" (J. M. Bennett, & Salonen, 2007, p. 48). The five orientations are Denial (the tendency to avoid and/or not recognize cultural difference); Polarization (two different types: the first, Defense, is the tendency to perceive one's own culture more favorably than that of others; and the second, Reversal, is the tendency to perceive other cultures more favorably than one's own); Minimization (the tendency to experience difference through subsuming it into one's own familiar cultural frameworks, with the result that the individual experiences more commonality than difference); Acceptance (the ability to recognize and experience cultural difference without denying, defending against, or minimizing it); and Adaptation (the ability to shift cultural frameworks and to adapt behavior to new cultural contexts) (Hammer, 2011). Within the context of this developmental framework, an individual becomes more competent interculturally as his or her experience of cultural difference becomes progressively more complex (J. M. Bennett, & M. J. Bennett, 2004). We used the Intercultural Development Inventory (IDI) to measure these orientations (Hammer, 2007, 2011; Hammer & Bennett, 2001), administering the instrument to students at the beginning and end of each voyage. We discuss the results of this IDI pre- and posttesting later in this chapter.

Experiential Learning Theory

ELT, developed over the past several decades by David Kolb and others, defines learning as "the process whereby knowledge is created through the transformation of experience. Knowledge results from the combination of grasping and transforming experience" (Kolb, 1984, p. 41). In chapter 6 of this book, Passarelli and Kolb explain that individuals grasp the world through either concrete experiences (sensing/feeling) or abstract conceptualization (thinking). They transform the way that they perceive the world through either reflective observation (watching) or active experimentation (doing). In other words, individuals have a preferred way of grasping and transforming: They tend to engage the world through either feeling or thinking, and to transform their experience through either reflection or action. Individuals develop as they become progressively more able to grasp the world through both concrete experience and abstract conceptualization, and to transform it through both reflective observation and active experimentation.

The ideal experiential learning process proceeds, then, through a learning cycle or spiral in which the learner is exposed to and is asked to experience all four learning modes: feeling, reflecting, thinking, and acting. Concrete experience provides opportunities for observation and reflection, which can then be transformed into abstract concepts, which can in turn be applied to the creation of new plans for action. People tend to start the learning cycle based on their own preferred learning style preferences (Joy & Kolb, 2009), preferences that can be identified through the Kolb Learning Style Inventory (KLSI) (Kolb, 2007). In TSS, we used the instrument as a foundation for inclusive teaching and program design. The KLSI helped staff and faculty facilitate multicultural groups more successfully and inclusively, in particular because it helped them understand the very different ways that individual students, and groups of students, were experiencing the world.

Intercultural Conflict Styles

An individual's conflict style is, for the most part, learned during early socialization, within his or her cultural or ethnic groups. It is the community, in other words, that informs an individual's sense about the appropriate and inappropriate ways that the individual should react in situations of conflict. The Intercultural Conflict Style Inventory (ICS) (Hammer, 2005; Hammer 2007) identifies the extent to which an individual tends to resolve conflicts on the one hand, by being more direct or indirect, and on the other, by being more emotionally expressive or more emotionally restrained. TSS used the ICS in intercultural classrooms and as a tool for staff development.

Integrative Learning

TSS also embraced the concept of integrative learning, which as Newell (2010) defines it, "subjects theory to the reality check of human experience" (para. 4). The concept helped us frame learning as "an understanding and a disposition that a student builds across the curriculum and cocurriculum, from making simple connections among ideas and experiences to synthesizing and transferring learning to new, complex situations within and beyond the campus" (as cited in Newell, 2010, para. 4). For our purposes, this meant that the TSS cocurriculum consisted of every intercultural element of the program, all those onboard and onshore activities, programs, environments, and experiences that placed students in situations in which they needed to respond to cultural differences and commonalities. These out-of-class situations allowed them to test and process what they were learning in class as they encountered new and different perspectives that required them to stretch outside their individual comfort zones and begin to integrate these new perspectives into their own. Transnational life on the ship in fact provided an around-the-clock intercultural context in which students were not only in "contact with people who [were] *inside* [author's emphasis] the complex situation" (Newell, 2010, para. 6), but were *themselves* the insider participants—and cocreators—of the transnational community in which they were living and learning. Onshore, students were additionally provided opportunities to experience themselves as outsiders as they proceeded from port to port, learning and interacting with people in the host countries that they visited. TSS provided intercultural frameworks that helped students understand the complex situations in which they found themselves, on board and onshore. Their intercultural classes gave them the conceptual frameworks and a common vocabulary to use in making sense of and explaining these complex situations, while at the cocurricular level, structured activities and programs gave them the tools to process and synthesize these situations.

Personal Leadership

In addition to providing students with classroom and other structured opportunities to develop intercultural competencies, TSS's Office of Onboard Life (OBL) taught students "Personal Leadership" (PL), a methodology designed to help individuals "better interact with the new and unfamiliar" (Schaetti, Ramsey, & Watanabe, 2011, p. 2) that they encounter in intercultural situations. PL offers a mindful approach to engaging cultural differences, a set of six practices that allows individuals to discern creatively the best right action at any given moment. These six practices are framed by two principles: *mindfulness*, "a quality of presence that allows us to access the full scope of our intelligence: thoughts, feelings, and physical sensations" (Schaetti, Ramsey, & Watanabe, 2008, p. 33); and *creativity*. In the PL context, "creativity" has two meanings. The first is constructivist, acknowledging that individuals are creators of their own experience and therefore responsible for the choices that they make in response to external stimuli. The second implies the ability to respond to external circumstances based on those circumstances, or, as Schaetti et al. (2011) put it, based on the "particular dynamics of the situation in which we find ourselves" (p. 26).

The six PL practices are attending to judgments, attending to emotions, attending to physical sensations, engaging ambiguity, cultivating stillness, and aligning with vision. The first three inform individuals in ways that allow them to explore the meaning they give to their external experiences in an intentional way. The last three specifically allow individuals to develop capacities that help them attend to and discern right action in complex intercultural situations. Each of the six focuses on the development of competencies that are, then, intercultural. PL also offers the Critical Moment Dialogue (CMD), an inquiry-based process that supports the application of the six practices and poses questions related to each of them in order to guide and deepen the understanding of an intercultural event as an individual experiences it.

PL methodology and practice proved invaluable to students and staff alike. In a culturally diverse environment, ambiguous by its nature, and made stressful by the uniqueness of the experience of being on a ship for days in a row, multiple possibilities for misunderstanding arose. PL invited the individuals to take uncomfortable or difficult events (what Schaetti et al. [2011] call the "something's up" moment) and systematically apply the six practices in order to clarify what they were feeling—physically as well as emotionally—and thinking, and to discern what the right action in that context might be. The OBL team offered this process to students as an alternative to their reacting mindlessly (i.e., without attention) to events in the ways that they habitually reacted to them. The team asked the students to apply the CMD—for example, in responding to conflicts between roommates—as an alternative to mediation, one that allowed the students to take more ownership of their conflict and their experience of its resolution.

The Four Pillars

TSS was a complex system that consisted of four separate but interdependent areas or, as they were called, pillars: academics, onboard life, port programs, and research initiatives. Each of the pillars focused on one or more of TSS's main goals, while they built on each other.

The First Pillar: Academics

First and foremost an academic program, TSS designed a curriculum based on topics related to globalization. Academic themes were organized through *learning circles*—the rough equivalent of a university department or division. There were five learning circles at the undergraduate level: worlds of art and culture, conflict studies, international business and communication, sustainable development, and global cultures and global change. There were also three at the graduate level: international business, international relations, and international communication. Particular fields of study were associated with a specific learning circle; for example, within the international business and communication circle, students could take classes in business administration, tourism, advertising, communication, and public relations, among others. Students selected classes from course offerings in a single circle.

In addition to enrolling in courses within one of the learning circles, all of the undergraduates were required to take a 200-level intercultural communication course offered onboard by intercultural communication faculty. TSS additionally offered a 300-level course for students who had already completed the equivalent of the 200-level course at their home institution. At the graduate level, only the international communication students were required to take the graduate equivalent to these two intercultural communication courses.

The primary learning outcome of the 200-level intercultural communication course was "to enhance students' awareness and understanding of cultural differences to facilitate their acceptance, adaptation, and integration of these differences" (The Scholar Ship Student Subject Outline: Intercultural Communication   TICT201). One of the many positive student comments about this course suggests the extent to which students were gaining in self-awareness: "I've realized the depth to which my communication styles are ingrained and I've started to realize why." (We review empirical data about the participants' intercultural development later in the chapter.)

The intercultural communication class was divided into 20 sessions and organized around nine topics: foundations of the intercultural field and definitions; cultural values; verbal communication and communication styles; nonverbal communication; cultural adaptation and culture shock; ethnocentrism, prejudice, and stereotypes; conflict resolution; intercultural relationships; and cultural identities and globalization. The faculty of these courses relied on ELT to provide a theoretical foundation for the selection of learning activities. They taught through lectures; pair, triad, and small-group conversations; games; simulations; role plays; peer teaching; films and film content analysis; inventories (students completed the IDI and the ICS); port journal writing; the collection of cultural symbols from the ports; free-writing about classroom experiences; and research on board about different intercultural topics. The students took a midterm exam and completed a written final project, which they presented to the rest of the students in the class.

The course, designed and delivered strategically, served as both a stand-alone element and a support for the larger TSS teaching and learning system. As a stand-alone element, the intercultural communication course, grounded in ELT, allowed the students to experience situations, reflect on those experiences, develop theories about those situations, and test their theories by applying them in the world outside the classroom. As a part of the larger TSS design, the course represented the formal academic structure for the program's integrative learning approach, providing the students with theories, concepts, and vocabulary to help them understand and frame their onboard and onshore intercultural experiences. Students were required to do guided reflective journaling about most of the countries they visited. These journals provided an important link between the class and their onshore encounters as the students reflected on those encounters and applied the specific intercultural concepts that they had learned about in the class. Two examples illustrate the technique. First, while students were in South Africa, they were asked to write about the intensity of their adjustment experiences by analyzing these with reference to Paige's (1993) intensity factors. Second, while they were in Thailand, students were asked to frame their observations of local cultural differences and similarities by applying Hofstede's (2001) value dimensions. Following the students' time ashore, faculty also asked students during discussions in class to frame their observations about what they had seen and experienced through these and other intercultural concepts.

The Second Pillar: Onboard Life, a Transcultural Residential and Social Community

The OBL, the equivalent of a student life office at a U.S. university, was staffed by an onboard life director, three intercultural resident counselor (IRC) coordinators, eight IRCs (all IRCs specialized in one of three areas: residential life, experiential education, or intercultural communication), a recreation specialist, and a psychologist. As part of their training, all IRCs were required to attend one of the intercultural communication courses during their voyage, and to attend workshops on Kolb's ELT, applications of the ICS and the IDI, and PL, each offered during the voyages. The goal of this training was to help staff understand that it was important for them to support the learning of their students, to encourage students to engage actively in potentially challenging cultural situations and, more generally, to take actions that would support both the students and their own intercultural development.

Each residential community (RC) consisted of an IRC and 20 students. The RCs were designed to provide a relatively small community that would help students feel at home, encourage them to share their experiences, and allow them to learn from each other—three desired outcomes that were supported by an IRC who had been trained to facilitate residentially based intercultural learning and development.

The OBL made every effort to expose students to cultural difference and to provide opportunities for self-discovery and processing of the intercultural experience. The exposure to cultural differences worked on many levels: on board through the matching of roommates from different cultural backgrounds; during meals, in classes, and during cocurricular activities; and on land through having students explore new cultures at every port while working to create connections and relationships with their hosts. Within the RCs, students participated in intercultural simulations and activities and processed their experiences. The IRCs planned such activities in partnership with the intercultural communication course faculty. The students were able to participate in facilitated discussions in the larger TSS community as well. An important topic that emerged during both voyages was the impact of privilege, or their perceived lack of it, in their own lives. This topic emerged when some students shared their own experiences with hunger and poverty during the Oxfam America Hunger Banquet (Oxfam America, 2009) that took place during the ship's first voyage. The Hunger Banquet, facilitated by OBL and students and attended by the entire TSS community, triggered unanticipated discussions that helped participants learn about socioeconomic differences within the TSS community. As OBL Director Alfred Flores said, "The most powerful intercultural learning happens when unexpected things happen" (personal communication, July 17, 2011).

OBL offered two workshops to the group at large: Personal Leadership, and Power, Prejudice, and Privilege, both through five consecutive sessions. Attendance at these workshops was voluntary; approximately 20% of the students participated. OBL additionally created opportunities for students to meet with Society for Intercultural Education, Training and Research members in a number of the different ports of call.

The Third Pillar: An Academically Integrated Port Program

The port programs played an integral role in meeting TSS's mission of developing the intercultural competence and leadership potential of its students. Students had an array of options from which to choose ranging from the academic (academic field programs [AFPs]) to the touristic (shore excursions and independent travel).

The AFPs were three- to five-day mandatory onshore programs arranged and organized first by academic level (undergraduate or postgraduate), then by learning circle. Students were required to participate in at least three of these programs as part of their academic curriculum. The AFPs enabled the students to examine overlapping social, political, environmental, cultural, and business issues across cultures and countries by providing lectures, orientation to the city, visits to relevant organizations (nongovernmental organizations [NGOs], corporations, government agencies), various project and tourist sites, and participation in service-learning and other experiential activities that were designed and led by TSS staff in collaboration with local facilitators. The shore excursions were organized by a TSS-appointed service provider. These excursions were voluntary and allowed the students to explore various destinations in groups with a guide. They were also encouraged to wander the world—or at least the ports and surrounding areas—on their own.

The Fourth Pillar: A Strategic Research Initiative

Aiming to support the students by offering opportunities to practice their academic skills, TSS created a research institute whose focus was to conduct natural and social science research on critical global challenges by harnessing the expertise of global academic partnerships. Although some undergraduates were involved in this research, it was mainly the graduate students who conducted research under the supervision of Research Institute faculty.

Commitment to Training

TSS offered both a pre-departure and an on-site orientation for students. Faculty and staff received on-site training to improve their facilitation skills before the students arrived on the ship. As we have already noted, both groups had other types of opportunities to develop interculturally throughout the voyages. At the end of both semesters, reentry sessions and reentry preparation activities were also conducted to make the process of returning home as academically and interculturally enriching as possible.

The pre-departure orientation, which was delivered online, lasted between 5 and 10 hours, depending on the students' English-language proficiency. Every student was required to complete this orientation before boarding the ship. The aim of the pre-departure orientation was to provide students with opportunities to begin developing interculturally while giving them information about TSS's four pillars. It in fact served as an introduction to the intercultural communication class, presenting key intercultural concepts (culture, values, verbal and nonverbal behavior) and exercises not only to test comprehension, but also to allow students to put concepts into practice through various scenarios. TSS staff members monitored the students' progress and contacted them as needed in order to remind them to complete the orientation before the program began. Faculty and staff were welcome to participate in this orientation, but their participation was not required.

Once students were on board, they began a second orientation that lasted several days. This orientation not only covered logistical issues about the ship and ship safety, but also maintained its continuing intercultural communication focus. Both orientations were designed to stimulate students' interest in becoming active members of a learning community from their first day on the ship.

Faculty and staff participated in their own five-day onboard orientation as well. It resembled the students' onboard orientation: They learned about the ship, reviewed safety issues, learned more about intercultural communication and the program's four pillars, and received information about the courses that they were going to teach. This orientation also provided time for the faculty members to meet each other and to work within their assigned learning circles. The OBL staff also participated in an onboard orientation program that focused on programmatic issues relevant to living and learning in RCs. Intercultural communication facilitators led all of these orientations for students, faculty, and staff.

Student Demographics

The TSS's transnational community consisted of students from 40 nationalities: 51% from North America (the United States and Canada), 20% from Europe, 11% from Asia, 9% from Mexico and South and Central America,

5% from Africa, and 4% from Australia. Their age ranged from 18 to 78, although the majority of the students were in their early to mid-20s. Students came from widely diverse socioeconomic backgrounds. TSS provided full and partial scholarships to a large number of students from a wide variety of countries.

Programming Developmentally

The program's developmental focus, grounded in the DMIS and in our use of the IDI to document student progress, extended across all aspects of the program. Faculty members, students, and staff completed the IDI prior to arrival to the vessel, and members of the OBL team received one to two hours of required individual coaching about their personal IDI results. During these sessions, team members looked at how their own developmental orientation was informing their own behaviors, values, work outcomes, and relationships with others. Faculty and students were also able to participate in optional individual IDI coaching. In addition, the OBL team participated in a workshop that trained the team members in applications of the DMIS when facilitating culturally and developmentally diverse RCs, and each IRC received an IDI group profile of the RCs that they were leading. The IRCs made extensive use of this profile when planning activities for their RC. They were also trained to take developmental orientation into account in conversations with individual students and in working with groups. The IRCs were taught not to stereotype the students based on their developmental orientations.

TSS's judicial process also benefited from this developmental approach. Designed with the DMIS in mind, the judicial process put theory into practice when staff responded to disciplinary infractions, taking into account the cultural backgrounds and DMIS worldview of individual students. For example, when a U.S. student whose worldview was at Denial found himself in several judicial hearings, staff recognized that he was not developmentally able to engage with culturally different others because he simply had little or no awareness of or ability to experience alternative viewpoints. When it became clear that he could not understand the values of TSS nor wished to follow the rules governing the community, he was asked to leave the ship. In another case, a Moroccan student at Minimization committed a minor policy infraction. When meeting with staff, the student explained that he was guided by another set of "higher" values and that he did not believe the rules of the ship were worth following. Through working with the staff member, he was initially surprised to learn that a lot of others on the ship did not share his values. At the end, this student came to understand that he was going to need to adapt to a set of values that the community agreed would govern disciplinary issues.

IDI Data Analysis

To assess the extent to which participating in a semester on board was influencing the development of their intercultural competence, students were asked to complete the IDI prior to the ship's departure and at the end of each voyage. The prevoyage IDI was administered online before they came aboard. The post-IDI assessment was conducted on board, using the paper-and-pencil version, during the last week of the voyages.

Our analysis of the IDI results includes the pre- and posttest data from both voyages. Of the 349 students who were enrolled in TSS during those two semesters, 136 completed both tests. We are offering two different types of data: first, average gains in intercultural competence; and, second, the extent to which students changed, across developmental orientations, between pre- and posttest. We thank Mitchell Hammer for contributing the IDI data analysis for this chapter.

Version 3 of the IDI (see chapter 5 of this volume) measures an individual's or a group's overall intercultural competence, which is represented numerically through a developmental orientation score (DO). This developmental score indicates the individual's or group's primary orientation toward cultural differences and commonalities along the IDC (Hammer, 2011). Figure 15.1 shows the average intercultural competence scores of the 136 students for both the pre- and posttest. The students' average pretest DO was 92.40, locating the group in low Minimization. The group's average posttest DO was 97.69, indicating that the students developed during the program by an average of 5.29 points, to the middle of Minimization, which represents more than a third of a standard deviation (SD = 15 points), and moves the students, normatively, from the 35th to the 47th percentile. This represents a significant gain in intercultural competence after only four months of international education.

Figure 15.2 presents the change in the specific developmental orientations of the students from pre- to posttest. There is virtually no difference between the small number of students who entered the program with a

FIGURE 15.1
Pre- and posttest DO scores

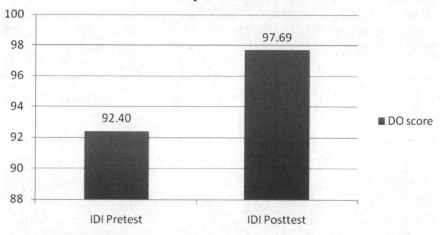

FIGURE 15.2
Specific percentage developmental change between pre- and posttest

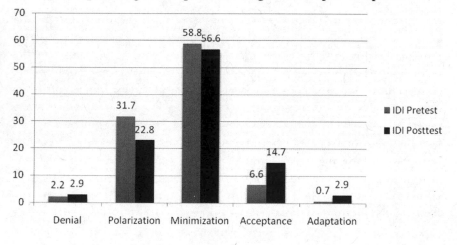

Denial orientation (2.2%) and those who were in the same orientation at the end of the program (2.9%). That is, very few students entered or left the program with a developmental orientation that provides little capacity for recognizing and experiencing cultural differences. The percentage of students who entered with a Polarization orientation (which means that they were experiencing cultural differences from a judgmental "us" versus "them" perspective) was 31.7%, with only 22.8% remaining in Polarization at the conclusion of the semester. This represents an important reduction in prejudice, bias, and a sense of superiority of one's own cultural practices over other cultures' values and practices.

The majority of students (58.8%) were in Minimization at the beginning of the voyage; this figure had reduced slightly, to 56.6%, by the end of their study abroad experience. Students at the Acceptance and Adaptation levels had the largest percentage gains in intercultural competence, with 6.6% of the students profiling in Acceptance in the pretest and 14.7% in the posttest. Although the numbers are relatively small, the students with an Adaptation orientation at the beginning of the program comprised only 0.7% of the population, a figure that increased to 2.9% by the program's end.

Figure 15.2 shows a consistent trend: students moving away from the more monocultural mindset of Polarization and increasing their intercultural competence in the direction of multicultural Acceptance and Adaptation orientations. That is, TSS not only helped reduce prejudice and bias among students as a group (Polarization), but also helped them substantially increase their deeper understanding of cultural differences and commonalities (Acceptance) and, to a lesser extent, increase their ability to shift cultural perspective and adapt behavior to cultural differences (Adaptation).

These significant gains reflect the students' experience during only the two semesters when TSS operated—that is, during the time when staff and faculty were only beginning to learn how to teach and facilitate this complex and multifaceted student learning and developmental program. As chapters 2, 12, and 16 of this volume suggest, it normally takes staff and faculty more than one or two semesters to master developmental and experiential teaching and training. As we discuss in the next section, there were several factors that we believe slowed the students' intercultural development during the voyage.

The Challenges

Implementing a transnational program on a ship was of course met with all sorts of challenges; in this chapter we focus on two that especially influenced student learning: the environment and human interaction. Regarding the environment, life on a vessel and the transnational nature of the community heightened the psychological intensity of the experience for faculty, staff, and students alike, sometimes bringing uncertainty and stress to the voyage. As we have noted, the learning curve for teaching developmentally and experientially was also steep. In addition, there were challenges that went beyond the fact that faculty and staff had not taught the new material before: Customs officials did not always clear teaching and office materials that had been shipped to various ports; infrastructure on board supporting teaching and learning was being created while the ship was sailing; a culturally appropriate judiciary process was being developed at the same time as it was being implemented; and students sometimes had to leave the ship for health or behavioral reasons, which affected the community and even the route of the ship.

Where human interaction on board was concerned, daily life on the vessel was unique, certainly very different from what students most commonly experience while studying exclusively on shore. They were constantly surrounded by people in an environment that was strictly limited by the walls of the ship, which was itself surrounded by open ocean. Their exposure to cultural differences was therefore not only intense but inescapable, with little or no rest for those in need of their own cultural space. In Paige's (1993) description of intensity factors, "which can raise the level of psychological intensity for sojourners" (p. 4), "cultural difference" appears at the top of the list. Paige suggests that "the greater the degree of cultural difference between the sojourner's own and the target culture, the greater the degree of psychological intensity" (p. 5). Although the support mechanisms in the TSS model were numerous, the challenges posed by the many dimensions of cultural experience that students were experiencing were still very high, perhaps too intense for some in spite of the intensive support structure.

The students encountered cultural differences everywhere they turned. Faculty, staff, and students had to adapt to a complex U.S.-centric organizational culture, and non-U.S. faculty and students had to learn to teach and learn using what are, to some extent, U.S.-centric pedagogies, including expectations about student participation and the debriefing of activities. Non-Australian faculty and students (96% of the entire population) had to adjust to the Australian grading system because Macquaire University, the school of record for the program, required that its own grading system be used. Differences in cultural concepts and practices were ever-present: differences in the treatment of time, in expectations about dress, in communication and conflict management styles, in views and practices. Students also shared a cabin with someone from a different national culture. Even in this small, private space, students were exposed to cultural differences.

Add to this ubiquity of cultural differences the fact that 93.33% of the students and the majority of the faculty and staff held an ethnocentric world-view at the beginning of the voyage. Paige's (1993) insight that "the more ethnocentric the sojourner, the more psychologically intense the experience will be" (p. 5) highlights the extent to which the intercultural capacities of the learners themselves served to intensify the sense that cultural differences on board were inescapable. Language ability was yet another issue on board. Paige suggests that it is inversely proportional to psychological intensity—that is, the lesser the language proficiency, the more stress a student may experience during a sojourn. Although English was the lingua franca, not everyone spoke it at the same level of proficiency. TSS did address this through English as a second language support to students struggling with the language. Differences in socioeconomic class created another sort of cultural issue for some students, reflected especially in the amount of money individual students did or did not have to spend both on board and at the different ports of call. Although the RCs helped students process this particular cultural issue, which manifested itself in obvious ways, it remained a significant challenge for some.

Our experience suggests that "environment" in fact be added to Paige's (1993) list of intensity factors: The more physically and culturally different the environment, the greater the psychological intensity of the experience. The many and complex differences of life on board a ship provided more than enough psychological intensity to go around. During its short two-semester existence, TSS was working to lessen the intensity created through the convergence and omnipresence of so many physical and cultural challenges. For example, planning for the third voyage included a requirement that staff and faculty score at Minimization, as a minimum, before being hired to participate in the program. In retrospect, we also wonder whether it made sense for students to be required to have a roommate from another national culture. Sanford's (1966) Challenge and Support Hypothesis suggests that learners need to experience both challenge and support, and the Georgetown Consortium study has shown that students abroad do not develop interculturally when they are experiencing more cultural difference than they can cope with (Vande Berg, 2009; Vande Berg, Connor-Linton, & Paige, 2009; chapter 2 of this volume). Had the program continued to mature and improve its systems, we have good reason to believe that TSS would have offered students an even more effective intercultural learning opportunity.

Best Practices and Recommendations

> I have come to appreciate and realize that people have different intercultural conflict styles, which are not always the same as mine. I have learned that it's always a good thing to realize this fact and appreciate, tolerate, and respect other people's decisions and the way they solve conflicts and avoid regarding mine as the only best style. (TSS student)

What follows is a list of recommendations, based on our experience with TSS, for those who are interested in designing and delivering effective intercultural teaching and learning experiences for their own students. To create this list, we asked TSS colleagues who were either intercultural communication teachers or OBL team members to share their thoughts with us.

- *Use learning outcomes and program goals as guiding principles for program design in all areas.* We "reverse engineered" this new program (see chapter 12, p. 285, this volume), first identifying what it was that we wanted students to know and be able to do when they were leaving the program, and only then proceeding to develop the specific courses, activities, and program support elements that would help students achieve those learning outcomes. Having clear learning outcomes from the outset made assessing the impact of the program possible through systematic data collection and analysis.
- *Require all undergraduate students to take an intercultural communications course or seminar.* The TSS course, among other things, provided a common base of knowledge and vocabulary that allowed all concerned to understand, process, and build an effective teaching and learning community.
- *Provide a space where a capable facilitator can help students safely process their experiences throughout the program.* This was a vital aspect of TSS's experiential learning cycle that helped students make sense of what they were feeling and sensing, and gave them information about next steps in their learning.
- *Combine theory, practice, and process using an integrative learning approach.* TSS created recurring intercultural cocurricular experiences

that paralleled what students were studying in class and provided opportunities to integrate them.

- *Take into account all learning styles—as laid out in ELT—in designing, programming, and teaching your different programs and intercultural communication courses.* In TSS, once we were clear about the program learning outcomes, we turned to ELT as we began to design the learning program that would help students meet those outcomes. We used the ELT principles to frame community-building activities; for example, some students enjoyed sporting events, craft nights, and service-learning; others were more interested in informal open spaces and parties; and others benefited from reflection. Providing multiple activities to choose from different contexts created learning opportunities for every kind of learner.

- *Take steps to make sure that faculty has reached an appropriate level of intercultural competence.* A capable facilitator is needed to help students make sense of the contradictions inherent in intercultural encounters, face their own fears and feelings of threat and inadequacy, and integrate the knowledge gained through their new experiences. In TSS, we observed that faculty members with lower developmental scores had difficulty managing the intensity of the ship's diverse living and working environment. They were the ones who received negative student evaluations and who had grievances and conflicts with other faculty and staff members. Our experience suggests that faculty with monocultural worldviews can become a hindrance for student development. Because it is not realistic to expect that all interdisciplinary and globally diverse faculty and staff will already be well versed in developmental theories and be able to facilitate learning from an intercultural worldview, we believe that professional development programs should be made available. The IDI is a tool that is useful for creating developmental programming for not only students, but faculty as well.

- *Make sure that your staff and faculty share the values behind stated program goals and are aware of how their behavior and attitude can affect the extent to which students achieve those goals.* Throughout the course of this initiative, not all staff and faculty had the same commitment or level of experience in dealing with a culturally diverse group of students, which created some disconnect among them, the students, and TSS goals and outcomes.

- *Be developmental in planning and carrying out the learning and teaching program.* TSS made an intentional effort to meet the students where they were developmentally, and to help them develop at their own pace and ability. During TSS's first semester, students complained that they were doing too much processing. There was nothing surprising about this, given the fact that more than 30% of the students were at Polarization—and thus experiencing considerable anxiety whenever they were asked to focus on cultural differences, many of which they were already rejecting. Moreover, almost 60% of the students were minimizing cultural differences and were thus not interested in having facilitators bring such differences into awareness during courses and activities. We needed to learn to present cultural differences in appropriate ways and to differentiate our presentation according to individual capacities to deal effectively with such difference. By the second semester, the RCs were starting to learn to do this.
- *Teach program staff the PL methodology, and make it accessible to students and faculty.* During both voyages, the CMD process was valuable at all levels, including the judicial system. Most important, the OBL staff reported that PL helped them maintain their sanity since its use allowed them to process the experience systematically. The students applied PL as well in, for example, resolving conflicts between roommates.
- *Leverage student, staff, and faculty diversity.* At TSS, everyone who was willing was welcome to participate and bring his or her strengths to the community. Focusing on student diversity allowed us to help students understand that diversity is not limited to differences in national origin—that in building learning communities many other types of diversity (differences in learning style, cognitive style, communication style, conflict style, and along such cultural dimensions as power distance, individualism and collectivism, etc.) are in fact at least as important as, if not more important than, differences in national origin.

Conclusion

Many TSS alumni are connected to each other through social-networking media and have regular reunions around the world. They are successfully applying intercultural skills in their current lives (Yamaguchi, 2011) and are working for international corporations, NGOs, and academic institutions. They are participating in the Peace Corps and other service-oriented programs. Some TSS alumni have established new organizations such as the Global Stewards Institute and Recrear. The Global Stewards Institute is an experiential international educational program that integrates leadership, intercultural competency, service, and research in a unique sea-faring environment. Recrear is an organization that trains and inspires young people to lead international development projects. We close with the words of one of Recrear's founders, Gioel Gioacchino, as she describes the impact that the TSS program had on her:

> In short, TSS has definitely been a crucial turning point in my intellectual and personal growth. During Recrear.beta, we really tried to integrate the TSS appreciation for the power of sharing and manipulating ideas in diverse groups. Meanwhile, principles of intercultural communication and understanding are an important base for all the work we do. We are trying to apply intercultural communication principles to the development projects there is a lot to explore and think about! (personal communication, July 28, 2011)

References

Bennett, J. M., & Bennett, M. J. (2004). Developing intercultural sensitivity: An integrative approach to global and domestic diversity. In D. Landis, J. Bennett, & M. Bennett (Eds.), *Handbook of intercultural training* (3rd ed., pp. 147–165). Thousand Oaks, CA: Sage.

Bennett, J. M., & Salonen, R. (2007, March/April). Intercultural communication and the new American campus. *Change Magazine*, 46–50.

Bennett, M. J. (1986). A developmental approach to training for intercultural sensitivity. *International Journal of Intercultural Relations, 10*(2), 179–196.

Bennett, M. J. (1993). Towards ethnorelativism: A developmental model of intercultural sensitivity. In D. Paige (Ed.), *Education for the intercultural experience* (pp. 21–71). Yarmouth, ME: Intercultural Press.

Hammer, M. R. (2003). *The Intercultural Conflict Style Inventory* [Instrument]. North Potomac, MD: Hammer Consulting Group.

Hammer, M. R. (2005). The Intercultural Conflict Inventory: A conceptual framework and measure of intercultural conflict styles. *International Journal of Intercultural Relations, 29*(6), 675–695.

Hammer, M. R. (2007). *The Intercultural Development Inventory, Version 3* [Group Profile]. North Potomac, MD: Hammer Consulting Group.

Hammer, M. R. (2009). The Intercultural Development Inventory. In M. A. Moodian (Ed.), *Contemporary leadership and intercultural competence* (pp. 203–218). Thousand Oaks, CA: Sage.

Hammer, M. R. (2011). Additional cross-cultural validity testing of the Intercultural Development Inventory. *International Journal of Intercultural Relations, 35*(4), 474–487.

Hammer, M. R., & Bennett, M. J. (2001). *The Intercultural Development Inventory, Version 2* [Instrument]. Portland, OR: Intercultural Communication Institute.

Hofstede, G. (2001). *Cultures consequences: Comparing, values, behaviors, institutions and organizations across nations* (2nd ed.). Thousand Oaks, CA: Sage.

Joy, S., & Kolb, D. A. (2009). Are there cultural differences in learning style? *International Journal of Intercultural Relations, 33*(1), 69–85.

Kolb, D. (1984). *Experiential learning: Experience as the source of learning and development.* Englewood Cliffs, NJ: Prentice Hall.

Kolb, D. A. (2007). *The Kolb Learning Style Inventory: Version 3.1* [Instrument]. Boston, MA: Hay Group.

Newell, W. H. (2010). Educating for a complex world: Integrative learning and interdisciplinary studies. *Liberal Education, 96*(4). Retrieved from http://www.aacu.org/liberaleducation/le-fa10/LEFA10_Newell.cfm

Oxfam America. (2009). Oxfam America Hunger Banquet Event Toolkit: Tools for hosting a high-impact event. Retrieved from http://actfast.oxfamamerica.org/uploads/OA-HBToolkit.pdf

Paige, R. M. (1993). On the nature of intercultural experiences and intercultural education. In R. M. Paige (Ed.), *Education for the intercultural experience* (pp. 1–19). Yarmouth, ME: Intercultural Press.

Sanford, N. (1966). *Self and society: Social change and individual development.* New York: Atherton Press.

Schaetti, B., Ramsey, S., & Watanabe, G. (2008). *Personal leadership: A methodology of two principles and six practices.* Seattle, WA: FlyingKite Publications.

Schaetti, B., Ramsey, S., & Watanabe, G. (2011). *Training of facilitators seminar* [Workshop materials]. Crestone, CO: Personal Leadership Seminars.

Vande Berg, M. (2009). Intervening in student learning abroad: A research-based inquiry. *Intercultural Education, 20*(1–2), 15–27.

Vande Berg, M., Connor-Linton, J., & Paige, M. (2009). The Georgetown Consortium Project: Interventions for student learning abroad. *Frontiers: The Interdisciplinary Journal of Study Abroad, 8*, 1–75.

Yamaguchi, M. (2011). *The role of international cross-cultural experiential knowledge in enhancement of students' world-mindedness* (Unpublished doctoral dissertation). The Ohio State University, Columbus, OH.

16

AN EXPERIMENT IN DEVELOPMENTAL TEACHING AND LEARNING

The Council on International Educational Exchange's
Seminar on Living and Learning Abroad

Michael Vande Berg, Meghan Quinn, Catherine Menyhart

For the past six years, the Council on International Educational Exchange (CIEE) has been developing the Seminar on Living and Learning Abroad (the Seminar), a credit-bearing elective course for students on CIEE semester programs abroad. The course represents one organization's efforts to apply theory and research on human learning and development across a broad array of programs and program types. The Seminar is designed to help students abroad learn to shift cultural perspective and to interact more effectively and appropriately with culturally different others. Insights from education, cultural anthropology, Experiential Learning Theory (ELT), developmental learning theory, intercultural communications, and social psychology have informed the course's development, as have findings from several research projects, including the Georgetown Consortium study (see chapter 2; see also Vande Berg, 2009, and Vande Berg, Connor-Linton, & Paige, 2009).

We have responded to three principal challenges in developing the Seminar: designing effective curricula that allow instructors abroad to help their students learn and develop while living and studying in a culture different from their own, motivating students to value a structured opportunity to develop their intercultural capacities, and meeting the significant training needs of the instructors.

Laying the Groundwork for the Seminar

Although the Seminar project officially began in the fall of 2005, following the arrival earlier that year of Michael Vande Berg (one of this chapter's authors) as CIEE chief academic officer (CAO), former CAO William Cressey and Martin Hogan, executive vice president for International Study Programs, had already begun to lay the groundwork for the project. Responding to increasing U.S. college and university concerns about student learning abroad, they and other staff at CIEE's headquarters in Portland, Maine, had begun encouraging instructors at Study Centers—where lectures were often the norm—to introduce more interactive teaching methods. In the spring of 2005, Cressey had hired two consultants, faculty members from two U.S. universities, to conduct "learner-centered" workshops to help CIEE staff and faculty explore the implications of shifting the focus of teaching from "the teacher and the content" to "the learner and the process of learning" (Bransford, Brown, & Cocking, 2000; Fink, 2003; Taylor, Marineau, & Fiddler, 2000; Weimer, 2002).

Vande Berg came to understand, through observing these workshops, that developing learner-centered teaching practices would require a very different approach to staff and faculty training. The two consultants had done a good job introducing learner-centered methods; however, when they had urged staff and faculty to change their teaching practices, they were met with resistance. Recalling that they had for years been told that students' home institutions in the United States expected them to learn from being exposed to or engaged in the "new and different" abroad, CIEE resident staff and faculty wondered—not unreasonably—why the consultants now seemed to be asking them to teach U.S students abroad in the same ways that they were taught at home. If the value of study abroad lay in exposing students to difference, would this not include different ways of teaching? When the consultants responded by discussing research findings that showed "learner-centered" teaching to be more effective than "teacher-centered" practices, some resident staff and faculty then wondered aloud whether these studies had been conducted by U.S. educators—and whether CIEE was thus implying that U.S. teaching methods were superior to those in other countries.

The consultants had framed their work as pedagogical and represented pedagogical research as culture neutral. The faculty and staff, though, in supposing that these new ideas were somehow exclusively "U.S. American," were experiencing the issue as intercultural. Vande Berg recognized, however, that the real division was not between national cultures, but between competing educational paradigms. Instructors in many parts of the world were coming to embrace experiential/constructivist perspectives, moving beyond the positivist or relativist paradigms that had once informed teaching and learning virtually everywhere. These new perspectives were rapidly coming to inform teaching practice in, for example, Australia, Canada, and Japan (see chapter 10 of this volume), along with many of the countries in the European Higher Education Area—a transition that the Bologna Process's 2007 *London Communiqué* describes as the "move toward student-centered higher education and away from teacher-driven provision" (p. 8). At the same time, though, faculty and staff in many parts of the world were continuing to base their own practice either on the positivist assumption that educators deliver knowledge in prepackaged forms to students who are willing and able to benefit from such information transfer, or on the relativist assumption that students who are "immersed in" a new culture adapt on their own to any differences that they encounter because teachers and students are essentially the same everywhere in the world. The challenge for CIEE, then, was to create conditions that would allow staff in Portland and staff and faculty at Study Centers abroad to reach a common understanding—an intercultural understanding—about what kinds of educational experiences would most benefit U.S. students studying abroad while still respecting the educational culture of each host site.

Project I: Identifying Learning Outcomes

In the spring of 2006, CIEE announced the "Student Learning Program" and launched the first of three interrelated projects designed to support the program's broad goal of helping students learn to shift cultural perspective and to adapt behavior in new cultural contexts. Vande Berg and his Portland colleagues asked CIEE Resident Directors (RDs) to identify individually a set of learning outcomes tailored to the learning needs of students at their particular programs. Identifying such outcomes seemed to offer a sensible way for staff in Portland and resident staff and faculty abroad to reach a common understanding: All involved would be committed to the goal of identifying what students should be learning through studying in a particular program abroad.

The learning outcomes project began with workshops designed to help RDs develop outcomes that would be "effective" in three different ways. First, the outcomes statements would clearly identify what students should know, understand, and/or be able to do by the end of a program. Second, the statements would be framed in ways that would allow RDs or other educators to observe or measure the extent to which students were meeting them. And third, they would be reasonably challenging. As a guide to the latter, RDs were asked to consider whether a "clever tourist," someone with a normal amount of curiosity and energy, could likely meet an outcome simply through spending several weeks at the program site—and if so, to revise the statement to make it more challenging. When by the fall of 2006 many RDs were finding the project more difficult than anticipated, Vande Berg shifted to working with them via telephone and e-mail. By spring 2007, most RDs had progressed through drafting three increasingly effective versions of their program outcomes, producing statements that identified what students would be expected to learn in three or four "domains": academic and intellectual learning, local and global awareness, intercultural learning and development, and (where appropriate) second-language acquisition.

Early in the process of drafting these outcomes, several RDs had produced similar versions of an "academic and intellectual" outcomes statement: "Students will learn and acquire knowledge at the host university." The statement was insufficient, and not only because it was not observable, measurable, or sufficiently challenging. More important, it was grounded in a basic positivist assumption: that because the environment imprints itself on learners (Maturana & Varela, 1992; see also chapter 1 of this volume), students will naturally learn in new and different ways as they come into contact or engage with new and different behavior, ideas, customs, institutions, and so on. However, as numerous authors in this volume have discussed, individuals learn and develop through creating and cocreating their experiences, and they naturally frame those experiences in the context of their primary cultures.

To be effective, then, RDs would need to revise the academic or intellectual outcomes statement, "Students will learn and acquire knowledge at the host university," by taking two basic intercultural competencies into account. First, the RDs needed to understand that students abroad are asked to bring into awareness what is for most of them very much *out* of awareness when they go abroad: that is, the norms and values governing how they learn and how faculty teach at the program site, which are often very different from those at home. Second, they needed to understand that the events around teaching and learning that students are experiencing require them to shift their perspective and adapt their behavior to this new context— intercultural capacities that, as research was showing, most of the students had not developed prior to going abroad (see chapters 1 and 2 of this volume; see also Vande Berg, 2009; Vande Berg, Connor-Linton, & Paige, 2009). Revising the outcomes statement to read, "Students will be able to provide several examples of differences and commonalities in teaching and learning between their home and host institutions, describing how they have come to reframe their awareness of themselves and culturally different others through their learning experiences," offered one way of taking these essential intercultural competencies into account. Changing it to, "Students will have developed practical and effective strategies that allow them to successfully engage the host academic system, and they will be able to discuss several such strategies in intercultural terms, making reference to specific value differences in teaching and learning between the home and host cultures," offered another.

The learning outcomes project allowed Portland-based staff to see that most RDs, even after working to draft outcomes statements for several months, were still not framing student learning around desired outcomes. The concrete benefits of explicitly presenting outcomes to students, and then concentrating program resources on helping students achieve them, were not well understood. Many resident staff and faculty still expected that good students would learn, naturally and normally, through studying abroad. They believed that their students would absorb the content their professors delivered, and that they would acquire skills—linguistic, social, cultural, or otherwise—almost inevitably through being exposed to, or, better still, through being "immersed" in, events outside the classroom. It was simply "in the nature of things" that professors taught and students learned, whether at home or abroad. And if students failed to take advantage both of the expert teaching and of the "rich linguistic and cultural environment" around them, they had no one to blame but themselves.

The learning outcomes project finally led Portland-based staff to understand that if CIEE students were going to learn more and better than recent research was suggesting, resident staff and faculty were going to need to do more than simply identify learning outcomes. As we have seen in this book's introductory chapters, a number of studies, including the Georgetown Consortium project, had by this time provided empirical support for the emerging view that far too many students were not learning and developing in ways that many members of the study abroad community had long believed they were. This growing body of evidence was undermining both the positivist assumption that humans learn directly from "experience" and the relativist assumption that students learn best through being "immersed" in another national culture through such practices as living with host families, committing themselves to speaking only the target language, and enrolling in regular university courses. The research evidence and disciplinary evidence also strongly suggested that unless someone or something intervened in the learning of students abroad, helping them become aware of how they habitually frame events, and helping them develop the capacity to reframe events in ways that are effective and appropriate within a new cultural context, most of them would continue to experience events through that original frame.

In short, the learning outcomes project allowed Portland-based staff to see that if students enrolling in CIEE programs were to learn and develop effectively and appropriately, resident staff and faculty were going to need to train them to develop the intercultural capacities that would allow them to meet their particular program's learning outcomes. And because few resident staff members or faculty were familiar with the basics of intercultural teaching and learning, Portland staff would have to develop an intercultural course curriculum for that purpose. First, though, more groundwork was needed.

Project II: On-Line Pre-Departure Orientations

In the spring of 2006, Vande Berg initiated the On-Line Pre-Departure Orientation (OPDO) project, the second step toward the development of the Seminar on Living and Learning Abroad. This project began as a pilot at six programs whose RDs had, through drafting their program learning outcomes, quickly grasped the implications of a learner-centered approach. He asked the pilot RDs to work within the structure of a common template, which they all adapted to their particular sites. The OPDO sessions offered each group of students a live, 90-minute online meeting with their RD several weeks before their arrival at the Study Center site. During these meetings, the students were introduced to resident staff, academic requirements and procedures were reviewed, cultural issues that past students had often found puzzling or challenging were presented, and considerable time was devoted to having students work with the learning outcomes for their program. Each RD facilitated two interactive activities, one familiarizing students with the outcomes that the program was asking them to achieve, the other asking them to identify their own learning outcomes—or "what they wanted to get out of the program."

Student evaluations of the OPDOs were strikingly similar across the six pilot programs. Students rated the discussions of academic requirements and cultural differences highly. They were especially enthusiastic about interacting with their RDs, almost uniformly ranking the item "I appreciated the chance to meet with the Resident Director" more highly than any other. The RDs valued the OPDOs as well; they reported that students who participated tended to have fewer problems on-site with the issues that had typically challenged students in the past. (It is also worth noting that two very experienced RDs were initially mystified when some of their students arrived at their sites behaving as if they had already formed a meaningful relationship with the RD through the single online session—perhaps illustrating different generational expectations about online learning.) Now, five years later, RDs from virtually all semester programs facilitate OPDO sessions; students continue to evaluate these orientations very highly, and both students and RDs now typically report that they benefit from the relationships that they have begun to form online.

Despite the overall positive response, problems with the OPDO also emerged. First, almost half of the students enrolled in the pilot programs had not attended this required activity. Second, the majority reported that they were simply not interested either in hearing about the program's learning outcomes or in identifying their own—in fact, they had collectively rated these lower than any other OPDO activities. This disappointing trend continued for two more semesters. By spring 2007, with 18 RDs now offering OPDOs, student responses to the learning outcomes activities were still so persistently negative that Vande Berg and his Portland colleagues decided to delete them from the program—an ironic decision because one of the primary motives in developing the OPDO in the first place had been the belief that working with outcomes prior to departure would serve to help students very consciously frame study abroad as a learning experience.

The learning outcomes and OPDO projects had, then, highlighted two issues that continue to test us today. First, the process of training RDs to identify effective learning outcomes had revealed that many resident staff and faculty were framing student learning in traditional ways. Neither their academic training nor their earlier experiences with U.S. students had prepared them to start teaching their students interculturally—which, as we have seen, they were going to have to be able to do if the students were to learn and develop in their courses, in their second-language learning, or in any other learning domain. Vande Berg and his Portland colleagues understood, too, that they were going to have to work intensively with resident staff and faculty if they were going to learn to help students achieve the desired outcomes; that is, simply asking RDs to identify outcomes was not going to do much to increase the likelihood that their students would achieve them. Second, the OPDO evaluations highlighted a divide between our expectations and those of the students. Even as we worked to frame their upcoming sojourn as a series of learning opportunities, student evaluations indicated that the students had very different ideas about what study abroad might mean for them.

Portland staff had by this time come to understand that only the development of an intercultural course—what came to be called the Seminar on Living and Learning Abroad—would help us meet these persistent challenges. Staff or faculty would presumably learn how to teach such an intercultural course by following a curriculum that we would provide, and students would presumably wish to participate in the course's activities once they understood that the new knowledge, perspectives, and skills that they were learning and developing would help them meet their own personal goals.

Project III: The Seminar on Living and Learning Abroad

We had come to view the Seminar, then, as more than just the continuation of a process that had begun earlier with the development of the student learning outcomes and OPDO projects; we believed that the course might help resolve serious problems that had surfaced during these two preparatory phases. In the fall of 2007, Vande Berg hired Meghan Quinn to join him in developing the course. Quinn's formal academic preparation—she was working toward completion of an MA in teaching and learning when she came on board (and has since completed the degree)—and her experience teaching in the United States, Japan, and Thailand complemented Vande Berg's own formal academic preparation and his experience as an intercultural instructor and trainer in the United States and abroad. Together they developed the first version of the Seminar during the 2007–8 academic year. The course curriculum and all associated materials were stored in a password-protected intranet site accessible only to teachers and related staff.

The Seminar curriculum was built on principles drawn primarily from pedagogical theory (chapter 10 of this volume), ELT (chapter 6), developmental learning theory (chapter 3), intercultural relations (chapters 4 and 5), and social psychology (Sanford, 1966). First, the course would be learner centered. Among other things, this meant that teachers (usually but not always RDs) would introduce new material by first working with what students already knew; help students apply what they were learning in class to their lives outside class; assess students throughout the course, giving them prompt and frequent feedback; and help students stay focused on learning outcomes—both the intercultural outcomes that we had identified in designing the Seminar and those that the students would themselves identify early in the course. Second, the Seminar would be developmental—that is, instructors would facilitate a series of lessons and activities designed to "scaffold" the students' intercultural learning (chapter 10), from less to more challenging material. Third, the course would be experiential rather than simply interactive—that is, in introducing each concept or idea, instructors would guide the class "around the wheel" of Kolb's learning cycle (chapter 6) through structured debriefs, helping students reflect on what they had experienced through an activity, become aware of how they made meaning of these experiences, and focus on the extent to which the meanings that they attached to the experiences were allowing them to interact effectively and appropriately with others. Fourth, the course would ask instructors to balance challenge and support, an application of theory (Sanford, 1966) and research (see Vande Berg, Connor-Linton, & Paige, 2009; and chapter 2 for discussions about findings from the Georgetown Consortium study which show that too much intercultural challenge leads to student burnout, while too much support allows students to remain in their comfort zones and avoid the sorts of tensions and disagreements that Kolb has identified as a key feature of effective learning). Finally, the Seminar would ask instructors to teach holistically (chapter 6)—to focus as much on the affective, behavioral, and perceptive as on the cognitive dimensions of their students' learning. They would work to help their students bring this "whole-person" approach into awareness, for example, by asking them to comment about when they experienced strong emotional responses to particular activities, so that they would come to understand how they characteristically responded in the face of various types of cultural difference.

The curriculum included a mix of lectures and activities; readings and writing assignments; individual, pair, and small- and large-group work; and homework tasks designed to push students to engage actively in local communities. Although traditional in some ways—the final assessment was a final exam—the course required both instructors and students to do significant intercultural "stretching," particularly those who had had little or no prior exposure to experiential, developmental, and holistic teaching and learning.

Ten RDs, including all of those who had participated in the OPDO pilot, taught the Seminar in spring 2008. And because theory and research suggested that all students would presumably benefit if educators intervened in intentional ways in their learning, all students enrolled in the 10 programs were required to enroll in the course, for a single credit.

Student and RD responses to this first version of the Seminar almost immediately made it clear, however, that the course as designed and delivered would, in and of itself, not be able to meet the challenges that CIEE was facing. In fact, faculty and student complaints about the course, which began during the first weeks, were more widespread and acute than anything Vande Berg had encountered in introducing the learning outcomes and OPDO projects. Some students pushed back hard against the course's experiential activities, and many of the RDs complained that this was not "teaching" as they understood the term. In short, neither group was well prepared for an experiential, developmental, and holistic learning experience.

To help assess the extent to which students were meeting course learning outcomes, the RDs had administered the Intercultural Development Inventory (IDI) to all of them within the first few days of the semester, and a second time a few days prior to its end (chapters 4 and 5 of this volume). The IDI post-test results confirmed what the student and RD feedback had suggested: The Seminar was not helping students develop their intercultural competence as much as Vande Berg and Quinn had hoped. As we have seen, the 1,150 students who had been enrolled in 61 programs abroad in the Georgetown Consortium Project had gained, on average, only 2.37 IDI points during their time studying abroad (chapter 2). We used this Georgetown Consortium finding as a baseline measure, comparing the intercultural development of the large number of students in that study with the development of students enrolled in the Seminar. During the fall semester of 2008, Seminar students showed average gains of only 4.03 IDI points—statistically no greater than the gains of the Georgetown Consortium Project participants. There was, of course, a key difference between the two groups of students: The great majority of those studying abroad in the Georgetown Consortium Project had received little or no structured intervention in their intercultural learning (the exception was the 109 students enrolled in the American University of Provence program, who gained an average of 12.47 IDI points during the study; see chapter 12), while the students in the pilot Seminars had enrolled in a new course intentionally designed to help them learn to shift cultural perspective and adapt their behavior to new cultural contexts. And now the course was not meeting that overarching outcome, at least not to the point where CIEE believed that it should.

Improving the Curriculum

Vande Berg and Quinn immediately revised the course, using the student and instructor evaluations and the IDI findings to guide them. First, they changed the course structure; all involved had agreed that the workload was too much for a single academic credit (one semester hour of credit). The course had met for a total of 26 hours and required regular reading and writing assignments and other homework; CIEE therefore decided to award two credits for the course in the future. Second, they adjusted the curriculum; students had complained that the course was not teaching them enough about local culture. Vande Berg and Quinn had anticipated that the RDs, with their deep understanding of local cultures, would be able to develop their own culture-specific material that they would integrate, as concrete examples, into the course's cultural-general content and activities. It was by this time becoming clear to them, however, that very few people can easily identify underlying cultural values or behavioral patterns in their own cultures, or connect these with observable behavior. If it were easy to identify such cultural patterns in our own or other cultures, more people would write books such as Edward Stewart and Milton Bennett's *American Cultural Patterns* (1991), Gary Althen's *American Ways* (1988), or Raymonde Carroll's *Cultural Misunderstandings* (1990), or they would produce the sort of culture-specific material that Dianne Hofner Saphiere (2004) and her collaborators continue to produce for the *Cultural Detective* (CD) series.

Vande Berg ultimately decided to incorporate CD material into the Seminar. Over the past three years, as the number of CIEE programs offering the course has grown, CIEE has purchased site licenses for those cultural "packages" that correspond to most of the national cultures where the Seminar is being offered (and a few other cultural packages, including *Islam, U.S.,* and *Self Discovery*). Since spring 2009, CD has helped Seminar teachers and students meet the course's three main outcomes. First, CD deepens students' understanding of "subjective culture," helping them become more aware of their own cultural values, beliefs, and behavior. Second, CD material and activities complement the students' development of "cultural literacy," the set of perspectives and skills that allow students to recognize the connections between observable behavior and the "deeper" or "hidden" cultural values and beliefs that underlie and inform that behavior. Third, CD helps Seminar students understand that to interact effectively and appropriately in a new cultural context, they need to learn to "bridge cultural difference" by applying key intercultural concepts and foundational intercultural skills, including understanding the relationship between culture and identity, differentiating stereotyping and cultural variability, identifying links between cultural values and behavior, sharpening observation, suspending judgment, sitting with discomfort, and shifting perspectives. RDs and other Seminar teachers also facilitate the CD debriefing method, one of several taught in the course— including Description-Interpretation-Evaluation (Bennett, Bennett, & Stillings, 1977); the Four As (National School Reform Faculty, n.d.); and the "Kolb-Thiagi" debrief, a series of questions formulated by Vande Berg that represents an amalgam of Kolb's experiential cycle and a six-step debriefing method developed by Sivasailam Thiagarajan ("Thiagi") (Kolb, 1984; Thiagarajan, 2004).

The course as a whole applies familiar intercultural design principles in proceeding from less to more challenging material—that is, material that frames the nature of "culture" precedes information and activities about "perception," which in turn precedes work on learning styles, stereotyping, communication styles, values, intercultural adaptation, and so on. The Seminar also presents culture-general before culture-specific material, with one exception: It introduces the CD material very early in the semester. We understand and to a large extent accept the familiar training principle that culture-general should precede culture-specific material; however, we have learned through hard practice that students respond much more positively to culture-general material when we offer them a taste of the specific first. Students who have just arrived in Buenos Aires, for example, generally want to learn particulars about Argentina before they are ready to take on culture-general concepts. In fact, this is often why students sign up for the Seminar in the first place; while our own understanding about teaching and learning continues to evolve, most students still believe, at least early in the course, that learning is about acquiring externally provided knowledge, and not about the process of reflecting on and cocreating meaning.

Over the past three years, Vande Berg and Quinn have continued to revise the Seminar regularly, with Catherine Menyhart joining them in the fall of 2010. As was the case with Quinn, Vande Berg hired Menyhart because her formal education and prior experience—an MA in teaching and

learning and work with educational programs in the United States and Senegal—had prepared her well to contribute to the continuing development of
this course. The Seminar has now been revised five times in four years,
with Quinn assuming the major responsibility for revisions starting with
substantial changes to the third version, in the spring of 2009. Student and
teacher feedback, as well as IDI scores, has continued to guide these revisions
significantly. As the course has developed, the curriculum has become progressively more experiential, developmental, and holistic, an evolution
reflected in the way that we have now come to describe the course's learning
outcomes. By the end of the course, students who engage actively in the
course material and activities will

- *Become more culturally self-aware.* As the Seminar instructor helps students develop the habit of self-reflection, they become more aware of
  who they are as "cultural beings"; the source and nature of their
  values; the ways that these values characteristically manifest themselves in their beliefs and actions; the ways that they characteristically
  respond to cultural difference and commonality; the ways that they
  prefer to learn; and so on.
- *Develop cultural literacy (or the habit of construing the experience of
  culturally different others).* As the instructor helps students learn more
  about the new environment (the people, values, beliefs, objects, ideas,
  and institutions that make up the unfamiliar cultural contexts that
  they are encountering) and helps them develop the habit of asking
  themselves why individuals within that cultural context believe, feel,
  and act as they do, students develop the capacity to understand, to
  accept, and eventually to empathize with culturally different others.
- *Bridge the gap between self and other.* As the instructor helps students
  develop the capacity for self-awareness, as well as their awareness of
  others in their own cultural contexts, the students come to recognize
  that considerable gaps—in values; in beliefs; in thinking, feeling, and
  behaving; and ultimately in the ways that others experience themselves and their world—exist between themselves and others. As the
  instructor fosters this growing awareness and helps students develop
  strategies for dealing creatively with cultural difference and commonality, they begin to develop the capacity to shift perspective and adapt
  behavior to different cultural contexts, and to interact more effectively and appropriately with culturally different others.

Yet even as we have continued to revise the Seminar curriculum, to make it more accessible to and effective for students and faculty alike, we have come to understand that no curriculum, no matter how well designed, can in and of itself resolve two fundamental issues: first, that most students are not particularly interested in learning either the culture-general content or the reflective techniques that the Seminar offers; and second, that most instructors struggle in learning to teach a course that is experiential, developmental, and holistic.

Marketing the Seminar to Students

While we are confident that our changes to the Seminar curriculum have strengthened the course, these changes have unfortunately had little or no impact on student enrollments. When we had required students to enroll in the course pilot in the fall of 2008, a significant number had pushed back hard against the requirement. When we converted the course to an elective, enrollments dropped to less than a fifth of students enrolled in programs where the Seminar was offered, and the participation rate has since then not exceeded 20%. While these rates are due in part to the logistical challenges of scheduling the course at a time when students are not enrolled in other courses, we believe the more significant problem is a lack of student interest. Over the years we have classified student rejection of the Seminar into six types of responses—the sorts of patterned responses that signal a common source in deeply held cultural values. Negative student perceptions of the Seminar tend to take the following forms:

1. *"I didn't come here to spend all my time in classes."* It is no secret that some U.S. students go abroad seeking a reprieve from what they perceive to be the rigors of studying at their home campuses. These are the students who wonder out loud why their courses abroad are as challenging as the ones back home—and they are likely to be just as vocal in pushing back against a Seminar course that asks them to sign up for additional hours of class, homework, and serious engagement. They have come abroad to experience other things they value more—perhaps new friendships, travel, romance, or simply "the freedom" they feel they lack at home.

2. *"What's the point of talking about all this stuff?"* Despite increasing acceptance of intercultural relations as a legitimate field of academic inquiry, most U.S. students have had little or no experience with

intercultural teaching and learning. Many study abroad offices incorporate a few intercultural activities into pre-departure orientations, but for students, intercultural concepts may seem as "foreign" as many other things that they encounter in their new and unfamiliar home. And as research findings grounded in the Intercultural Development Continuum (IDC) show, not all students respond positively when they encounter the new and different (chapter 2 of this volume).

3. *"What do my feelings have to do with learning? I'm doing just fine—and my personal life is nobody's business."* Intercultural learning requires that students learn to look inside—to develop an introspective habit about their intentions, hopes, expectations, and fears. The Seminar asks them to reflect on themselves as individuals whose values, beliefs, and behavior have evolved within the context of their own cultural contexts. Such introspection does not come easily to many U.S. students, and especially to those who have been accustomed to learning in primarily cognitive, externally focused ways that do not recognize the experiential and constructivist nature of learning.

4. *"I don't have to work this hard in the other classes I'm taking here."* While the number of U.S. faculty teaching experientially has grown significantly, those who rely primarily on traditional lectures probably still outnumber them. It is likely, then, that many students have still not had much experience learning experientially in their classes back home. They are more comfortable sitting quietly in a classroom taking notes and receiving knowledge via lectures than they are with an approach that asks them to learn more actively—for example, to work in groups, to engage in the community outside the classroom, and above all to be self-reflective and accept responsibility for their own learning.

5. *"Why do I need to be here—I learned this in a class at home."* As noted, some students may go abroad after encountering a few intercultural training activities during, for example, a pre-departure orientation on the home campus. They may believe that because they have been exposed to an intercultural activity at home they have learned all they could learn from it, and repeating what they perceive to be similar activities abroad is thus a waste of time. Students who complain that they "have already done this" fail to understand that experiential, developmental, and holistic learning is more about *practicing* self-reflection in order to deepen self-awareness than it is about acquiring a set of facts and then moving on to another.

6. *"I didn't come here to learn from a bunch of other Americans."* U.S. students who go abroad seeking an "immersion" experience may resist studying alongside other U.S. Americans, and especially in a course that asks them to introspectively identify U.S. values, beliefs, and behaviors—things about U.S. culture that they may be trying to avoid. A student might feel the Seminar is an "American bubble" for various reasons. Viewed from an IDI perspective, it may be, for example, that the student is in a state of Reversal—that he or she is embracing the values and culture of the host culture and rejecting many things associated with U.S. culture. Or it may be—to consider the student's attitude through the lens of Experiential Learning Theory—that he or she enjoys meeting new people and is inclined to see "yet another course" with Americans as time that would be better spent meeting local people or having other "authentic" experiences outside the classroom.

These six responses suggest, as we have noted, a common cultural source—what we have taken to calling "student abroad culture," which is deeply grounded in positivist and relativist assumptions about teaching and learning. Some students appear to be unconsciously or consciously embracing what amounts to a positivist assumption that learning proceeds directly from experience, and that the more they experience, the more they will learn. Others seem to be embracing a relativist perspective, seeking to find common humanity—rather than more challenging cultural differences—through "immersing" themselves in the host culture. Our main obstacle in convincing students to enroll in the Seminar is that so many fail to grasp that either raw "experience" or "immersion," without cultural self-awareness, cultural literacy, and the capacity to bridge cultural differences, is ultimately self-limiting. In this regard, working with many of our students is more than a little bit like trying to talk with someone about cultural difference when they are not developmentally able to perceive much difference at all. We are still working to figure out how to demonstrate the values of the Seminar to many students who experience the world through a Polarization or Minimization lens. In fact, our lack of success in attracting more students has led us to redirect our focus toward helping Seminar instructors understand more fully how this course can help students achieve their own goals abroad, so that the instructors themselves will be able to make more direct and compelling appeals to the students.

Training and Coaching the Faculty

When after launching the Seminar in fall 2008 we found that students had not developed interculturally as much as we had hoped, we resolved to do three things: revise the curriculum, increase enrollments through better marketing to students, and coach Seminar instructors differently. Although we have continued to focus on all three, the third has over time become our most important focus. We attribute the continuing improvement in student IDI gains that we are seeing—by spring 2011, students enrolled in the top 13 Seminars had gained, on average, 9.0 IDI points, compared with the 4.03 points of average gain for the pilot courses in fall 2008—more to changes in our training and coaching of the instructors than to curriculum revisions or improved marketing. In short, while curriculum revisions and marketing appeals are necessary, the key to unlocking the Seminar's success lies in individually coaching each instructor.

During the Seminar's first semester, we had believed that instructors would learn to teach the course through attending workshops in Portland and at annual conferences (many CIEE resident staff attend the latter), or through attending the occasional workshops that we offered at CIEE Study Centers abroad. During spring 2009, we began to complement these group training workshops with individual coaching sessions (typically lasting 60–90 minutes, by phone or via Skype) that took place every few weeks. We now understand that most instructors struggle to teach the course without this coaching, so those who have never taught the course before, or who have taught it only once, now receive coaching every two to three weeks. These sessions focus on the key elements of our experiential/constructivist approach to teaching and learning:

- *Learning is developmental.* In our experience, most instructors are not explicit about what they expect students to learn in their courses. In fact, although identifying learning outcomes has become more widespread in the United States, most of the courses that U.S. students take at their home institutions—like most of the courses that students take abroad—still fail to identify what the students are expected to know, understand, or be able to do by the end of the semester. As noted, the Seminar differs in this regard in providing clear learning outcomes that we believe students need to develop in order to interact effectively and appropriately with culturally different others. But beyond simply identifying these outcomes, the Seminar recognizes that different students increase self-awareness, develop cultural literacy about cultural norms and practices in the new culture, and learn to bridge cultural difference in various ways and at varied paces. As the IDC has taught us (chapters 4 and 5 of this volume), some students respond to cultural difference by responding defensively, persistently re-creating an "us" and "them" dynamic in their interactions with others. Other students respond to difference by minimizing it, so that they experience the things that they have in common with others as more important, more "real," than any perceived differences. Others, the ones who recognize and experience commonalities and differences in a more balanced way, are in a much better position to engage effectively and appropriately with culturally different others. We coach the Seminar instructors to develop the ability, over time, to recognize and work appropriately with students at all intercultural levels so that each student can develop to full capacity during his or her time abroad.

- *Learning is experiential.* The Seminar distinguishes clearly between "interactive" and "experiential" learning. Interactive instructors who ask learners to be active while they learn—through such things as discussions or field trips—are for many, perhaps most, learners more effective than instructors who depend primarily on classroom lecturing. However, simply asking instructors to be "interactive" will not help their students achieve desired intercultural outcomes. We train the instructors to guide their students "around" Kolb's experiential cycle (chapter 6) so that each reflects on and becomes aware of how he or she characteristically makes meaning of his or her experiences, and how culturally different others make meaning of those same experiences. For example, while an instructor of an "interactive" class for students enrolled in a program in Madrid might simply take them out of the city to tour El Escorial, an instructor of an experiential class might ask the students to work in small groups, to take photographs of the site that speak to Spanish values about hierarchy, beauty, or spirituality, and then to compare their findings with how they think such values are expressed at home. Reflecting on our experiences, becoming aware that the meaning we assign to experiences may be very different from the meanings that culturally different others assign to those same experiences, is one of the keys to being able to shift perspective and adapt behavior, and ultimately to interact more effectively with culturally different others.

- *Learning is holistic.* Most U.S. students have been conditioned by their experiences at home to approach learning as largely, if not exclusively, a cognitive experience. Taking a page out of Experiential Learning Theory (chapter 6), the Seminar intentionally incorporates multiple learning domains: affective, behavioral, perceptive, and cognitive. Part of a Seminar instructor's work involves helping students bring learning domains that have remained dormant into conscious awareness. In practicing mindfulness, for example, students learn to attend to the affective dimension; in describing sensations of emotional or physical discomfort, they may over time come to understand that such feelings or sensations often signal the presence of a challenging cultural difference. Rather than simply complaining about their "annoying" Spanish host mother, then, they are asked to name the feeling and perhaps some accompanying physical sensations as an "uncomfortable experience of difference," and to explore the contrast between the host mother's values and their own. In short, the Seminar embraces the view that to learn well and deeply, our students need to develop and practice their capacities to learn through all the domains—and that Seminar instructors need to learn how to integrate each of these domains into their teaching.
- *Learning depends on the resolution of cultural tensions and disagreements.* ELT also tells us that in order to learn deeply, students need to bring tensions into awareness, and then to learn to resolve them (chapter 6). A Seminar instructor can help students discover through self-reflection that—as with the student and the Spanish host mother—a value they hold conflicts with a value common to the host culture, or even that some of their own values conflict with each other. We ask instructors to introduce tension strategically into the learning experience. For example, in working with students whose dominant learning style is concrete experience (and who thus tend to prefer learning through immediate sensory experience, close emotional identification with others, and sharing of stories), instructors may ask them to "stretch" and learn to learn in ways that students whose dominant style is abstract conceptualization typically do. That is, instructors will show dominant concrete experience learners how to distance themselves from immediate experience, to learn more "objectively," and to frame their learning through abstract theory rather than concrete examples. Seminar instructors provide students with opportunities to practice resolving these experiential tensions

in class so that they will be better prepared to work effectively and appropriately with intercultural tensions in their daily lives outside the classroom.

- *Learning depends on good assessment.* The Seminar incorporates three different types of assessment: needs, formative, and summative. First, instructors conduct a needs analysis using the IDI and Kolb's Learning Style Inventory, both of which provide valuable information about the capacities and learning preferences of individual students and of the group as a whole. Second, instructors give frequent written and oral feedback throughout the semester. Such "formative assessment" helps students monitor their progress toward the course's desired learning outcomes, as well as their own personal goals. (We have over time increased the volume of assignments in the curriculum to provide instructors more opportunities to give students prompt and systematic feedback.) Third, we ask instructors to carry out a "summative assessment" at the end of the course by re-administering the IDI and giving a final course exam. In our final coaching conversations with instructors at the end of each semester, we compare these summative results with the instructor's perception of each student's growth to gauge the accuracy of his or her ability to perceive intercultural development. In other words, layered assessment practices help instructors learn to recognize the many manifestations of (or, sometimes, the lack of) intercultural development in their students.

During the past four years, it has become increasingly clear to us that an instructor's effectiveness in facilitating student learning through the course is to a large degree a function of his or her own developmental worldview. It is very difficult, if not impossible, for students to develop interculturally when the students are more developed than the teacher. This is not a minor issue; we know from the Georgetown Consortium Project—and our own IDI testing during the past three years has confirmed—that U.S. undergraduates, on average, begin their semester abroad at lower Minimization (Vande Berg, Connor-Linton, & Paige, 2009). If an instructor, then, is herself at lower Minimization, she may not be able to do much to help most of the students in a typical seminar class. The limitations of her own worldview—the ways that she characteristically finds ways to "subsume cultural differences into more culturally familiar categories" (Hammer, 2009, p. 208)—will influence and ultimately constrain those students who are at lower Minimization themselves, as well as those who are more interculturally developed.

As we have become increasingly aware of this connection, the focus of our coaching has become more developmental. Version 3 (v3) of the IDI has significantly influenced us in this regard; as IDI Qualified Administrators, we have been trained to use v3 debriefing methods that are proving very effective in helping Seminar teachers further their own development. Whether we are conducting an IDI feedback session with a new Seminar instructor or helping a more experienced instructor debrief an incident that has occurred in his or her class, we frame the discussion by taking him or her through one of two series of questions (Hammer, 2011). The first, which we use in discussing an individual instructor's own IDI results, follows this sequence:

1. What are your goals?
2. What types of challenges are you facing (that is, what is preventing you from achieving those goals)?
3. What strategies are you using to meet those challenges?
4. What types of support are available that may help you meet your goals?

We use the second sequence, and encourage the instructors to use it themselves, in debriefing incidents with their students. Like the first, this sequence is grounded in a basic experiential/constructivist assumption: that the meaning of an event is not in the event itself but is created—and within the context of the person's own cultural groups is cocreated—by the person who experiences it:

1. What happened?
2. What did you do?
3. How did you do this?
4. What were the consequences?
5. What might you have done differently?

We find that this sequence, and especially the final question, helps individuals realize that in order to address successfully the cultural issue that they are facing, they must take into account the perspective of "the other," and work to shift their own frames of reference.

We have good reason to believe that the Seminar instructors are benefiting from our coaching. First, some of those who are "getting" the course content and developing the intercultural capacities to teach it are successfully addressing the challenge of low seminar enrollments in creative ways. One whose students face scheduling challenges has begun using the online service Doodle (n.d.) to identify times when interested students are free; two others are informing students, prior to their arrival, that they have taken the liberty of registering all of them in the course (the students can opt out, but few do); another is emphasizing the social advantages of attending the course; and so on. In other words, once instructors both understand the meaning of the course and experience the ways that it positively affects their students, they start to find creative ways to "market" it to the students. Empirical evidence also supports our belief that Seminar instructors are benefiting developmentally. When 30 instructors who have taught the course for at least two semesters recently completed the IDI for a second time, we were pleased to learn that they had improved by an average of 14.54 points. Within the context of the IDC, this means that instructors who were, for example, at mid-Minimization when they began to teach the course have now reached the cusp of Acceptance. The data suggest, then, that an effective way for instructors to develop interculturally is to engage actively and regularly with students who are themselves focusing on their own intercultural development—and to do this while being coached to teach experientially, developmentally and holistically.

For readers who are thinking about developing a course similar to the Seminar on Living and Learning Abroad, we offer four conclusions based on our own experience:

1. Students benefit significantly when the course, first, helps them become aware of their habitual responses to cultural commonality and difference; and, second, teaches them to reframe their experience consciously. Students enrolled in the Seminar learn to reflect on, make meaning of, experiment with, and adapt to events within unfamiliar cultural contexts. The habit of self-reflection leads to both self-awareness and awareness of others situated within their own cultural contexts, a "double awareness" that then positions students to build the sorts of reciprocal bridges that will allow them to cross the cultural gap between self and others.

2. Instructors need to facilitate student learning *throughout* the study abroad experience. Pre-departure orientation is important, as are orientations that take place at the program site. But to learn and develop effectively through studying abroad, most students need to meet regularly—ideally, at least once a week—in an explicitly defined learning space, with an instructor trained to facilitate intercultural learning, so that they can share and debrief

their experiences with cultural difference and commonality in their daily lives outside the class.

3. The curriculum should be soundly designed. Material should be sequenced from less to more challenging, should present sufficient cultural-general content before introducing culture-specific content, and so on. At the same time, educators need to be sensitive to students' needs, and to adjust the course curriculum to meet those needs. We did this, for example, when in redesigning the Seminar we "front-loaded" the CD material because students were clamoring for culture-specific material early in the course.

4. The single most important step that an institution or organization needs to take in designing and delivering a course such as the seminar is to invest heavily in the training of the instructors. Designing an effective curriculum is critically important, but only a well-trained instructor who knows how to teach experientially, developmentally, and holistically, and who knows how to balance challenge and support for learners, individually and in a group, will be able to make even the best curriculum work. We have learned that instructors typically need to teach the Seminar more than once before their students' post-IDI scores will show that they are learning and developing more than they would if they were simply left to develop interculturally on their own. However, once instructors learn to teach the Seminar effectively, and to adapt the curriculum to their own cultural land-scapes, both their own and their students' IDI scores tend to improve dramatically.

Conclusion

We close with the old adage, "You can lead a horse to water, but you can't make him drink." Or to put it in study abroad terms, recent research tells us that we can lead students to new and different places abroad, but we cannot make most of them learn deeply while there. Our experience with the Seminar confirms the wisdom of the educator and writer Maryellen Weimer (2002), who has given the old adage a pragmatic twist: The next time you are planning to take your horses to drink, "salt their oats" first—they will be a lot more likely to drink when they get to the water (p. 103). The Seminar, grounded in experiential/constructivist perspectives and supported by recent research and interdisciplinary insights, provides a concrete example of how one organization is going about salting those oats.

References

Althen, G. (1988). *American ways: A guide for foreigners in the United States.* Yarmouth, ME: Intercultural Press.

Bennett, J. M., Bennett, M. J., & Stillings, K. (1977). *Description, interpretation, evaluation.* Retrieved from http://www.intercultural.org/tools.php

Bologna Process. (2007). *London communiqué.* Retrieved from http://www.coe.int/t/dg4/highereducation/ehea2010/London%20Communique%20-%2018-05-2007.pdf

Bransford, J. D., Brown, A. L., & Cocking, R. R. (Eds.). (2000). *How people learn: Brain, mind, experience, and school* (expanded ed.). Washington, DC: National Academic Press.

Carroll, R. (1990). *Cultural misunderstandings.* Chicago: University of Chicago Press.

Doodle. (n.d.). Retrieved from http://doodle.com/

Fink, L. D. (2003). *Creating significant learning experiences: An integrated approach to designing college courses.* San Francisco, CA: Jossey-Bass.

Hammer, M. (2009). The Intercultural Development Inventory: An approach for assessing and building intercultural competence. In M. A. Moodian (Ed.), *Contemporary leadership and intercultural competence: Exploring the cross-cultural dynamics within organizations* (pp. 203–217). Thousand Oaks, CA: Sage.

Hammer, M. R. (2011, June). Intercultural Development Qualifying Seminar: Kingston, Ontario: IDI.

Kolb, D. (1984). *Experiential learning: Experience as the source of learning and development.* Englewood Cliffs, NJ: Prentice Hall.

Maturana, H., & Varela, F. (1992). *The tree of knowledge: The biological roots of human understanding.* Boston, MA: Shambhala.

National School Reform Faculty. (n.d.). *Four a's text protocol.* Retrieved from http://www.nsrfharmony.org/protocol/doc/4_a_text.pdf

Sanford, N. (1966). *Self and society: Social change and individual development.* New York: Atherton Press.

Saphiere, D. H. (2004). *Cultural Detective series.* Retrieved from http://www.culturaldetective.com/products.html

Stewart, E. C., & Bennett, M. J. (1991). *American cultural patterns: A cross-cultural perspective* (Rev. ed.). Yarmouth, ME: Intercultural Press.

Taylor, K., Marineau, C., & Fiddler, M. (2000). *Developing adult learners: Strategies for teachers and trainers.* San Francisco, CA: Jossey-Bass.

Thiagarajan, S. (2004). *Six phases of debriefing.* Retrieved from http://www.thiagi.com/pfp/IE4H/february2004.html#Debriefing

Vande Berg, M. (2009). Intervening in student learning abroad: A research-based inquiry. *Intercultural Education, 20*(4), 15–27.

Vande Berg, M., Connor-Linton, J., & Paige, R. M. (2009). The Georgetown Consortium Project: Interventions for student learning abroad. *Frontiers: The Interdisciplinary Journal of Study Abroad, 18,* 1–75.

Weimer, M. (2002). *Learner-centered teaching: Five key changes to practice.* San Francisco, CA: Jossey-Bass.

PART FOUR

CONCLUSION

17

INTERVENING IN STUDENT LEARNING ABROAD

Closing Insights

Kris Hemming Lou, Michael Vande Berg, and R. Michael Paige

We started this volume with a promise: that we would address the confusion surrounding competing claims about student learning abroad by considering and sharing credible evidence. We argued in chapter 1 that the evidence that many members of the study abroad community have for decades offered would not stand up to careful scrutiny. We identified three types of common claims about student learning. first, that students learn effectively abroad through being exposed to new and different experiences, or especially through being "immersed" in those experiences; second, that reports from some returning students about being "transformed" provide evidence that being exposed to or immersed in experience is in fact effective; and, third, that because students are normally learning effectively abroad it makes more sense to focus more on getting larger numbers of students abroad than on working to improve teaching and learning.

In place of untested assumptions, student narratives, and reports on enrollment increases, we have offered three different types of evidence that together represent a new and very different story about student learning abroad: knowledge from a wide range of academic disciplines and traditions, knowledge from recent research, and knowledge from successful study abroad courses and programs.

Each form of evidence takes shape within the paradigmatic structure presented in chapter 1. We borrowed from Thomas Kuhn, applying his groundbreaking work on the history of science to the field of study abroad.

His profound insights into the nature of scientific revolutions enabled us to examine past, present, and emerging knowledge claims about student learning in a new light. Broadly speaking, we could see and better understand those claims and counterclaims when situated within one or another of the three paradigms situated in that chapter. We also drew from another discipline, critical theory, for insights about the nature of "master narratives"— accounts of knowledge shared by members of particular human communities. Applying these to study abroad allowed us to see two things more clearly: that members of our study abroad community have long been sharing stories with each other about student learning, and that the community's master narratives are continuing to evolve over time.

Knowledge From the Academic Disciplines

The first source of evidence is knowledge from the academic disciplines. The authors in Part Two, "Foundations of Teaching and Learning," are representatives of disciplines that offer key insights into the nature of teaching, learning, and human development that are relevant to student learning abroad. This body of work helps us better understand, theoretically, how learning occurs and points to ways that we might better support learning abroad. The chapters in Part Three allow us to see how the traditions of a discipline—its ways of knowing, theoretical frameworks, and knowledge claims—can shift dramatically over time. This vantage point also provides a historical perspective that shows how individual disciplines, over the course of the past century, have intertwined and converged to inform the more current experiential/constructivist theories and practices discussed in this volume.

Recent Study Abroad Research

The second source of evidence presented in this volume is recent study abroad research. In chapter 2, Paige and Vande Berg provide a detailed review of the relevant study abroad literature and identify a new set of knowledge claims based on these studies. Perhaps the most important claim is that students learn more "effectively and appropriately" when educators provide comprehensive and intensive intervention that includes cultural mentoring, as opposed to their sending students abroad with the expectation that they will learn simply through being exposed to or immersed in new and different environments.

While the studies described in chapter 2 use a number of different instruments to assess student learning and development, all of them rely on the Intercultural Development Inventory (IDI), underlining an important characteristic of the emerging paradigm: the use of valid and reliable instruments across studies and the subjecting of models, theories, and practices to rigorous empirical testing. More and more researchers are turning to the IDI as one means of validly determining to what extent students are learning effectively and appropriately while abroad. This increasing reliance on a common instrument is also allowing researchers to compare the learning of students across different courses and programs of study. Within the experiential/constructivist paradigm of study abroad programming, these courses and programs increasingly share at least one outcome: that students will have made meaningful progress in developing interculturally. Or to put this in the context of the IDI, students will have made significant progress toward Adaptation, the developmental orientation associated with a growing ability to shift perspective and change behavior in different cultural contexts.

Knowledge From Successful Study Abroad Courses and Programs

The authors of Part Three, "Program Applications: Intervening in Student Learning," provide the third type of evidence as they describe six courses and programs that are successfully intervening, in strategic and intentional ways, to help students develop their intercultural and other capacities. These case studies demonstrate how theoretical knowledge from the academic disciplines and empirical knowledge from the study abroad research literature can be converted into successful interventions that support student learning.

Recommendations

We close this volume by fulfilling a second promise that we made at the beginning: to offer recommendations to faculty and staff who are interested in drawing from one or more of the six interventions discussed in Part Three in order to maximize their own students' learning abroad.

First, be clear about what you want your students to accomplish through studying abroad. Student learning is often assumed and claimed to occur as a result of study abroad, but the nature of that learning is often not well articulated. If learning outcomes are not clear, then it is going to be difficult for students to achieve them. Since the 1970s, higher education in the United States and many other parts of the world has been sharpening and increasingly embracing the distinction between "surface" and "deep" learning. Surface learning is typically associated with, among other things, instructors transferring knowledge in the form of facts to students, who absorb and memorize but do not critique them. Deep learning involves faculty and students coconstructing knowledge, with teachers helping students become more self-aware and able to shift frames of reference (Fink, 2003; Taylor, Marineau, & Fiddler, 2000).

Considered in the context of this volume's three-paradigm framework, surface learning aligns with positivist and relativist, and deep learning with experiential/constructivist, perspectives. We have seen that some authors in Parts Two and Three have discussed "deep learning" (see chapters 6 and 14), but they and others have used a variety of other terms as well. That is, in the context of the emerging paradigm, the phenomenon of "deep learning" is often also described as "experiential," "constructivist," "developmental," "dialectic," and "holistic" learning.

Our second recommendation: Identify learning outcomes and then design programs that will help students achieve these. This is not how study abroad programs have traditionally been designed. Five of the six training courses and programs described in Part Three were, however, developed in just this way—that is, only after the designers had first identified the learning outcomes that they wanted their students to achieve.

Of the six training programs, the one that was not designed with learning outcomes foremost in mind, the University of the Pacific's pre– and post–study abroad courses, dates to 1976. La Brack was an early innovator in what would come to be experiential/constructivist training methods; he was developing a training approach well before most of the concepts and practices discussed in this volume had been developed—including the identification of learning outcomes. Over the years, as he and his colleagues have integrated the pre– and post–study abroad courses into the School of International Studies (SIS) curriculum, they have come to identify the sorts of learning outcomes that we see in the other five cases.

The American University Center of Provence (AUCP), almost certainly the first study abroad program to be designed through "reverse engineering," and The Scholar Ship (TSS), designed more than a decade later, offer examples of entire study abroad programs that were designed only after specific learning outcomes had been identified. The Maximizing Study Abroad project evolved uniquely, where the use of learning outcomes was concerned.

The first step that Paige and his colleagues took in this regard, with the Maximizing Study Abroad project, was exploratory: They researched the culture- and language-learning literature to refine their understanding of particular learning outcomes. They then conducted research both to test a promising intercultural assessment instrument and to study culture teaching in the language classroom. By this point, they had identified clear learning outcomes and were ready to develop a curriculum and a program that would support language and intercultural development. Lou and Bosley's Intentional, Targeted Intervention (ITI) training model as well as the Council on International Educational Exchange's (CIEE's) Seminar on Living and Learning Abroad also began with the identification of learning outcomes before the course curricula were developed.

Our third recommendation: Familiarize yourself with the recent research on student learning abroad. The studies presented in chapter 2 provide us with valuable information that can be used to design effective study abroad programs. For example, the research shows us the limitations of immersion strategies such as homestays and direct enrollment in host university courses, strategies that the study abroad community has long favored. These studies also show that the key to making these and other strategies work more effectively is to support students through intentional mentoring and guidance that is designed to help them learn to reflect on themselves as cultural beings, and to become aware of the ways that they characteristically respond to and make meaning within different cultural contexts. The research might also help us to convince skeptical colleagues why we are so strongly encouraging that particular elements be included in the design and implementation of our programs. The assumption that immersion is the key to learning abroad is strong and persistent; it probably engenders more resistance to experiential/constructivist perspectives than any other belief. As we have seen, however, recent research clearly shows that for most students, immersion is a necessary, but not a sufficient, condition for learning abroad; only when immersion is combined with intervention in the form of cultural mentoring across the study abroad experience do most students learn and develop in meaningful ways.

Our fourth recommendation: Embrace the principle that "intervention" is necessary, but that there is no best or single way to intervene. Each of the six training approaches in this volume does rely on a cultural mentor or mentors who are trained to facilitate intercultural learning and development, but the *form* of the mentoring intervention can differ dramatically from one course or program to another. Both Lou and Bosley's ITI model and The

Scholar Ship's training approach create learning communities that bring students from the United States and other countries together in "productive spaces" where cultural mentors can help them understand intercultural concepts and learn to make sense of challenging intercultural encounters. These two training programs, however, are structured very differently. Lou and Bosley's courses are taught online and asynchronously, with the mentors physically situated on the Willamette and Bellarmine campuses, whereas TSS's program had cultural mentors facilitating student learners face-to-face.

The University of Minnesota's Global Identity course is taught online by trained instructors located on the Twin Cities campus, in contrast to the AUCP and CIEE's Seminar on Living and Learning Abroad, both of which feature face-to-face cultural mentoring at program sites. The AUCP approach, moreover, employs a comprehensive intervention structure that includes a required intercultural training course at the site, while CIEE's approach features two phases: an elective intercultural relations course at program sites and an On-Line Pre-Departure session that all students are required to attend prior to departure. The University of the Pacific program, alternatively, involves two courses, both required of students at SIS, that are offered prior to and after study abroad, with no organized facilitation occurring while the students are abroad.

Our fifth recommendation: Train cultural mentors in the theory and practice of intercultural teaching and learning. This investment of time and other resources will ensure that those serving as cultural mentors will be effective in this challenging work. All of those who are implementing the six study abroad programs have been trained through one or more currently available training venues. The University of the Pacific, the University of Minnesota, and CIEE invest heavily in training instructors, and TSS went to considerable lengths as well to train faculty and staff in intercultural theory and practice before and during the two semesters that the program was offered.

While space considerations prevent us from listing all of the available training venues, we cite three that are playing important roles in helping faculty and staff to learn intercultural theory and concepts, and to teach these in ways that may be unfamiliar to them—that is, experientially, developmentally, and holistically. The Summer Institute for Intercultural Communication (2001) has each July for more than three decades offered a wide variety of three- and five-day training courses in Portland, Oregon. The Canadian, European, Japanese, and U.S. chapters of the Society for Education, Training and Research offer training workshops at their annual conferences. And the IDI Qualifying Seminars, offered in various locations in the

United States and abroad, teach individuals basic intercultural theory as well as training in the use of the instrument.

Our sixth recommendation: Develop and carry out an effective assessment program that uses valid and reliable instruments and rigorous methodologies. If the necessary first step in course or program development is the identification of challenging learning outcomes, the second is the identification of the assessment methods and instruments that educators will use to determine to what extent students are meeting those outcomes. We have seen that all six training courses and programs rely on pre- and post-testing of students, use a variety of instruments to do this, and share a common commitment to using the IDI for assessing intercultural learning. Each of the six includes two other forms of evaluation as well: needs assessments and formative assessments. As these courses or programs begin, instructors conduct needs assessments that help them understand what their students' developmental learning needs and capacities are, what their preferred learning styles are, and so on. They use the results to make adjustments in the materials and approaches that they will use during the course or program. Most of the six rely on one or more instruments that are already in wide use, including the IDI (Hammer, 2009), Kolb's Learning Style Inventory (Kolb & Kolb, 2005), and the Intercultural Conflict Style Inventory (Hammer, 2009). Finally, for the formative assessments, the instructors use written assignments, short reaction papers and quizzes, peer-to-peer check-ins, and other techniques (Weimer, 2002) to keep track of how their students are progressing, so that they can offer frequent and timely comments to help the students understand to what extent they are on track in meeting desired learning outcomes.

Final Thoughts

The study abroad community has long expected students to learn in ways that they will not if they stay at home. However, as this volume has shown, insights from a wide range of academic disciplines, empirical research, and six training courses and programs together provide evidence that all too often our students are not learning in the ways that we have traditionally assumed that they do. This is especially the case where the community's core expectation is concerned: that when students study abroad, they normally and naturally learn to understand and get along with the people who live in this culture that is new and different to the students. The evidence tells us, though, that students do not learn as the force of "the environment" imprints itself on them—even when that environment is a different culture; even when the students are exposed to sights, sounds, smells, tastes, and textures very different from those at home; and even when educators have taken steps to immerse them in these and other rich experiences. Finally, the evidence tells us that when trained cultural mentors intervene in the education of students throughout the study abroad cycle, they learn and develop more effectively and appropriately—much more than those who either stay at home or enroll in programs abroad that do not provide cultural mentoring.

The evidence asks faculty and staff not only to frame learning and teaching abroad very differently, but also to change long-established practices in designing and delivering programs. For educators at many institutions, this will mean realigning operations so that the focus of their efforts will be directed more to student learning abroad than is now often the case. That is, staff and faculty will need, among other things, to identify clear learning outcomes, provide for the mentoring of students, and assess their learning—in addition to attending to other current responsibilities, including the recruiting, selecting, and orienting of students prior to departure. We understand that some readers may find this challenging, to say the least, given the current economic stresses at many of our institutions, and the fact that study abroad office budgetary allocations are still often tied to annual increases in study abroad enrollments. We have included six courses and programs that are successfully maximizing the learning of students in very different ways in the belief that members of our study abroad community will be able to identify one or more models that will match their own institutional needs and profiles. And we hope that readers will find the evidence in this volume helpful in articulating, for their institutional colleagues, a vision of how study abroad can fulfill its promise of educating students in ways that will finally allow them to learn in ways that they will not if they stay at home.

References

Fink, L. D. (2003). *Creating significant learning experiences: An integrated approach to designing college courses*. San Francisco, CA: Jossey-Bass.

Hammer, M. (2009). The Intercultural Development Inventory: An approach for assessing and building intercultural competence. In M. A. Moodian (Ed.), *Contemporary leadership and intercultural competence: Exploring the cross-cultural dynamics within organizations* (pp. 203–217). Thousand Oaks, CA: Sage.

Kolb, A., & Kolb, D. (2005). Learning styles and learning spaces: Enhancing experiential learning in higher education. *Academy of Management Learning & Education, 4*(2), 193–212.

Summer Institute for Intercultural Communication. (2001). Retrieved from www.intercultural.org

Taylor, K., Marineau, C., & Fiddler, M. (2000). *Developing adult learners: Strategies for teachers and trainers.* San Francisco, CA: Jossey-Bass.

Weimer, M. (2002). *Learner-centered teaching: Five key changes to practice.* San Francisco, CA: Jossey-Bass.

Laura Bathurst, PhD, is assistant professor of anthropology and director of the MA in Intercultural Relations in the School of International Studies at the University of the Pacific, Stockton, California. Laura provides intercultural consultation and training to students, faculty, and staff at Pacific, and assists with programmatic efforts to implement and assess intercultural competencies throughout the university. A former director of the Pacific Institute for Cross Cultural Training, she is on its executive board. She is a qualified IDI administrator and past fellow of the Summer Institute of Intercultural Communication. Laura received her PhD in sociocultural anthropology from the University of California, Berkeley, and has conducted research in Bolivia, Spain, and the United States. Her specialties include lowland South America, controlling processes, and the pedagogy of cultural difference.

Milton J. Bennett, PhD, is a founding director of the Intercultural Communication Institute in Portland, Oregon, where he was previously associate professor of communication studies at Portland State University. He currently is director of the Intercultural Development Research Institute (Hillsboro, Oregon, and Milano, Italy), teaches for the IDRAcademy (www.idrinstitute.org), and holds an adjunct faculty appointment at the University of Milano-Bicocca (Italy). He has consulted with more than 150 colleges and universities on topics of intercultural learning in international education and domestic diversity programs. Milton is well known for his Developmental Model of Intercultural Sensitivity (DMIS) and its measurement, the Intercultural Development Inventory (IDI). He is coauthor of *American Cultural Patterns: A Cross-Cultural Perspective*; the contributing editor of *Basic Concepts of Intercultural Communication*; a contributing editor of *Handbook of Intercultural Training*, 3rd ed.; and the author of a seminal chapter on intercultural learning in *A History of U.S. Study Abroad: 1965– Present* commissioned by the Forum on Education Abroad.

Gabriele Weber Bosley, PhD, is director of International Programs and Professor of Global Languages and Cultures at Bellarmine University, where she guides the SACS/QEP campus-wide internationalization initiatives as chief international officer. Gabriele founded and chaired the Foreign Languages Department from 1995–2008 and developed and implemented Bellarmine's BA degree in Foreign Languages & International Studies and the minor in International Studies. She is the founding director of Bellarmine's International Programs Office and has served in that capacity since 1995. She is the recipient of numerous regional and national grants and awards, and a regular presenter at international education conferences. Gabriele currently serves on the boards and advisory councils of various regional, national, and international education associations and has served on the boards of the Association of International Education Administrators (AIEA), ISEP: International Student Exchange Programs, and as president of the Kentucky chapter of the American Association of Teachers of German. Her research and publications focus on intercultural education, curriculum development, and foreign-language acquisition. She is president of Hemming & Weber Consulting, LLC, which provides intercultural consulting services to educational institutions.

John Engle, PhD, is cofounder of the American University Center of Provence. He received his PhD in English from UCLA and is currently Maître de conférences, or associate professor, at the Université du Sud Toulon-Var, where he served for many years as director of Erasmus University Exchanges. He has written extensively on modern and contemporary literature, film, the history of education, and cultural communication; his work on international education has appeared in, among other places, *Frontiers: The Interdisciplinary Journal of Study Abroad* and *The Chronicle of Higher Education*. He is currently writing about the French filmmaker Abdellatif Kechiche.

Lilli Engle has been active in international education since 1980. Raised in Europe and the United States, she completed a master's degree (1978) and PhD coursework (1980) in Comparative Literature at UCLA. She is cofounder and director of the American University Center of Provence (AUCP), with study abroad programs in France and Morocco. Educator and administrator, Lilli has designed intercultural training programs for U.S. students and international business professionals, and she has taught in both French and American university settings. She has published numerous articles on intercultural communication and program design and frequently leads intercultural workshops. A founding member of the Advisory Council of the

Forum on Education Abroad, Lilli also served as a longstanding member of the Board of Advisors of Experiment in International Living (France) and is the founder/director of The American Center, one of the largest independent language schools in the south of France.

Mitchell R. Hammer, PhD, is the founder of several organizations that focus on intercultural competence development, conflict resolution, critical incident management, and crisis negotiation and resolution. He is also professor emeritus of International Peace and Conflict Resolution in the School of International Service at the American University in Washington, D.C. His work has resulted in the Intercultural Development Inventory (IDI), an assessment of intercultural competence; the Intercultural Conflict Style (ICS) Inventory, a measure of cultural differences in solving problems and resolving conflict; and the S.A.F.E. model of hostage/crisis negotiation for resolving crisis situations.

Tara A. Harvey is a PhD candidate in the Comparative and International Development Education program at the University of Minnesota. She earned a BS in communication studies and Hispanic studies from Northwestern University, an MA in international relations from the Instituto Universitario Ortega y Gasset in Madrid, and an MA in journalism and mass communication from the University of Wisconsin–Madison. Tara has worked in International Student Services at Texas A&M University and at the University of Wisconsin–Madison. One of her primary interests is helping undergraduate students learn and grow through intercultural experiences. In that regard, she has taught two study abroad intervention courses at the University of Minnesota—the university's well-known Global Identity course and a semester-length reentry course for study abroad returnees—and is now consulting at the Council on International Educational Exchange (CIEE), coaching teachers of CIEE's Seminar on Living and Learning Abroad.

David A. Kolb, PhD, is professor of Organizational Behavior at the Weatherhead School of Management, Case Western Reserve University. He received his BA in psychology, philosophy, and religion at Knox College and his PhD in social psychology from Harvard University. He is best known for his research on experiential learning and learning styles described in *Experiential Learning: Experience as the Source of Learning and Development*, which he authored. He has also coauthored *Conversational Learning: An*

Experiential Approach to Knowledge Creation, Innovation in Professional Education: Steps on a Journey From Teaching to Learning, and *Organizational Behavior: An Experiential Approach.* He has authored many journal articles and book chapters on experiential learning as well. David currently serves on the editorial review boards of *Academy of Management Learning and Education, Human Relations, Simulation and Gaming,* and *Journal of Management Development.* His current areas of research include team learning, the cultural determinants of learning style, and experiential learning in conversation. He is involved in a number of learning-focused institutional development projects in education and has received four honorary degrees recognizing his contributions to experiential learning in higher education.

Bruce La Brack, PhD, professor emeritus of anthropology and international studies, University of the Pacific, Stockton, California, is a South Asian specialist and intercultural anthropologist. He has been involved with study abroad for more than three decades, including designing and directing Pacific's innovative and integrated orientation and reentry programs. He has published extensively on culture-learning issues and trains regularly on intercultural adjustment related to international educational exchange. Bruce is primary author and editor of *What's Up With Culture?*, a free Internet resource for preparing U.S. American study abroad students going to and returning from study abroad. He has traveled to more than 85 countries and conducted research in India, England, Uganda, Japan, and the United States.

Kris Hemming Lou, PhD, has been director of international education and associate professor of international studies at Willamette University since 2003. He is an active member of the Association of International Educators (AIEA), CIEE: Council on International Educational Exchange, the European Association of International Education, the Forum on Education Abroad, ISEP: International Student Exchange Programs, and NAFSA: Association of International Educators. He presents frequently on issues of intercultural learning abroad and has taught in the United States, Austria, and Japan. Kris previously held faculty and administrative positions at Aquinas College (where he established the international programs office as the college's assistant dean of International Programs & Cultural Studies), the Oregon University System, and the University of Innsbruck. His education includes studying abroad as both an undergraduate and a graduate student for more than three years in Germany (Tübingen and Munich) and the

Soviet Union (Leningrad), culminating in a PhD in political science (international relations) from the University of Oregon. Kris is CEO of Hemming & Weber Consulting, LLC, which provides intercultural consulting services to educational institutions.

Kate S. McCleary, MEd, is the director of International Programs at Washington College and a doctoral candidate in Comparative and International Development Education at the University of Minnesota. From 2006 to 2011 she coordinated and taught the Maximizing Study Abroad and Global Identity courses at the University of Minnesota. Through this work she explored the online teaching of intercultural learning and the role of instructors in one-on-one teaching environments. Kate's research interests focus on gender and education, as well as on social justice and equity issues that youth confront in the United States and Central America. She has been the recipient of fellowships from the Fulbright Foundation, CARE USA, and Save the Children, which have sponsored research relating to gender and/or education in Madrid, Spain; Chinandega, Nicaragua; and Tegucigalpa, Honduras, respectively.

Adriana Medina-López-Portillo, PhD, is assistant professor of Intercultural Communication and Spanish in the Department of Modern Languages, Linguistics and Intercultural Communication at the University of Maryland, Baltimore County (UMBC). She is a member of the Center for the Advancement of Intercultural Communication (CAIC) at UMBC, an associate faculty at the Summer Institute for Intercultural Communication (SIIC), and the founder of the Baltimore chapter of the Society for Intercultural Education, Training and Research (SIETAR). She is a qualified IDI administrator and a Personal Leadership and Emotional Intelligence facilitator. Adriana is an accomplished intercultural trainer, having designed and led workshops for higher education, not-for-profit, governmental, and corporate clients in the United States and abroad. Among her favorite appointments are training for The Scholar Ship, a transnational academic program housed on a passenger ship, and offering pre-departure and on-site orientations for the King Abdullah University of Science and Technology (KAUST) in Saudi Arabia.

Catherine Menyhart has worked in international education since 2002. She is currently the manager of Academic Assurance & Support at the Council on International Educational Exchange (CIEE), coaches instructors of the Seminar on Living and Learning Abroad, facilitates intercultural trainings, and supports various research projects. Previously, she worked as resident coordinator at the CIEE Study Center in Dakar, Senegal. Catherine holds an MSEd in teaching and learning from the University of Southern Maine and received her BA in international relations and French from Grand Valley State University. She taught French at a public high school in Portland, Maine, and currently tutors English Language Learners.

R. Michael Paige, PhD, is professor of international and intercultural education in the Department of Organizational Leadership, Policy, and Development at the University of Minnesota. He is the cofounder of the university's Comparative and International Development Education (CIDE) program and the EdD program for International Educators. His research in recent years has focused on the impact of study abroad, the development of intercultural competence, the internationalization of higher education, and global engagement. He has codirected or served as a research consultant on a number of major studies including Maximizing Study Abroad, the Georgetown Consortium Project, CIEE's Transformative Power of Study Abroad, and Study Abroad for Global Engagement (SAGE). An active scholar, he has coauthored the *Maximizing Study Abroad* volumes, coedited *Culture as the Core: Perspectives on Culture in Second Language Learning*, edited *Education for the Intercultural Experience*, and authored numerous research articles.

Angela M. Passarelli is a doctoral candidate in organizational behavior at the Weatherhead School of Management, Case Western Reserve University. She holds an MS in educational administration with a focus in college student development from Texas A&M University and a BS in psychology and general business from James Madison University. Her research explores the impact of human connection on individual learning, vitality, and performance. She has coauthored several scholarly articles and book chapters on coaching, experiential learning, leadership development, and strengths-based education.

Meghan Quinn received her BA from Barnard College and her MSEd in teaching and learning from the University of Southern Maine. Before joining the Council on International Educational Exchange, she taught English language learning (ELL) in Japan, in Thailand, and at a chicken-processing plant in the United States; directed a traveling study abroad program in Thailand and Laos; and taught English and ELL in various Maine high schools. She has been the manager of instructional development at CIEE since 2007, where she develops intercultural course curricula, coaches faculty to teach the Seminar on Living and Learning Abroad, and trains staff to facilitate other intercultural interventions. Her recent interests include contemplative education and Mandarin Chinese.

Jennifer Meta Robinson, PhD, studies how people learn to be themselves, as individuals and as members of a community, uncovering systems of value, socialization, and implementation. She teaches courses on performance in everyday life and ethnography in the Department of Communication and Culture at Indiana University and publishes on environmental humanities and on education. She was the fourth president of the International Society for the Scholarship of Teaching and Learning and directed the Indiana University scholarship of teaching and learning initiative, which won the Hesburgh Award in 2003, and she coedits the Indiana University Press book series *Scholarship of Teaching and Learning.* Her publications include *A Cultural Approach to Interpersonal Communication* (Wiley-Blackwell 2012) and *The Farmers' Market Book* (Indiana 2007).

Riikka Salonen, MA, brings more than 18 years of experience as an intercultural leader, facilitator, and consultant in corporate, governmental, academic, and nonprofit contexts worldwide. She is currently a program manager for diversity and inclusion at Oregon Health & Science University (OHSU) in Portland, Oregon, where she leads the diversity and inclusion strategic planning for more than 6,500 OHSU Healthcare employees. She is also a cofounder and managing partner of Global Inclusion Consulting, LLC. Previously, she served as a member of academic teaching staff for intercultural communication and an intercultural residential counselor coordinator on The Scholar Ship. Prior to this, she was the associate director of assessment and research at the Intercultural Communication Institute (ICI). Riikka received her master's degree from the University of Jyväskylä, Finland, majoring in speech communication, organizational communication, and intercultural relations. She also holds the Professional Intercultural Certificate from ICI and is a qualified IDI administrator.

Victor Savicki holds a PhD in psychology from the University of Massachusetts. He is currently a professor emeritus of psychology from Western Oregon University, where he taught for 33 years. His courses spanned several areas of psychology including clinical, industrial/organizational, and crosscultural. Victor has taught in study abroad settings many times and has several publications addressing intercultural adjustment, as well as stress and coping in cross-cultural contexts, including the book *Developing Intercultural Competence and Transformation.* His current research interests focus on the psychological and educational processes that study abroad students navigate during their encounters with a foreign culture. He is also interested in assessment of study abroad outcomes.

Douglas K. Stuart, PhD, is director of Intercultural Training & Development at IOR Global Services. His focus is the developing field of intercultural assessment instruments, and he is licensed to deliver and interpret a variety of such tools. He authors position papers on the assessment and development of intercultural competence and presents at conferences and workshops internationally. His experience includes Educational Specialist in Andersen Worldwide's Performance Consulting Group; full-time faculty positions at the Illinois Institute of Technology in Chicago and the Economics Institute of the University of Colorado, Boulder; and education management positions in Algeria and the United Arab Emirates. Doug earned his PhD at the Illinois Institute of Technology and pursued postgraduate studies at the Illinois School of Professional Psychology and at Naropa University. He has a diploma in Client Centered Therapy and a Master Certification as a developmental coach and consultant with the Interdevelopmental Institute.

Michael Vande Berg, PhD, is vice president for Academic Affairs at the Council on International Educational Exchange. He completed his PhD in comparative literature at the University of Illinois at Urbana–Champaign. He has held leadership positions at several institutions that are unusually committed to the international education of their students, including Georgetown University; the School for International Training; Michigan State University; Kalamazoo College; and el Instituto Internacional, in Madrid, Spain. Michael has authored a wide range of international education, intercultural relations, and comparative literature publications, including Spanish-to-English translations of two classics of 20th-century Spanish literature. He has been the principal investigator of several study abroad research projects, including the Georgetown Consortium Project; frequently consults with faculty and staff about international education topics; and leads intercultural workshops in the United States and abroad. A founding board member of the Forum on Education Abroad, he now serves as a senior faculty member of the Summer Institute for Intercultural Communication.

James E. Zull, PhD, is professor of Biochemistry, Biology, and Cognitive Science at Case Western Reserve University (CWRU) in Cleveland, Ohio. He is also founding director emeritus of the University Center for Innovation in Teaching and Education (UCITE). He received his doctorate in 1966 from the University of Wisconsin and has published more than 60 papers in biochemistry journals. He has also written two books for educators: *The Art of Changing the Brain* (Stylus 2002) and *From Brain to Mind* (Stylus 2011). His teaching career has spanned 45 years and he has been nominated for numerous teaching awards. In 2001, James received a "teacher of the year" award from the Greek Organizations at CWRU.

INDEX

431

McCleary, Kate S., 325–26
Mead, Margaret, 194, 196
Meagher, M., 311
meaning making, system for
  brain for, 180
  communication research and, 31, 97, 189,
    199–200
  dynamic equilibrium and, 78–79, 86
  experience for, 332, 336
  reflection as, 21, 69–71, 146, 394
  as subjective, 184
*Measuring Hidden Dimensions: The Art and
    Science of Fully Engaging Adults* (Laske),
    69
memory
  emotions and, 167, 170, 173–75, 178, 181
  as implicit, 182
  as pillar of learning, 170, 173–75, 178
  reflection on, 174, 181–82
  as selective, 181
mentoring, cultural. *See also* Georgetown
    Consortium Project; on-site programs;
    research
  AFS and, 45
  experiential/constructivism and, 38
  Internet for, 30
  learning and, 21
  preparation for, 46–47
  for study abroad, 129, 133, 412, 415
  training for, 46, 53, 82
  value of, 53
  WIM and, 47–48
Menyhart, Catherine, 47, 130, 394–95
MERLOT: Multimedia Educational
    Resource for Learning and Online
    Teaching, 253
metacognition
  awareness of, 183, 186
  experience as, 172, 183
  learning cycle and, 139–50, 156, 158,
    169–70, 172, 183, 186, 312
Mezirow, Jack, 22–23
Mikk, B. K., 311
Miller, G. A., 217
mindset. *See also* worldview
  Acceptance as, 123–24, 363, 374–75

Adaptation as, 123–24, 363, 374–75, 413
  as Denial, 120–21, 363, 372, 374–75
  IDC and, 118–19
  as Minimization, 118–19, 122–23, 363,
    372–75, 402–3
  as monocultural, 119, 363
  as Polarization, 121–22, 363, 374–75
Mintz, Sidney, 198
Moon, J., 327
Morais, D., 210
morals and perspectives, self-related stages
    of, 62
Morgan, Lewis Henry, 193
Moss, D. M., 52–53
motivation
  AUCP and, 287
  intervention for, 155
  for language, 315
  of students, 82, 155
  teaching role for, 153
multiculturalism, experience of, 106
Myers-Briggs Test, 67

NAFSA: Association of International
    Educators, 90, 200, 203–4, 254
narrative therapy, 217
National Academy for the Integration of
    Research, Teaching and Learning, 243
National Association of Foreign Student
    Advisers. *See* NAFSA: Association of
    International Educators
National Institutes of Health (NIH), 81
National Science Foundation, 252
National Security Education Program, 4
Navy, U.S., 200
near equilibrium, 86
negentropy, laws of, 86
Nelson, A., 245
Newell, W. H., 364
Newton, Isaac, 92–93
NIH. *See* National Institutes of Health
Nishida, Hiroko, 201

Obama, Barack, 115
OBL. *See* Office of Onboard Life
observation. *See also* reflective observation
  anthropology for, 192

Also available from Stylus

Building Cultural Competence
Innovative Activities and Models
Kate Berardo and Darla K. Deardorff
Foreword by Fons Trompenaars

For college administrators, diversity trainers and study abroad educators, human resources directors, and corporate trainers this book provides a cutting-edge framework and an innovative collection of ready-to-use tools and activities to help build cultural competence—from the basics of understanding core concepts of culture to the complex work of negotiating identity and resolving cultural differences.

Building Cultural Competence presents the latest work in the intercultural field and provides step-by-step instructions for how to effectively work with the new models, frameworks, and exercises for building learners' cultural competence. Featuring fresh activities and tools from experienced coaches, trainers, and facilitators from around the globe, this collection of over 50 easy-to-use activities and models has been used successfully worldwide in settings that range from Fortune 500 corporations to the World Bank, nonprofits, and universities.

This new, research-based, 4-stage model works for developing cultural competence in any environment, and for designing effective cultural competence courses. Education abroad administrators will be able to use these activities in their pre-departure orientations for students going abroad. Corporate human resource professionals will find these activities invaluable in cultural competence building programs.

International Service Learning
Conceptual Frameworks and Research
Edited by Robert G. Bringle, Julie A. Hatcher, and Steven G. Jones

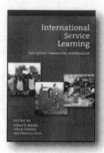

This book focuses on conducting research on ISL, which includes developing and evaluating hypotheses about ISL outcomes and measuring its impact on students, faculty, and communities. The book argues that rigorous research is essential to improving the quality of ISL's implementation and delivery, and providing the evidence that will lead to wider support and adoption by the academy, funders, and partners. It is intended for both practitioners and scholars, providing guidance and commentary on good practice. The volume provides a pioneering analysis of and understanding of why and under what conditions ISL is an effective pedagogy.

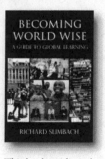

Becoming World Wise
A Guide to Global Learning
Richard Slimbach

"Slimbach's book raises an important question about the rush to internationalize college students' educations. He asks, 'Globally competent for what purpose?' and proceeds to give some thought-provoking responses. He describes education as a public and common good that should be applied to improving the human condition. His words challenge students and international educators to make choices that will foster full cross-cultural engagement in their communities. Addressed directly to students going abroad, it discusses both questions of purpose and direct practical concerns of students preparing to study overseas. He invites all of us to use our international experiences to make a difference." —***Mell Bolen***, *President, BCA Study Abroad*

This book guides independent and purposeful learners considering destinations off the "beaten path" on connecting with a wider world. Whether traveling on their own, or as part of a group arranged by an educational institution, humanitarian organization, or congregation, this book will enable them to make their international encounter rewarding, authentic, enriching, and learning-oriented.

Becoming World Wise offers an integrated approach to cross-cultural learning aimed at transforming our consciousness while also contributing to the flourishing of the communities that host us. While primarily intended for foreign study and service situations, the ideas are just as relevant to intercultural learning within domestic settings. In a "globalized" world, diverse cultures intermingle near and far, at home and abroad.

Sty/us

22883 Quicksilver Drive
Sterling, VA 20166-2102

Subscribe to our e-mail alerts: www.Styluspub.com